Family in Towne

by

Kaye Naybor
(Pam Rohman)

author**HOUSE**™

1663 LIBERTY DRIVE, SUITE 200
BLOOMINGTON, INDIANA 47403
(800) 839-8640
WWW.AUTHORHOUSE.COM

First published by AuthorHouse 10/21/05

ISBN: 1-4208-8743-2 (sc)

Library of Congress Control Number: 2005908528

Printed in the United States of America
Bloomington, Indiana

This book is printed on acid-free paper.

"The Naybors"
Back row left to right: "Tom," "Ellen," "Kaye," "Dale"
Front row left to right: "Drew," "Mike," "Meg," "Beth," "Kate"

Permission to publish these columns has been given by the Publisher of Lansing Community Newspapers, owner of The Towne Courier.

Contents

1970

1971

Introduction

[Note: Pam Rohman, alias Kaye Naybor, wrote the column entitled "Family in Towne" for eight years, 1965-1973, for the East Lansing, Michigan, Towne Courier. She never got around to writing her own introduction to these wonderful sketches of family life in that era before she died November 23, 2004. But the following column she wrote on Thanksgiving, November 24, 1970, for the fifth anniversary of Family in Towne, serves nicely as her introduction.]

It seems like yesterday, if you'll pardon my grammar.

In reality, it was 5 years ago this Thanksgiving week that I introduced my Family in Towne to you.

At that time, our baby, Drew, was 2; now he is 7, and no baby. Our big girl, Ellen, was 14; now she is a young lady of 19. Between them are Dale, now 17; Kate, now 13; Beth, 10; Meg, 9; and Mike, 8. Lim Tai Hi, who lives in Seoul, South Korea, and has been a part of our family for the past 4 years through the Foster Parent Plan, Inc., is now 8.

Our dog, who 5 years ago was not even a member of the household, now rules it with a furry paw.

As for Tom and me, five years may have made us older and, hopefully, wiser, but the price has been a loss of energy and patience.

A family changes in five years. When the children were smaller, our main problems were physical--keeping them fed, clean and safe, and of course, letting them know they were loved.

Now that they are older (and larger!), our house bulges with separate lives lived under one roof. Our concerns now are with less tangible things--hoping they are challenged, understood and fulfilled, but, as before, letting them know they are loved.

It was more important in those early days to know where they were, than who they were. And if you thought it was rough keeping up with where they were, you should see us trying to keep up with who they are!

But "it seems like yesterday" is what people say when time has passed not only quickly, but pleasantly, and that's the way I feel about our five-year friendship with you.

You've been generous with calls, letters and comments, saying you've enjoyed having us in the neighborhood, and that you've been glad to provide a listening ear for our trials and our joys.

Many of you have said, "I'm not sure if all the things you write about really happened, but I can tell you that the same thing happened to us in almost the same way just the other day. When we read about it happening to you, we laughed about it all over again."

Most of the things I write about really did happen to us or our family or friends. I'm not above a bit of literary embroidery (creative snitchery, you might say), but the human race is so honestly amusing, that it is seldom necessary.

No family's existence is an unending round of gaiety, but because I knew you'd expect it of me, I leaned over backwards through the years to find a bright spot in every happening. As a family, we've had our share of worry, grief and regret, but in trying to present hopeful faces to you, we have been rewarded with hopeful hearts.

It has been fun living down the block from you and we hope to go on doing so for many years to come.

Happy Thanksgiving from our Family in Towne to yours.

Who Was "Kaye Naybor"?
by
D. Gordon Rohman
Her Loving Husband of 54 Years

In 1965 Pam was a happily-married mother of seven children who was "looking for something to do"!

We had lived in East Lansing since 1958 when I was employed in the Department of English of Michigan State University. In 1962, Harry Stapler had started a weekly home-town paper that he called *The Towne Courier.* Pam, who was an experienced journalist, got the idea that a small town newspaper should have a regular column about family life in town.

It would be light-hearted but truthful about the joys and trials of a large family growing up in that time and place.

Pam wrote a sample column for Harry and he was delighted. And the rest, as they say, is history. She named it "Family in Towne" and wrote under the pseudonym, Kaye Naybor. She gave me and all our children fictitious names so that no one in town would know who the "Family in Towne" was.

In the eight years of doing them, she wrote an incredible 230 columns! In the beginning, the *Courier* paid her $8 for each column. (She did get a raise later after the column proved to be a success with readers.)

Pam kept her typewriter set up on the dining table in our home. (Remember typewriters?) In between making meals, doing the laundry, cleaning, shopping, and shuffling kids in and out of the house on their way to and from school and school activities, she would sit at the table and peck out her columns. Often one of our older kids would be sent on their bike to the downtown office of the *Courier* on Albert Street with last-minute copy in time to meet the paper's deadline.

Over the years, several of her devoted readers would write the paper saying they looked forward each week to hear the latest news from our very own "Family in Towne." A few people guessed who "Kaye Naybor" really was but most of her fans never did. Pam was often part of conversations where people were guessing (wildly).

Each column took up some event that was actually drawn from her family's daily life told in such a manner as to make her readers smile and say, "Yes, that's how it is (or was) in our family." Her columns tell the story of her around-the-clock on-the-job training as a wife and mother of seven. She wrote about an amazingly wide range of subjects from Christmas Past to Christmas Present, trailer trips and blimp rides, dressing kids up and dressing kids down, babies, teens and "inbetweens," April Fools' Day and Groundhog's Day, Doctor Spock and "Doctor Mom," going to Church, going to the White House, going to California, going to Europe.

Ostensibly her columns were about her beloved family. But Pam was really the main character in all of them. She was like that person in every family who takes all the photographs but who seldom appears in any of them because she is always behind the camera. But the presence of that person is revealed in every snapshot by what she selects to photograph and from what angle she chooses to see it. Pam was the implicit subject in every column she wrote. Her sharp wit, her funny scenes, her home-ly puns all reveal her character. You might say that she was the direct object of all the little verbs running around in the run-on sentence of her "Family in Towne."

3

Her columns reveal her great love for her family, a keen and dry-eyed insight into family life at ground level, an engaging style and a richly comic imagination. (I especially admire her playwright's skill with dialogue with which she puts kids and others into lean sharp focus.)

Although her pockets were full of wry and her cheek full of tongue, her heart was always full of love. Hers was what C. S. Lewis called that kind of mature married love that gives to a man and a woman, but especially to the woman "a power of seeing through its own enchantments and yet not being disenchanted." Pam never ceased to be grateful for the astonishing miracles of all those lives that filled our home. An incorrigible wonder child, she was untiringly thankful to God for her life, her family, and her friends.

I present these columns as a tribute to my beloved wife, and as a gift to our children, to our many friends and to the legion of Pam's devoted readers in loving memory of a great wife and friend, a great mother, a great writer and in gratitude for that too-brief period in our lives when we all were part of a great "Family in Towne."

Okemos, Michigan
June, 2005

P. S. I would like to say a heart-felt thank you to Nancy Seebeck for helping me edit these columns. Nancy and Pam were best friends who worked together for many years in the libraries of East Lansing Schools. Nancy brought to this task not only the sharp eyes of a good editor and the passion for accuracy of a good librarian but also a loving heart and a great joy at being able to help bring to publication the work of her friend.

Pam's Letter Proposing the Column

August 18, 1965

Harry Stapler, Editor
Towne Courier
East Lansing, Mich.

Dear Mr. Stapler:

I have an idea for a "friendly neighbor, over the fence" type of column which I think your readers might enjoy seeing in the Towne Courier. I am

4

enclosing a few samples for your consideration. The general theme is one of family life in a college town, although the individual columns would deal with ideas as diverse as chauffering for a family, to feeding the neighbors' errant cat while they vacation. As you can see from the samples, the accent would be more on wit than wisdom.

But I have neglected to introduce myself. Professionally, my experience consists of seven years on the Utica (N.Y.) Observer-Dispatch, a Gannett newspaper. I began work as a copy girl, during the 1945 war-caused shortage of copy boys, but within a year I was offered a job on the copy desk. For the rest of my time on the paper I read copy and wrote headlines. In the last three years of my stay, I also originated, wrote and edited a page for women. In this capacity I also covered semi-annual fashion showings of the New York (City) Dress Institute. After I left the paper to begin my family, I played "back-seat newspaperman" while my husband worked for five years on the Syracuse (N.Y.) Post-Standard.

In private life, I am the mother of seven children, ranging in age from 2 to 13. They were born in an 11-year span of our 14-year marriage, during which I followed my husband as news-paper wife, Army wife (in trailer), graduate student wife, faculty wife, writer's wife, and now dean's wife. Since March I have watched him bringing to life MSU's new Justin Morrill College, I hope with as much patience as he showed while I was bringing to life the little subjects of my proposed column.

I'd like to call the column something catchy, like "Please Don't Eat the Daisies," by Jean Kerr, but that might involve infringement of a sort, so I'd settle for something like "Over the Back Fence" or "Family in Towne." And for the sake of that family, I'd like to sign it Kaye Naybor.

If you think my offerings might be an addition to the neighborly Towne Courier, I'd be happy to talk to you about the possibilities.

Yours truly,
Mrs. D. Gordon Rohman

Harry Stapler and *The Towne Courier*

The Towne Courier was the brainchild of Harry Stapler. The first issue came out on Nov. 14, 1962. As an article in the paper on the occasion of its 10th anniversary states, that first 16-page issue "was the culmination of a year's concentrated effort and several years of half-formed dreams and plans." Stapler was an experienced newsman who had worked as a sports writer for the Associated Press, the Detroit News and the Lansing State Journal. Stapler and his wife Kit sold their home and borrowed on their life insurance to get the paper going. They hired a skeleton staff. Margaret Lauterback was managing editor. The paper employed 8 other part-time workers. Their first office was a single upstairs room on the corner of MAC and Grand River avenues. The office was later moved to 423 Albert St. The Courier prospered and gained prestige in the community and even in the nation through numerous awards. The paper set a record in 1971 for winning nine National Newspaper Awards in one year. Stapler sold *The Towne Courier* in 1973 He died on May 6, 1987.

1965

Thanksgiving in a Nutshell
November 23, 1965

The pies are cooling, the turkey is thawing, the house is sparkling, and my feet are aching. It looks like a good time to sit and make a centerpiece for the Thanksgiving table. Most years I forget all about this nicety and we end up with two slightly bent Christmas candles stuck rakishly in a bowlful of grapefruit and bananas left over from breakfast. But I have reformed.

And now, with a 3-month collection of magazine and newspaper ideas before me, I am ready to create.

The trick is to study the pictures and then adapt the ideas into a centerpiece meaningful to the Naybors.

For instance this majestic composition of pomegranates, avocados and pheasant feathers may mean "The bountiful day in this land," but my crew would miss the symbolism. To them "bountiful" means a mound of hamburgers centered on a raft of peanut butter sandwiches, crowned with a ring of hot dogs surrounding a nest of spaghetti. The whole thing should be afloat on a vat of chicken soup.

But maybe another idea using "Joyful Mementoes of the Family's Past" would adapt better. The lady who thought of this suggests using grandmama's cut glass compote filled with mother's wedding pearls wound among blue and green grapes, and set upon Great-Aunt Harriet's gossamer antimacassar.

The closest I can come to this is a baby food jar filled with multi-colored chips, the remains of 5 different sets of dinnerware, long since demolished. I could highlight the chips with my unique collection of 45

7

luggage keys none of which fit any of the luggage upstairs. And I could circle the arrangement with bowls of mementoes of meals of long ago, all of which have mellowed in the refrigerator.

Hastily passing up that plan, I fashion a cornucopia and toy with the thought of filling it with cherished trifles--such as the receipt of the final payment on the washer, our 3rd washer and the first to outlive its payments; one wedding ring, now 2 sizes too small, but still cherished; the tongue from Mike's shoe (I hunted and hunted for it and found it the day after I threw out the shoes); a pencil stub, not sharp but the only one that turns up when I need one.

Dale, who is 12 and perpetually famished, thinks he'd be properly thankful if I copied the pyramid of cream puffs shown on a pedestal plate. Kate, our Brownie Scout, likes a perky turkey made from pine cones and pipe cleaners. But Ellen, who is 14 and romantic, is entranced by an intricate balancing of shimmering footed goblets. I suspect the theme of this one is "I dare ya, with seven kids," and the thankfulness comes if you get through the meal without a misguided sneeze.

Finally, realizing my limitations, I decide to settle for a traditional bowlful of fruits and nuts and send out for fresh candles. As an afterthought I shell a handful of walnuts and carefully tape the empty halves back together.

Late in the day, after the turkey and dressing and gravy have gone the rounds, and the pies have been sampled, we'll sit and nibble at my centerpiece. And each time someone complains about an empty walnut shell, I'll say, "Look again. It's filled with thankfulness—thankfulness for 7 children, strong and bright-eyed; for 4 grandparents and a great-grandfather, too, still on earth to enjoy; for Daddy's work which challenges and fulfills him; for Drew's recovery when each labored gasp seemed weaker than the last; for good neighbors and warm friends; and for days such as this on which to pause and remember.

That's Thanksgiving—in a nutshell.

Christmas Shopping With the Kids
December 21, 1965

In any house where there are children, this is surely the most joyous season of the year. And Christmas morning is the very best time of all at our house. Picture the neat little stacks of presents for the nine of us. And look again 2 minutes later at the ear-to-ear grins and the wall-to-wall carpeting of wrappings!

But first comes the suspense. Santa and I have worked hand in hand so I know what the kids will be getting. I even know about the bills Daddy will be getting. What I don't know is what I will be getting. And I can hardly wait to see.

Shopping for each other and especially for Mommy and Daddy is almost as much fun for the kids as Christmas morning itself. For two weeks we had a long line of volunteers for each household job that promised a "salary." Finally came shopping day, purposely late so the excitement would last. They went in shifts, for privacy, but also so store clerks should not be besieged with the jingle of 7 piggy banks at once.

Because of my privileged position in the household, I supervised most of the buying. I tried not to pry into the details of that "one more present" each seemed to need to buy for me, of course. Ellen loftily informed me that she bought my present "ages ago," but that if I wanted to hint she'd see that Daddy got the word. Dale, an impulse buyer if there ever was one, said he had lots of ideas. But Kate tried to trick me with 8-year-old ruses.

"If Santa brought things to mothers, what would you wish for?" she asked.

I lifted my head briefly from my pre-holiday surprise (a Beaumont Tower of grated cheese which Mike thoughtfully constructed under the breakfast table), and snapped, "A 3-month vacation--with pay!"

Later as they all gathered to help me splash frosting on the cookies, elbows and walls, she sensed that I was in a better mood so she tried again. This time I volunteered to make a list, just as they did weeks ago at the crack of the first Christmas commercial.

"Put down exactly what you want," urged Beth, who made no secret of the fact that she did not get exactly what she wanted in the kindergarten exchange. "I got 52 cents," boasted Meg.

Thus forewarned, I ruefully discarded the list that begins "Cherry dining table and ladder back chairs, $695.98 complete," and considered for a fleeting moment "Hummel crèche figures, $89.95, plus stable, $14.95." Even "Vermont pie basket, $4.98," is out of allowance league, so I tried to think small and came up with a list to fit any budget:

"Ball of gum, one penny; pencil, 5 cents; rubber bands, 10 cents; funnel, 15 cents; spatula, 19 cents; bobby pins, 29 cents; washcloth, 35 cents; twine, 59 cents; toothbrush, 89 cents, and apron, 98 cents." I assured them that I need all of these things just as much as I needed the cutter that Daddy helped Dale buy several years ago when they shared a giant craving for French fries.

9

Well, Ellen shopped for Mike and Drew, and I engineered the wrapping and hiding. I spent the week trying to change the subject every time a little voice started to say, "Mommy, you'll never guess..."

Some people complain that the real meaning of Christmas is lost in our modern whirl of commercial glitter. But I think that if children have walked with Christ in the other seasons, no amount of tinsel will obscure their vision of Him now. And as for those children to whom He is a stranger, perhaps even the most chilling carol distortion can be forgiven if it serves perchance as an invitation to His "party."

We try to remind our children that material giving should be but a reflection of the spiritual giving of themselves. This makes it an important part of "Jethuth Birsday," as Drew lisps it.

Now the money is spent and the bows are tied. All that remains is for me to be both pleased and surprised as I receive my "bounty," and prove, as mothers have for centuries, that it truly is more blessed to give (joy to youngsters) than to receive (their gifts).

Merry Christmas to all from your Naybors, Tom, Kaye, Ellen, Dale, Kate, Beth, Meg, Mike and Drew.

1966

Going for a Ride
February 22, 1966

"Everybody get ready--we're going for a ride."

Comes Sunday afternoon, and fathers coast to coast are stricken with the same bright idea. And, coast to coast mothers know it's either that or a gray afternoon on the TV sidelines of college ball, pro ball or golf ball, with Dad growling, between snores, "Of course I'm watching."

The idea hits Tom in the middle of a bleak February day. At first my built-in hotline sends out a frantic warning, stirring memories of rides last fall. But after weeks of too much clean, new snow, alternating with too much dirty, old slush, my resistance is low. My failsafe device, blurred by the monotony of my winter limits of Burcham Drive, Hagadorn Rd. and East Grand River, flashes a "Go, Go," instead of a "No, No." And then the fun begins.

"Everybody get ready," I echo. This is the signal for chaos.

"Where are my boots?" (They fell down the cellar stairs.)

"Who took my other mitten?" (It's behind the refrigerator, but we won't know that until a hot day next summer when the chiller starts making chilling noises and the repair man finds it--at a cool $7 an hour.)

"Do we need snow pants?" (If they wear them, we have to turn off the heater, which means I freeze to death. If they don't, we will pass a perfectly wonderful snow slope and everyone will weep if they can't roll down "just one time.")

"I gotta use the bathroom." (This urgent cry can quickly be traced. It is always the only child who is completely dressed.)

11

At times like this I want to dash off huge bouquets to all kindergarten teachers in the snow belt. They need to know someone realizes what they go through morning, noon, night and recess.

Tom is more practical. I returned from the store one snowy Saturday to hear him declare, "Anyone who can't dress himself stays in until spring." It works for him, but I am the one they stay in with, and I may not last until spring.

Finally everyone is ready. I'm weary, but Tom says a nice quiet ride is just what I need. It may be what I need, but it's not what I get. The makers of our bus say it holds 9. They are modest. Before Christmas we jammed in all 7 kids, Uncle Don, Tom, me and an 8-foot Scotch pine. Only the tail of Beth's coat hung out.

But in spite of all this space, each trip starts with a game of musical chairs. The bus has so many windows I feel like I'm a display manikin, but to hear them argue you'd think it was a paneled truck.

Once out of town we see, in quick succession, a beautiful stand of pine, a picture book farmhouse, a horse pulling a cutter, and a skier tracing a graceful pattern down a white slope. That is, Tom and I see all this. Ellen is filing her nails. Dale, in protest of the filing, has his hat over his eyes and his fingers in his ears. Kate, who plays school endlessly, is penciling a new syllabus. Meg and Beth are fighting again—or still. Mike stands, sound asleep, wedged between the rear doors and the last seat. And Drew coos, "Me see cows?"

After 20 miles of squeeze, squirm, push, prod and nosebleed, we head home via the "soak yourself" car wash. It is the highpoint of the trip. Besides the splashy fun, we discover that: No, the rust spots are not dirt, and they won't wash off. And: Yes, the right front door does leak, and my feet are soaked.

Back home the earlier scene of snowsuit-itis is repeated. This time the one who has to you-know-what is the one who can't get his boots off. I trail his snow-wet, muddy feet across kitchen, hall and bathroom floors. But the zipper on his snow pants jams and we don't make it.

Twenty minutes later as I swallow a couple of aspirins, I notice Mike is missing. Tom finds him still sound asleep on the back seat where Dale has hoisted him. He brushes his eyes open and says, "Daddy, you said we would go for a ride."

Dress Up
May 15, 1966

With the Easter Parade and the Community Ball just past, spring is a big time for fashion in East Lansing. But while most folks are showing a spring-born interest in new clothes, the Naybor kids are more excited over old ones. One of their favorite games is called "dress up," and their fashion parade goes on the year around. There are no rules and any number can play. The basic requirement is a boxful of old dresses, aprons, blouses, gloves, hats, shoes, scarves, jewelry, and perhaps a feather, or an artificial flower or 2. A discarded petticoat makes an enchanting ballerina dress. Skirts, the longer the better, adapt to any role from Red Riding Hood to fair Juliet.

Any mother worthy of the title can be persuaded to part with a bright red hat--especially if she is sorry she bought it. (It was so expensive I couldn't admit I hated it after I got it home.) Another good contribution is the slinky green dress that made mother feel like Cleopatra last year. (This year it makes me feel more like Cleo's barge.)

Big sisters, aunts, grandmas and friends are fair game for donations too. Invariably their contributions are plushier than mine, and give the wardrobe a dash of *haute couture*. At other times, however, I gasp at what the neighbors must think of my taste in fashion--for instance, when they see Meg trailing down the street in a ball gown of purple velvet with chartreuse bows.

At times like this, I'd like to drape a sandwich board over her declaring, "The fashion opinions expressed here are not the ideas of this child's mother." Or simply, "My mother wouldn't be caught dead in this orange hat."

On the other hand, when Kate swaths herself in a mink stole and Beth wears her fox collar, just think how my stock must go up. Imagine having all that to give away! Unfortunately, I didn't. As a matter of fact, I thought these items from a richly-garbed Haslett friend would add a little class to my own wardrobe. But I couldn't talk the kids out of them.

If you dig deep into the "dress-up box," you'll find cowboy suits, Indian war bonnets, an old Zorro cape (from pre-Batman days), and other such masculine regalia. But Mike and Drew, and Dale long before them, seem to pick by color rather than sex. They don long skirts, fluffy hats, all the jewelry they can find, and end up looking like the male peacock—the more colorful and decorative of the species.

13

Favorite items with both the boys and the girls are high-heeled shoes. Ellen has her own now, and Dale has graduated to stilts, but none of the others can resist the lure of tottering on what Meg calls "high hills."

"Look at me, Mom!" is usually followed by, "Click, click, click ... boom ... ouch!" But they learn quickly.

There is a "History of Footgear" piled in the playroom right now. Remember wedgies--and babydolls? Shades of 1939!

One pair of toeless, backless, sling pumps, made of black velvet, date back to 1951. They cost $17.95, and I get nostalgic when I see them because they went on my honeymoon. Another pair is made of wine-colored, scaly reptile. They must have been the hit of the war years with their platform soles, a full one-inch high. The heels, of necessity, I imagine, are 4 inches high. (This pair was NOT mine, I swear it on a stack of old Vogue magazines.)

Most exciting of all the shoes we have ever had "for play" was a pair of clear plastic sandals. Their high "crystal" heels had a starburst design embedded in the plastic. Dale found these discarded atop a trash barrel back in the days when every rubbish heap was a treasure trove to be explored on the way to school. My first impulse was to promote them to our trash barrel, but on 2nd glance I found them irresistible. Surely, this is what Cinderella's glass slipper must have looked like!

The children wore them out trying them on "stepsisters." But Ellen and I always wondered what Orchard Street belle wore them first. And where she might have danced.

And what happened to her pumpkin coach ... ?

Vacation Syndrome
July 19, 1966

At first the doctors thought a strange new illness had hit town. Mother after mother staggered into their offices with the same awful symptoms. There was tightening of stomachs, ringing in ears, glassy looks, sudden bursts of shivers, and would you believe tears?

When the mothers started to babble about slamming doors, piercing screams, broken limbs, perpetual fights, 11 o'clock breakfasts, 12 o'clock lunches and round-the-clock snacks, the doctors isolated the malady. They call it the "vacation syndrome."

For the first time since September, the kids wake up without being called--and at 6 a.m. You've got to understand how it is. They've been penned in so long. And they have so much to do now that vacation is here.

When you hear the list of all they hope to accomplish, you agree that they are right--vacation should be a month longer. At least.

By 2:30 p.m.--3:45 at the latest--the bloom is off.

The air rings with cries of "What a dumb summer."

"What a dumb town."

"What a dumb family."

"What is there to do in this dumb family in this dumb town this dumb summer?"

The doctors, especially the ones with kids, prescribe military camp for the mothers with the worse symptoms. One mother misunderstood and she went instead of the kid. She wrote back to say it was the best summer she ever had.

In less critical cases, the doctors recommend the kids go on a trip to Grandma's or a visit to that friend who owns the lakefront cottage.

With a little planning and quite a little money, we managed to fix it so that the kids will leave at 8 a.m. each morning and return just in time for supper, if they run the last block from the high school.

Actually the syndrome doesn't hit our family as hard as it does some. After all, when you've still got 3½ children at home, it's not such a shock when the other 3½ stay home too. (Beth goes half days)

And there are some benefits, like Ellen who suddenly is available to babysit in the middle of the day, and no school dresses to iron for Kate. Drew, Mike and Meg go around in as little as the law allows, and Dale does his part by not changing at all, until I get wind of it.

All in all, our house was more shaken by the last 3 weeks of school than by the advent of vacation. To put it mathematically, if 3½ children attend 2½ different schools, and 4 children take 3 different kinds of lessons, and 3 children belong to 5 different clubs, and 5 children go to Sunday school, how many rehearsals, concerts, recitals, picnics, award ceremonies, farewell parties and playlets will a family of 9 be late to?

One event in this burst of culture and Kool-Aid paid for itself in laughs. The Girl Scouts have a dignified ritual to mark the day a Brownie "flies up" to Junior Scout. A ring of younger Brownies circle the honored girl and sing her on her way to higher things.

But the day Kate got her "wings," 34 other little girls got theirs too. You might say the dignity of the rite was diminished a bit by repetition.

By the time the 26th girl was on her way, the "ring" was more like a drunken Conga line, and the fledglings were being shoved like reluctant baby birds, and "flying" like tired pelicans.

The mothers (and one brave father) in the audience fidgeted politely on their church basement chairs. But the little sisters and brothers, who came along for the promised cookies and punch, started a ritual of their own.

One future plumber took it upon himself to check the valves on all the radiators. A future Brownie waddled up to join the sorority in their ceremony. Another spotted her older sister and hissed, when she was ignored, "You stinkpot!" And over all the hubbub, one charmer yelled at the top of his lungs, "I already did shut up, Mama."

To top it all off, the cookies ran out.

With memories like that to look back on, what's a little thing like a summer vacation?

Ah, September, October, November, Bailey, Red Cedar, St. Thomas, Central--can we survive?

Going Camping
August 16, 1966

We're going camping on our vacation again this year. From our experiences last year, what I ought to say is: We're going camping again this year, and in my book, that's no vacation!

Seasoned campers (which includes half the people in Michigan from the crowds which jam the campsites) assure me that camping gets easier and better each time you go.

But the discouraging thing is that there is always the first time.

And if the first time comes after you have 7 children, an automatic washer and dryer, an electric stove, a garbage disposer and 2 bathrooms (which you treasure in that order), it may be too late.

I made my first mistake when I admitted to the family that I had never been camping. My second came when I agreed to try it.

"You've never, ever, ever been camping?"

"No, not day camp, nor school camp, nor scout camp, nor boot camp, for that matter!"

After the children worked on me for a while, I finally realized how positively un-American I had been. I decided to take the plunge.

We borrowed equipment, and for a whole weekend it was to be Family Camp.

Five days after the big weekend, when all the towels were back on the shelf and I had set the Final Loss Tally at 1½ pair of socks, 2 washcloths, one funnel and at least 7 hours of sleep, I discovered my third mistake.

There, right in the 2nd paragraph of a 6-page "Guide to Family Camping," sat the clue:

In the best camping everyone shares in the chores. Dad and Mom aren't the do-it-alls. Each member of the family does what he or she is capable of. "Capable" seems to be the important word here.

Well, the 2 little boys did a lot of eating. And the 3 little girls did lot of swimming. And the 2 oldest did a lot of swimming and a lot of eating.

It seems I picked the wrong capabilities.

Further down in the article was this gem: "Family camping is not an endurance contest." Ha!

Not that it didn't have its moments.

Forget the 2 days packing before and the 6 loads of laundry after.

Forget the general impression of having worked twice as hard to do all the jobs I thought I was getting away from in the first place.

Forget the night of thunder, lightning, wind and rain when it was too hot and sticky to zip up the flaps.

Forget the next morning and the 2 wet sleeping bags, one soggy wool blanket, and my very dampened spirits.

Remember the sun. (The boys whined all day because we made them wear shirts in the water, and the girls cried all night from sunburn because we didn't make them wear theirs.)

Remember the smell of bacon in the woods. (It takes skill to juggle 2 pounds of bacon and 18 eggs on 2 balky burners, but boy, those camp appetites.)

Remember the lake. (I saw it twice.)

But there was hope. The article promised, "After each trip you'll be prepared for something more ambitious."

Somehow I was outvoted and we decided to try it again later in the summer.

In the weeks between, I read all the camping articles I could find to convince myself that, indeed, camping is "a good, cheap, way for a family to enjoy life, while eating simply, and being close to nature where the living is easy."

We bought a tent, 9 sleeping bags, a camp stove, a lantern, a water jug, a shovel, miles of rope, and 2 car top racks.

Even I could see how cheap it was all going to be, compared to the Hilton, that is.

Tom made up a kit of bug spray, insect repellant, poison ivy salve, bandages and probably a little snake bite antidote. Even I could see how close to nature we would be.

We packed the tent, 9 sleeping bags, camp stove, lantern, water jug, shovel, rope and Tom's "disaster kit" into the two car top racks on the one car.

Even I could see how easy it was going to be, if we could find room for the pots, pans, food, clothes and the 9 of us in the car.

But then came the 3 big surprises: We found the space. We went. I survived.

And now it's time to go again. Excuse me---I've got to go find some more convincing articles to read.

Fifth Child Goes to School
August 30, 1966

Another bird is ready to fly. September is almost here and the school bell beckons to another fledgling from the Naybor's nest. Meg was five last month and she is more than ready to answer the call. The question is, is mother ready?

You might think that by the time the fifth child in a family started kindergarten, a mother would be more than ready. You might think she would be pounding at the schoolhouse door at the dot of 8:30. You might think she'd spend the rest of the day celebrating that there are "only" 2 left at home.

But it hasn't hit me that way. I still get weepy.

I spend most of my days moving them towards independence, I hope. So what the cause of my tears comes down to is hope that in school they are bitten by the bug and pursue one discovery after another. Like Isabella, I can only wait on the home shore and hope that it will be the Indies.

And maybe for Meg, in about 20 years, the ship, that starts this month in kindergarten, will indeed sail home with riches of knowledge, and spice for life. I devoutly hope so.

Meanwhile, mother has more immediate problems. The book fee, I remember alarmingly, was doubled last year. It doesn't take the new math to show me that at $6 a head it will take $30 for our five just to walk into school on the first day.

And somewhere in this box, there should be a birth certificate for that child.

But wait, there aren't any here for the other three Michigan-born babes either. Can it be . . ? Yes, a call downtown confirms it: certificates are not sent out automatically in this state.

But you don't need to go all the way downtown—just send $1 for each one you want. It may be a little late, but teacher will understand, I hope.

I seem to have forgotten another little detail. I thought about the pre-school physical all summer, but somehow summer is over and thinking wasn't enough. But we're in luck and the doctor can take her on Wednesday—just under the wire.

School clothes are something else. Each fall I look longingly towards Jake's and Knapp's, then come back down to earth and start re-hemming last year's dresses.

Ellen's clothes come down to Kate; Kate's come down to Beth; Beth's come down to Meg.

That's how it should be, but this year Beth stayed slim, while Meg got tubby.

A conservative estimate of the situation shows that if I let down three hems and let out 4 waists we can make it to Thanksgiving, with a little bit of luck and a lot of washing and ironing.

Now all I have to do is remember to bring my little black book to registration.

Most people use a little black book for phone numbers.

I use mine for such notations as, "Meg: 4/15/65, db, n/p, bst tts." Translated that means that Meg went to the doctor on April 15, 1965, because she was bitten by a dog (db). The skin was not punctured (n/p), but she got 4 booster tetanus (bst tts) shots anyway.

Anybody knows you can't fill out the registration card without that kind of information.

But after all, this is my fifth kindergartener. I know all about cigar boxes, painting smocks, rest rugs, gym-shoes and milk money by now. There won't be any problems.

No problems, that is, unless Meg comes home weeping as did an older sister on her first day of school. She had heard that soon she could go to school where children learn to read. She spent a whole morning in school, and "I didn't learn to read . . . boo hoo hoo hoo."

Grampy's Visit
October 18, 1966

Grampy is coming to visit. And Mimi is coming too. They came in the spring, and we went to see them in August. But 3 times a year isn't half often enough to see people you love.

When the children were younger, between visits they would forget just who Grampy and Mimi were. I would spend days getting them familiar with the names so that when the faces appeared, there would be no shyness. That wasn't enough, and often the visit was half over before the little ones could warm up.

But that's no problem anymore. Even 3-year-old Drew remembers all about them from trip to trip, and the difficulty now is keeping them from bursting with anticipation.

Our children have 2 grandfathers, 2 grandmothers, and a great-grandfather. They have trouble remembering whose mother is whose, etc., but no trouble knowing that all of them are very special people.

There are lots of wonderful things about grandparents. It's best, of course, if they live just down the block. But hardly anybody's do anymore. So you have to cram a lot of grand-fathering and grand-mothering into a few gatherings each year.

And the kids are always ready to do just that. When we go to visit Grampy and Mimi we sit at the breakfast table and watch the freshly-milked cows amble out of the barn on the farm across the street. There is a row of neat white houses on Grampy's side of the street, but across the way Mr. Parker's farm stretches as far as you can see.

Mr. Parker keeps ponies for his grandchildren, and if Grampy goes along, all our children get to ride too. By the time all 7 have had a turn, Grampy has walked 2 miles around the corral. When Grampy has had enough of the horses (long before the children are ready to leave), he puts up 2 swings beneath the apple tree. He knows how to make them out of rope and a notched board. One is always lower than the other, for the shortest legs in the family. Grampy also has a hammock in the backyard. It's fun to tumble out of it onto the soft grass.

Both Grampy and Mimi make things. At home Grampy makes sauerkraut. He has crocks and a very old shredder and his kraut is coarse and crisp, the best you've ever tasted. Once Grampy packed a double quart jar of kraut in sawdust and styrofoam and mailed it to us. It didn't break. But the kids laughed for weeks thinking how the smell would have startled the postmaster if it had.

Mimi makes big, fat, soft sugar cookies. And crispy chocolate chip ones. And flaky rhubarb pies. And wonderful lumpy applesauce. She makes mittens, too. Mimi likes to knit in challenging patterns, so all the pairs differ. There are single cables, double cables, twists, ribs, diamonds and plains in our drawer. All of them are soft to the touch. All of them are warm. Mimi made sweater sets with tiny caps for each baby to wear home from the hospital. And each of the children wore Mimi's knitted bootees until they began to walk.

The children are never fooled by Grampy's pretended gruffness. If he grumbles at them, they look him straight in the eye and say, "Grampy, read to us." They know he always will. He always does.

They know, too, that the first morning after Grampy gets in East Lansing he will rise before any of us is awake and take his walk around the campus to see what's new. Something always is. He gets back in time to walk the little girls over to Bailey School. Mike and Drew go along for the walk. Grampy never minds leading a parade.

When Grampy comes we have bananas for breakfast, because that's what Grampy likes. And if you come into the kitchen at just the right time, you might catch Grampy having his 2nd cup of coffee--and you can beg a doughnut.

Later there will be trips to the store, and you can get to ride in Grampy's car, but you mustn't put your muddy feet on the seat.

Grampy always brings his tool chest when he comes. In the beginning there were always jobs waiting for someone to get at them, and Grampy always took care of them. But now I collect jobs and save them for him because he gets restless if he is not busy. If he starts a job, he'll stay until it is finished, and that means his visit will be longer. The kids love it when Grampy is making something. That always means the truck will come from the lumber yard. And you can't beat a truck with 50 feet of 2x4's for excitement.

Grampy and Mimi's visits are always too short. After they've been with us for a while they long for the peace of their own quiet, orderly home. After they get home, they write that their home sometimes seems too quiet and orderly. After they go, our house is still noisy, messy and busy. But we all look forward to the time when we can say again, "Grampy is coming to visit. And Mimi is coming too."

Halloweening
October 25, 1966

To hear the Old Timers tell it, today's Halloweening is more treating than tricking. It is true too, if you stop to think about it. In a town like ours, only the truest witch would turn away a bunch of bag-toting ghosts and Batmen. The stores make it easy to be a generous giver.

Early in October (nay, early in September) the packets of "72 individually-wrapped" you-name-its show up in stop-or-trip-over-it displays

21

in the supermarket's main aisles. No need to bake, pop or wrap goodies--the stores have done it all for us. And for the purist who disapproves of candy-giving, there is nature's own ready-wrapped treat, the apple.

It is kind of an unwritten rule in East Lansing that only the little kids can be open-bagger-beggers. If you are more than 2 times as tall as the bag, you automatically get a dirty look, and half as much candy as the others.

However, our Ellen, who is at least 3 times as tall as the bag, and only went along last year as guardian angel to our little ones, found herself besieged to "take some too." She came home as laden as her charges..

But for the most part, the junior high and high schoolers can't be bothered with "treating" and spend the evening at school or home parties. Some take time out before or after the party for a little dirty tricking, but most of it is innocent fun. There are exceptions--a few known trouble makers, and their "fun" is better known as vandalism.

When I first heard the Old Timers tell about their pranks, and how they got away with it all, I wondered if today's kids had become soggy Milquetoasts. But now that 7 of today's kids live under our roof, I know better.

The kids aren't soft. They are smart. Instead of saving all their tricking for one night a year, when the juvenile authorities are snapped to attention, they spread it out over the whole year. And instead of spreading their mischief out over the whole town, they confine most of it to the limits of our own house. This mother and father team has been tricked aplenty. And by the sweetest little angels, in or out of costume, you ever saw.

Take the time Dale, now 12, but then only 4, learned to tie knots. We were pretty proud of him. His knots were strong and tight and he always made about 8, just to make sure. One rainy morning Tom loaded an assortment of 9 school children into the car, started up and backed out of the garage. Well, he almost backed out. He stopped with a jerk, just short of pulling down the garage, and the adjoining house with it. Dale had tied a hawser to the rear axle and anchored it to the overhead door braces. He meant to show Daddy his strong, tight 8 knots, but he forgot. Daddy and 9 school children were a bit late that morning.

Another trick that won ample notice was pulled by sweet, gentle Meg. Not wanting to be caught chewing gum in bed, she quickly slipped the offending wad under her pillow and fell asleep. By the time I found it, sheet, pillow case and a stray tissue were firmly and permanently cemented.

Once we heard Kate yell "Fire!" It thrilled us to see her grab a garden hose and extinguish the blazing basket of trash by the back steps. That night I found a book of matches in her slacks. Her blaze of glory gave way to a blazing bottom.

Ellen once presented me with a handmade pin cushion on Mother's Day. The material looked familiar, and I traced it to a gaping hole in the middle of a favorite tablecloth.

The best trick of all was almost an international incident. One year as we entered Canada, a customs official stuck his head in the rear window of the car and asked Dale where he was born. Dale looked up—and vomited! Never were we waved through customs in such a hurry.

All in all, I can't fear Halloween. If other children are like ours, Halloween should be a "treat" compared to the rest of the year.

Keep your spirits up.

Foster Child
November 22, 1966

Lim Tai Hi is a 4-year-old boy who lives in Korea with his father, mother and brother. We have a snapshot of Tai Hi. It shows a freshly scrubbed and combed little boy. He looks sturdy. His cheeks are baby-plump. His eyes are bright and curious. He seems to be wondering who wants his picture, and why.

Tai Hi isn't old enough to know it, but for the Naybor family he is an extra reason to be thankful this Thanksgiving. He doesn't know Ellen, Dale, Kate, Beth, Meg, Mike or Drew. He doesn't know Tom or me. But we, all 9 of us, are the difference between light and dark for Tai Hi and his family.

Tai Hi is now our foster child. His parents need help to feed and clothe Tai Hi and his brother. We are able to help. For that the Naybors are thankful.

Tom and I have long admired the work of the many foster parent groups which strive to help needy children. What wonderful opportunities, we thought, for the wealthy or those without children of their own to help some child, somewhere. Since we were up to our elbows caring for so many children of our own, we felt we were already doing our share. But gradually we began to feel an urgency to help one of these needy children too.

Surely, we decided, we who have been given so much pleasure through our own children, have the greatest debt of all to the needy children of the world.

Finally Tom wrote and asked for more information about "adoption." For $15 a month, we learned, we could provide food and clothing for an unfortunate child in a country of our choice. We decided that as soon as we could spare $15 a month we would apply for a child's name and our whole family would become his foster parents.

But what family of 9 can spare $15? One month things looked promising, but then the refrigerator handle broke. Another month 3 of the kids went right through the toes of their only shoes. The next month was new mattress month. And so it went. There never was $15 left over. There never would be.

The more we thought about the matter, the more we knew what the answer had to be. We decided to take out the $15 first and then make do with what was left. That sounds a bit rash, considering the price of food these days, but for us there is always peanut butter or hamburger. For Tai Hi there might be only hunger. His father is blind and his mother has been ill. Neither of them is able to work enough to buy the bare necessities for their family.

When our family sits down to eat Thanksgiving dinner there will be more than $15 worth of food on the table for that one meal alone. Our gift of $15, which would do very little for a family of 4 in East Lansing, stretches through the buying powers of the foster parent group and provides food, clothing and a few other necessities for the whole Lim family. Without this help, the family would be shattered. With it, Tai Hi will grow up with those who love him. He will eventually go to school. Perhaps someday he will find a way to help someone else.

Strangely, while our $15 buys peace of mind for the Lims, it also buys something for us. It makes us aware of our blessings and reminds us to be thankful for them. On days when Tom and I are ready to strangle 3 of the kids and drown the other 4, we suddenly remember Mama Lim and how she must worry about the future of her boys. When we tuck in our brood on a cold, snowy night, our minds travel to Korea and we wonder if Tai Hi is warm. When I scrape food off a plate I worry that the little bit I am throwing away might have been enough to save someone somewhere from starvation.

When you open your heart to one outsider, the whole world slips in with him. One family can't help the needy of the whole world. But one family can help one little boy, and on this Thanksgiving Day, when we give thanks to God for our many blessings, we will count Tai Hi among them.

A Teenage Boy
November 29, 1966

Whoosh! Out went 13 candles and in came a new era for the Naybors. We are now parents of a teenage boy.

Along with the cake, there were presents for the boy and condolences for the family. Still shaky from the calamity of 2:30 school dismissals, we braced for the inevitable disasters of the months and years ahead.

The first shock came the morning after Dale's birthday. That day he made his bed without being told. The next day he did not make his bed until he had been told. And told. And told. And told.

But we have another teenager (a girl which is a calamity of a different color and another story entirely), so we realize that the change from child to teenager does not occur overnight. As a matter of fact, as I look back over the past few months I can see several signs or forebodings of approaching teendom.

For example, there is the matter of Dale's hair. One day last spring I scraped up the necessary ransom and sent Dale to the barber shop. When he came back I uttered several choice phrases and ordered him right back again. He pleaded for arbitration and we compromised on combing the bangs back off his forehead.

Since then the bangs have been down more often than up, and the time between haircuts has steadily lengthened. Just as I was about to blow the whistle again, Dale crossed a gigantic threshold in life---he discovered shampoo.

Twice a week he disappears into the upstairs bathroom. Half an hour and 40 gallons of hot water later, he emerges with sparkling bangs. Our shampoo bill is shattering.

Some of the signs of Dale's maturity have been more comforting than dismaying. For instance, he does his homework more willingly lately. He remembers his horn and his books in the morning. He tells me if he has a game after school. He fixes his own flats on his bike. He changes his shirt once in a while. And he manages, most times, to get 2 socks into the hamper instead of losing one under the bed, behind a chair, or up in the light fixture.

As a result of these slight advances, my lip gets a chance to heal occasionally. What does my lip have to do with Dale? There was a time in Dale's life when every time I looked at him I sputtered. Frequently I even boiled over. If it wasn't something he did, it was something he didn't.

"Hang up your coat."

"Get your muddy foot off the couch."

"Don't touch that cake."

"Do you have to put the whole slice of bread in your mouth at once?"

"What do you mean you forgot to wait for your sister and you don't want to walk all the way back to St. Thomas?"

"You swallowed WHAT?"

Well, I haven't been going to child study club for 6 years for nothing. Even I know you can't talk that way to a boy every time he hails into sight. So I learned to bite my lip once in a while. I tried to keep from exploding except over truly vital issues.

"You mean the jacket we bought yesterday?"

"But why the curtain, Dale?"

"I said get it out of here and NOW!"

"Clean it today or I'll call the Board of Health."

"Don't bleed on the carpet."

You've got to admit that Dale is trying. Dale accidentally broke 3 windows in 4 months. Dale eats 3 helpings of whipped potatoes and gravy at a sitting. Dale goes through the knees of every pair of pants he owns. Dale brushes his teeth 4 times a year. Dale gets a "D" when he could get a "B". Dale wears a tie for one hour and ten seconds every Sunday. Dale takes out the garbage the 3rd time I tell him.

But Dale is a loving son. Dale forgives without question. Dale is generous. Dale is good to our little ones. I've got to admit that Dale IS trying.

One day I asked Tom, through bleeding lips, "Why couldn't we have had a normal boy?"

Tom, who remembers being a normal boy, said, "Dale is a normal boy."

Now, if Dale turns out to be a normal teenager... well, I hear plastic surgeons can do wonderful things with lips these days.

Dolls at Christmas
December 13, 1966

If Santa should be forced to specialize some year and pick one international toy to fill his sleigh on Christmas Eve, the best choice would have to be the doll.

Children the world over love dolls, and no barrier of language or culture ever comes between the two. What is more, boys like them as well as girls.

Dolls have been made from every material imaginable: rocks, potatoes, spools, crab-claws, cornhusks, clothespins, pine cones, animal skins, rags, seed pods, leaves, stalks, wax, clay, china, cork, and of course, today's life-like plastics. Some Indian tribes used apples for doll heads, and that trick probably came down from Mother Eve.

The earliest dolls, historians say, were objects such as stones or roots which resembled humans in shape. They were considered good luck charms and were strictly for adults, or were used as tomb companions for the dead.

The word doll can be traced back only to the 1700s, but before that children had adopted them and called them babes, babies or puppets.

As a paid up member (until the January bills come in) of Santa's Helpers Inc., I've run into quite a few dolls lately. And let me tell you, they've come a long ways from those old good luck charms I was talking about.

If your memory of dolls goes back to the days when the newest thing was a blonde be-curled moppet that looked like Shirley Temple in "The Little Colonel," it may come as a big surprise to you to find that today's dolls not only look like people, they act like people.

My favorite is one called Cheerful Tearful. I walked up to this charming darling and it almost broke my heart to see her smiling lips actually turn down into a tearful pout. Another babe, named Tickle Tears, stops crying when you tickle a magic button on her tummy.

I must admit Tiny Thumbelina, who wiggles like a real baby, makes me a little nervous. She looks like our babies used to look just before they wailed for that 2 a.m. feeding.

Many of the dolls can be fed (with the usual damp results), and little Snugglebun comes with a bottle "warmer" which lights up when her bottle is ready. Tiny Baby Pattaburp even burps when the feeding is over.

Real Live Luci is a doll with temperament; she turns away from spinach, but loves her bottle. Katie Kachoo really sneezes. Baby Teenietalk runs off at the mouth in 11 different sentences, but Answer Doll can only nod yes, or shake her head for no.

A whole flock of precocious young lady dolls have taken to ambulating. In addition to Goody Two Shoes, Baby Walk Alone, and Suzie Steps, all of whom walk, there is Baby First Step who roller skates as well.

Trolls at 1½ inches and Liddle Kiddles, 2½ inches, are probably the smallest dolls in season. Close behind are the Pee Wees, all 4 inches of them dressed in delightful costumes symbolic of Springtime, Flowertime, Schooltime, Angeltime, etc.

I saw what I thought was a doll as big as Daddy (6'4" in his socks), but the clerk said that was a mannequin and I was drifting into the wrong department. However, she did show me a little girl doll who was a yard long if she was an inch, and a stuffed Saint Bernard who was definitely breathing DOWN my neck.

I fell in love with a bevy of soft-eyed dolls from Italy, and some elegantly dressed mam'selles from France. An old-fashioned doll in calico and long black stockings had saucer eyes like a Keene painting.

Big sorrowful eyes are also the trademark of the waif of the year, Miss No Name, a woe-be-gone urchin dressed in patched burlap. If you're the type who picks up strays, you've as good as adopted this one the moment you see her.

Character dolls range from Alice, Mary Poppins (followed dutifully by Jane and reluctantly by Michael), Smokey the Bear and Flipper the Dolphin to Pooh, Piglet and Eeyore, whose tail is removable.

Sure to be a hit with the boys are stuffed velour replicas of Batman, Robin, Superman, Zip the Chimp, Lassie the Collie and Ida Da Spida---the last a 5-legged creature with orange hair and a webby smile.

G.I. Joe doesn't have to fight alone this year. He's got an army of friends now including the Man of the Green Beret, and Fighting Tigers with such names as Bugle Ben, Big Ears and Machine Gun Mike. German, Japanese, Russian, Australian, British and French action fighters can be had for a real international force.

If you are interested in an investment instead of just a doll, there's always Barbie, Ken and their crowd, expensive to dress as any teenager in town.

Scooba-Doo is a real hep-talking beatnik, and there are 7-inch Go-Go dolls, one of which comes complete with guitar.

If like me, all of this makes you long for the good old days when all dolls were good for was to love, you'll be happy to hear that two old favorites have survived "progress."

Sure enough, almost every store in town still stocks Raggedy Ann and her pal Andy.

And if you wait until the clerk isn't looking, and peek under Annie's pinafore, you'll find the same old heart on her chest, embroidered with the same old sentiment. "I Love You."

Trimming the Christmas Tree
December 15, 1966

We trimmed our tree last night.

It stands by the living room window, and every few minutes one of the kids goes in to check on it. Each one comes back to echo Tom's verdict--it's a perfectly splendid tree. Actually, it's a trifle lopsided, greatly overloaded, and probably too big for our living room. It'll never make the pages of

Better Homes and Gardens, but I have to agree: it's a perfectly splendid tree (and ours!)

It's not stylishly modern, but neither is it formally old-fashioned. It's more of a Naybor-fashioned tree, for the whims of each of us are clipped to its branches. If the tree has any theme at all, it has to be friendliness-- some one of us has a special feeling for each shiny ball, tinkling bell, or beat-up snowman on it.

Every year I wonder if this is the year we should buy an artificial tree and be done with all the fuss. Some of the new ones look more like Michigan scotch pine than Michigan scotch pine, and are a good bit cheaper. The silvery ones are pretty too. I saw one synthetic white flocked tree that would be absolutely breathtaking with blue and green teardrops, or maybe striped candy canes and bright red velvet bows.

My long-drowned dream of grandeur and elegance flares at the thought. But then I remember the kids. Kids are fresh, bold, vibrant, sticky, prickly and even a little bit smelly. Nature makes trees that are a perfect match for them. They even shed like the dog. So every year we buy a real live tree. And each tree leaves a memory in the family book.

Getting the tree is half the fun. I remember, but Tom would rather not, the year all the trees on the lot seemed to be frozen solid. The dealer assured us that a day in the garage would bring all the branches down to perfect gracefulness. When our "popsicle" thawed, we discovered it had no grace at all, and what's more, the "best" side had an empty spot a foot high. Tom got out the brace and bit, sawed off a back branch and filled in the spot Nature forgot. After we got 3 boxes of tinsel on it, you could hardly tell.

Another year the only spot not cluttered with play pen, high chair, or dirty laundry, was a shallow corner between bookcases. I set out to look for a skinny apartment tree. The fellow at the gas station lot said, "Lady, they don't pick that kind." But up the street I saw just "that kind." Leaning on the fence, apart from all the others was a giant tree freak. The bottom was full and bushy, but midway up the trunk the branches shrunk. The whole thing looked like a green tenpin. The man gave it to me for a dollar. Tom sawed it in half. The top made a perfect corner tree, and the bottom made 2 wreaths and a spray.

After moving to Michigan, we were bitten by the urge to "chop our own." We spent a glorious hour in the woods, found the perfect tree and tied it to the top of the station wagon. We sang the 40 miles back to East Lansing, and just as we approached the city limits, a gust of wind grabbed the tree and flung it, twisted and broken into a gully. We went into town and bought a replacement.

The closest we ever came to glamour and elegance was our "pink year." We spotted a real tree which florist had flocked to cotton-candy pinkness. We paid the $8.50 before we knew what hit us. We didn't fully realize how expensive our tree really was until we got out the box of trimmings. Nothing in that box went with that tree. We ended up buying 60 pink bulbs and 35 pink balls, at specialty shop prices. The tree was a dream, but using up all those miserable things has been a nightmare.

Ever since the kids have been big enough to help, we've had a family tree-trimming party. I unlock the freezer and bring out the cookies I've sworn will last until Christmas, or else, and Tom buys a case of pop. We have candy and nuts and poinsettia napkins--the works.

Then while Tom and Dale unkink the wires and test the lights, the rest of us carefully lift each ornament from its cocoon of old tissue and memories. This is the best time. As each imported flocked ball, or school-made paper chain goes from box to branch, a tapestry of our family comes to life. The room rings with cries of, "Oh, I remember that pink angel. Let me hang it." Or, "Oops, there goes that pretty striped one!"

Each year a few trinkets slip to oblivion, and each year we buy or make a few more. Always there are too many for sophistication, but we put them all on anyway. When the boxes are empty and the tree is full, its sparkle reflects our daily life: often lopsided, frequently overloaded, sometimes sticky, prickly and a little bit smelly, but always fresh, bold, vibrant, alive, friendly and full of wonderful memories.

Merry Christmas to all from your Naybors—Tom, Kaye, Ellen, Dale, Kate, Beth, Meg, Mike and Drew.

1967

House Rules
January 17, 1967

The first month of the year is rather like the first day of the week. I'm full of plans, and I know that it's time to get started, but somehow I can't seem to get over that Monday morning feeling. January is supposed to be a great time for making resolutions, paying bills, balancing budgets, and starting new regimes. I've been trying, but so far I have run out of will power for the first, money for the 2nd and patience for the 3rd.

On top of that, the vacuum cleaner keeps finding more pine needles to choke on, and I've still got some ironing left over from 1966. In the matter of new regimes, I may make my breakthrough. Actually I'm not thinking of another city hall sit-in, nor even a march down East Michigan to the Capitol. When I talk about new regimes, I'm only interested in making a few changes in what might be called home rule.

Just the other day I came across a set of regulations which, provided I can enforce them, could guarantee a happier, and certainly cleaner, 1967 for the whole family. Just take a look at these ideas for "Care of Living Quarters":

"Everyone must share in maintaining clean living quarters." (That means Mother, Daddy and all 7 kids; you can see immediately what a sweeping program this is.)

"Quarters must be ready for daily inspection at 8 a.m." (Now I'm a reasonable woman—let's make that 8:30. I don't focus too well before that.)

"Every Saturday all sinks, toilets, windows and floors must be washed and cleaned." (Up and at 'em, kids!)

"Living areas are not to be littered." (Get those shoes and that hammer off the couch.)

"No excessive amount of newspapers or magazines are allowed to accumulate." (That goes for gum wrappers, too.)

"Bedding must stay on beds at all times." (If you make a tent out of that new blanket again, the roof will fall in.)

"Nothing is to be hidden under mattresses." (That goes double for gum.)

Under "conduct" is this noteworthy suggestion:

"Loud talking, whistling, singing, profane language, scuffling or fighting are prohibited." (Some of you even breathe too loud.)

In regard to "Personal Cleanliness," I second the following:

"All members must keep themselves in a state of personal cleanliness at all times." (That means wash your face even if it is Saturday and there is no school.)

"Shoes are to be worn at all times, except when retiring." (The next person who comes into this kitchen barefooted, gets it.)

"Members must be clean shaven at all times." (Oops, skip that one.)

"Equipment for laundering personal effects is available upon request." (If you need that blouse tomorrow, put up the board and iron it.)

While some of these may seem harsh, remember this is only January and it's a long way from May to September. Besides, these "privileges" should make up for any hardships:

"Everyone may have visitors." (Better ask before you bring back that kid with the cleats though.)

"Everyone may receive and send mail." (The stamps come out of your allowance, and if you get a pink envelope that smells of essence of gardenia, it may be opened by the censor.)

"One personal telephone call is allowed." (And make it short, girls.)

The more I check over this list, the more convinced I am that this is the right way to get the household started on a new year. Tomorrow I'm going to post the whole folder of ideas on the bulletin board.

I'll entitle it, "Naybor Residence Rules and Regulations."

The folder begins by saying, "These rules, which explain what is expected of you, are intended to insure safety, decent living conditions and fair treatment for all. Any infraction may result in loss of privileges or more severe disciplinary action."

If I cut off the part that says "Wayne County Jail, Rules and Regulations for Inmates," no one will know I stole the ideas from the Sheriff of Wayne County.

And if all the inmates in my cellblock cooperate, there may be time off for good behavior.

The Great Snowfall of '67
January 31, 1967
[A special column on how one family survived]

Snow, snow, snow, snow!

Late Thursday night we listened to a newscaster list the school closings for Friday.

"Let the kiddies sleep, Mom," he urged.

"Let Mom sleep," I begged, as they rose at the crack of dawn.

Snow! Twenty inches, dawn report. But from a frosty upstairs window it might have been 20 feet. Sidewalks, curbs, streets—indeed all the familiar guidelines of daily life—were buried under the swirls and drifts. The snow on the porch roof was mounded to the middle of the window. I stood Mike on the windowsill to see. A squirrel scurried between two trees. In a few seconds his tiny prints disappeared.

Snow.

Time to hibernate, decided Tom. He hugged his pillow and plowed back under the covers. By 9:15, 2 of the kids had asked him and one had asked me, "If Daddy's not sick, why is he still in bed." Time for cereal, begged Drew, proving that his 3-year-old appetite was not snowed under.

Snow!

Time to check the milk and bread, worried Mother, proving that mothers worry every chance they get. I took the milk card back in and wondered what the man would do with the 4 gallons I usually take on Fridays.

The kitchen range, flustered by its important role in this emergency, blew a fuse. There was one left in the box.

Snow!

Time to break trail, decided Dale. Out he ventured, a tall, slim boy, sinking up to his hips into the drifts and leaving the first imprint of man on Mother Nature's Marshmallow Surprise. Wearing 2 pairs of pants, 3 pairs of socks, mittens over his gloves, boots, sweatshirt, jacket, and 2 hats, he walked in the snow. Why? Because it was there. In a few minutes we saw him sitting on our toboggan in the middle of where the street should be. He paddled with his hands; his unlikely craft was a reluctant canoe in midstream.

Snow!

"What a gyp," moaned Ellen. "The East Lansing High School kids were going to have the day off, and now there's no school anyway.

"Why couldn't it have been Wednesday--when I had my chemistry final?"

By noon, 2 neighbors had called to cancel baby-sitting jobs, and she moaned some more. But soon she was testing her skill on a neighbor's snowshoes. The boy across the street, home from Purdue for a semester break, wandered over, and her day was a success after all.

Snow!

New neighbors moved into the block on Wednesday. From Tallahassee, Fla., they said.

"The kids have never seen snow and they can hardly wait," the father said. By noon on Friday they had walked, jumped, rolled or fallen through enough snow to last them a lifetime. By nightfall the snow in their yard was 10 inches lower than in ours, packed solid by their happy frolicking.

Snow!

Beth put Ellen's size 8 boots on her size one feet because, "They go all the way up to my knees."

Meg donned slacks, snow pants, jacket, mittens, hood, scarf and boots--and came back in after 10 minutes because her nose was cold.

Mike and Drew disappeared from sight in the narrow canyons the older kids carved out. From above they looked like mice in a maze.

"Think of the mint I'll make shoveling," gloated Dale. But now all his clothes were soaked through, and it was hours before he could go out again. By then Mike had joyfully re-shoveled the snow back into the narrow path to the back steps, and it all had to be cleaned out again.

Snow!

Tom made it to the Albert St. Min-a-Mart on Friday for milk and bread. He offered to try for Prince Brothers on Saturday "if you can think of something light and easy to carry."

It wasn't easy to make a "light" list for a family that normally eats 6 cans of soup for lunch, or 4 pounds of meat loaf and 5 pounds of potatoes for supper. Tom said it was Father's Day at the store.

Drew got a switch from our usual "hungry orphans" sermon with his lunch: "Don't waste a bite, it's a long walk to the store."

Thursday morning I had made brownies and fudge to take to a shut-in. By Saturday morning my own shut-ins had consumed them all. "Let them eat brownies," I decreed in queenly fashion.

Snow!

I decided I wasn't the outdoor type and watched Claudette Colbert weep her way through 2 husbands and 2 wars on TV. I decided to let the laundry go for one day. The reek of wet wool in the basement was making me turn green.

I tried to get up a work party to clean the playroom. Nobody wanted to help.

"Gosh, Mom, 'sno fun"

[The following was a feature article that Pam wrote about the great snowfall of '67.]

East Lansing became a small town again Sunday morning. For the first time since the "old days," you could look from a window and see people in the streets.

They walked down the narrow channel opened by the plows, almost as people walked down the dirt roads of yesterday. They walked just to walk--there was no place to go.

They stopped to talk, and shoveling neighbors were glad to stop their work. The shovelers chipped away at their driveways, but without haste. They had all day.

Dogs and children tunneled through the snow. Fathers were home. Mothers were home. There were plenty of people to help pull sleds, make snowmen, build forts. Nobody really had anything more important to do.

A few people managed to get to church. When it was over there was plenty of time to talk to friends. There was no irritating jam in the parking lot. There were no cars at all. Friendly groups walked leisurely homeward. It was a quiet Sabbath. The few stores which opened became meeting places. Strangers compared notes on how their families had fared in the storm. Shoppers bought newspapers hungrily and later they would read each page instead of scanning hurriedly.

Knots of walkers gathered to worry about a rooftop overburdened and in danger of collapse. There had been fire sirens early in the morning, and everyone wondered if some family were homeless this cold day.

The sun glistened on the snow, and East Lansing was "our" town again. Everybody cared about everybody and everybody had time to be friendly. It was Sunday in a small town.

How Staff Produced This Souvenir Issue

The Towne Courier's staff of reporters, photographers and editors combined in producing this souvenir issue of the Great Snowfall of '67 for the Towne Courier's readers. Stories were written by news editor Barbara Kincaid, Alice Schmid, Nick Sharkey, Miley Lane, George Colburn, Joan Boyer, Lee Premer, Romi Chaffee and "Kaye Naybor."

Photos were taken by Boyd Shumaker, Bob Smith, Pete Cornell and Harry Stapler of the Towne Courier staff, and by John A.Yunck, of 4536 Cherokee Way, Okemos, a resident who volunteered a number of pictures he made in the Okemos area.

Marriage on Ground Hog's Day
February 7, 1967

The children's favorite family joke is the one that started it all--Tom and I were married on Ground Hog's Day. I agree that it is hardly as romantic as Valentine's Day, but 16 years ago it seemed like exactly the right day. And although it was as gray and dreary a February 2 as any ground hog ever saw, the years have been sunny and bright.

What amazes me is that 16 years seems so short to me and so long to the kids. It seems like last year to me, but the children are quick to set me straight. We look at snapshots and Dale says, "Look at that car! If you had kept it, we'd have a real antique." Ellen groans, "My gosh, Mom, that dress is practically down to your ankles."

Tom takes a ribbing over his padded shoulders, wide ties, and slack slacks. But a picture of me in the outdoor girl's uniform of the day--rolled up blue jeans and red plaid shirt--really rolls them in the aisles. Just when I begin wishing for another outfit like that "good black suit" I wore on my honeymoon (and for 4 years afterwards), somebody spots the seams on my stockings and I am dated again.

Kate is amused by the fact that our first dinnerware was service for 4. Beth and Meg think it must have been wonderful to set the table for only 2 instead of for 9, as they have to do.

Mike and Drew simply keep wondering where they were when all of these things were going on. Which proves that a lot can happen in 16 years.

As brides go, I was about as inexperienced a housekeeper as any of them. But egged on by memories of grandma's coal stove and of chickens bought live-weight and unplucked, I experimented with every new appliance, mix, or short cut food as soon as it hit the market. I was, in 2 words, the Modern Bride.

Yet I can see that the years have made it even easier for today's newly-wed girl. Her first biscuits will be as light as a feather, the best that Pillsbury can pack into a bake-and-serve tube. She probably will never in her life cream shortening, separate eggs or siphon cream from the top of the milk bottle. She won't own a flour sifter.

She will think a spider is a long-legged bug instead of a black fry pan. With Teflon on the job, she never will lose half her scrambled eggs to the pan. Chances are she will never can a tomato, pickle a pickle or marmalade an orange.

She will never get her hair caught in the wringer of a washer, or break a fingernail on a scrub-board. She will use an automatic washer and dryer either at home or in a Laundromat from the start of her marriage. Which means that she will never stand in the sun to hang her sheets, nor dash out in the rain to retrieve them. (Does anyone remember the sight of long johns frozen rigid in a March wind?)

Her husband's shirts will iron themselves, as will her sheets, tablecloths and curtains. She will never prick her finger on a curtain stretcher. Nor recognize one. She will be spared the agony of setting trouser creases, or of wrestling with ornery pants stretchers.

Her pre-treated blankets will never shrink down to crib size. Her reds will stay red, her blues will stay blue. She'll never cook starch or boil a diaper. She'll know new ways to do things that her grandma never dreamed of, and I'll try to keep up with this new Modern Bride. But I'll be nostalgic because the simple art of pressing a baby girl's sleeve sideways to make it puff will pass forever.

Meanwhile, I'll look forward to many happy returns of Ground Hog's Day, and be glad Tom and I didn't pick April 1.

Losing a Shoe
February 15, 1967
[Editor: I could find no date for this column. This is a likely place for it.]

Drew has lost his shoe.
Not shoes.
Just one shoe. Remember the nursery rhyme?
> Little Betty Blue
> Lost her holiday shoe.
> What can little Betty do?
> Buy her another,
> To match the other,
> And then she will have two.

If only it were that easy. We'd walk into the store and say, "One left shoe, please. Yes, to match the pair we bought last month."

It does seem as if at $8.99 (plus tax) a pair, a store could afford to sell half a set. You know, $4.50 each, or $8.99 a pair.

But so far I haven't been able to convince any local managers. They must all be bachelors. Surely any father would understand and arrange the convenience.

This is an especially bad time to lose a shoe. In the heat of summer a mother could look the other way while a two-year-old ran barefoot through the soft grass. But at this time of the year a Michigan boy might get blue from the cold one day, and black from the mud the next.

It seems there are only 2 possible solutions: buy a new pair of shoes— or equally drastic, spring-clean the house and find the vagrant.

A quick glance at the check book rules out the first course until pay day.

I can't get very excited about the housecleaning idea either. It sounds like work. And it's a long shot. At the rate I work my way from room to room and floor to floor, the shoe would turn up just about the day Drew is ready for the next size.

Needless to say, this is not the first shoe to be lost in the Naybor household. Based on earlier hunts over the years, we know precisely where the shoe will not be. It definitely will not be in any of the places where lost shoes have been found before.

That rules out the playroom trash pail, the ironing basket, the apple drawer of the refrigerator, the Salvation Army carton, and the sound box of the piano.

Experience has taught us 2 other tricks to shorten the search. The first trick is to quick lock up the shoe that is not lost so we will know where that one is, when and if we find the other.

The 2nd trick is to check the day's schedule for dentist appointments, tests at school or anything else a child might want to miss.

Once, eager to leave on a trip, we posted a reward for the return of a shoe. Within 12 minutes Dale came to claim the dollar, shoe in hand.

It seemed like a wonderful technique until we heard him speculating that a smart man could make a million "hiding and finding."

The other kids join in the fun and assure me they know exactly where we will find the shoe. They are so doubled up with laughter over their perennial gag line that they can hardly tell it:

"Mother, it will be in the last place you look!"

With this in mind I prowl through the closets once more, demand that Kate check the Bailey School lost and found, call Grandma long distance to see if she packed it into her suitcase, ask Daddy's secretary to check the carton of books that just went over to the office, and pray it wasn't in the mountain of junk the trash men hauled away yesterday.

Meanwhile Drew stays in the house and has great fun seeing how fast he can walk out of his slippers each time I put them back on.

Then he pulls off his socks. The object of this game is to see how long he can paddle around before he is caught.

He boasts that he has "my barefeet on."

By nightfall he is sneezing and coughing. Tom hauls out the vaporizer again.

Neatly tucked in the box, among the germs from Meg's last cold, is the shoe.

Mother composes a new nursery rhyme:

Drew has found his shoe;

Let's put it on with glue!

Bohemians
February 28, 1967

"Bring a dish to pass, and your own table service." Does that sound familiar? Of course. It's the classic invitation to a Bohemian. If you are new in town you probably need to be told that a Bohemian is to Michigan what a Pot Luck is to a Westerner and a Covered Dish is to an Easterner. It's a buffet supper to which each participant brings part of the meal. It's the meal the casserole was invented for, the place to try out a new salad, and the time to discover who makes the best pie in town.

If you belong to any kind of a group, club or guild, you are sure to get at least one such invitation each year. If you happen to have 3 children in elementary school, you may end up passing dishes as a steady diet. In East Lansing, the class Bohemian is as much a part of parenthood as cough syrup and lost mittens. Mothers accept it philosophically, fathers submit stoically, and children think it is the next best thing to Christmas and the Easter bunny.

Each year at the classroom conferences some brave parent rises to urge, "Let's skip the Bohemian this year." The others in the group are stunned to silence. Each one is thinking what this would mean to him.

Mother, thinking: "No more rushing to feed 6 kids, clean up one kid, heat a casserole to take, gather up service for 3, and get there by 5:45."

Father, thinking: "Ah, I can just come home, rip off my tie, eat a quiet dinner and take a little snooze."

Just as the whole group is ready to sound a resounding "aye," a mother in the back timidly puts up her hand for attention.

"I dunno. My Gracie looks forward to her Bohemian."

Well, of course her Gracie likes it. All the kids like it. It's their big night. If it's 4th grade night, only the 4th grader in the family can go. The other kids in the family get a cold supper and a babysitter, but the lucky Bohemian child gets the royal treatment. No parent in the room can bear to be the one who puts an end to that night of special privilege.

Mother, thinking: "Maybe, Pete will be sick that night and we won't have to go."

Father, thinking: "The Farmer's Almanac is talking about another big snowstorm this month. Maybe we won't be able to get out."

Mother and Father, thinking: "Anyway, the food is always good."

The food is always good--you can count on that. And there will be plenty of it. Every once in a while the last 6 families in line get to the table in time to find a choice of 16 salads and 14 desserts, but no meat. But usually the word goes out to bring "anything you like to fix," and by some strange magic this provides a fine balance of meat, casseroles, salads and desserts. Each time you go you'll learn 7 new ways to use hamburger, 3 new ways to fix ambrosia, and 2 new reasons to go off your diet.

The program for the evening depends on the teacher involved. One friend of mine who teaches at Marble School really "sings" for her supper. She rehearses her charges for a week and presents quite a dramatic production. Some teachers hold open house in the classroom after supper. Most of them feel the occasion demands at least a skit or a musical number, but one brave teacher at Bailey prefers to simply come as a guest.

"I have them the rest of the day," she says. "Let the parents be responsible for them tonight."

Even when there is no formal program, it can be quite a "happening." The kids seem to know teacher won't scold in front of mother, and mother certainly won't yell in front of teacher--and the sky's the limit.

While the parents are having coffee, the girls get together and giggle and the boys get together and run. Then the boys giggle and the girls run. Finally the girls giggle and run and the boys giggle and run, and it's a good thing when a room mother stands up and shouts that it's time for introductions.

The introductions can be a floor show in themselves. Each child is supposed to stand, give his name and introduce his parents. Suddenly the redhead who was screaming like a drill sergeant on the stage a minute ago is fresh out of words.

"Uh, I'm Jim, and this here's my mom and this is my dad. "

It turns out there are 3 Jims in the class and none of them remembers his last name tonight. When it is your child's turn, you suffer a little sympathetic stage fright. But she loudly and clearly recites her name, your name and his name, and sits down gracefully.

As you sit down, you spill the rest of your husband's coffee into the teacher's lap.

One good thing about a classroom Bohemian--it breaks up early.

Springtime and Mud
March 28, 1967

Does a little bird tell you? Is it something in the air? Or do you go strictly by the calendar? My first sign of spring is mud.

It happens every year. Day after dull, gray winter day, I send my Eskimo-wrapped toddlers out into the cold to play. Day after day they trudge right back in, noses frosty and mittens white with snow.

Then one afternoon it happens. Instead of hurrying back in, they stay out for hours. As a matter of fact, they stay out so long and seem to be playing so peacefully, I get ambitious and decide to mop the kitchen floor. Just as I'm getting out the wax for the finishing touch, in they troop.

Their noses are frosty, their mittens are not white. Eskimo babies they are not. Mud babies they are. Closer inspection proves they have walked in the mud (up above their boots), sat in the mud (their jackets are chocolate coated), and done headstands in the mud (anyway, it's in their hair).

I react with wildness. I grab--no, not a child. I grab a rag, glass cleaner, a pane of the nearest window, and yes, it's true. I see spring! It may be only one muddy patch, still surrounded by ice and snow, but it is mud. And if mud comes, can spring be far behind? After this tried and true harbinger, I watch for other signs and daily the list grows. In a period of a week the following spring-like things happen:

Ellen catches her first cold of the year.

Tom forgets his rubbers in Chicago, and subsequently brings home a little MSU mud each day to mix with our own garden variety.

Dale comes home from school without his hat, which is in his locker where it will stay until he cleans it out in June.

The East Lansing High track team sprints down the middle of the street, followed by 3 dogs and my neighbor's 3-year-old boy. The sprinters go home and collapse, but the 3-year-old has enough energy left to run his mother a ragged race until 2 hours after his bedtime.

Mike and Drew have a fight with the little boys up the street. The fight is over a sled which they have been pulling over the bare sidewalk.

Traffic increases on E. Grand River, and one day when the thermometer gets up to 52, a convertible flits by--top down!

The young high school couple who walked briskly through the streets despite the Big Snow, now walk more slowly, and they look at each other a lot.

I come back from the store one afternoon and there are 3 tricycles blocking the driveway. Only one is ours.

The slush, slush, slush of boots fades away, and the brisk staccato of high heels is heard again in the supermarket.

The paper boy tries to make up for lost time by throwing the paper at the porch, instead of placing it behind the storm door. He misses and it lands on the roof.

A big pile of snow starts to thaw at last, and it turns out to be less snow than trash, hidden since the blizzard. The dry cleaners find Beth's ski jacket which they misplaced in February.

She has had a growth spurt and it now fits Meg--but it won't next winter when she needs it.

Dale escorts Kate to the police station to buy a license for her Christmas bike which she finally gets to ride.

Tom takes the lining out of his coat, and I buy some patent leather shoes. Every dress I take out of my closet smells of the Easter basket chocolate eggs that were stored on the shelf.

Can you trust March to stay spring-like? Of course not. It will freeze, snow and blow again, despite the equinox.

But the mud will be here until the 4th of July.

Learning to Read a New Way
April 25, 1967

I never thought the day would come when all I could read on my first grader's school paper was the star! But the day came. And as a former champion apple polisher and board washer, I felt pride had suffered a blow, magna cum laude. I don't expect to keep up with the older kids.

The moment they hit junior high, I clean out their ears and warn them to catch every word in class. If they expect help from me with their geometry and chemistry, they aren't as smart as they think they are. I didn't understand those things when I listened!

But the Three R's? I stopped looking at the school as a safe, handy, dependable baby-sitter, and decided it was time to audit a few pint-sized seminars. Of course, I had heard about the new math--but I had dreamed that I might reach the protective arms of Medicare without actually having to figure out what was new with 2 and 2.

After all, if you can calculate what size jersey to buy a 5-year-old (try a 10, it's sure to shrink in the dryer), and you know within a lick of mustard how many hot dogs to cook for 9 hungry people (only 16, if 4 kids finagle you out of a "raw" one just before dinner), what else is there to arithmetic?

Apparently there is now a good deal more to it. As if it wasn't enough just to produce the right answers, now you have to understand what you are doing. And it seems that the new method makes the understanding easier, and thus the learning faster.

For an adult, hoping to look wiser, or as wise as his 9-year-old, a whole new vocabulary is a prerequisite. Among the important words these days are factoring, prime numbers, set concepts, bases, properties, number lines, subsets and intersection.

The kids in our house toss these off like Mother Goose rhymes. I give them lots of encouragement, and any day now I expect to understand what they are talking about. I tell them that the reason I am so slow is because I have a lot to unlearn before I can catch up to them.

There is one consolation. New math or old, nothing adds up right unless the kids have learned the basic facts of arithmetic "by heart," as we used to say. So it's all right to be an old-fashioned mother when it comes to making them memorize the same old combinations we had to learn.

But to get back to that first grade mini-scholar and her all-star paper. She is in a class that is testing the use of Initial Teaching Alphabet (ita) as a beginning reading tool. Two such classes are in operation in East Lansing, one under Mrs. Opal Wong at Marble, and one under Mrs. Marlene Cosgrove at Bailey.

Mrs. Cosgrove tells me that the effectiveness of the new method in her class is to be tested next month. But I don't need to wait that long to know that for our first grader, it is a great success. I can't always read what she writes in ITA, but through ITA she can read what she writes, and a great deal more besides.

The ITA alphabet was created by Sir James Pitman, a grandson of Sir Isaac, inventor of shorthand. The new alphabet consists of 44 characters of which 24 are letters of the regular alphabet. The letters "q" and "x" are the omitted letters. Most of the new symbols cannot be made on a regular typewriter, but the children learn to make them easily. One character, which looks like an "e" riding piggy-back on an "a," is read like the "a" in face. There are also run-in symbols for such sounds as "sh," "ch," and "th."

The main advantage of ITA is that every time the child sees an alphabetical symbol, he knows the sound will be the same. He is spared the confusion that ordinarily takes place as a beginner tries to read the sound "i" when it is spelled in these varied ways: aisle, height, choir, eye, pie, cry, sigh, buy, guide, island, and other combinations. Also, all lower case letters are used, so that they appear the same at all times.

Most children adjust quickly and easily to normal spellings after having begun to learn to read in ITA. In the beginning, all class signs are in ITA, and often parents are bid "Welcome" to the room in a combination of letters they can't read. As the year progresses, the teacher adds a 2nd sign next to the first, and the child can see the word as he has learned it and as the adult world knows it.

Later, the ITA sign is discarded completely, just as the need for its help is discarded by the child. As in the math, the end results are the same only the approach is new. There are many new keys being used these days to unlock the old secrets of learning. A smart parent adds them to her key ring so that she won't be the one who is left out.

Parent-Teacher Conferences
May 16, 1967

No, Jean, I don't for one minute believe that silly rumor about that nice Mrs. Startley.

You can say what you want about parent-teacher conferences, but would a teacher threaten to quit just because of a few little conferences?

Sure, I know this is her first year of teaching. And I know how it is with first graders. But after all these months of wiping noses, tying shoelaces, unsticking zippers, separating fighters, stopping nosebleeds and translating "my looth tooth juts camed out," what's a few differences with parents? Besides, the May conferences aren't the first--Mrs. Startley survived 2 weeks of conferences last November, remember?

You say it's the memory that started her shaking? I never dreamed. And it all started the other day when three mothers sent in notes asking for changes in their schedules?

After all, Jean, a teacher has to be reasonable ... Oh, they each wanted to stop by for a minute at noon--couldn't make it any day between 2:30 and 4:30.

And they all got angry when she said she usually went home for her lunch, and besides she thought it might take more than just a minute to discuss certain problems. It was the word "problems" that set them off, I suppose.

Oh, Mrs. Startley told you she didn't really have any problem children, just problem parents.

That nice Mrs. Startley.

You don't mean it? Three mothers actually brought the child right along to the conference and Mrs. Startley had to whisper all her comments. I see.

And 8 other mothers brought their pre-schoolers along and let them keep busy messing through all the children's desks. And the library shelf.

But some mother had to ... what? Oh, she didn't mind that so much. The paints bothered her. You don't say? Right on the bulletin board, too, huh?

What's that about teachers, Jean? You mean 15 mothers started off the interview by asking if this was her "first year, Dear?"

Then they told her all about when they were teaching. Nine of them taught first grade? And all the children in their classes were reading by January?

I suppose that was a bit unnerving.

But not as bad as what? You mean one father actually introduced himself as John Smith, Ph.D.? I don't believe it.

Oh, in psych. You say it's a case of the shoemaker's son, eh?

What mother didn't believe that her little boy was late 37 times so far this year? Thought she made the whole thing up, I suppose. Finally agreed to check her clock--well, I should think so.

Overslept?

My problem? Now, Jean. Nothing like that. It was that day I overslept, and then she dropped her toasted muffin in the gutter right by the corner. And when she was picking it up a truck went by and splashed her.

Jean, she was there by 9:15. And it only happened once.

One little boy did what? Oh, couldn't find his shoes. But couldn't his mother... Oh, she leaves the house before him. It must have been awfully hot in those galoshes all day. Smelly, too, huh?

I always say, it's all part of a teacher's job to ... what's that? Oh, what she really minded was the note the mother sent her after she suggested the boy stay with his grandmother in the afternoon because the kids teased him so in the morning.

She said Mrs. Startley was making the child feel rejected? And Mrs. Startley bit her lips and didn't tell her?

It all builds up, I suppose.

45

No, I didn't hear about that. Yes, she is a rather bright child. Came over to play one afternoon. Not really play, you know. She didn't seem to know how. Just kind of stood around and looked at things.

A suggestion. Mrs. Startley suggested the child be left alone at home. Oh, not so much reading. You don't mean the encyclopedia? Every night? Breakfast? And the parents told Mrs. Startley the child was a genius, and who was a young upstart?

Oh, I see.

Which father challenged the tests? Him?

Did she tell him she didn't make them up?

And then asked where she went to school, huh?

Gosh, Alice, do you think she'll really quit?

You didn't tell me that. When is it due?

Ha, ha, ha, ha!

What's funny? I was just thinking that in a few years she can go to conferences and tell the new teachers all about how it was when she taught, and how bright HER Suzie really is!

Class Reunions
June 20, 1967

Next to hot fudge, a class reunion must be the hardest thing in the world to resist. The announcement comes with the bills one day, but the post mark is from a town 20 years away. The return address is headed Mrs. D. R. Clark. You never heard of her. You open the letter and take a quick look at the signature.

Elizabeth Miller Clark?

Elizabeth Miller Clark!

Can that be good old Betsy Wetsy Miller? Sure, it's got to be.

The letter says Betsy Miller Clark, Duggan Price, Beverly Walters Amill, John Webster and Rusty Gabbler have been remembering the good old days and they say it's time the good old class got together again for a good old reunion.

You show the letter to Tom and he says, "I'm free that weekend, want to go?"

"Of course not. Whatever for? Go all that way with 7 kids just for a class reunion? That's silly."

But you take another look at that list of names and it stirs up 30 or 40 other names and you are hooked.

"Gee, I wonder what ever happened to Helen Groves? Did I tell you that I heard Ruth and Norm and Am are still single? And they were all so popular back in high school."

"Tom, do you think we could go? I think I'd like to. You know, I really would like to."

The town is a mixture of "remember that?" and "when did all that spring up?" The high school which graduated you and 79 others that year, graduated 364 this year.

The fire station has an addition that is bigger than the original. The old Episcopal church has been painted red and is an amateur theater now. Ye Olde Colonial Diner is still there, but the sign says 24-hour Laundromat. Wet wash fills the air instead of the smell of burgers and fries.

With a renewed feeling for the passage of time, you pull your new dress carefully over your fresh hairdo, and wonder if you will be able to sit in your snug new girdle.

The club brings back memories of Stardust, strapless evening gowns and camellias in a wrist corsage.

Like everything else, the club is bigger and more affluent looking. The tiny bar you remember is gone and a tiered carpeted lounge replaces it.

As you walk in, you spot a familiar face. You smile. He smiles. It takes a minute for the names to come to both of you. Then you introduce your Tom, and Jim Ramsey, class president, introduces his Claire.

The next half hour is a jumble of faces, names and memories. By the time dinner is announced, you remember almost everyone in the class and you are counting noses to see who got here.

There are nonsense prizes: the greatest distance come, the biggest bigwig, the baldest head, the grayest head, the most children, the oldest and youngest children, the most grandchildren, anybody pregnant?

There are few surprises. The most likely to succeed did, and the least likely didn't. The most beautiful girl is still quite a dish, and all 3 of her former husbands thought so too. The best athlete played college football and admits to a little golf now and then.

You are struck by how little people have changed. They are fatter, thinner, grayer, older--surely. But obnoxious little Lester High is now obnoxious old Lester High. Mousey Jane Brown is now mousey Jane Williams. Vivacious Shirley Higbee is vivacious Shirley Jones, and a grandmother to boot.

The boy you dreamed about, who never looked your way 20 years ago, is full of pretty compliments--and liquor. The dream fades and Tom looks better every minute.

In the parking lot you make letter promises you won't keep as Ruth zooms off in her racy sports car, all alone.

Everyone vows to make it a bigger and better party come '77.

You snuggle close to Tom as you drive away.

"Hope you didn't mind meeting all those strangers, Tom."

"Good party, Honey," he says. "They were a bunch of very friendly strangers."

Friendly strangers. You decide that after 20 years that's all your good old classmates can be to you, too.

Built-In Babysitter
July 11, 1967

I'm the envy of the neighborhood.

My house? Messy.

My figure? Floundering.

My wardrobe? Forget it.

My family? You're getting warmer.

Actually, it's my baby-sitter that makes my sister housewives and mothers green-eyed.

I have a built-in baby-sitter and it's the greatest thing that's happened to me since I stumbled into motherhood. It's nice in royal families for the first child to be a boy.

I'm happy for Lucy too. But for middle-income, no-Nanny families, I vote for a girl for a starter.

Ellen, our first born, is 15 ½ and she loves children.

She also is experienced, willing and cheap. What's more, MY credit is good with her and no matter how low my funds may go, I can leave.

Like the milkman, she collects at the end of the month.

When Ellen herself was small, Tom was in the service and we never seemed to be in one place long enough to find any sitters.

As a result she went along or we stayed home. We carried her in a pink-lined grocery basket--to church, to the post movies, to the supermarket, to the drive-in; and even one momentous evening to Luchow's famous German restaurant in Manhattan.

But as the family grew larger, it was getting AWAY from the children that seemed to be the important thing. For many years we found willing sitters among Sparrow's student nurses. When that school closed, we had a series of MSU coeds. None of them seemed to need the money very much--one arrived in a bright red convertible and told us cheerfully as she left that she'd had a blast.

We switched to "older ladies." One was hard of hearing and after a restless evening of wondering whether she would hear the baby, we crossed her off our list.

Another slept through our return home, the dog's welcome and our initial efforts to waken her. She came to when we switched off the TV.

Just about this time, our neighbor's daughter flowered into a conscientious, attentive, baby-loving angel. Instead of crying when she arrived, the kids whooped with joy. She gave bottles to the babes, read stories to the middle ones, and made the older ones feel needed and important.

We enjoyed every half-dollar's worth of time she gave us. Then she discovered boys. End of chapter!

One of the nicest things about the built-in sitter is that she already knows the rules of the house. She knows about treats, bedtimes, drinks of water and where to look if a pajama top is missing (under the bed? behind the dresser? in the bathtub?).

She knows where we are going and how to reach us. She knows that in case of fire it's only the kids who are important. She knows which neighbor to call in an emergency.

Just being able to skip all this briefing gives me a head start on a happy evening.

The other important thing is that I don't have to knock myself out cleaning the house before she comes. I can remember thinking, "I can't go out. I'm too tired to clean the house for the sitter."

Silly? Sure, but I'll bet you do it too.

Once we alerted all the neighbors, and left Ellen in charge overnight. As we traveled we heard reports of a tornado hop-scotching in the Lansing area. We called home, but got no answer.

Keep trying, we told the operator. Still no answer. We sped home and arrived to find all seven children safely in bed, the excitement over.

"Why didn't you answer our call?" we gasped.

"We heard the phone ringing, but the TV said to stay in the basement, so we stayed there until the all-clear."

Such a sensible girl.

There is one catch. She is in such heavy demand among the neighbors, I have to get my bookings in way in advance to get her services.

Also, that bit about boys hovers menacingly.

But I may have that beat too. If I can keep Ellen's services just a bit longer, Kate will be old enough to take over and I'll still have it made.

Summer Food
July 25, 1967

Thoughts about food on a summer day:

--People eat less in summer. That's what all the ladies magazines tell me. But my food bill is higher. Can it be because the "light, refreshing" supper menu they suggest actually costs more than winter's heavy but hearty casserole supper when you are feeding 9?

--Our charcoal treats have been especially good lately. After 16 years of marriage, I recently learned that the reason Tom ruined so many steaks and roasts was because he resented the job.

"The barbeque grill is a feminine plot," he says.

Now I'm the chef--inside and out--and Tom can't get enough of the charcoal flavor.

--It's fun to go to the farmers' market these days. The kids can't understand why we can't buy the first peaches we see. But half the fun for me is to walk through both sheds first, spotting the good peaches or the best buy in melons.

Then we go back and make one purchase at this stand, 2 at the next, and maybe one each at 4 other places. Pretty soon everybody is carrying a bag. When we get home I discover that I bought everything at the peak of readiness and we'll have to have a fruit festival to eat it all up while it's good.

--Our little kids won't eat canned spaghetti in any shape or form, but my recipe is one of their favorite foods. For the 9 of us I cook 8 quarts of sauce and 3 pounds of spaghetti. That leaves enough for a small lunch the next day. So far it's a toss-up as to whether they like it better freshly made, or warmed over.

--After my grandmother died, my grandfather found that most of his sons and daughters made a habit of stopping by "to see Pa" after Sunday Mass. Grandpa learned to make the visit interesting for his restless grandchildren by mixing up a large batch of Italian meatballs and cooking them up as the children arrived. Grown now, they still talk about Grandpa's meatballs, sizzling hot on the tip of a fork. (The Italian trick is to add freshly grated cheese to the raw meat mixture. Good!)

--When Tom is out of town, the children's favorite treat is burgers and fries from the nearest "take-out." Three kids eat seconds on the burgers and we buy 3 extra bags for everyone to share. The boy behind the counter always snickers when I order "12 burgers and 12 fries, please."

-- I stopped making homemade cookies except at Christmas and other special occasions. I like to make them, but by the time every child has one to taste, a 3rd of the batch is gone. My favorite homemade cookie is a large soft sugar cookie topped with lemon rind. Tom likes oatmeal with nuts and raisins. But for the kids, it's chocolate chip every time.

--My favorite summer meal is corn on the cob, green beans with fresh mint, and sliced tomatoes dressed with salt, pepper, crushed oregano and a touch of vinegar and oil. We like our corn before the sugar turns to starch, so we call ahead, put on the pot, and then ride out to a farm for the corn.

--Few restaurants seem to know what to do with vegetables. Some skip them altogether and offer only salads. Others offer a choice of mundane peas, mediocre corn or frankly overcooked green beans. In Detroit the London Chop House offers a choice of 10 or 12 vegetables, each cooked in a special way. We resisted steamed artichokes with drawn butter sauce, and tried the French fried zucchini. It was crisp and pungent, and one order was enough for three people. We'll go back.

--One year we were up at Old Mission just after the peak of an over-productive cherry season. Most farmers still had whole fields of trees laden with fruit the economy dictated they should not pick. We took the family into one such orchard and even the smallest child could reach up and gather a handful from the bending branches. We picked as many as we could use. The farmer at first waved away our offer to pay, but we insisted we owed him something. Not for the cherries--but for the delightful experience.

Family Glossary
August 8, 1967

Communication is a "now" word. It's on the tip of everyone's tongue these days. Everyone who talks knows that the world is badly in need of more and better listeners. Everyone who listens knows that what we really need is fewer, but better talkers.

As a parent I spend a lot of time talking and listening, but I'm discovering that talking and listening to children is not always communicating. Granted, I learn fast. When a 4-year-old tells me his grapefruit is "grinny," I don't waste time trying to find that word in the dictionary. I simply agree that he's chosen a fine description for grapefruit, or even lemons or limes, and pass him the sugar.

When his younger brother asks me to "inside it out," as he hands me his pajama bottoms, I see at a glance what needs doing. But when one of our teenagers interprets a firm "no," to mean "keep trying, and if she doesn't give in, try Dad," I begin to fear that the lines are down and I am not getting through.

At times like this I can see the need for a family-type glossary. The kids could define all the words and phrases parents commonly misunderstand. This should include phrases such as "I'll be home early," which apparently really means when they are good and ready, and an hour and a half after you have given them up as maimed or worse.

I'm forced to admit that parents are as guilty of double talk as are children. What mother, saying "later," means anything but "the answer is no, but I can't think of a reason right now, so ask me again later." Every family speaks its own brand of "forked tongue," and there's danger that communication will break down completely unless every member has the latest list of meanings.

Here's a random sampling from our family's vocabulary of double talk:

A baby: What you are when you want to do something that scares Mommy, and what you aren't anymore when Mommy wants you to do something that scares you.

Your fair share: In a family of 9, it's always less than you want.

A room of my own: What most of the 9 of us don't have and "need desperately."

Disaster area: Any room in the house after a rainy day, and the playroom any day.

Dangerous activity: Anything you want to take up that costs more than your allowance.

Healthful and rewarding: Anything you can do that's free.

Allowance: A fund given to children so that parents can borrow it back when things get tight.

Mommy's money: The grocery money.

Vacation fund: The grocery money plus anything we can borrow from the credit union.

A long trip: The last 7 miles to the nearest gas station rest room.

A long, long trip: Any distance you travel with children.

Walking distance: Anywhere the kids need to go (this side of Haslett or Okemos).

Too far to walk: Anywhere Mom needs to go.

The flower garden: a 2-foot strip between the swing set and the fence where nothing blooms until 2 days before the first frost.

The neighbor's yard: That beautiful stretch of lush green that makes our house look as if it is surrounded by an acre of parched Nebraska plain.

Meddling Mother: Their own.

Attentive mother: Their friend's.

Well-organized: What other mothers always are.

An important career: What you tell the kids you gave up to have them.

A clean house: What you really gave up when you decided to have them.

The cook: Mommy.

The cleaning lady: Mommy.

The dryer: The last hope when it's 2 minutes to school time and 3 kids have one sock apiece.

Too many kids: What it's impossible to have some peaceful, loving days. And what you know you've got when they ask how something was "in your day," and you know they mean back in prehistoric times.

Prehistoric times: If you think communication is tough now, you should have been here then!

Dream Vacation (1)
August 22, 1967

A dream vacation. Everyone has his own idea of what that would be. But suppose you had to dream one up for me? For a mother of 7, who has been just a wee bit tied down for the past few years, how would you dream?

Would you dream three weeks in Europe?

Would you say fly over?

Would you say leave the kids behind?

Would you say have a taste of England, France, Switzerland, Italy and Spain? Would you say look a little, shop a little, sun a little, swim a little? Worry? Well, just a little. But relax a lot.

It's time I admitted it. I took just such a vacation, and it seems like a dream now that it is over.

It all started with the usual bad jokes. Wouldn't it be nice, everyone said, if I could go with Tom when he went to Europe this summer. Yes, I'd answer, but "there are 8 good reasons why I can't--7 kids and an empty bankbook."

This set everyone to thinking, and the ones who were thinking the hardest were the other mothers of big families who seldom get to do exciting, adventuresome, selfish spur-of-the-moment things.

There must be a way, they'd say.

You owe it to us to prove it can be done, they'd say.

If you do it, maybe someday we can, they'd say.

The more they said, the more I'd think about it. The more I thought about it, the more I talked about it. Suddenly, I HAD to go.

Then things really started to happen.

I talked about the possibility of getting a young student couple to move in with the kids. One of my friends echoed my thoughts--in exactly the right place at the right time--and the next thing I knew, the right couple had come along.

The children liked them immediately. Soon they were talking about "when you go," instead of "if you go," and with a feeling of eager anticipation.

I began to get cold feet about the whole project. I couldn't believe it was really me buying walking shoes and folding hangers and dresses that weighed next to nothing and promised to pack without a wrinkle.

These are all things I really need, I told myself. Folding hangers? Well, I don't expect to go, but just in case things should work out. . .

I remembered that the house needed painting, the kitchen needed a new floor, and the upstairs bathroom sink was threatening to leak again. Everybody assured me all those things could wait.

I applied for a passport.

The couple to the right of me were there for a marriage license. The man at my left demanded loudly to know the exact date of his divorce. And suddenly the clerk was reading an oath of allegiance and I was mumbling, "I do," "Yes," "Amen," "I do so swear," hoping one of them was the reply she expected.

I told the doctor I might as well take the shots—again.

Just in case things should work out.

My arm stiffened up. I got sick all over. My vaccination festered and threatened to spill out onto my whole arm.

"If I don't get to go after all this, I'm going to resent it," I muttered.

The travel agency drew up an itinerary. Tom decided that because the children were still so young, we should travel on separate planes.

"I hear you're going to Europe with your husband," my friends said.

"Not really with him," I'd answer, "But I think we will get to wave at each other at airports."

I had never been up in an airplane before, and I'm still a bit uncertain about what holds them up. I decided to "put my affairs in order," as they say.

I cleaned out the medicine chest and a couple of messy drawers. I looked up our insurance policies and checked on Tom's will. The fire insurance policy was missing, and Tom's will was so outdated that it listed 5 children instead of 7 as his "sole heirs." I called the agency about the policy and our lawyers drew up new wills for both of us.

Then I paid up a few bills.

The whole affair was beginning to take on a pretty gloomy light..

Suddenly, it was Saturday and Tom was leaving. I was to follow on Monday.

"Tom, Tom," I gasped, "if I cable, you'll know I'm not coming. I don't think I can leave the kids, Tom. And Tom, I'm not sure I have the nerve to go all that way alone."

And Tom ...

By Sunday night, three kids were sick--one with a temperature of 103. I called the doctor. "Remember that vacation you've been telling me to take? What do I do now?"

Go, he said. Go, the couple said. Go, the children said.

Go, the neighbors said. Go, the other hopeful mothers said.

I went.

The kids got well. The couple managed beautifully. The neighbors kept me informed.

It was a dream of a vacation.

Dream Vacation (2)
August 29, 1967

I've been speaking English since I was a year old. With a background like that, it seemed like a smart thing to start my European travels in England.

On the flight from Detroit to London, I studied a currency converter. I'd been warned about "tuppence," "florin" and the non-existent "guinea," and I wanted to be able to make dollars and sense out of £5/4/6.

At the airport I sailed through the formalities and claimed my bag with the ease of a seasoned traveler. "Passport" sounds the same in English English as in American English, I discovered.

Friends met me and led me to their car. I promptly climbed into the driver's seat by mistake. It took me 2 days to get used to being on the "wrong" side of the road as we drove. I never did quite get over the feeling that we were on the brink of a head-on collision, so I learned to look out the side windows instead of the front.

Looking out the side window of a car in England can be a delight both in the country and the city. In the country there are green rolling hills, trim walls and hedges and delightful villages. Most of the village houses are simple cottages of repetitious red brick or gray stucco. Strangely, almost all the thatched roofs we saw were atop houses of pink stucco.

In the cities, most of the houses are row houses. Frequently the only variety in them is on the rooftops where TV aerials pose in many-limbed confusion. In contrast to the sameness of the houses are the gardens. In both the country and the city no home is complete without its garden. Every front yard, no matter how small, bursts with blooming color.

We saw roses 4 and 6 inches in diameter. Hydrangeas in all hues from pink to blue to purple bent heavily on laden bushes. Sweet peas on 8-inch stems spilled their delicate fragrance into the sunlight.

The temperature stayed in the 80's. We saw no sign of London fog.

"British weather is much maligned," our friends said.

British money is much maligned, I decided. I learned to spend it with ease. Understanding the language was something else again. I ran into unexpected difficulties.

"Shall we meet Tom in Norwich?" I asked.

"Yes, if you mean Nor'ich," laughed my friends.

I picked up the unused "W" and pocketed it along with the leftovers from Worchestershire sauce.

The British use international road signs and I quickly learned the wordless signs for Men, Women, no passing, no left turn, etc. It was the signs written in English that often left me wondering.

First there was "round-about." Simply a traffic circle I was told.

The warning "verge," I learned, signified merging traffic.

"Safe lay-by" brought chuckles until it was explained it means a good place to pull off the road.

"Fly Posting Prohibited" is the equivalent of our Post No Bills.

"Dead Slow" was as amusing to our British friends as it was to us, but they missed the humor in "Please Mind the Step."

One sign, "Drive in Constant Use," made us jump back in haste, but we passed it 5 days straight without seeing any sign of traffic at all.

We understood, but found terribly formal, the proclamation: "Car will be impounded for improper parking."

"Jumble Sale" turned out to be a highly descriptive term for a rummage sale in progress in a church yard.

In the subway was a sign condemning litter. It read "It's not nice for you. It's not nice for us."

Straight and to the point was a railroad sign, "To prevent draughts, do not open window."

One charming lady whom I met on a train to Brighton told me she was a Rambler. Ramblers, it seems, are people who like to walk, and there are many Rambler Clubs in the country.

She told about a famous Ramble for Charity in which her father had taken part when she was a girl. She said the walkers went the 60 miles from London to Brighton in 2 days.

Later in our own "rambles," we met a man whom our friends considered "shirty," meaning he was a bit of a stuffed shirt, ye know.

Their description of the country inn we spent a night in was equally good. They said it was "pricey" for the services offered.

My favorite sign was on the fence surrounding a small, neat cottage out in the country in East Anglia. It read: "Please set the gate firmly, small child loose."

The image of a small child, loose, and against whom a gate must be set firmly, will dance in my head forever.

Dream Vacation (3)
September 5, 1967

The first time Tom went to Europe, he spent five days in Switzerland and never saw a mountain. It was winter, and fog and mist made a myth of the peaks he should have seen. His plane skirted a shrouded Mont Blanc. He stayed in Geneva, surrounded by the Juras, but fog blanked them out. He traveled to Zurich, but still no mountains. This trip, Tom discovered that the Alps are really there, and even got the age-old urge to do a little climbing.

We left Geneva by train early in the morning. The route along the north shore of Lake Geneva took us through vineyards, rolling farms, sharp foothills, and beautiful, clean villages. Each village was clustered around a church and nestled along the lake. A few new apartment buildings towered over the older tile-roofed houses. But most of the houses had a timeless, sun-bleached look--as if they had always been there. At each stop we marveled at the attractive stations, each with flower planters or formal gardens tumbling colorful "bouquets" into view of the passing trains.

A simple sign, "Chillon," identified the castle where Francois de Bonnivard, Lord Byron's famous Prisoner of Chillon, was actually held captive. The castle lies between the rail tracks and the lake. Part of it seems almost to sit on the lake itself, and one imagines the double punishment of being in a dungeon and of missing the magnificent sight of the sun or the moon-mirrored lake.

A few miles along, the French railway signs gave way to German. At Visp, in this German-tongued sector of Switzerland, we boarded a cog railroad for the uphill ride to Zermatt. The train was bright and new and took the sharp ascent in graceful sweeping curves. Around the bend we would go, our ears would pop, and then the breathtaking sight of miles of sloping valley would open into view below us.

Peak after peak came majestically into sight, until finally the train pulled into Zermatt, a picture-book town at the foot of the mountain we had come to see--the Matterhorn! There are no cars in Zermatt. Horse-drawn carriages meet the trains and carry passengers and luggage to the hotels which line the village streets. The merry tinkle of harness bells warns aside the tourists who stroll through the town, in the middle of the streets. There is much to see. There are chocolate shops, pastry shops, clothing shops and restaurants with gay umbrella-topped tables. Every street leads out of the village and turns into a mountain trail. Knickers and climbing boots are the uniform of the day. Even children wear the boots. Women, who apparently are only going for a little stroll, don their heavy footwear but wear delicate sun dresses above--a comic contrast.

From Zermatt we took a slower-moving cog to Riffelalp. We got off at the tiny cliff-side station, walked up a curving trail, and there it was--the mighty, glistening Matterhorn. We sat, enthralled by its awesome beauty for 15 or 20 minutes, and then the show was over for the day. A cloud of mist descended over the peak like a last-act curtain. It was almost as if someone had decided a longer view would have been too much for mere mortal man.

Coming down the mountain from Zermatt to Visp, the train came to a sudden stop. After half an hour of craning from the windows, a few brave passengers walked the narrow track to find out what the trouble was. Word came back, mostly in German with an occasional smattering of English, that the train was in trouble. The river which raced down the mountain had burst its banks, spilling silt and rocks across 30 feet of track.

The train backed up to a call box on a pole a few feet up the mountain. Then, because night was fast falling, all the passengers were asked to leave the train and walk the narrow track to a grassy clearing some 50 yards below.

The lucky boot-wearers trudged on ahead, but those of us in everyday shoes inched along the track, sliding in the mud and wincing at the rocks. The track went over the river in 2 spots and all courage deserted me as I approached the first crossing. There was no bridge, no side rail. The track crossed nakedly and the river thundered in raging haste some 20 feet below, clearly visible between the wet and slippery ties.

My feet froze. Tom urged me forward, but my heart and head rebelled, and my knees melted in fear. Suddenly I heard a strange, rapid gait beside me. A man on crutches was limping along on the tracks, his one shoe and 2 crutches finding solid footing as surely as a mountain goat. That did it. I clutched Tom's waist and followed behind him, slipping, sliding and praying.

A soft drizzle fell and it grew dark. We sat for 2 and a half hours in the grass and wondered at the power of the mountains, and the composure of our fellow-sufferers. Many had small children whom they carried over the same perilous trestles which had almost stopped me. They sat in small family groups and talked quietly. One group complained loudly and we were embarrassed to find that they were Americans. We gave our chocolate bars to a mother with 4 children, as if to ask forgiveness for our loud-mouthed, thoughtless countrymen.

At last a trail of light wound up the slope--our rescue train. At Visp, the stationmaster put some of us aboard a "refugee special" bound for Geneva. It was long past midnight. It was too dark to see the towns and the lake as we sped along. I'd had enough scenery for one day anyway. I cuddled up against Tom and put down my purse and the small white box I was carrying.

Small. White. Square. Box.

Apparently, all the while I had been fearing for my life as I inched over the slippery trestles, I had tightly clutched my box.

"I thought you were going to drop your purse once or twice, but you never lost your grip on that chocolate torte," teased Tom.

The University Is Where Daddy Works
September 26, 1967

Our 7 children are college kids. What's that you said about the poorhouse? Perhaps what I should have said is that they are college-town kids. They're not old enough to be enrolled yet, and we're still a few years from the bankruptcy of sliding-scale tuition.

But as faculty children, they have lived on or near a campus all the years they can remember, and MSU is a big thing in their lives. It sets the pace for their education and recreation, their dress, their view of the world, and the tone of the town they live in. But most of this happens without their awareness.

Ellen, Dale and Kate are old enough to use the pool and the ice rink and cheer for State at football, hockey and basketball games. Occasionally, we take them to a concert, play or travelog. They think the planetarium is interesting, and when pressured, they even look things up in the university library.

But the younger children aren't too sure just what a university is. I suspect they see it as a place with a lot of grass to run on, a lot of flowers to smell and a lot of buildings between the grass and the flowers. They like to feed the ducks, ride in the canoes or throw rocks into the river. They tolerate the art center, enjoy the museum and adore the steam engine.

They know it's a fine place to take grandmothers and other equally important guests to see the gardens. They know it blooms with purple, pink, yellow, white and new-green shrubs in the spring, and blazes with yellow, red and rusty brown trees in the fall.

Students? Ideas? Breakthroughs? Technology? Protest? Oh, yeah, all those things, but what the university really is, is the place where Daddy works. It may come as a surprise to the taxpayers of Michigan, the Board of Trustees, President Hannah and some 40,000 students, but to 7 junior-sized citizens of East Lansing, MSU is "Daddy's university," and I guess that automatically makes it theirs.

Like every kid who thinks it's a special treat to visit Daddy's office, Daddy's store, or Daddy's factory, ours like to visit Daddy's university. When we first came to town, we used to take the children for walks through the park-like campus almost every Sunday. That is, we walked. They ran, skipped, chased, climbed and fell.

But that was before the enrollment exploded and PDA sprang up beneath every bush and behind every bank. PDA is Public Display of Affection, and as far as college students are concerned, any day in the year is spring and any place or any time is right for love. Now, unless we happen to be talking about the birds and the bees anyway, we stick to the main paths. The area around Cowles House is fairly safe and the power plant seems unromantic enough.

"Why do they call it Kissing Rock," we ask Mike.

"Cause if you pass it, you gotta kiss it," he says.

There are 2 times when you can take the family on campus without blinders--the time it's most crowded, like a football afternoon, and the time it's least crowded, like last week, just before the students came back from vacation.

Last week the summer terms and seminars were all over and the fall term was still several days away. A few students had begun to trickle in, and in the day drums and air hammers beat out a rhythmic duet. But at twilight, things were so quiet that only Beaumont's chimes and the mechanical brains in data processing seemed to be working.

Students? Ideas? Breakthroughs? Etc.? The computers seemed to be clicking out a reply: Next week! Registration! Enrollment! Classes! Etc.!

Beth, Meg, Mike and Drew and I rode over with Tom one such twilight to return a car to the garage under the stadium. The arena was hauntingly hollow, like an empty honeycomb. The kids yelled as loud as they dared, and giggled as their echoes rang through the ramps.

"What's a stadium," we asked Drew.

"It's where the gas station is, and all those cars with stickers on 'em!"

We walked over to see the ducks. Usually they are too stuffed to look up, but when students are gone the pickings are poor and they came waddling for hand-outs. As we left, a parade of 20 or 30 ducks followed us over the grass and up the path, hoping for more.

We strolled over to admire Wells Hall, brand new and expectantly empty. The building, up. The grass, in. The trees, tall. The students, coming. The kids played Indian, and stalked down a bike path. We rushed them across Circle Drive, out of habit, but there were no cars. We sat beneath the tower and watched the big hand edge up to 8 o'clock.

"Why doesn't it ring?" pleaded Beth.

"It will, the minute you turn away," we warned.

She looked away. It rang. There was no answering throb of life.

"What's a multiversity, Peg?" we ask.

"Does it have something to do with students," she wonders.

"Something," we murmur.

Football Fan
October 6, 1967

Some days it's hard to be a lady. In the supermarket I'm all sugar and spice.

"You overcharged me on the spinach? Well, it's only a few cents. Don't let it worry you."

"Yes, my heel does hurt where you slammed your cart into it, but I'm sure I was at fault."

I'm equally polite on the phone.

"Of course I'll answer 53 questions for your survey on 'Grits in the Northern Diet.' Just wait until I bind my dripping hair up in a towel."

I'm even a ladylike driver.

"Get up off the floor, Honey. No, that man didn't stop, but I'm sure he didn't mean to make us jump the curb."

But don't be misled by my housewifely Good Conduct Medal. All it takes to make me forget myself is a home game at Spartan Stadium.

Give me 2 choruses of MSU's fight song, squeeze me cozily amid 75,000 other crazy nuts, and I'm a disgrace to the memory of Emily Post.

I yell at the coach, the teams, the officials and even the spectators.

I yell when we're winning (remember last year?), and I yell when we're not (or would you rather not talk about it?).

I start the afternoon with my calling-the-kids-while-the neighbors-are-watching voice, but by the end of the last quarter, I'm putting everything I've got into my calling-the-kids-and-the-heck-with-the-neighbors howl.

To the coach, when we're ahead: "Atta boy, Duff, old boy, you call 'em!"

To the same coach, at other times: "Hey, Duffy, quit kidding, send in the real team."

To the team, anytime: "'If you can't do anything else, fall forward!"

To the refs: "Pick up that hankie, you butterfingers, you."

To a critic: "Drop dead."

To a noisy plane overhead, "Drop."

To a boy on his first trip over my toes: "Why didn't you eat at home?"

To the same boy on the second trip: "Why didn't you drink at home?"

To you-know-who, the third time: "Why didn't you--aw, hurry up, you're blocking the view!"

To Tom: "Whaddyamean I missed it? A touchdown?"

To the stadium, the campus, Mason, Grand Ledge and points East: "We made it! We made it! We made it!"

In between insults and entreaties that would put a fish wife to shame, do I sit demurely, breath abated, as the action resumes? Not this gal. I hop, jump, clap, stomp and then I toss in a few blocking motions, fast passes and quick kicks for good measure.

When it's all over, win or lose, I slink out of the stadium, restored to sanity, and hoping hopelessly that nobody I know heard or saw me.

P.S. To the lady in the red hat: Gosh, girl, I'm sorry about that umbrella.

[The following is a reply sent to the *Towne Courier* to this column October 24, 1967]

I don't often volunteer advice. Not any more. (I admit to having lived that long.) But I can't resist a word to Kaye Naybor. Her lady-at-a-football-game woes touched a sympathetic heart.

My advice for her: Next game manage to sit next to or even near--or for that matter, on the same side of the field as--a football player's mother.

Before Kaye has had a chance to lose her "calling-the-kids-while-the-neighbors-are watching voice" she'll discover that this is her hey-day. She can yell, screetch, scream, stomp, or roar. Next to the football player's mother, she'll look like Mrs. Prim-and-Proper herself.

I know this for a fact. I'm one of those mothers. A brand-new one. (I shudder as I look ahead into the long years of this.) Early on game day I can feel myself becoming a bit edgy. I chatter. To my son, Mike: "Now don't over-exert yourself--the other children can do your chores. How's your knee feeling?"

"What should you eat? Nothing greasy, something solid but not heavy, nothing sweet, nothing sour. What about that bruise on your arm? Is your duffle bag packed? What time are you to be at the gym?"

The frenzy inside mounts. I must be out of my cotton-picking mind to go along with this! He's so skinny. Tall, yes--but skinny. This is sheer madness. I should have thought of all this when I married a football player. Maybe the game'll be cancelled. That's it. Rain, maybe? Snow? Sleet? No-- face it, they don't call off football games.

At game time, the opposing team trots out on the field. I wail for the enemy across the field to hear:

"They're giants! What are they doing in this league anyway? Put in their little brothers."

I shout at the refs. I yell at the players. I beseech the crowd to join me in demanding justice.

Our team comes onto the field. For one fraction of an instant I'm quiet. They actually look BIG. It must be the pads. There's Mike. Now, why did I ever think he was skinny? Look how he handles himself--so sure and confident. Come on, fellas, this is our day. Get in there and fight.

The whistle blows--there's nothing else in the world but MY team. They kick, I kick; they tackle, I tackle; they pass, and my hands are stretched high in the air to catch.

I plead with them; I scold them; I praise them; and if one should happen to be a bit slow in getting up, I groan in agony. Best friends go unrecognized. My other children (who are always there en masse) are ignored. My husband's reassurances go unheeded. The game's the thing--the only thing.

I don't reach sanity, till I get back home. Hoarse throat, shot nerves, drained of all energy, I collapse. Hey, Kaye, wanna join me next week?

A football mother

Five-Year-Olds
November 14, 1967

[Editor's Note: This column was written for the 5th anniversary of The Towne Courier.]

What's that about a 5th birthday?

Wait until I finish getting this chewing gum off the rug and I'll tell you all about 5-year-olds.

Of course, I don't claim to be an expert, but I have a 5-year-old now. And I had 6 before him. And one mad year we had 2 of them--Meg and Mike are less than 11 months apart. Boy, that was a year!

I'm no Spock or Gesell, but have I had EXPERIENCE!

Talk about the "Terrible 2's." Wait until you live through the "Fiendish 5's."

A 5-year-old is innocent and conniving, all at once.

He's baby enough to have winning ways, and man enough to exasperate.

He alternately demands your protection, and demands that you let him jump his fences and try his wings.

He wants you to allow for his tender years, but respect his wisdom.

He loves praise, but begins to accept criticism, reluctantly.

At times he is annoyingly timid. On other days, he is embarrassingly bold.

He's just becoming aware of his appearance, and he begins to enjoy dressing up for something special.

Some days he droops before his day is done. Other days he has sparkle enough for 2 days in one.

Sometimes he is righteous; other times he's just plain stubborn.

At one time he's a sophisticated bore. At others, he's alive with imagination and creativity.

He can be complimentary and attentive or distant and remote.

He knows you are important to him, but he isn't sure he wants you to know that he knows.

He alternately loves his peers, and hates them with fury. He competes with them even when he likes them.

He respects his elders, but you have the feeling that he wouldn't if he didn't have to.

He's torn between being a fresh, young kid forever--or leaping too soon to maturity.

Hide something, he's sure to find it.

Invite him to take something, he's suspicious.

Demand he take something--well, you'll soon learn that NEVER works.

Spiteful? Almost never.

Quick-tempered? Sometimes.

Possessive? More than he likes to admit.

Boastful? Only a bit.

You know what he does best at this age? He grows!

By the way, what do you call your 5-year-old?

"The Towne Courier."

Towne Courier? Boy, that's some name to give a kid!

I wonder what the future holds for him?

What's A Good Day?
November 21, 1967

"Did you have a good day?"

"Wonderful! How about you?"

"Well, let me think."

It is better than Friday. On Friday the leg broke off the kitchen table--during breakfast.

It was a better day than Monday. On Monday the bill came to cut down the 2 elms.

It was better than a week ago Thursday. A week ago Thursday, Beth got sick all over the settee. When the seat covers came back from the cleaners, the seams had parted in 4 places.

It was better than the day the paper clip got stuck in the kitchen disposer.

It was loads better than the day I got a flat in the middle of the intersection at East Michigan and Pennsylvania Ave.

And any day when the phone rings 11 times and none of the calls is (a) a wrong number, (b) a sales pitch, (c) a request for money, or (d) a good friend, who has done a million favors for you, asking you to serve on yet another committee—well that's got to be a good day.

A capital letter Good Day is something else. That's the kind of a day when something terrific happens.

Such as:

--You go to the dress shop and they have three dresses you like, all in your size. You try the nicest one on, and lo and behold, it's too big. The clerk finds the right color the next smaller size and it fits perfectly. You take it to the cashier and she notices that the tag is marked "10% Off." You take it home and your teenage daughter looks it over, scowls momentarily, and then says, "Hey, that's a real smart number."

--The electrician comes and tells you (for free), that all you need is a 35-cent switch which he's sure your husband can put in himself.

--You find a parking place right smack in front of the Towne Courier, and there is half an hour left on the meter,

--Tom invites a special guest for dinner and calls to ask (at 5:15), if it's all right. Wonder of wonders, the house is spotless, and a 10-pound turkey you just happened to be cooking is within half an hour of being done. Would you believe fresh apple pie, too? Well at least sherbet in the freezer.

--Sally at the beauty parlor raves over the "the natural waves" she thinks she sees, and says she doesn't think you're nearly speckled enough to dye yet.

--Tom has a meeting, Ellen takes a lunch, Dale has student council and Kate eats with a friend. With only 5 for lunch, yesterday's leftovers go around with ease, and just happen to be everybody's favorite dish.

--Drew leaves the water running in the bathroom sink but the plug is up and the outgo stays 2 drops ahead of disaster.

--Your meeting runs overtime but you just have to stop at the store. You pick the shortest check-out line--6 people. It turns out three of the people are together, two others are buying cigarettes only, and the 6th one forgot to get bread and drops out to let you go ahead. The cash register does not jam, you easily slip out of the parking lot into practically no traffic on Grand River Ave., and you get home just in time to let the dog out before you know what happens to the kitchen floor.

--The checkbook balances.

--Tom looks at you in that special way that makes the wrinkles fade, the pounds melt, and the years fall away.

The Santa Calendar
December 19, 1967

December has 31 days. But to the kids at our house, only 25 of them count. Take December 26, for instance. Was there ever a worse day? The day AFTER Christmas is a child's idea of a bad dream.

"Mommy, what can I do?"

"Play with your Christmas toys."

"I did that yesterday."

"Well then, play with your brother's Christmas toys."

"His are all broken."

"What did you do last week, before you had all those new toys?"

"Oh that was different. Last week I was busy waiting for Christmas."

"Good, you've got 364 days to wait for next Christmas and you can start right now."

It doesn't work. Everyone knows you begin waiting for Christmas on December 1. That's the day the big feed store calendar (if you're lucky enough to have a farmer in the family to send you one) goes up on the kitchen wall.

"Now kids, I want you to pay attention. Here's today, see December 1. And here's Christmas, way down here. From now until Christmas I want you to know I'm keeping track for Santa, so you better be good."

The calendar rules change every year because their memory is short and Mama's heart isn't really in it.

I mean it takes a lot of nerve to look at a 4-year-old in the eye and put his name in big black letters. Five names and Santa drops one present off your list.

I use the calendar, but mostly as a warning.

"Stop that kicking right now. Where's that black marker?"

The kicking stops. Actually, I hide the marker, but once in a while the kids find it and bring it to me. They find it faster if they are the injured party.

"Mike ripped my school picture and Daddy didn't even see it yet. Here's the marker, Mom."

When I'm forced to, I defile the calendar with a dishonored name.

Meg and Beth react with embarrassment. They know one name is quite a ways from 5 so they don't worry too much.

Drew, the "baby," is always the most upset. He melts into hot hears and deep sobs fill his breast.

At times like this I wonder if it's all worth it. I mean, after all, what's a little torn wallpaper?

Mike, the 5-year-old, reacts with deep down worry, but on the surface he's all bravado and spunk.

"Ha, who cares if I don't get any presents. I don't care if all I get is coal and wood (his sisters' warning). I like coal and wood. I like it. I like it. I like coal. Mama, what's coal?"

The calendar hovers over us every waiting day.

"Dale, Mama says take the trash out right out. You better, too, Dale, or Mama says she'll put you on the calendar." (Mama didn't say that.)

"Daddy, did you forget to pick up your suit from the cleaners again? Bet Mama's gonna put you on the calendar." (Mama isn't gonna.)

"Mama, Ellen forgot to take Ginger out and Ginger did a mess on the floor."

"Mama, does Ellen's name have to go on or Ginger's?" (Mama says both to Drew's delight and Ginger's canine unconcern.)

"Mama, my teacher scolded the wrong boy today. Will Mr. Lewis put her name on his calendar?" (Mama explains that the Santa list is only for children); grownups have to be good for the sake of a better world, not for presents. Mike ignores this and assures Meg that he's seen Mr. Lewis' calendar and there are "lotsa names" on it.

Mom and Dad come home after the children's bedtime one night and find they are both blacklisted. At breakfast we get the indictment.

"Ellen said we could because you promised to be home in time for a story and you weren't."

As December 26 drags on, someone remembers the calendar.

"What does Santa do with the toys we don't get?" wonders Meg.

"He gives them to the poor kids," says Kate.

"Gosh, Mama, when we wrapped those things to give away you said some poor kids get hardly any presents."

"Do you think we should have been naughtier so they could have had more of our good stuff?"

Ellen comes to the rescue.

"It doesn't work that way. It's better to be good because every good deed is a present for Jesus. How many like to give presents to Baby Jesus?"

All the sticky hands shoot up.

Maybe next year we can forget about the Santa calendar.

Mother to Santa
December 25, 1967

Dear Santa:

I know things are as hectic around your place this week as they are around mine, but I thought I should write a few words in regard to the children's letters this year.

For years I had to write them all myself, but this year all the children but Mike and Drew wrote their own.

I consulted on some words like 'Etch-a-Sketch' and 'Gobble-de-Goop,' but when Kate got stuck on Ouija she was smart enough to get out the mail order catalog and look it up.

As for Ellen and Dale, I didn't even get to see their letters. One of the things I wanted to be sure to remember to tell you was that if Dale asked for that $535 set of drums he saw in the book, you're to forget it.

That's right, don't (do not) bring them.

Tom and I feel that if a 14-year-old boy wants something that costs that much, he'd better work for it himself.

Besides, he has a snare already and you should hear the racket he can make on just one drum--and the set has 6!

Mike and Drew made me write super road-race on their letters, but you can draw a line through that too, on both lists.

It's not that I don't trust your judgment, Santa. But I thought you might get confused in such a big family and forget that they are only 5 and 4 and at that age their eyes are bigger than their toy chests.

Meg is to get the bike. We promised it to her for her birthday, but if you remember that was when Tom and I were away and when we got back we got busy with school clothes and such things and she never got the bike.

The thing is, if Meg gets a bike, Beth should have one too. Beth is the one who went from the middle-sized trike to Ellen's 26-inch bike without a tumble in-between.

She was only 5, but she was so determined she could ride that big thing that we let her keep it.

But now, it's in pretty bad shape.

Ellen got it when she was in the 3rd grade and she's 16 now. So better figure on 2 bikes again this year.

By the way, the bike you brought Kate last year gave us no trouble at all, but the "English" you brought for Dale has been in the shop 3 times already.

Which brings me to another thing I wanted to call to your attention.

I hate to have to bring it up, but the quality of Christmas toys just isn't what it used to be. I know that with the population what it is these days you just can't make all your own toys anymore, but maybe you'd better supervise your sub-contractors a bit more strictly.

One manufacturer who used to make all-wood toys has substituted plastic screws on that little work bench the boys always like so much.

Dale's lasted through Kate, Beth, Meg and Mike, but last Christmas you brought a new one for Drew and the screw broke the first time he took it apart.

We complained to the company and they replaced the screw but by the third week 2 more had broken so we gave up.

Another thing--Tom is resigned now to greeting each Christmas dawn with pliers and hammer in hand, but he does get a bit upset when the screws don't come out even.

It isn't too bad if there is one missing; we can usually find one to match. But when one is left over, it sometimes takes hours to find out where we goofed.

So tell the boys at the factory to count carefully.

Like I said, I didn't get to read Ellen's letter, but I know she must have asked for clothes.

She understands how much it costs to feed and dress this clan, so I know she hasn't asked for anything unreasonable.

So if you can manage a groovy sweater in addition to the things she really needs, I'm sure she'd be delighted.

Be sure the books you pick for Kate are advanced for a 5th grader. She read the Narnia fantasies by C. S. Lewis and loved them, so we know she's ready for something meaty.

But she's only 10, so don't forget to bring her some little-girl toys too.

Don't be surprised at the 2 extra stockings on the mantle this year. The kids decided to hang one for Ellen's dog, Ginger.

Doggy boots might help my floor problem, but a gift certificate for the MSU clinic might be appropriate in view of what it costs for all the care she needs.

The last stocking will be Uncle Don's. He's a junior at the university, so don't be surprised if he hangs up a pair of fishnet tights and asks you to fill them with something size 10 and blonde.

Be sure to notice the university tree as you come down Abbott—it's such a pretty sight. And if you're not too busy dodging traffic on Grand River Ave., give a look at the pine roping and red bows on the lamp poles--they're delightfully old fashioned and tasteful.

Give our love to Mrs. Claus and wish a Merry Christmas to all from your Naybors--Tom, Kaye, Ellen, Dale, Kate, Beth, Meg, Mike and Drew.

1968

Party Time
January 2, 1968

It's the season for partying.

I think parties are great, no matter what the season or the reason. But to tell the truth, I'm a little bit behind in my entertaining.

About 4 years, to be indefinite.

This means that when I finally do get around to having a party, it has to be an open house. Open barn would be even better.

But my idea of elegant entertaining is the small dinner party--say for 8 or 10 at the most.

The table should be sparkling, the food exotic, the candles lit, the company witty, the conversation brilliant, and the children absolutely absent.

None of this comes easy in a house where normally the table is crowded, the food leftover, the candles for birthdays only, the company witless, the conversation mostly through stuffed mouths, and the children absolutely abundant.

But the ladies' magazines are a lot of help. They don't have too many ideas about how to pretend 7 children aren't around, but they are loaded with ideas for parties.

Month after month they have new ways to be festive.

In March it's "Keep Up with the Joneses, Give a Brunch." In June it's "Keep Up with the Smiths, Give a Pool Party."

In August, it's "Keep Up with the Johnson's, Give a Texas Barbeque."

I keep waiting for "Keep Up With the Housework, Give a Cleaning Party."

They make it all sound like fun, and over the years as I tried to keep up with the diapers and the mending, I've collected helpful hints to graciousness.

Enough of "Lunch for 63 Made Easy," "Souperior Suppers," and "Leaning Tower of Pizza" parties.

I'm beguiled by "Ways to Winning Wining," "Corking Cocktail Capers," "Escargot-a-Go-Go," or "A Loaf of Bread, a Bottle of Wine and Roquefort."

But now it's winter entertaining time and one authority challenges me to be "The Perfect Hostess." What's more, there is a step-by-step path to perfection to follow.

It's such a good plan that I'm passing it on to you. We may soon lose Lenore [Romney] to Washington, and the rest of us should be ready to carry East Lansing's torch of hospitality.

Just one thing more. If you don't happen to have 7 active children, a forgetful husband, a playful puppy and a meager budget, you can forget about my parenthetical notes.

Step 1: Set a date, preferably a month away.

(Preferably a million months away, but if you've really decided to go through with this, better make it next week before you lose your nerve. Whatever you do, don't choose Friday or Saturday night. The kids don't have school the next day, and they'll never stop licking at the dip and go to bed.)

Step 2: Make up a guest list of interesting and compatible people who know how you live and will not expect a style beyond your means.

(Don't invite your sister-in-law. She knows all too well how you live and you don't want that kind of a party.)

Step 3: Choose a menu that is easy to prepare, quick to serve and elegant to taste.

(If you can't manage all that, stick with "easy to prepare." Foreign dishes are good. If it comes out a bit queer, you can say it's a provincial variation a native taught you.)

Step 4: Check linens and wash to refresh. Check silver and polish. Check china and replace broken and chipped pieces.

(No, paper won't do this time. And if you haven't used the coffee service since the first baby was christened, you may need more than polish to restore it.)

Step 5: Pretend you are a guest and walk through the house in a kind of preview of your party. Can you think of anything that would make your home more hospitable?

(Yes, but it's too late now for wallpaper and new furniture.)

Step 6: On the 3rd day before the party, shop for all the groceries you will need.

(Pick up some eggs and cereal in case the family gets hungry sometime.)

Step 7: On the 2nd day before the party, clean house completely.

(If that looks like more than a one-day job, clean the downstairs and put a quarantine sign on the 2nd floor landing.)

Step 8: The day before the party, make the molded salad, prepare the sauce for the vegetables, marinate the meat, and bake the dessert.

(In your spare moments, feed your family the eggs and cereal you stocked up on.)

Step 9: The day of the party, set the table, make a centerpiece, and clean the bathrooms before lunch. After lunch, whip the topping, chill the wine, and start the meat cooking.

(At 5, feed the kids some more eggs and cereal and banish them to the quarantined area. Better clean the bathrooms again.)

Step 10: Bathe and rest with your feet up for 30 minutes at least before you greet your guests.

(When the doorbell rings, send your husband to answer it while you take the racing cars off the dining room table, stir the finger holes out of the dip and give those bathrooms one more swipe.)

Steps 11 to 20: Be warm, cheerful and relaxed. Enjoy your party and your guests will too.

(If you're too warm, cheerful and relaxed, better slip upstairs and take your temperature. If it's over 101, take my advice: next time you feel a party coming on, hire a baby sitter and take the whole crowd to a Chinese restaurant.)

Ginger
January 23, 1968

It's June in January around our house. Starry-eyed suitors are crowding our doorstep, and it isn't even spring.

The object of all this affection is going around in a lovesick whirl. The rest of us are going mad. But for Ellen's sake we're gritting our teeth and facing the facts of life, and courtship, with less grumbling than we feel.

After all, Ellen was our first born, and we owe her an extra measure of understanding and patience at a time like this.

It isn't every day (thank goodness!) that your daughter's dog reaches the charming and alarming age of puberty and the whole family finds itself face to face with sex. Or as Mike puts it, "We can't let Ginger out because all those boy dogs will give her puppies and Mama says one dog is too many already."

No doubt about it, Ginger has put spice in our lives. When she first came to live with us, she was a handful of golden fluff, and you had to be careful you didn't step on her. Now you have to be careful she doesn't step on you. For 9 months she has feasted on expensive canine fodder and the unrestrained adoration of 7 kids. This exhilarating mixture has turned her into a 2-foot-tall, gangling, clumsy-pawed, hardheaded, furniture-eating, leash- straining pet-type pest.

I mean does your dog eat the wallpaper off the wall? Besides wallpaper, she also favors redwood benches, shoe insoles, cookie boxes (preferably full), mittens, plastic toys of any size or shape, and anything off the table or out of the kitchen wastebasket.

But kids need a dog, Ellen kept telling us. She wished, wheedled and wept. And when we found out that she had $40 saved toward a "marked down" $200 St. Bernard at the pet shop, we gave in. Not to the St. Bernard, but to Ginger.

All we know about Ginger's lineage is that her mother was part cocker, and her father was friendly--and large.

Ginger herself was irresistibly cuddly, helpless and responsive. Also, she was free. She seemed the perfect pet, guaranteed to engage all the kids in lessons of love and responsibility.

She came to us on a Friday. All day Saturday and Sunday the kids carried her up and down the back stairs to the yard, and learned dozens of lessons of love and responsibility.

But then came Monday, and the dawn of truth. During school hours Ginger was all mine--love, responsibility, trips to the backyard, and accidents on the floor, included. It was like having a new baby.

Summer vacation brought eager volunteers, plus the added adventure of neighborhood chases whenever Ginger decided to pit her new-found strength against that of the tenderfoot on the other end of the leash.

Trip-planning took on a new dimension. The kids were sure Ginger would love to go along. After we priced the boarding kennels, even we were tempted. But money seemed unimportant when we gave a thought to the prospect of sharing the car with 7 kids and a dog during a hot and humid shower.

From the very start, we all agreed that training is important if a dog is to fit into a family rather than disrupt it. It wasn't easy, but we all worked hard. Today I can honestly say that it has paid off. There is instant response. (We come the minute Ginger signals.)

Never is a stick of butter stolen from the table. (We've learned to put it way out of reach.)

We have no more problems about the dining room rug. (We've learned to keep that door shut or else.)

Only once did we come down in the morning to find chewed potatoes all over the floor. (We keep them on a high shelf now.)

She doesn't chew hats anymore. (We bribe her with treats until she lets go.)

She never jumps on the neighbors when they walk in. (They all know enough to come to the front door now.)

Boy, are we trained!

Learning to Drive
February 6, 1968

Say "Abracadabra." Or "Open Sesame." Or "Temporary Instruction Permit." The first two are kid stuff, but that last phrase has a magical ring for every 16-year-old in the state of Michigan, and ours is no exception.

She comes home, walking on air.

"I passed. I got it. I can drive!" she bubbles.

"You passed. You got it. Who says you can drive?" her parents bristle.

But Honorable Parents are only quibbling. If she got her "TIP" it means that Mr. Dolan thinks she can drive well enough to try for a license. And as all East Lansing high schoolers know, Mr. Dolan is the last word when it comes to young drivers. Martin Dolan directs the high school driver training program, and if he says you're ready, how can any parent disagree?

The object of driver education is to produce safer drivers, through information and experience. In the classroom, the talk includes traffic and insurance laws, car buying, accident statistics, and enough knowledge about cars themselves to instill respect for their power, and for their ability to maim and kill.

In simulators, students get a chance to face every possible traffic situation in safety. On the range, they get their first taste of a real car. Then comes the road. It's the later phase that tends to be hard on parents. The first morning Ellen went out on the road, I had the crazy impulse to dash over to the school and mount road blocks along her route to protect her from all those nasty "other drivers." Later, I got calmer. I kept my preschoolers out of the streets, and every 5 minutes I called the police to ask if there had been any accidents lately.

"Do the kids get any experience in driving in unusual weather?" one parent asked at Parents' Night.

"We take what the good Lord sends us," said Mr. Dolan cheerfully. "But we never cancel a class because of weather."

Remember that first snowfall in November? That morning Ellen left the coddled womb of the range and drove out into the real, slushy world.

Remember that super soupy, foggy day before Christmas? That day our sweet young thing was propelling 350 horses along I-96.

I resisted the urge to call for a state police escort.

Don't get the wrong idea; I'm not a nervous driver. Sometimes my passengers get nervous, but never me. Well, almost never.

You know that watery feeling you get when you go for your road test? One day recently I had that feeling all over again. That was the day I drove part of Ellen's driver-training class to their "survey post," a busy intersection where they were supposed to observe traffic conditions. I don't know what they saw at the corner, but I know what they observed on the way over--me. Six pairs of eyes followed my feet, my hands, my eyes, my every move.

"Why do you brake with your right foot?" asked one observant observer.

"If you try to use the left on this bus, you hit the steering col—Ouch! Well, you can see what I mean."

I hated to tell her that way back when I learned to drive we used the left foot for the clutch. I was afraid she would ask me to explain what the clutch was for. I wasn't too sure about that way back when I used to use one.

But now Ellen's training is over and I can breathe easier.

All I have to worry about now is her driving.

Anybody know any good 2-lettered answers to the query, "Mom, may I take the car?"

Borrowing
February 20, 1968

"Try Mary first."

"I will, Mom."

"And if she doesn't have any, try Winnie."

"And don't spill any."

Talk about borrowing and everyone quotes Shakespeare: "Neither a borrower nor a lender be."

Polonius delivers the line, but everyone knows he's nothing but an old fool. After awhile Hamlet takes care of him.

A better quote is from the Sermon on the Mount. It goes: "Give to him that asketh thee, and from him that would borrow of thee turn not away."

Anyway, I'm glad Polonius didn't live on our block.

What good would he be in a real emergency?

Here's the picture--it's 2 minutes past 6, the meat loaf is done and Daddy is home.

"Mr. Mayor" and "The Flintstones" have just ended.

You can tell because one by one all 7 kids stream into the kitchen with the same lament, "I'm starved, when do we eat."

Daddy says Grace, and then comes the crisis.

"Amen," says Dale, "where's the butter?"

Amen, indeed!

"Try Winnie--or Mary--or Ann. But don't try that old fool Polonius!"

A neighbor is for borrowing from and lending to--and if you don't have that kind of neighbor all I can say to you is, "Have you thought about moving?"

The item most often borrowed around our corner is bread. A loaf is best, but half a loaf is better than a trip to the store at noon.

If you have a freezer, it's your neighborhood obligation to keep it stocked with "plain, white sliced."

After a time the kids get used to eating frozen bread for lunch. If it happens too often, you make grilled cheese sandwiches and the secret is yours.

Butter is second on the "10 Most Wanted" list. It's understood that margarine will do. Except when there is company.

Onions and potatoes enjoy a brisk exchange, but hardly anybody feels obligated to pay back an onion. Or vanilla.

Some items demand special borrowing techniques. For instance, if you need two eggs and nobody is around to get them but the 4-year-old, you send along a covered plastic jar.

When the 4-year-old gets home with the eggs, they are already slightly beaten and ready to go into the batter.

If what you need is a small dose of cough syrup, your safest bet is to send the cougher to get it. Then all your neighbor has to do is say: "Open wide."

Hair spray works the same way. You call and say, "I'm on my way, could you..."

Then one squirt and you're off.

Sometimes it's more of an exchange than a lending transaction that takes place. If you have 3 cans of vegetable-beef soup and one can of cream of mushroom, sometimes you can swap the mushroom for some turkey-noodle, which everybody knows will blend in with the veg/beef and then you'll have enough to feed 9 if your friend can spare some soda crackers too.

Money is something else again. Usually I borrow money only from credit unions or banks--corner or piggy.

But the other car-less noon, Ellen needed $10 immediately. I checked Dale's newspaper collection box and that yielded $3.75. 1 found a bit more in the piggy banks, but I was still short $5.50.

Coat pockets, the penny jar and the couch made up the 50 cents, but I was out of luck for the last fiver.

Finally I called around.

"If I give you a check for $5 can you spare the cash?"

Mary could, and Ellen dashed off with her $10 and 10 minutes to spare.

Do you want to know the real reason women cry when they move?

It's not for the houseful of memories they are leaving behind, it's for the cup-of-sugar credit they'll have to build up all over again.

A Dream of the White House
February 27, 1968

It was the craziest dream. Even for an election year.

There I was in the White House having breakfast 30 feet down a walnut table from Tom.

"What did you say, Dear?" I cupped my hand so my voice would carry.

"I said, what's this white stuff next to the sausages?" Tom didn't cup his hand, but his bellow was coming through loud and clear.

I tasted the white stuff.

"I think it's grits. Don't you like it?"

"No, I don't like it. Didn't you tell the cook that we're from Michigan, not from Texas?"

"Well, you see Tom, I haven't really talked to the cook yet. I can't find the kitchen, but I think I'm getting warm. I distinctly smelled barbeque sauce in one hall I was in yesterday. Now if I can only find that hall again ..."

"Okay. Say, where are the kids?"

"The helicopter came for them. They've gone to school."

"What school do they go to?"

"Why, don't you remember? Ellen and Dale go to the high school and Kate, Beth, Meg and Mike go to Bailey."

"Bailey? All that way?"

"Well, it didn't seem right to switch them just for the length of a dream."

"Tom, what will you be doing today?"

"Just the usual capital whirl--a couple of speeches, several meetings, an important luncheon. How about you? Anything special on your agenda?"

"Mostly routine. But Drew does need shoes. I thought I'd try to work in a quick shopping trip. Of course, it'll have to be Knapp's--they are the only ones who carry his width."

"Speaking of shopping, Kaye, have you straightened out that business with the budget yet?"

"No, we're still short. To tell you the truth all those zeros throw me a little. But you know how good I am with money, Tom. I'll manage to balance this one yet. I'll save a little here, borrow a little there, and maybe we'll end up with a little left at the end of the year even."

"You sure have the touch, Kaye. By the way, are you having any regrets? I mean I'm glad we decided to come into politics. How about you?"

"Oh, yes, Tom. You were right. And our country does need a good firm hand."

"Operator, I'd like to speak to the cook. Can you tell me what extension that is? Number 33? Fine, could you ring it now, please? Oh, I see. Yes, here's the white one. Yes, I'll remember not to use that red one again."

"Miss Nixon? You say you're my new secretary and your name is Miss Nixon? Oh, Gladys Nixon. For a moment...well never mind. Who do I have to see next? Oh, that man about the fighting. Was it Dale or Mike this time? I see, not the children's fighting. Yes, send him in."

"Please sit down Mr. Rusk...are you related to Sally Rusk? She teaches at the university? Oh, I see. Well, about this fighting, Mr. Rusk. I never can see much sense in it. Nobody wins."

"When Mike had that fight with Benjy Hill, I told Clara Hill, 'Clara,' I said, 'the important thing is to stop the fighting. First let's break up the fight, then let's talk.'"

"Then we shared a nice hot pot of tea and a fresh coffee cake, sour cream, it was. Does Mrs. Rusk make sour cream coffee cake? I'll give you the recipe. But you must promise to stop that fighting."

"Tired, Tom? It was a long day, wasn't it? All those committees and meetings and phone calls! We have so little time together."

"I know, Kaye, but that's politics. Say, let's go to a late movie. You see if Ellen will sit with the little kids, and I'll check in so they'll know where to reach the President in case of an emergency. Operator, give me the Vice President. Hello, that you, George? Say, Kaye and I want to dash out to a movie. Will you and Lenore take over? Fine, we'll be back around 12:30."

"That was a good movie, Tom. And if I do say so, you're still fun to be with, politics or no politics."

"Good night, Madame President. You're fun too."

Lost Child
March 19, 1968

It has happened dozens of times. There is a milling crowd; so much noise you can hardly hear your own words. You recount heads and renew your warning for everyone to hold someone's hand, and for Heaven's sake, stay together.

Suddenly the loud speaker blares. It's hard to hear all the words, but you get the gist--a little boy is lost. You know it's not one of yours, but your heart jumps anyway. You have just counted heads, but you hastily do it again, twice. You renew the old warning and grab as many moist little hands as you can hold. You turn a corner and there's a refreshment stand. You tell Tom to make it carmel corn and 2 popcorn. But wait. That's only 6.

You count again, but already your throat is dry and your chest is tight.

"One (where's Drew?), 2, 3, 4 (has anyone seen Drew?), 5, 6. Tom, Drew is lost. I know he's lost. Oh, Tom, in all this crowd, in this huge place. Oh, Tom!"

It has happened dozens of times. But each time the fear is fresh, the pain is new. Your mind flashes pictures of all the lost children, your own and others, who have wrung your heart. In your mind you can see Drew's

4-year-old brashness and boldness melt into trembling fear. But because it has happened dozens of times, you waste no time on useless panic.

"I'll look here," yells one child. "I'll look there," yells another.

"No one will look anywhere," I yell as you toss your invisible net over the whole crew and bind them to you.

"But Mom, poor Drew will cry and cry."

"Don't you want to find him?"

"Yes, I do, but I don't want to lose any of you while I'm finding him. So if you really want to help, sit down, don't move and shut up."

Tom goes straight to the officials. Because it has happened dozens of times you know this is the best and safest way. In minute the heart-scalding words come over the speaker.

"A little boy is lost. His name is Drew and he is 4. He is wearing a brown and white shirt, brown corduroy pants and cowboy boots.

"If you see him, please bring him to his father at the loudspeaker booth."

For endless minutes you sit and scan the crowd. Mindlessly you carry on a firm argument with the older children who are sure they could "find him in a minute if you'd just let me go to look."

Beth drops her popcorn and pouts for more.

"You'll have to wait," you bark sharply.

Meg confides a biological emergency.

"You'll have to wait," you whisper hopefully.

All your experience tells you that what you are doing is right. But deep within, your panic and fear fight to be heard: "Look for him! Run over here; run over there! Scream his name--Drew, can you hear me? Drew, come to Mommy! Drew! Drew! Please, God, help us!"

"Mom."

"Oh, not now Dale, just pray."

"But Mom, I think I see him. See over there. Drew! Hey, Drew, here we are."

There he is, fighting his way through a jungle of unfriendly, unseeing, unyielding adult knees. There he is, brown and white shirt, brown pants, cowboy boots and a dirty, tear-stained, funny-nosed, lovable face.

Your heart bursts. You fight back tears. Your whole being surges into silent choruses of Thank you, God, Thank you, God!

As you pick him up and hug him, you swallow the lump in your throat and you say, "Tell me Drew, do you want carmel corn or popcorn?"

And that's the last time you take kids to a zoo, park, show, exhibit, circus, carnival, fair, arena, skating rink, supermarket or department store--until the next time.

Giving Up for Lent
March 26, 1968

Mike gave up suckers for Lent. I doubt that it was his idea. I know it wasn't mine. He came home from Sunday School one day with his intention written on the back of his lesson sheet.

The message, printed in his own uncertain letters, was: "Mike gives up suckers for Lent." The unwritten message, meant for me, was: "Deliver Mike from temptation; buy gum drops, licorice or toffee, but no suckers."

All in all, I expect it is easier for him to give up suckers until Easter, than to give up hitting his sisters (which was my idea of real sacrifice).

Meg set everyone straight on the hitting business.

"You can't hit anyone for 40 days, except on Sundays when Lent doesn't count," she reported.

But Beth set her straight.

"You can't hit on Sundays either," she corrected, "because that's the day of rest."

The girls aren't the only ones who have trouble interpreting The Word.

Drew, for instance, is so pleased that God loves him even when he is naughty, that he sees little reason to be good.

He listens carefully while I explain about God and love.

After I have touched on people who are different, people who are far away, people who are near, and even people who are your brothers and sisters, I make my big point.

"Love is the most important thing there is," I say, lovingly.

"No, candy is," Drew answers, positively.

He is making great progress with his prayers, though. He no longer starts out, "Our Father, mother of God ..."

He likes my idea that you can talk to God anytime you feel like it, and in any kind of words.

"Hi God," he says, "Mama says I'm thinking about you."

Both little boys are more impressed by Samantha Stevens' ability to "twitch" bewitchingly on TV than they are by the idea of a supreme being who is everywhere and knows everything.

"Mike, do you realize that God knows everything you do?"

"Yeah. Probly he has a big computer," reasons Mike, whose tomorrow is the 21st century.

And when I spy my first shy crocus on a Beech Street lawn, I wonder myself at the magnitude of that computer.

Then, reinforced with the wonder of the fatherhood of God, I find new strength to tackle again my favorite theme, the brotherhood of man.

The kids see through me, though. They know that while I talk about peace on earth, what I really want is a little quiet at the dinner table.

I remind them to be thankful to be part of a large family because it gives them so many opportunities (preferably over the Lenten tuna casserole), to practice brotherly love.

But, they think this coloring book verse catches the spirit of brotherly love better than I do:

You're lots of fun
A wonderful brother
If you're bad today
I won't tell Mother.

I Remember When
April 2, 1968

I've decided to start lying about my age. My family assures me that I look no older today than I did last week--in spite of a birthday which tumbled me unmercifully into another decade.

Ellen says, with newly-acquired 16-year-old tact, that it isn't my gray hairs, my wrinkles, or my brood of 7 which tell my secret. She says the dead give-away to my approaching senility is my "I remembers."

She's right. But I'm hooked on the game and I can't help repeating that I remember when there was parking on E. Grand River Ave.

I remember when the library was next to the fire station. I remember when State had "only" 18,000 students. And I remember when there was hardly a duplex or an apartment building in town.

I remember when Franklin Delano Roosevelt was president (all 3 times). I remember trolleys, the Depression, the NRA and the CCC. (Ha, look those up, you younguns!)

I remember Pearl Harbor. Up until then, when anyone spoke of "the war," they meant World War I. My parents had been teenagers during that crisis and I remember being annoyed that their memories of it were so hazy.

Suddenly, there was a new war and I was a teenager. Now my memories are a bit hazy.

Aside from the sorrow of a paratrooper uncle killed after the D-Day jump, what I remember most are the shortages: no gas for the prom, no senior trips, no stiff covers for our yearbook, no sugar for punch, and no interesting boys except at the USO dances.

I remember the World's Fair. To me, that was the one in New York City in 1939. I had (and still have somewhere) bobby pins bearing the symbols of that event, the Trylon and Perisphere.

The trip to the Fair was also my first visit to Manhattan and the beginning of a love affair with the big city that has lasted to this day.

Between the Fair, the Bronx Zoo, the Bowery, the Cloisters, Wall St., and Coney Island, I wore out 2 pairs of brown and white saddle shoes. (I remember saddle shoes.)

One Sunday, we walked the entire length of the Triborough Bridge--I don't remember why, but I do remember having Italian ices and pastry on the "other end." For some of those I'd walk that far today.

I remember running boards. My father's first car was a Model T Ford, but I remember the Model A that followed it better.

We had an extension gate on the running board, and when we went on a picnic, half the lunch was packed behind this gate. When my father felt the car couldn't make a hill, he turned it around and went up in reverse.

On the way down, we always turned off the ignition and coasted. When I was about 8, I got to ride in a rumble seat. It was the treat of the year.

I remember crank telephones. A farm family we visited had one installed in a hall closet, the first telephone "booth." For years I thought all phones were supposed to be in closets.

Later I noticed that most people put them in the living room. Much later, things got really practical and I know one family that has one in 5 different rooms of their 9-room house.

I remember the Marcel. Several of my mother's friends had them, but my mother wore her hair wound in a knot until the late '30s.

By that time the machine permanent had been invented and although most of the women suspected it was harmful to the hair, most of them gave in to temptation and tried one.

Up until the time I was 10, I had my hair cut by the same barber who did my father's. The style was known as a shingle, and it was shorter than most boys wear today.

I remember the birth of Venetian blinds. I hated them on sight, and my hate grew when my parents bought them for the whole house and decided I was the logical one to clean them. I still hate them.

I remember radio. Every day I listened to Little Orphan Annie and Jack Armstrong, the All-American Boy. In the evening, there was Eddie Cantor, Charlie McCarthy, Burns and Allen, Fred Allen and The Shadow.

None of our friends ever missed the Lux Theater on Mondays or the Hit Parade on Saturdays.

I remember a birthday cake with only 8 candles. But, as you can imagine, that was a heck of a long time ago.

Debts We Owe
April 9, 1968

There's a new baby in the neighborhood. All the mothers on the block have been in to "Oh" and "Ah."

"How sweet," they say, "how tiny, how lovable, how precious."

Nobody says, "How demanding."

But as they look at the mother with her sweet, tiny, lovable, precious darling in one arm and its 24-hour needs in the other, you can tell they are remembering. At about this point they count their little dependent blessings and turn to me with the inevitable wonder, "Gosh, how do you manage with such a large family?"

There isn't any official classification table for the size of families, but most people figure it this way: 1 to 2 children make a small family; 3 to 5 is a medium sized group; 6 to 9 is large; 10 to 12 is very large, and over 12 is idiotic.

Luckily, East Lansing has a lot of families that rank in the large to very large grouping. On a really bad day only the thought that somewhere down the street someone is coping with 10 keeps you going with 7.

Most people are very diplomatic about the size of our family.

"How many children do you have now?" asked a visiting 11-year-old. I started to toss off a whimsical "I have seven, I think," but faltered when he continued with "My mother says you must be nuts."

Many people say "large family" with capitals.

"Meet my dear friend Kaye," says the hostess. "She has a Large Family."

The "L" and "F" immediately identify me to all listeners as a dropout from planned parenthood, from the battle for equality of the sexes, from the fight to keep school taxes down, and from any activity involving brains, time or even a carefree attitude.

So the question comes up again: "How do you manage with such a large family?"

If you are not Ethel Kennedy, who manages her "very large" family of 10 by being cheerful, patient, efficient and wealthy, you manage by going into debt.

In the beginning you owe the obstetrician, pediatrician and the druggist. Over the years you owe a bank for your house, a credit union for your car, a furniture store for lots of bunk beds and every shoe store in town for shoes, sneakers, slippers, boots and rubbers.

But as time goes on, you find there are other things you are in debt for besides money.

For instance you owe your closets a spring cleaning (last spring's).

You owe the kitchen walls a coat of paint (3 years overdue).

You owe to your husband a good breakfast. (He hasn't had one since that first baby came 16 years ago).

You owe to the family a chocolate cream pie. (Ice cream is so much quicker).

You owe to your mother-in-law a letter. (Her days are long and lonely while yours are crowded and short).

You owe to your oldest son a talk on sex. (Can he be 14 already? It may be too late.)

You owe to yourself time to read something deep and thoughtful. (Or even something wild and frivolous).

You owe to your neighbor a cup of coffee. (And an open ear).

You owe 9 pairs of shoes a good polishing. (They wear out so fast, it's hardly worth it).

You owe the lawn a barrel of seed. (A dime to anyone who remembers where the lawn used to be).

You owe your taste buds some homemade pizza (with black olives and anchovies).

You owe to your marriage some time, patience, and a bit of honey. (It's got to outlast the kids).

You owe your club a couple of chairmanships. (How long can you beg off?)

You owe your city your interest (and opinion).

You owe your schools your support at home. (The Naybors think any child, be he 13 or 3, is old enough to know that neighbors can be white, brown or polka dotted.)

You owe your God a million thanks (for another Easter full of hope).

The only one you don't owe is the Bureau of Internal Revenue. With 7 children you manage very well to deduct enough to make them owe you a refund.

Waiting for the Right Season
April 23, 1968

For 3 weeks now I have resisted watermelon.

Mike and Drew showed no interest in the colorless slabs that appeared off and on during the winter. But suddenly the supermarket filled a whole counter with shiny, dark green "footballs," and that was a melon of a different color.

"Buy watermelon," they begged in chorus.

"Watermelon in April? Don't be silly."

"We want some. Buy a watermelon, Mom. It looks so good."

"Say, it does look rather good. That split one is rosy and firm. Maybe--what does the price tag say? $3.86? Oh, Mike, forget it!"

"Don't cry, Drew. We'll buy something else. Oranges? Bananas? Stop crying, boys. How about bubble gum?"

Each time we go to the store they spy the melons and it's the same story all over again.

One day they looked so good to me that I even considered buying a quarter piece. But it was 90 cents.

In summer you can buy a whole melon for that. And a quarter means just a sliver apiece when you are serving 9. Talk about impulse buying!

So I told the boys the truth: "It's just too expensive now, fellows."

"Aw, Mom, you always say that."

So I lied: "Anyway, guys, it's the wrong season for watermelon. You know how turkey is for Thanksgiving? Well, watermelon has a special time too."

"When?"

"Uh--Memorial Day."

"Memorial Day?"

"Yes, and the 4th of July and Labor Day. And any time in between if the price is right--say, 89 cents apiece."

"Is Memorial Day pretty soon?"

"No, it's quite a long way off. But it won't hurt you to wait."

When you think of it, it won't hurt them to wait. But nobody today is used to waiting for anything.

Do you remember when there seemed to be a time and a place for everything? You had turkey on Thanksgiving, watermelon for the 4th, oranges and nuts for Christmas, and jelly beans for Easter.

If you saw asparagus on the market, it meant it was spring in your valley. Nowadays, it just means that a refrigerated shipment has arrived from Florida.

People were used to waiting. You waited for the strawberry season for strawberry shortcake. You waited for the first tomato to ripen in August. You waited all year it seemed for that first bite of corn on the cob.

You even waited until that magical third date to let a boy kiss you.

Nobody waits for anything anymore.

"Dad, Jean and I want to get married," says Junior.

"Wonderful," says Dad. "What year were you planning on?"

"This year, Dad. Next week. Why wait?"

An aunt in our family waited 10 years to marry her beloved. The first 5 years they kept steady company. Then they were engaged.

Each was the oldest child in an immigrant family caught in the hopelessness of the Depression.

Each worked to help feed sisters and brothers too young to work.

Each put aside a little money each week for their future life together. When there was enough money, they got married.

I know why they waited, but I don't know how they waited.

But it seems like such a strong thing to do that I intend to go on resisting those watermelons until Memorial Day.

Unless the price goes down.

Taking Messages
April 30, 1968

When things get real dull around here I scoot over to the library for excitement.

Actually, the ride down Abbott Road is far from a visit to Peyton Place. And the library itself is no Grandmother's.

It's when I get back home that the mystery and intrigue begin.

"Any messages for me?"

"Ask Kate."

"Kate, did you answer the phone?"

"Yes."

"Was it for me?"

"Yes."

"Was there a message?"

"Yes."

"Did you write it down?"

"No."

"Well, do you remember it?"

"She wants you to call her."

"Who?"

"I dunno."

Honestly, it makes you feel as if your cable has been cut.

All of which gives you an idea of why I tell friends, "If you call and I'm not home DON'T leave a message. Just call again later."

It isn't that there aren't plenty of people around to take messages. Our answering service is well-staffed. What it lacks is quality-control.

Take Meg. For a first-grader, she has a wonderful telephone-side manner.

"Naybor residence," she coos. "Who is this please?"

Then she makes a very careful note, but it's not in any language I can read. It's in "ita," the initial teaching alphabet.

It's fine if Meg is here to translate, but if she should be at school when I find the note, the "Toun Kereeir" will have a long wait for my call.

Dale, whose long legs usually get him to the phone 2 giant steps before the runner-up, answers in monosyllables.

"'Lo. No. Yep. Who? Hudson? Bye."

The message comes out, "Mom, call Mrs. Hutsin befor the lungon."

Spelling was never his strong point

Tom spells well. But like many another husband, he forgets and stuffs the note into his own pocket.

Days later, when he wears that suit again, he puzzles his secretary by wondering what "Woodingham, not after 5" can possibly mean.

Drew and Mike, neither of whom has completely conquered the alphabet yet, usually solve the problem by dangling the receiver and yelling "Mom" as loud as possible.

Then they run off to more important things. Hours later we discover the poor instrument, dead by hanging.

Beth is fairly reliable as a "Hello Girl." But once, after taking a message, she turned the paper over and drew an elephant. It was so good we put it on the bulletin board.

Several days later, under questioning, she remembered the message on the elephant's backside.

Ellen has a good batting average, but once she wrote her memo on a note-pad, closed its cover and put it safely back in the telephone desk. I missed the meeting.

So if you can't get me by phone, write me a letter. The mailman is reliable.

Although one day he--oh, I'll tell you about it when you call.

Mothers' Day Cards
May 7, 1968

The sign over the card rack said, "Mother's Day, General," and we all had a good laugh over it.

But I got to thinking: Is there anything more "general" than a Mother's Day card?

Study a whole motherhood-full and you'll discover you have been wished "the best of," you've been sent "special wishes," you mean "so much" to someone, or you're in someone's thoughts.

Cards made by children, on the other hand, are specific and to the point.

Cherished is the mother who receives a card that says, "I love you, Mother, and when you buy me that ball you promised me, be sure it is red."

When you think of it, it's crazy that greeting card companies hire adults to write Mother's Day cards.

Of course many adults do have mothers, and those who don't probably remember when they did. But an adult sees mothers with eyes dulled by sentiment and time-glossed memories.

A child, any child, sees mothers with the cold, clear eyes of a seeker of wisdom and truth and a conniver who usually gets caught.

Roam all of the card and book shops along E. Grand River, and see if you find just one card that says:

I love you, Mother,

And wish you a happy day

Even if you did

Take my slingshot away.

When you become an adult you forget all the truths you ever learned about mothers. You know that they are subject to green bottle headaches and need more iron than a teenager, but you forget that it was they who invented itchy sweaters, washcloths, pediatricians, probably cauliflower, and certainly Mother's Day.

(Have you noticed there isn't any Children's Day?)

What the card writers need is a juvenile board of advisors so that henceforth Mother's Day cards can be beautiful on the outside and truthful on the inside, like the ideal mother herself.

Then when a mother (still breathless from climbing to the garage roof to rescue Jimmy who had fun going up but chickened out when he looked down) gets a greeting, she would know that she was loved not simply because she cares, guides, aids, or just "is."

She would know she was loved because she loves, and in spite of the fact that a mother is someone who:

Can see that you are playing in the street, even if she is not looking.

Thinks that when you and the boy next door are playing out front, he ought to use his bathroom rather than yours.

Makes you scrub the "suntan" on your neck until it rubs off like dirt.

Winces when the doctor gives you a shot.

Can tell by looking at the thermometer whether you need a sweater.

Says your artwork is out of this world and makes your big brother shush when he agrees that it is unearthly.

Almost always knows exactly what birthday present would bring you most joy.

Will hug you and wash your cut even if you got hurt doing something you were warned not to do.

Is vague on anything scientific except the power of soap over germs.

Cooks 2 vegetables you hate, and thinks she is giving you a break when she says you only have to eat one.

Peels 2,467 potatoes a year, and is glad you like rice occasionally.

Knows automatically which of 7 equally guilty-looking kids ate the last candy bar without asking.

Puts gigantic patches on the knees of your jeans, but thinks pocket holes are unimportant.

Knows all along that the pot, flower seed and dirt you need for school is for a Mother's Day plant, but is surprised anyway when you come home with a flourishing lima bean.

Or lends you money to buy her a present.

And alternately kisses and spanks you for the same reason--because she loves you.

What's for Dinner?
May 28, 1968

I like to think our children are good eaters.

I like to think that, and it helps me to make it from Sunday to Saturday.

"The kids will eat anything," I tell my neighbor who offered to give them lunch the day I am away.

"Okay. How about tomato soup and tuna sandwiches?" she asks, reasonably.

"Uh. Well, Ellen and Mike will eat both of those and love it all. Kate and Dale will eat the sandwich, but not the soup. Meg likes the soup but no tuna. And Beth and Drew--say, how about switching to peanut butter?"

"Fine, will they all eat that?"

"You had to ask."

From the size of my grocery bill (you groaned at the national debt?) you can tell that quantity isn't the issue at hand.

The checkout girl at the supermarket always asks, "Having company?" as she loads the sixth bag.

"I hope not," I mumble.

When I come back 3 days later she alerts the manager. She figures I'm some kind of Agent 99 sent out by the company to check on the help.

Ask me what my family likes to eat and all I can answer is "Lots!"

Ask me if they're picky, choosy, fussy, and all I can answer is that it preserves my sanity to pretend they're not.

I manage the suppers fairly well. I cook a balanced meal every evening--meat they like, balanced by vegetables they hate; potatoes they love, balanced by salads they tolerate; and liver balanced by chocolate fudge cake.

Lunch is the real headache.

"Do you want baloney, ham loaf or salami?" I ask as they troop in.

"Do you have any leftovers?" they ask.

"Leftovers? Let me see. Yes, I have half a cup of peas, but I had my heart set on tossing them into tonight's stew."

"What else have you got?"

"Baloney, ham loaf and salami."

"Ugh! I'll take peanut butter."

The day I'm big on peanut butter, I'm greeted with, "Kathy's mom has leftover spaghetti today."

Leftover spaghetti is manna to leftover lovers. Let the Olympians have their ambrosia, let the Beautiful People have their caviar. But in a certain house on a certain street in a certain Midwestern university town, the peak of culinary perfection is leftover spaghetti.

But a certain mother gets heartburn at the mere mention of the name.

"Leftover spaghetti! We had it yesterday."

"I know. I like it. Besides, I was the last one home and there was only a spoonful left, remember?"

I remember. It's the same every time. On spaghetti night I cook enough to serve 20, according to package estimates. The package underestimates.

I serve 9 nicely at supper, but the amount left for the anticipated gourmet lunch is always below expectations. The slow runner gets a baloney sandwich, and I get protests.

Next time I take the pop bottles back to the store, I'm going to donate the refund to science. The sooner they invent a meal in a pill the better.

Letter to the Board of Education
June 4, 1968

Dear Board of Education

Normally I'd be the last one to accuse you of going around making trouble.

But some of my neighbors have been avoiding me for the past few days, and I think it's all your fault.

It's not that I think you are picking on me, but after all, 18.6 mills? And just because all 7 of our children will be in school next year!

You can talk all your like about only 4.1mills of that being an increase and the rest being a renewal of last year's funds, but I can see right through that ruse.

Not 2 days had passed after I registered Drew for kindergarten and there you were having coffees to explain to everybody about the "increased enrollment."

I can see right through the language in that little yellow bulletin you're passing out to all the voters, too.

You call it "Plan for Continuing Progress," but I know that between the lines you're calling it "Plan for staying even now that the Naybors are all in school."

I caught that dig about "improvement of the math curriculum in all grades through the services of consultants etc." too.

I know you've been angry all along because I wrote that note to Kate's teacher. But you've got to understand that after 7 times 12, it's just a maze of wrong numbers to me.

And that business about the new primary science program. You heard about the hamsters having .5 babies, didn't you? So I was wrong about Simon (oops, Simonetta) and Garfunkel. So sue me.

As for your aim to "reduce class size, where possible," that one really hit home. Dale even offered to drop out of school if that would help balance things.

But his grandfather told him education is more important than preserving the family honor, so he decided to stay on.

93

He goes around calling himself a "fringe benefit," but we think he's more of an "intramural sport."

Speaking of Grandpa, don't be surprised if you meet him on the street handing out "Vote Yes for 18.6" flyers.

Gramps is retired and his fixed income doesn't stretch easily for things like tax hikes. But Gramps is proud of his town, and he says well-educated children are its future.

My husband Tom doesn't think you really blame us for all these new expenses. He says most of the money goes for salaries and those would have gone up even if we hadn't enrolled Drew for next year.

He may be right but I just know you need those 2.3 extra clerks because I forgot to put our social security numbers on all those white cards I had to fill out. Ellen is excited about the increased independent study and Work-Study opportunities you are talking about for high school students. She says this sort of thing "goes a long way toward keeping some kids in school."

She even seems to think you don't resent our 7 kids. She says you're all for kids and that's why you are going to all this trouble.

So I'll make a deal with you. All you have to do is spread the word that the budget is based on a desire to continue quality education, and that all the citizens of our town will benefit from that.

In return, I'll vote "yes" in the June 10 election.

By the way, if you're adding 7 new janitors just to pick up after our 7 children, let me warn you--that's not nearly enough.

Assassination of Robert Kennedy
June 11, 1968

"What are you watching?"

"Just the news, Mike. Run out and play."

"Okay. But why are you crying?"

"It's a tragic world."

"What does that mean, Mama?"

It means Mama's tired. Run along and find Drew now and we'll talk about it later if you want to."

"Okay. But Mama, why are you crying?"

I'm not really crying. I'm just blowing my nose."

"Are you crying because that man died?"

"What man?"

"That man who wanted to be president, and he had more kids than us, but someone shot him. That man."

"Yes, but where did you hear about all that?"

"We talked about it in school."

"In Kindergarten?"

"Yes. Mama, do we have any popsicles?"

"What?"

"Popsicles."

"Popsicles? How can you think of food at a time like this?"

"I'm hot."

"No."

"No what?"

"No popsicle."

"Okay. Did the children cry?"

"What children, Mike?"

"That man's children."

"Have a popsicle and we'll talk about it at prayer time."

"I would cry if some bad guy shot our Daddy."

"I know darling. And if you really want to, we can talk about it right now."

"No. Later."

Then Ellen came in:

"What are you going to tell him?"

"I didn't know you were listening. Actually I'm hoping he'll forget and I won't have to tell him anything."

"He won't forget. There's hardly anything else on TV."

"I know. But what can I tell him?"

"Tell him how you feel about it. That's what he really wants to know. That's what I'd want to know if I was 5."

"But you're 16. Is that what you want to know, how I feel about this and the other killings, about Vietnam and Resurrection City and the trouble right down the street on campus?"

"I have my own ideas. But the little kids, they're just puzzled by all this emotion and upset. They want to know what you and Daddy think about all these things. That's how it is with kids."

"But what can we tell them beyond the fact that we are deeply troubled and our hearts ache for peace, for justice, and for love?"

"I don't know. Maybe that's enough."

All Birthdays on Sunday
July 2, 1968

"When is Mike's birthday?"

"Sunday, of course."

"Good. I was afraid it might be Friday. I have a lawn job for Saturday morning and after that I'll have enough money to buy him a present. Lucky for him his birthday comes on Sunday."

"All the birthdays in our house come on Sunday."

"Gosh, that's right. I forgot."

If you are checking your calendar, don't bother. Our birthdays don't really all come on Sundays. It's just that Sunday is the day we celebrate birthdays except for Drew's. We celebrate his on the 4th of July.

Which doesn't make much sense either, because he was born on the 3rd.

So I take a few liberties with our pursuit of happiness. You would too, if the candles and cake bit came up 9 times every year.

It's pretty hard to make something special out of an occasion that recurs that frequently.

Not that I didn't try.

In the beginning, birthdays were master planned affairs with red and blue balloons, pink and white cake, green and yellow Jello, black and blue kids, and carpets to match.

But as the children, and the family, grew, the "master" planned less and less well.

"Tuesday is Kate's birthday. The party is after supper."

Dale: "Gosh, Mom, I have a game Tuesday. I won't be home until 8:30, maybe 9 even."

Ellen: "And I have a baby-sitter job. At 5:30. 1 promised Mrs. Clark a month ago."

Two down and 7 to go.

Tom: "Evaluation meeting Tuesday. But it will probably break up early--will she still be up at 10?"

Three down.

Kate: "Guess what? The whole troop is going to Detroit Tuesday morning. We're gonna sleep at the 'Y.' Can I go, Mom?"

"But Tuesday's your birthday."

"I know. Can I go?"

"May I go, not can I go."

"Well, may I?"

"If that's what you want, I guess it's all right. I'll give you a rain check on the party. How about Sunday?"

"Whoopee. I can go! And you know what, Mom, Sunday parties are the best anyway because they last all day, not just after supper like weekday parties. And everyone's always here on Sundays."

So now all birthdays have been moved to Sunday. Except for Drew's.

Most days are as good as the next when it comes to being born. Most days, but not July 3rd. July 3rd is a nothing day.

But the 4th, now there's a day!

Flags fly. There are picnics in City Park. The Community Band plays. There is dancing on the tennis courts. There is cotton candy, ice cream on a stick, carmel corn, cold pop, and to top it all off, fireworks.

If you're 4 going on 5, you know better, but you can still pretend it's all for you.

And that makes a red-letter day on anyone's calendar.

Wondering Why
July 9, 1968

I stopped work on the ark.

It wouldn't have helped anyway. Our family of 9 just doesn't work out 2 by 2.

Now I'm alternately digging out sweatshirts, or concentrating on getting through the days when it's even too hot to wonder:

WHY: Michigan weather is either extremely hot, extremely cold, extremely dry or extremely wet, and seldom just fair-to-middling pleasant.

WHY: in a house boasting 2 refrigerators, we are always on the last tray of ice cubes.

WHY: when the storm kills the lights in only one part of town, it's ours. has to be our part.

WHY: no matter what brand I buy, when an appliance breaks the repairman tells me I bought "the one that is hardest to fix."

WHY: if our trash is out early, the truck comes at 3, but if we forget, the truck goes by at 7:45.

WHY: the kids who vow they are on the brink of keeling over from hunger, disappear the moment supper is on the table.

WHY: the dresses that were just the right length last year, seem to have grown a couple of inches hanging in the closet over the winter.

WHY: our dog snuggles up to every child in town, but threatens to bite the head off any meter man who comes around.

WHY: the housework you haven't done is so much more noticeable than the housework you have done.

WHY: if one kid gets the "bug," at least 4 others have to get it too.

WHY: when the kid with the bug vomits, it's on the carpet instead of the linoleum.

WHY: the couple with no children stays in the same house forever, but the family with kids the same ages as your kids moves away just when the kids are "best buddies."

WHY: there is a white plastic tenpin on the floor in the corner of the bathroom.

WHY: when you come back from your 3,412-mile trip everyone you meet that week made the same trip last year and saw twice as much as you did.

WHY: people with big yards and swimming pools never seem to have the time to stay home to enjoy them.

WHY: your own husband still seems so much more interesting to you than anyone else's husband.

WHY: some fathead down the block has to use his power mower at 6:30 on Saturday morning.

WHY: rough leather sandals don't murder the feet of all the delicate little blondes who wear them.

WHY: when you pass by the playground the counselors are sitting around talking to one another and the kids are off unsupervised.

WHY: when you finally remember to buy and wrap a romper for that new baby who is already 6 months old, you misplace the address and can't mail it.

WHY: none of the other 8 members of the family ever figures out why you blocked the stairs with a basket full of laundry to go up that they are forced to climb over.

WHY: the fall and winter clothing catalog arrived on what seemed to be the hottest day of the year.

WHY: the store windows are filled with wools and tweeds instead of cool, sleeveless shifts.

WHY: if you are planning a seaside holiday in August, you'd better buy your swimsuit in May, and

WHY: not bothering to wonder is almost as exhausting as wondering.

Visiting Grandparents
July 16, 1968

We packed the Bingo game.

We also brought Scrabble, Monopoly, 3 decks of cards, 10 puzzles, 5 new coloring books, 78½ old crayons, 2 Nancy Drew books, 4 Hardy Boys books, 3 paperback mysteries, a book of crossword puzzles, and enough play clothes, PJ's and undies for 6 days.

We overpacked, and it was my fault.

Nana and Grampy live a quiet life, and frankly, I thought our 6-day visit would be nothing but Capital "B" Bother for them and Capital "D" Dullsville for the kids.

I was wrong. It is hard to say who had the better time, the grandparents or the kids.

Who can say what made the magic?

Part of it was love, of course, and I don't pretend to know how that works.

But another part of it was give-and-take, a series of little offerings, and gracious acceptances.

I think I have the system figured out.

The grandparents started by offering complete admiration. The kids accepted this, and countered cautiously with reserved respect. This the grandparents acknowledged, and dignified with an offer of trust. The kids lived up to it and the stage was set for a wonderful visit.

I watched and enjoyed the whole drama and picked up a few pointers to store away for the day when my own grandchildren, hopefully, will come to visit me.

First of all, I observed, it's terribly important to show the children that no matter whether there are 2 of them or 10, you think their family is wonderful just as it is and you are glad they ALL came. (If there really are 10 of them, 3-day visits are better than 6-day visits; however if they live very far away, settle for 6, but ask the doctor for a few tranquilizers.)

Lay in a large supply of candy, cookies, pretzels, fruit and chewing gum and offer them liberally. (It's better to do this when the children's mother is somewhere else. You can rely on the children not to tell.)

Produce a box of stuff left over from your last white elephant sale. Tell the kids they are heirlooms, and ask if they think their mother would let them each pick one item to take home. (Make sure that by the time the mother hears about it, the child is firmly attached to his prize and there is no turning back.)

Do not mow the lawn before the children come, so that the older ones can "volunteer" to ride around on your sit-and-steer mower to "help you out." (Watch for the children's father because he has always wanted to try one of those mowers and the kids may never get near it if he spots it first.)

The day it rains, take an expedition up to the attic and let the children try on their mother's old ball gowns and anybody's old uniforms. (Or just a pile of stuff you forgot to give to the rummage sale.)

If it rains for 2 days, bring out every photo album in the house and be prepared to tell every good family story you know as you name off the relatives in the funny-looking clothes. (Be sure to remember something terrible their mother did; they'll love you for it.)

Keep a box of old, spare tools in the basement. Tell the boys the tools are very special but you don't mind if they use them if they are careful. (Their father is a bear about finding his tools rusted, blunted or missing, so you'll be a hero for sure.)

Keep up your friendship with Farmer John, so that when the kids come he will insist you bring them out to ride the mares, drive the tractor and come down off the hill perched on the last wagonload of hay. (Bring home blackberries from the hill for you-know-who so she won't notice the rips in the new jeans.)

Walk around toys as if you don't see them. Sweep only when the kids are out of the house. Leave your shoes in the living room once or twice. Pretend you always live in this state of confusion and clutter, and never, never wipe fingerprints off the wall while the kids are looking. (This helps their mother to have a good visit, too)

Keep remembering how quiet and clean the house will be after they are gone (to sustain you), and cry a bit when they all leave.

They'll be back!

California: Planning the Trip
July 23, 1968

The word is out. We're headed for California.

For a dime you can buy into the neighborhood pool with odds on how far we will get before we 1) run out of patience and 2) run out of money.

The wise money is on Charlotte for the former and Benton Harbor for the latter.

Otherwise, reaction is mixed.

"You're taking the whole family? How wonderful!"

"You're taking the whole family? How?"

How is a good question. Rocket ship would be best, but NASA wouldn't answer my letter. So we are driving, and hoping to See America First. (First--that means before interstate insanity sets in.)

Lodging is a problem, too, when you are traveling in a party of 9. Friends of ours made the same trip last year without spending a dime for bed or board. They got AAA to Triptik them through all the towns where they had friends.

I thought it was a bit too much to go to L.A by way of Tallahassee, but I couldn't knock the price.

"How did you get everyone to invite you?" I asked innocently.

"Just write. Let them know. Everybody's dying to see you."

So I wrote:

"Dear Jane and Jim,

We keep remembering the wonderful time we all had when you folks came to visit us 3 years ago. Wasn't it great? Guess what? We've finally decided to come out your way. Unfortunately, we can only stay 4 days, instead of 15 days as you did. Look for us on the 19th."

Dear Great-Aunt Mildred,

Isn't it awful how families get spread all over the country? I'll bet you don't even remember me--I'm Ann's daughter, remember? My husband and I are taking our little family to the coast this summer and we wouldn't dream of coming so close to your place without stopping to say Hello. The kids have heard so much about Texas ranches that they can't wait to stay on yours for a few days."

"Dear Eunice and Bill,

Somehow we've lost track of each other over the years. What a shame. I met Bill's mom at the market the other day and she happened to say that you live a stone's throw from Disneyland. What a coincidence. That's just where we are heading in a week or so. Of course we wouldn't think of imposing on you, but your mother did say you have a very large house and we thought you might not mind if we dropped in for 3 or 4 days. See you soon."

"Dear Wilsons,

You see we did mean it when we promised to look you up if we ever came through Dakota. We're coming that way on our return through Dakota. We have 7 children. By the way, Tom keeps insisting that it is Jim and Madge, but I know it is Jerry and Madge. We can't wait to get out there to see which of us has the better memory."

The return mail was slow, but the following looked promising:

"Dear Tom and Kaye,

Talk about poor timing--ours, not yours. Just the day your letter arrived telling about your plans to visit us for 4 days, Clark decided this was the year for us to visit Hawaii. Give us more warning, I mean notice, the next time you plan to pass through town."

"Dearest Kaye,

Have only a moment to jot this. Moving van at the door. So glad you're coming. Will send new address as soon as we are settled. By November for sure."

"Dear Sir:

The Claybornes you wrote to must be another family. We know no one from East Lansing, Ohio, much less a family with 7 children."

"Dear Mr. and Mrs. Naybor:

We are looking forward to your stay with us. Your rooms will be ready when you arrive, if you will send $35 deposit soon. Holiday Inn is always happy to be your host."

It's hard to disappoint all the people who are waiting eagerly for your visit, but sometimes you have to do it. I mean how can you decide who to turn down?

So Tom and I are looking at trailers.

California: Buying the Trailer
July 30, 1968

We set out to rent a trailer, but no dealer would cooperate.

"Yes Sir, this is a neat little job. All the comforts of home in 18 feet. And you're smart to rent. You know, see how you like it first, then maybe buy another year."

"Will it sleep 9?"

"Yes Sir, a neat little job. Of course it's booked up for the entire summer already."

"Do you have another one you could rent us?"

"All booked up. All booked up. Look Folks, I hate to be the one to tell you but nobody's gonna rent you a rig for 9 people. It ain't practical. Five, sure. Maybe even 6, but 9? Boy, 9 people in a trailer, you call that a vacation?"

Several times we had 9 people in a tent and called it a vacation. We had had the same 9 in a tent camper and called that a vacation. All things considered, 9 people in a trailer not only sounded like a vacation. It sounded like the next thing to first class.

(Everybody knows first class is without kids.)

We changed our strategy and changed our luck.

We found that when we started to ask about buying ($$$) trailers, suddenly that took on amazing properties. Chief among them was elasticity.

"Sleep 9? It's a cinch. I've got a 14-footer that would be just right for your little group."

We judged him an optimistic opportunist and went elsewhere to buy.

Elsewhere turned out to be some 15 dealers within that many miles of Lansing. The variety of trailers available is unbelievable. We saw high ones, low ones, short ones, long ones, fancy ones, plain ones, expensive ones and more expensive ones.

We decided to draw up our requirements. First, it must be tall. Tom is 6'4" and instantly rejected any trailer that threatened to decapitate him. Aside from that, we decided we needed only the barest necessities. We set out to buy as small, plain, and inexpensive a house on wheels as it was possible to find.

We failed miserably. The outfit we bought is 22 feet long (not small), has white sidewall tires (not plain), and cost 4 times what we set out to spend (not inexpensive)

It is tall. It's so tall, in fact, that when Tom brought it home it seemed to loom menacingly over the station wagon.

I began to wonder if maybe we should reconsider the tent.

But the trip we are planning is more traveling than camping, and the thought of a daily routine of packing (and unpacking), pitching (and unpitching), staking (and unstaking) to California and back, makes the trailer look like comfort and ease.

Wind resistance? Sure, but think about that sink and refrigerator.

Special brakes? Sure, but think about that 4-burner stove.

Low mileage? Sure, but think about that heater and thermostat.

Extra Insurance? Sure, but think about that bathroom and shower.

Want to back out? It's too late now. Besides, there is one big plus feature that makes it a very worth while piece of luxury--it sleeps 9 people.

California: Welcome to Trailering
August 6, 1968

"Welcome to trailering, Children. Listen carefully and watch Mama and we'll all have a fine trip."

The airlines have been so successful with this sort of briefing, I thought I would try it.

"Your pilot is someone you all know and love. Give him your trust and respect and never bother him while he's driving--even if he is your father."

"Can we talk to him?"

"No."

"Not even if he's making a wrong turn?"

"Especially not if he's making a wrong turn."

It's important for kids to know the rules, I always say. And say and say and say.

"There will be one rest stop before lunch. Please take advantage of it. Yes, Beth, that does mean go even if you don't have to."

"I wanna go to Disneyland."

"Hush, Drew, we're going to Disneyland (God willing), but it's a long way and you must be very good in the car or we'll just turn around and come home."

That's called bribery and threat and certain child specialists don't approve of it.

"Is Disneyland farther than Okemos?"

"Boy, is he dumb."

"Quiet, Kate. Yes, Mike, it's about 2,500 miles and two bottles of aspirin farther."

"Do I have to take aspirin?"

"Boy, is he dumb."

"Quiet, Kate. No, Mike, the aspirin is for Daddy and Mommy."

"I'll need 2 suitcases, Mother."

"That's the happy surprise, Ellen. No one takes a suitcase. We'll all share the trailer like one big suitcase."

"But Mother, will I be able to take everything I need?"

"Everything you need, but possibly not everything you want. Is that clear?"

"Yyeccch!"

"Stop that, Ellen. Think of us as a pioneer family about to make that great trek west in a covered wagon. Now that was real hardship. No laundromats or gas stations or supermarkets."

Every time I think about those pioneer women I itch all over. Linsey woolsey and no deodorant or bath powder. No bath, either.

"I'm hungry."

"That reminds me about food. We're planning 3 meals a day. I know that's a blow to those of you who have been living with one hand in the refrigerator ever since school let out. But you will have to make do. Kate, be sure to put the root beer barrels and the licorice in the car pack for emergencies."

"Which one is my bed, Mama?"

"Let me check the accommodations chart, Meg. Oh yes, you're in H-1. That's the front hammock. Beth has the other hammock. Dale, you're in the rear single. Ellen you have to share the rear double with Drew. Kate, you share the double berth with Mike. Be sure to put him next to the wall so he won't roll off. Daddy and I will share the dinette bed."

"What's that plastic shoebag hanging in the bathroom?"

"I was coming to that. It's for toothbrushes, combs, deodorants, anything you might need in the bathroom."

"Combs in the shoebag? Where do the shoes go?"

"The shoes go in that divided prune juice carton I got from the store, Dale. See, the pairs stay together and there's no scuffing."

"I'm almost afraid to ask, but where did you plan to put clothes?"

"In the wardrobe, of course, silly."

Most of them, that is. Things like shorts and shirts that fold will have to go in those laundry baskets under the dinette seat. And all the PJ's go in one drawer so they're easy to reach at night."

"What's this applesauce carton for?"

"Underwear and socks. I counted the cubbyholes and there are enough for everyone. In the morning we'll just haul out the box and everyone can take his choice."

"Gosh, Mama, you're clever."

"Thanks, Meg."

You don't admit to a kid that you're not clever, just desperate. Sleeping and feeding 9 people in a 22-foot trailer is a cinch. It's the packing that takes ingenuity.

"I wanna go play."

"Just one more thing, kids. About getting up in the morning. Check on Page 5 of the rule book and find out what your Rising Number is."

"Rising number? Can't we just get up when we feel like it?"

"The Wilsons tried that and 3 of them bumped heads and landed in a heap on the floor. Better mind the chart."

"Anything else?"

"No, but study your rulebook and be ready for countdown at 0700. Wait, one last thing. What's the password for privacy?"

"Turn around and close your eyes!!!"

"Fine. Westward-ho!"

California: Traveling West
August 13, 1968

America the Beautiful!

There is no way to say it better. Our land sings with beauty and anyone who has traveled it cannot help but join in the chorus. The story goes that a New England schoolteacher took her first trip west in the late 19th Century. So awed was she by the sights she saw that she wrote a poem to express her feelings. She caught much of the glory of the land in "America the Beautiful." Later it was set to music as a hymn.

Our own trip has led us from Michigan through Indiana, Illinois, Missouri, Kansas, Colorado, New Mexico, Arizona and Nevada to California. Still ahead of us are Utah, Wyoming, the Dakotas, Minnesota and Wisconsin. Our only regret is that we'll have to skip a few states this trip.

Because Tom and I are "showing" the states to our 7 children, we are seeing them twice, through our own eyes and through theirs. Some days, admittedly, we not only see things twice, we see them double, again thanks to the 7 kids. On those days, we wish we had taken the advice of the airlines who assure us that we "could have been there by now." But most days we are thrilled by the land, its mountains, its plains, its valleys, its similarities, its contrasts, and its constant surprises.

"Hey, it looks just like Michigan," shouts Beth in an area of Missouri.

We all look and see that the fields are green and fertile, much like home. Kansas offers the first real contrast on our particular route. Suddenly we are aware of a Big Sky, an endless canopy of blue visible in every direction over the flat plains,

We play "Who's First to Spy the Grain Elevators," and Dale holds the record for distance. We measure the miles and discover he has spotted some 10 miles away. Always the silos tower over the towns and the very heartbeat of the area seems confined within them.

The first sight of mountains, a misty image on the far horizon, greets us some 60 miles before we cross into Colorado. For miles we watch as the shapes clear and suddenly, in Denver, we are worshiping at the feet of the Rockies.

At Colorado Springs the Air Force Academy chapel sits like a spiked jewel in the lap of the mountains, its 17 spires soaring upward like the peaks behind it.

"I see Pike's Peak," exclaims Kate.

"Peek-a-boo, Pike's Peak," chants Drew.

New Mexico offers us rosy buttes and green-coated mesas. The kids see Indian silhouettes strung out along the tops, a result of too much TV, for sure. Real Indians offer silver jewelry and pottery at Santa Fe, a Spanish town where the pace seems to slacken and there is time for grace and charm.

The desert proves more alive than we had imagined it would be. Pinion, sage and yucca dot the sandy soil.

"Yucca, yucca, yucca," sing the kids, pleased with the way it rolls from the tongue,

As we head north in Arizona, we see tall pines, Ponderosa, for the first time in days and suddenly we realize how much we had missed the sight of tall trees. The road twists among the trees and without warning the canyon suddenly appears. The Canyon, and Grand it is. We are all but frozen by our first sight of it.

For 3 days we walk its rim, study its colors, descend into its depths, climb its walls, but the wonder never fades.

"It's a big pit," says Mike.

The rest of us find it harder to describe.

The canyon is a hard act to follow, but Hoover Dam manages to fill the bill. It fits so beautifully in its nest of rock that one wonders if man and nature did not originally plan the whole thing together.

We swim later at Lake Mead, courtesy of the dam. The water, the harsh land and the circle of sharp peaks convince us that we are in another world, a barren Twilight Zone where man has made lush flowers bloom.

The California desert is the bleakest part of the journey. The kids delight in the funny shaped cactus and the stunted look of the Joshua trees. But the rest of us live on ice and wonder how many early settlers got this far and then gave up in despair.

But California offers as much contrast within its borders as the country as a whole. Soon we are engulfed by rich green orange groves, busy freeways, snow-capped mountains, miles of sandy beach, and the mighty Pacific.

Imagine, all this and Disneyland, too!

California: Disneyland
August 15, 1968

Disneyland is for kids. And any adult lucky enough to have some kids to take to Disneyland should hurry up and do it.

Float a loan, mortgage your home, do anything, but go west, you young-in-heart men and women. And take some children. In summer, Disneyland opens at 8 each morning and closes at midnight, except for Friday and Saturday night when it closes at 1 a.m. Tom and I arrived with our eager bunch at 9:30 a.m., and lasted until 10 p.m., a record in endurance for our crew. If we live to be 100, none of us will know a day so filled with fun, excitement and beauty.

The first thing that hits you about Disneyland is that it is expensive. If you have to take 7 kids, it's even more "pricey," as the English say. If the 7 kids agree that it's the deluxe tour (admission plus 15 rides) or nothing, it's practically bankrupting.

Two adult tickets at $5.75 add up to $11.50. Two junior tickets at $5.25 mean $10.50. Five children's tickets at $4.75 make $23.75, and the total tab comes to $45.75 on anybody's fingers and toes. But 2 minutes in the park and even I never thought of the cost again, except to agree the next day that it was worth every penny we spent.

Disneyland is every beautiful childhood dream spun together and come true. Think of every amusement park, fair or funland you have ever visited. Then think how those places would be if they were as clean as your kitchen (when company's coming), as well-run as your husband says his office is, as pretty as a model village promises to be, and as exciting as being the winner in the Grand Prix.

Thinking? Well, Disneyland is cleaner, better run, prettier and more exciting than you can possibly think. What's more, Disneyland is magical. In that Magic Kingdom, our children were so spellbound, they forgot to get lost, hurt or tired and almost forgot to go hungry.

The Kingdom is divided into 6 parts: Main Street, U.S.A.; Tomorrowland; Fantasyland; Frontierland; New Orleans Square; and Adventureland. Each section has enough activities to keep you there for hours, so in only one day, it is best to adopt the smorgasbord technique and pick and choose what you think you'd like most (and promise yourself you'll come back again someday soon).

Ellen, Dale and Kate were afraid the little children would slow them down, so for a while they went off on their own. Tom and I each grabbed 2 of the junior members of the family and set off to have fun.

In Tomorrowland we scooted down an icy "Matterhorn" in speeding bobsleds. (I lost my courage and closed my eyes after the first turn, and Mike swallowed his bubble gum on the second swerve.)

On Main Street we rode a fire engine of early 1900 vintage through the streets of a typical U.S. town, past delightful shops and stores. Later, on foot, we went into the stores for penny candy, souvenirs, and the biggest, sourest, crispiest dill pickle this side of Great-Grandma Naybor's old blue and gray crock.

When we whirled around on King Arthur's carousel in Fantasyland, a real, live Mary Poppins, complete with highbutton shoes, sloppy hat and open umbrella rode 2 horses ahead of us to Beth and Meg's great joy.

Other storybook "Pals" also walked the streets and when we caught up with Dopey he posed for a snapshot with Mike and Drew which should be the hit of "show and tell" at Bailey School.

Drew looked a bit worried as the hatch closed on the submarine in Tomorrowland, but he relaxed as we journeyed past starfish, anemones and other "jewels" of the undersea world.

We took more rides than I can remember, but among them were a trip through Frontierland on Mark Twain's steamboat (with fruit juice mint juleps), a breathtaking jaunt into space on the rocket jets of Tomorrowland, a realistic jungle river cruise in Adventureland, a circle tour of the whole park on the Santa Fe and Disneyland Railroad, and a flight through the air of Fantasyland in adorable flying elephants, all named Dumbo.

Drew and Mike were charmed by trips through the looking glass into Alice's Wonderland, and into the Black Forest to the diamond mines where the 7 dwarfs were hard at work. The wicked witch lurked at every dark turn, but we managed to evade her evil clutches.

The hit of New Orleans Square, an area of charm and grace accented with wrought iron gates and balconies, was the ride through the pirate lands of the Caribbean.

Here the fierce baduns staged sea battles, looted and burned towns, cavorted with captive maidens and generally scared the living daylights out of our young foursome, who alternately gaped with joy and gasped in even more joyful "fear."

There is no picnicking in Disneyland, but every appetite can be satisfied at low cost. There are snack shops for hotdogs and drinks, or fancy restaurants where foreign flavors fill the air but dinners seldom top $3.50.

Much in Disneyland is free. Just looking is a treat in itself, but everywhere bands play, groups sing and the shows are open to the public.

At dusk there is a parade of bands and storybook heroes. After dark Tinkerbell flies through the sky to start a sparkle of fireworks over the Magic Kingdom. Behind all the fun and games, people work incessantly to keep the area clean, safe and pleasant. It is forever new looking. No paint peels in Disneyland. Even the trash bins are pretty and colorful.

All the employees, beautifully costumed to suit their jobs, seem to enjoy their work. Tom and I sensed a feeling of pride in Disneyland, almost as if someone dreamed a dream and charged his aides to go out and make it happen even better than the dream.

Disneyland is first class all the way, and a grand memorial to the late Walt Disney who dreamed so much better than most of us can.

California: Returning Home
September 17, 1968

"Are we there yet? Are we there?"

We must have heard that question 3 million times in our 8,700 miles of travel. But as we came down Trowbridge Road and the lights of the campus apartments greeted us, the question seemed to have a new urgency.

"There" meant home and home was suddenly an exciting place to be. Everything about your town looks good when you have been away. Travel is great, but after a while the lure of strange places and new faces wears thin. Suddenly it is good to be back where you know each one-way street, each hole in the pavement, exactly where to find the Ivory soap in the A & P, and how each of your neighbors feels about the perennial squabble over liquor.

The neat lawns, the pretty houses, the friendly stores, the beautiful campus, even students soon to swarm across E. Grand River--we missed them all.

Clara and I were talking about it. She and Jim got back the night before school started too.

"Boy, it was so great for the kids," she sighed.

"What, being late for school?"

"No, going away and seeing the country the way you all did. I keep telling Jim it's what we ought to do. But every year it's the same--to the lake, to the lake. The kids think there's nothing beyond Michigan but water. Now your kids, they've really seen something."

"They saw a lot, but kids are funny. It's hard to know if they will remember any of it."

"Oh, Kaye, you know they will treasure these memories forever."

"They'd better. I may never be the same again. Forty-three days in a trailer and I don't remember how to live in a house anymore. Yesterday when it rained I told Ellen to roll down the roof vents. And every time we go by the Sunoco station, everybody wants to stop and use the rest rooms. Tuesday I forgot we were home, and I let them."

"You can joke about it, but I bet their friends and teachers are hearing all about the trip right now. Wouldn't you love to listen in?"

"I don't have to. I can tell you just what each one is saying."

Ellen: "Gosh, Mary, I thought I'd die--sometimes I only got to wash my hair twice a week."

Mom's Version: I used to think it would be great if all the kids were old enough to fend for themselves on trips. But now I'm glad some of them were younger and didn't mind wearing the same outfit for 3 days running or sharing a comb with the whole family when theirs disappeared. If they had all been teenagers, we'd still be in the middle of Kansas, waiting to get into the showers.

Dale: "Boy, some summer. Forty-three days in a Mercury station wagon."

M. V.: The kids kept hinting that some mothers sit in the middle seat, but I staked my claim on the front seat and refused to budge. It was better for those in the back that I couldn't reach them as often as I felt like it.

Kate: "We saw some very interesting places, but the best part was that I got an Aggravation game for my birthday. It's a really cool game. We played it everywhere we went. We bought my birthday cake in Missouri, but when we ate it, we were in Kansas."

M. V.: Kate's favorite sights were the souvenir shops. She had her own money, but some of the little kids didn't. That meant that if she got to buy something, we'd have to subsidize the others. After a while we convinced everyone to collect post cards--they were 6 for a quarter and didn't break the family bank.

Beth: "In Nebraska they have Daisy Freeze instead of Dairy Freeze or Dairy Queen. It tastes the same, though."

M.V.: The day we crossed the Mohave the thought of a sandwich for lunch was more than I could bear. We bought banana splits and sundaes all around and called it lunch.

Meg: "Mama let us go in the lake in South Dakota even though it was freezing outside."

M. V.: I had lots of aspirin but no bathtub. Besides, the pool was heated.

Mike: "I got an Indian belt and a tomtom, and a helicopter and a airplane and some post cards of buffaloes and prairie dogs, but my tomahawk broke already."

M. V.: Thank goodness.

Drew: "It was so my turn to sit up front, but I stopped crying when Mama gave me candy."

M. V.: I'll be ashamed to take them to the dentist.

"Oh, Kaye, you're making that all up. You know perfectly well they'll always remember this look at the old west, the new west, the mountains and plains and deserts. Even the refried beans from the Taco Bell drive-ins. Why, they've learned a lot and you know it."

"Maybe so, Clara. I know one thing we all learned."

"What?"

"Dead skunk smells the same in Utah, California, Nevada, Michigan or anywhere else."

Seventh Child Grows Up
September 24, 1968

"Mama, come quick. Come see Drew!"

"Mike? Mike, what's wrong?"

"Nothing's wrong, Mama. Just come quick and see Drew."

"Is Drew hurt? Mike! Meg! Beth! Is Drew hurt?"

"Gosh, no. It's better than that. Come on."

"Better....?"

"Mama, just come see."

"I don't see anything. He's just riding that bicycle---riding the bicycle? Oh, he is riding! He is! Hooray, Drew. Mama sees you, Drew. Good for you, Honey."

That's how it happens. One bright September day your youngest child learns to ride a two-wheeler. After that nothing is ever the same again. He may fall and get hurt and come crying to mother. He may be sick and whimper for your touch. He may get lost and come home weeping. But he is not a baby anymore.

"Can we take his picture for Daddy?" asks Dale.

"Daddy has the only loaded camera with him. Besides Daddy will be home tomorrow and he can see Drew for himself."

"Yeah, but we really ought to have a picture of him on his first ride. You know, like the first day of school. You did take his picture on the first day of kindergarten didn't you, like you always do?"

"No, I didn't. If you remember it was so rushed that day, I just didn't get around to it. It was a dark and gloomy day anyway."

It was dark and gloomy the day that Ellen first went to school, too. But that didn't stop us from taking her picture. And then, just in case it didn't come out, we took another one the next day.

But Ellen was our first child and with a first child things are different. I sewed for weeks. I talked to Ellen and prepared her for the great adventure ahead. I re-styled her hair and I bought her new shoes. I rearranged my schedule to fit hers, and when the day finally arrived, I cried.

Then the next day, I cried again.

But Drew is the seventh child and the last of our babies (right, Lord?).

With the seventh child you are lucky if you get a chance to dust him off before he joins the gang and rushes off.

"Are you sure you don't want me to take you?"

"Naw."

"Not even this first day?"

"Naw."

"How will you know the way? I wouldn't have to walk all the way. Maybe just the first block."

"Naw."

"How will you know where to go?"

"Mother, he can go with Kate, Meg, Beth, and Mike. It isn't as if he's the only Naybor in Bailey School, you know!"

"I know, Ellen, hush. I'm just saying good-bye to him."

"Well, say it."

"Good-bye Baby."

"Bye."

"Good-bye, Sweetie, good-bye."

"Bye."

"Drew?"

"What?"

"Good-bye."

"You said that already. You want me to be late?"

In a way I did want him to be late, maybe even a year or two late. Anything to prolong his babyhood for a while longer. But you can't do that with a seventh child. You can baby him all you like, but the other six children will grow him up when you're not looking.

Day after day he tags along on the fringe of the doing-it group. They like him and you know he's safe.

Then one day you look out and there he is riding a two-wheeler and he's a doer too. He's not a baby anymore. All you can do then is stick your head out the door and let him know you love him and will be around if he needs you.

"Get out of that street and stay out of it until you're ten or I'll give that bike to the Salvation Army!"

A simple little statement of your love can be very reassuring to a beginner.

Supermarket and College Kids
October 1, 1968

Years ago a trip to the supermarket was the high point of my social calendar. Any week when I got to go to both church and the grocery store, I was really swinging.

Those days began and ended with bottle feedings and wet diapers as I coped with 3 children in school, one in the high chair, one in the playpen, one in the cradle and one "in the oven."

The night before "store day" I washed and set my hair. I sent Tom out late at night to check the tires and fill the tank. The morning of my "outing" I reminded him 5 times of his promise to come home early to babysit.

I made up extra formula and I even alerted the pediatrician's nurse to the fact that a sub would be manning the nursery.

Believe me, shopping was a real event.

But lately, it has begun to lose its thrill.

Part of my trouble is the fact that what used to be a weekly event is now an every-other-day chore. I simply can't cart home enough groceries in one trip to last my trenchers more than 2 or 3 days.

So Mondays, Wednesdays and Saturdays (or Tuesdays, Thursdays and Saturdays), there I am stocking up on bread, eggs, bologna and marinated artichoke hearts (to relieve the monotony).

That's how it was before the college students came back. But since they returned, things are looking up.

Have you noticed all the students in the stores lately? It used to be you met them mostly at the bank, the bookstore or at the post office where they went to mail their laundry cases.

But since so many of them have left the dorms for apartments, you are just as likely to meet them at the grocery, the laundromat and the discount stores.

They are fun to listen to and watch, and they don't seem to mind having an obviously over-30 housewife smiling at their efforts to be self-sufficient.

1 spotted one group of bachelor do-it-your-selfers in the grocery store, and listened in.

Number 1: "All right. So far we've got two pork steaks, pork chops, lobster and dried herring. We still need bread, eggs, cereal, 3 or 4 gallons of milk and 4 more suppers. Any ideas?"

Number 2: "I like sauerbraten. Any of you guys know how to make that?"

Number 3: "What about desserts? Maybe I should phone my mom in Hawaii and get her recipe for Pineapple Coconut Wahine."

Number 4: "Hey, you guys, are you sure $20 is going to cover all this?"

Two girls in the cereal aisle were trying hard to get to know each other's tastes.

Number 1: "Do you like oatmeal?"

Number 2: "I love it."

Number 1: "Shall I buy the large or small?"

Number 2: "Get Special K. It has fewer calories."

A boy and a girl with matching shiny gold bands on their fingers were in the produce department.

He: "What's that green stuff you're getting?"

She: "Kale."

He: "I never heard of it. I don't like it."

She: "How do you know you don't like it?"

He: "My mother never cooked it."

At the cashier's counter, one coed was asked to limit her check to the amount of her purchase. The tab came to 92 cents.

But these kids are smart, they learn fast and they help each other. One young man broke off from his all-male trio to speak to 3 girls he obviously had not met before.

"Excuse me, girls, but we've noticed that hamburger is 65 cents a single pound, but only 59 cents a pound if you buy 3 pounds. How about if you buy the chips and the buns and we buy the meat and we all eat together and save money?"

Two of the girls looked interested, but the 3rd twisted her engagement ring and suggested:

"Why don't you just freeze half?"

The boy returned to his group and asked, "Anybody for liver and onions?"

Fall Is a Busy Time
October 8, 1968

Mother Nature and I are working on different schedules.

I breathe the cold, crisp morning air of autumn and I think I am in tune with the season.

115

But then I see the leaves turn to red and brown, wither and finally drop, leaving branches bared and ready for snow, and I know nature and I are on different timetables.

Fall is an ending time in her domain; in my life it is a time of beginnings. She is preparing the maples for a winter of rest, lulling the forest creatures into seasonal sleep and coaxing the zinnias into one last burst of frost-defying bloom. In my world, the sap is up and the first stirrings of life are evident after summer-long rest.

While wild geese honk Mother Nature's "Farewell" and "Well done," the voices in my life herald the start of the annual family busy season.

"Hey Mom, don't forget my room conference tonight." (The school year is already more than a month old and thriving, thank you.)

"Kaye, don't forget to pack my socks this time." (The difference between summer travel and fall travel is that now Dad goes alone and first class.)

"'Mrs. Naybor, you do remember that you agreed to be guild secretary this year?" (Is it this year already?)

"Pre-schoolers, first and second graders come at 9:30, and grades 3 to 8 come at 10:45." (Now that Masses are in the new church at St. Thomas, a mother with 5 children in the Sunday School walks 2 miles between pickup, delivery and supplication.)

"I'm sorry, but these are B series tickets, and this is an A series performance." (So you missed one. There are a lot more lectures and concerts coming.)

"But Mother, I told you last week that I already had a baby-sitting job for Friday." (Jane saw Helen buying sirloin tip in the store yesterday, so you can't call and beg off now.)

"If' you can't sharpen the crease in these pants our whole squad will get demerits." (It's pitch black, the Trojans are in trouble again. Tell me, who cares about the creases in a clarinet player's pants anyway?)

"If you can't think of anything else, you can always buy me another skirt and sweater for Christmas." (Christmas! Don't bring that up yet!)

"And if I am elected. . ." (It's amazing how a winner's views change between November and January.)

"As you leave the school, please check the lost and found table." (Raincoats and rubbers I can understand, but isn't it a bit early for someone to lose their ski pole?)

"Now let me get this straight--recreation and drama meet on Tuesday, Scouts and Brownies and beginning guitar come on Wednesday, cooking and dog obedience are on Thursday, the games are Friday, and play practice is every night." (All right, but don't forget the dishes, you guys.)

"If you absolutely can't work that morning, we will understand. But be sure to send us all your rummage. We need it." (Do people who don't belong to clubs which have rummage sales ever clean out their closets?)

"It is cold enough for mittens--see, my hands are purple." (In another month or so, this same purple-pawed urchin will leave his mittens on the fence post while he makes a snowman.)

Maybe the geese are trying to tell me something. Maybe what they are saying isn't "Farewell." Maybe it's "Come with us and get away from it all."

I'm tempted.

Talking to the Refrigerator
October 15, 1968

"You don't like me."

"What?"

"I said you don't like me."

"I heard you, but I don't believe I heard you."

"Well, do you?"

"Do I what?"

"Do you like me?"

"Well..."

"Admit you hate me. Go ahead and admit it."

"I don't hate you. I..."

"'It's because I'm old, I know. I've lost my sparkle, haven't I?"

"Now that you mention it, you aren't all you used to be."

"There, I knew it. You hate me."

"I didn't say that. I said--Oh, what am I doing arguing with a refrigerator of all things? I must have a couple of screws loose."

"There you go, picking on me, just because I have a couple of wobbly parts you're ready to dump me."

"I'm not ready to dump you. I can't afford a replacement."

"You see, you don't have any loyalty at all."

"Loyalty? What's that got to do with buying a new refrigerator when you need one?"

"I've given you lots of years of good service. I make good ice."

"You're always out of it when we need it."

"I keep the ice cream firm."

"Only if we remember to put the carton flat on the floor of your freezer."

117

"I have lots of shelves."

"The metal ones have rusted and the glass ones are impossible to get at to clean."

"My freezer is nice and big."

"The freezer door is broken and you're so old the dealers can't get me a new one."

"That's not my fault, is it? Besides, I'm still good looking."

"You look overstuffed."

"I am overstuffed the way you cram stuff into me."

"I mean, you're not sleek and trim the way the new models are."

"I wouldn't talk if I were you, girl."

"That's enough. If there is anything I hate it's a fresh refrigerator."

"Do you hate me?"

"No!"

"Are you going to replace me?"

"Not for a while, that's for sure."

"How about defrosting my freezer?"

"I'm thinking about it."

"Thinking about it will get you nowhere."

"If there is anything I hate..."

"I know, it's a fresh refrigerator. Confidentially, what can I do to stay in favor around here?"

"Stop talking, for one thing."

"And another?"

"Cool it."

(Some days it's possible to spend too much time in the kitchen. Things get dull out there now that the Series is over.)

First Communion
October 29, 1968

Sister Joan Anthony says thanks.

Which leads us to wonder, what do we say to Sister Joan Anthony?

The kids in the first communion class always know right from the start that they are Very Important Pupils.

"I have a special note for you from Sunday School," informs Beth. "The others don't have a special note because they're only in the regular classes."

The special note is the first of several communiqués which find their way home. Only one of the notes goes astray, which shows you how special they really are.

The notes are mostly about times and dates and the need for extra class sessions. But along with the information there is another theme: God is real to children to the extent that He is real to the adults with whom the children share their daily life.

The charge to parents is clear--please parents, do your part.

Always the notes end with thanks. Thanks for your help and cooperation. Thanks for your patience and understanding. Above all, thanks for letting us help prepare your children to receive these holy sacraments of penance and communion.

Finally, the great day arrives. The children have already received the sacraments of penance, and now they march into the church for their first real participation in the celebration of the Mass.

Their eager responses show they have been well taught.

"The King of Glory comes, the nation rejoices. Open the gates before Him, lift up your voices."

The young voices rise in a joyous hymn, and it is easy to imagine that wings have sprouted from the boys' white shirts and beneath the girls' filmy veils.

But no, they are still only children, not angels. See that boy on the aisle? He has spotted his younger brothers sitting with his parents and now they all have the giggles.

Although a special "special note" has stressed that clothes are not important to this occasion, it is easy to see that all the little girls are very much aware of their white frills, and the boys are trying not to peek to see if their ties are straight.

We spot Beth beneath her pearly crown. She is quiet and pensive.

My heart stirs. Do you know, Beth, why we are all here today? I think you do.

Are you prepared as the church requires "to understand according to your capacity those mysteries of God which are necessary to salvation?" I hope you are.

We have talked (surely not enough), and you have answered confidently that you understand. But I wonder if I have taught you anything, if I have done my part.

We are quietly religious in our family. Perhaps we do not talk enough about such things. Now I wonder if you have known by any of my thoughts, words or deeds that it is most precious to me to be a child of God.

I know I have never been a good teacher, but I have tried to be a good mother. I keep hoping that from the things I do, the things I say and the things I ask of you, you will know that I am trying to serve God in a faithful and loving manner.

Whether I have succeeded, I cannot tell yet. When you are older we both will know.

Meanwhile, I can tell by your poise, confidence and pride on this important day that Sister Joan Anthony has been a very good teacher.

And if she says thanks to us, what can we say to her?

Elections
November 5, 1968

"Mama, did we win?"

"Win what, Mike? Eat your Crusts, Drew."

"You know, did we win the election?"

"Who left this milk? Every drop, please. Did who win the election, Mike?"

"Us, did we win?"

"No, we didn't win, Dopey. We weren't even running."

"Kate, that's enough of that sassy talk. Beth, don't mash that banana. Mike, the elections aren't like the World Series or a football game.

"You see, a lot of men were running for a lot of jobs and Mommy and Daddy voted for the ones we thought were best for the jobs."

"And did they win?"

"Some did and some didn't. Beth, stop playing with that banana."

"Are you angry about the some who didn't?"

"No, of course not. Beth!"

"But yesterday you said..."

"Oh, yesterday. This is today and the voting is all over now, so things are different. More toast, anybody?"

"Were there lots of people here last night?"

"Only a few neighbors. Pass the milk to Meg."

"Why did you have the TV on when you had company? You always make us turn it off when somebody comes."

"This was different. We were following the election returns. That's why the TV was on. Dale, you forgot your orange juice."

"Was the company glad when they found out who won?"

"Some were and some weren't. But we are all glad it's over. That's enough jam, Mike."

"Can I tell my teacher?"

"Can you tell your teacher what, Mike? Brush your teeth, if you're through, girls."

"Can I tell her about the election?"

"Oh, Mike, I expect she has heard all about that by now. Are you almost through with your breakfast?"

"I don't want anymore."

"You've got to eat it. Don't you want to grow up to be big and strong, and maybe get to be president, even?"

"No."

"You don't want to be president?"

"No."

"Why not, pray tell?"

"Because some people wouldn't vote for me."

"Some wouldn't, of course. But what difference would that make? You would still be president, if you won."

"But some people wouldn't like me."

"Oh, they would all like you when you were president."

"If they didn't vote for me, why would they like me?"

"Well, they might not like you exactly, but they would all respect you. You see, Mike, everyone respects the president once he is elected."

"Hmm."

"Hmm?"

"Then what was all the talking about?"

"Oh, Mike, you're going to be late. Zip your coat and run. And Mike."

"Yeh?"

"Ask your teacher to tell you about democracy."

"Is it fun?"

"The greatest!"

When Mom Gets Sick
November 12, 1968

Mothers have a right to get sick too! Naturally, there are strict rules governing the situation and most mothers, in an effort to uphold the standards of the trade, try to heed the regulations.

An important rule to remember is to make it short. (Anything over 4 hours is excessive.)

Another guideline is to keep it cheap. (No medication, visits to the doctor or emergency hospitalization allowed.)

Timing is important too. (In general, Sundays are best.)

A really considerate mother will get sick only after church and Sunday School are over and the roast is in the oven. She will pick a warm day so the children can play out most of the afternoon. If possible, she will also arrange for the Lions to be playing so her husband will not be lonesome while she is indisposed.

Conditions were exactly right last Sunday, and since it looks like a busy winter, I decided to get my sick day in early in the season.

After checking the roast and setting the table, 1 ran upstairs to vomit (quietly) and go to bed.

Later, with half an hour to go before my time was up, I was congratulating myself on the precision of my arrangements.

Just then, Dale came to my door.

"What's for supper?"

"Leftovers."

"Which ones?"

I lifted my head the better to concentrate on the specifics. That was my first error.

I went back to bed and didn't get better until Tuesday. Getting well was my second error. One look at the state of my motherhood—Dishes! Laundry! Dust! Peanut shells (?) and I was ready to be sick all over again.

But my turn was clearly over. Sicknesses always run in relays in our house and it was time to prepare the premises for infirmary duty.

Ellen got it first. Then Beth and Kate and Drew. Meg looks like it could happen any min…oops…It did.

Actually the children's illnesses aren't such disasters as they used to be. Most of them are content now to sleep and vomit through the first few hours, watch TV for the next half day and gradually coat their stomachs with coke, dry toast and soda crackers. They soon get tired of the whole routine and beg to go back to school.

In the old days even a mild upset signaled their "hold me all day Mommy" instincts.

I remember one day the phone rang, and I was holding Meg and Mike on my lap. Beth was in the playpen and Drew was in the carriage. All in the dining room—where else?

As I reached for the phone, Beth gulped, belched and let go.

"Hello, Kaye, this is Mother…"

"Hi, Mother."

"Kaye, is everything all right? You didn't write this week and I got worried."

"Fine, Mother, fine. I got a little busy, that's all."

I tried to reach Beth, squeezing Meg as I reached. She let out a yelp that reminded Drew it was time to yell for his bottle. As I swerved to rock his carriage, Mike vomited over my hand.

"Kaye? What's that funny noise? Sounds like water."

"I'm just rinsing out the receiver, Mother."

"Oh. Well, just thought I'd let you know I was thinking about you. Write, Kaye."

"I will, Mother, any day now."

Boy Actor
November 19, 1968

My son, the actor, makes his bow this week.

Who knows, it may be the start of a thrilling career. Acting is such an exciting profession these days.

And the field is wide open. Think of the opportunities on the stage and in the movies. Why, TV alone must hire thousands of talented young people every year.

Of course, in the old days actors had a bad name and were held in ill repute. You've heard of John Wilkes Booth, the bad actor?

But nowadays there is almost no limit to what an actor can do. Especially in California.

I must encourage my son.

"Dale, you got a part in the play."

"Yeh."

"How wonderful. Aren't you excited?"

"I guess so."

"Imagine my son emoting the world's great tragedies."

"It's not a tragedy."

"A comedy, then. I always knew you had the makings of a great comedian."

"It's not a comedy either. It's more like a musical."

"A musical. How wonderful. And you have the title role?"

"No, no. There really isn't any title role. The title is 'Brigadoon.' That's the name of a place."

"And you play the lead."

"Mom, no. I don't play the lead."

"So, it's the sub-lead. What matter?"

"It isn't that either."

"Never mind. I'm sure you will sing beautifully."

"I don't get to sing."

"Dance! I knew it, of course, with your grace you're the dancer. You'll capture us all with your joyful leaps."

"I'm one of the dancers, but I don't do many joyful leaps."

"But you'll thrill us with your cheerful personality."

"I have to sulk a lot, Mom."

"There, just as I thought, a character role. That's the best kind. All the best actors do character roles--Laurence Olivier, Christopher Plummer, Maurice Evans. I could go on and on."

"It's not all that much of a part, Mom."

"My boy, it's not the size of the part that counts. It's what you make of it. By the end of the play you'll be a hero."

"I die before the end of the play, Mom."

"You see, a hero's death. What a scene. I can see it now. How the audience will weep."

"It's not actually a hero's death."

"A coward, then, a really meaty part."

"Not a coward either. It's more like a villain."

"A villain?"

"Sort of like a villain."

"A bad guy."

"I guess so."

"And you die before the end of the play?"

"That's right. I get killed offstage."

"OFF stage? OFF stage? OFF?"

"Yes."

"You don't sing. You only dance a little. You don't get the girl. You're the bad guy. And you don't even get to die in front of the audience?"

"That's about it, Mom."

"My boy, have you given any thought to accounting? It's not exciting, but it's nice steady work. It may be that you're not cut out to be a governor anyway."

Things To Be Thankful For
November 26, 1968

Parents don't necessarily have more to be thankful for than other people. It just seems that way when they stop to consider the alternatives.

Take our family. Seven kids in 12 years? Be thankful; they might have been twins.

Three of the kids need new boots? Be thankful; the other 4 can make it through the winter with last year's.

There's always a waiting line for the bathrooms? Be thankful; there are no more diapers to change.

Two of the kids are sick? Be thankful; the other 5 are well.

Children seldom think this way. To hear them tell it (like it is, man), they have little or nothing to be thankful for. Our 3rd grader wrote in school that she is thankful for "my family, my dog, my grandmother, my grandfather, my aunt and my friends."

It's a typical statement, and it shows how much typical children can miss if their parents don't nag a little and keep pointing out the many blessings they tend to overlook.

Take our family (I keep offering, but nobody ever does).

Child: "I have a toothache."

Parent: "In one tooth?"

Child: "Sure, one tooth. Nobody gets a toothache in all his teeth."

Parent: "Be thankful."

Child: "I don't understand math."

Parent: "How are you doing in geometry and calculus?"

Child: "Silly, I don't take those."

Parent: "Be thankful."

Child: "Why do all our clothes have to be handed down from Ellen to Kate to Beth to Meg. I'm sick of getting everything 2nd hand."

Parent: "Who are you?"

Child: "I'm Kate. You know that."

Parent: "Be thankful you're not Meg. She gets everything 4th hand."

Child: "Why does it have to be so cold?"

Parent: "It's November."

Child: "I know it's November. If it was July I'd probably be boiling."

Parent: "Freezing or boiling--take your choice. And be thankful you can't do both at once."

Child: "You never let me do anything. I never see any good movies like the other kids do."

Parent: "Do you see any bad ones?"

Child: "Of course not."

Parent: "Be thankful."

Child: "I didn't get a prize in my Crackerjack box."

Parent: "Did you get Crackerjacks in your Crackerjack box?"

Child: "Sure."

Parent: "Be thankful."

Child: "I get a little sick of turkey every Thanksgiving."

Parent: "Have you thought of how the turkey feels?"

Child: "Turkeys don't have feelings."

Parent: "Be thankful, and pass the cranberries."

When Dad Goes Away
December 10, 1968

Breathes there a man with expense account so dead that never to his wife has said, "I have to go away on business for a few days. You'll manage, won't you?"

To which a dutiful wife can only answer, "Good-bye, have a good trip. And don't worry about us."

"Well, take care. And don't forget to call the plumber."

"Forget? How can I forget? The dirty dishes are crowding the back door now."

"I know. Gosh, it never fails. The moment I go away everything falls apart. This time it happened before I even get on the plane. Well, take heart, maybe this will be it for the whole 3 weeks I'll be gone."

Ha! That was Saturday. By Sunday night our catastrophes totaled 4: the plumber made a $25 dent in the Christmas money; the kitchen window broke; Mike woke during the night with an earache; and it snowed.

Ask any wife.

"Mrs. Blinker, you handle that plunger like a pro."

"I get lots of practice. Whenever Herkimer goes out of town, the toilet spills over."

"Is Herkimer gone much?"

"I wear out 2 plungers a year."

"Mrs. Collins, you seem to be stocking up on groceries this morning."

"Yes, Gerald left for Washington last night. Whenever Gerald goes away we get a crippling snowstorm."

"Surely, not every time?"

"You remember the time it snowed in late May?"

"You mean ...?"

"Right. Gerald went to L.A. for a week."

"Mrs. Andrews, how are the children?"

"Poor Claudie has the croup. Sammy needs to have his tonsils out tomorrow. But Jerome is really getting used to his crutches now."

"My, what a pity."

"No, it's not bad considering."

"Considering?"

"Considering Cyrus has been gone for 10 days already."

It never fails. The moment the man of the house departs every screw in the house shakes itself loose.

The bulb which has burned faithfully for 5 years suddenly flickers and quits.

If it is winter, the furnace heaves a sigh and drops dead.

If it is summer the car boils over on the freeway, 6 miles from the next exit.

If your husband travels often, I know this about you:

You know where the spare tire is, and how to get it out. You know what a bumper jack is.

You know the number of your safe deposit box, and where the key is. You pay all the bills (especially the life insurance premiums). You know a friendly store which will cash a check on Sunday night.

You know which druggist is open until midnight, and which one will deliver. You own a fever thermometer and know how to read it.

You have a small, handy tool that opens stuck jars. You know how to get the bathroom door open from the outside with a hairpin. You have a small boy trained to climb in the kitchen window when the back door jams.

Even if your husband only goes away once a year (say for 4 hours on a Saturday), you know how to change a fuse, the quickest route to Sparrow's emergency ward and the name of your car insurance agent.

Despite all this special knowledge, you've never learned how to fill all the gaps a husband leaves when he goes. And you'll never learn.

You do what needs to be done, but you jump when the phone rings; you toss and turn at night; you are alternately extra nice or very short with the children. You watch all the newscasts, especially the ones about crashed airliners; you almost never go out at night and you have to live one day at a time, no more.

And when he comes back from Japan, Maine, Timbucktoo or Battle Creek, your heart is glad.

"We managed," you say, "but we missed you."

Baking for Christmas
December 17, 1968

"I'll have to call you back, Jean. I've got cookies in the oven."

"But you were baking cookies when I called yesterday."

"Right. I'm almost done now though."

"Honestly, I don't know why you bother."

"Neither do I."

Christmas baking is out of style. I know because I read it. Somebody made a survey and found that most women will buy their holiday goodies this year.

Some of the local survey was made by phone:

"Madam, are you doing any holiday baking this year?"

"What are you, a nut or something?"

"No, Madam, I'm making a survey of baking trends. Are you planning any fruit cake?"

"Boy, you are fruity."

"Madam, please. How about gingerbread men?"

"George, is that you? What kind of a joke is this anyway?"

"Madam, I only want to know where your Christmas stollen is coming from this year."

"I'm getting it from Santa."

"Santa?"

"Yeh, Hermano Santa. He runs a bake shop downtown."

One canvasser came to my door:

"Madam, I'm making a survey of Christmas baking trends. Say, what's that I smell?"

"I'm making almond spritz. Come in and taste one."

"Wonderful, just wonderful. Do you do a lot of baking?"

"Mostly mixes during the year, and an occasional pizza. But at Christmas I go all out. Doesn't everybody?"

"Not anymore. Our survey shows most women are buying this year."

"Oh. Well, I thought of that. I almost didn't make fruitcake at all. What with Tom in South America and all, I almost decided to skip it. I'm only cooking for 8 these days and that stifles the incentive."

"What made you change your mind?"

"I guess it was the cherries. There they were in a clear plastic bowl. They just looked at me and shouted 'fruitcake!' So I bought some, and then some golden raisins and citron and pineapple--and nuts, too. First thing you know I had to triple the recipe to use it all up."

"My, my. What else are you going to make?"

"I've got to make cutouts for the children to paint. They like to say paint instead of frost. I make 14 dozen of those."

"Fourteen dozen?"

"Well, some break while the children are painting. Then there's the tasting. That kills a couple dozen more. I make 8 dozen nutballs too. And maybe 4 dozen date chews. They're rich. Then a double recipe of chocolate chip, some oatmeal nut, a few frosted brownies with sprinkles on top, and I'm done."

"Madam, please, you're confusing my whole survey. Isn't it more expensive to make your own goodies?"

"Yes."

"And isn't it a lot of work?"

"Of course."

"Then why? Why do you bother?"

"My mother always did it?"

"Oh, come now."

"Well, if you can't guess the reason, I'll have to tell you."

"Yes?"

"I like it when my children come home, sniff once or twice and say, Oh, boy, Mama's making Christmas cookies!"

"There's no place to write that on this form."

"There never is. Have another spritz."

"Thank you. I don't know when I've had such an interesting interview."

"Oh, this is nothing. Wait until you get over on Elizabeth Street. I know a lady over there who is making cranberry bread. Just sniff a little; you can't miss the house."

"I want to tell you, Mrs. Naybor, it's you odd ones who make this survey work interesting."

Old Presents and New
December 24, 1968

"How do you see Santa?" asks my neighbor whose first child is only now old enough to care.

"As I see him, he's a good-natured, well-meaning old fellow who has his own bag and does his own thing."

"I meant what do you tell the children about him?"

"We don't talk about it too much. Just a noun and a verb--believers get."

"And that satisfies them?"

"Sure. We've got a 17-year-old who believes like crazy and hangs a longer stocking every year. Would you believe pantyhose?"

"But what do you tell the little ones when they see Santa in Knapp's and Sears and every other store in town?"

"They have it figured out that the fellows in the stores are Santa's helpers, kind of a person-to -person ordering service."

"And they really believe?"

"Why wouldn't they believe? They've always gotten. Even I've begun to wonder how Santa does it. This year Drew and Mike have each got a list of 11 'musts'."

"Eleven toys! At that rate Santa would have to bring 77 presents to your house alone."

"Don't forget a tie for Dad and a scarf for Mom."

"Santa's sleigh will break down before he gets half-way around the block."

"Exactly what I told the boys."

It was as if I'd turned into Scrooge.

"Fellows, suppose we give Santa a break and ask for only 3 toys this year?"

"Three! I got more than that for my birthday. And this is CHRISTMAS!"

"Okay. Four."'

"Five, or I'll cry."

"So cry."

"Waaaaaaaaaaaaa..."

"All right. That's enough. But you boys have got to be reasonable. Let's say one big present and 4 small ones."

"Let's say 4 big ones and one small one."

"Oh, Mike. I'll compromise. Let's make it 2 big presents and 3 small ones. Now what 3 little presents can you think of Drew?"

"How about a real horse, a 2-wheeler and a road-race set?"

"I said 'little' presents."

"Those are little presents. Now I'll tell you the 2 big ones."

"Don't bother. The two of you go up and clean out your toy box. If Santa brings anything bigger than a whistle, it won't fit."

"I don't want a whistle. I wanta horse."

"I know. I know. So clean out the toy box. You may need it for hay."

Ten minutes later Mike bellows, "The box is empty." Over the mountain of rubble on the floor I can just see that the box is empty.

"I'll get some garbage bags and we'll haul this junk out to the trash."

"Garbage bags?"

"Trash cans!"

"That's the good stuff we're saving."

Chorus Twiddle-dee and Twiddle-dum.

"We've got to throw out something," I insist.

"Start with the broken things and then sort out the babyish things to give away."

"That fire engine is broke," says Mike.

"That's mine and I'm gonna keep it for ever and ever," wails Drew.

"All right," counters Mike, "then you can't throw out my locomotive with the rusty battery stuck in it."

"That's enough. Now I'll give you each a cardboard carton. You each get to keep whatever you can stuff into it. And not one thing more. Understood? Bring the discards down to the kitchen and I'll sort them to give away."

When they present their discards, I am ready to weep. The little blue lamb--why that was Ellen's, then Dale's, then Kate's--everybody hugged that at one time or another.

And I can't let them toss out the little red truck that Tom played with when he was little. It's practically an heirloom. Oh, the Raggedy dolls—I made them myself. Don't these kids have any feelings at all?

I decide to smuggle my sack of treasures up to the attic, but I am caught. "Mom, what's with the junk?"

"That's not junk. That's a collection of golden memories and I'm sentimental over every one of them."

"Mother!"

"Never mind. That's my bag and I'm doing my thing."

Merry Christmas from all your Naybors—Tom, Kaye, Ellen, Dale, Kate, Beth, Meg, Mike and Drew.

Predicting the New Year
December 31, 1968

Ready or not, here comes 1969. In some cultures it is customary to close out the old year's affairs in order to start the new year with a clean slate. Luckily, that's not the custom here.

Luckily! Some of my mending dates back to July. There's a jar of gravy in the refrigerator that went with Thanksgiving's turkey. (When Thanksgiving's turkey went, why didn't the gravy?) And the last entry in the diary I started on January 1, 1968, is dated January 3, 1968.

But why look back now? The new year is the one that counts, and having collected 8 calendars from the milkman, fuel company, insurance agency, etc., I'm ready to look ahead.

I wanted to talk to Jeane Dixon when she came to town in hopes of getting a really clear look at the future of the Naybor Nine, but somebody got the flu and I didn't "seer." Anyway, there is nothing more unpredictable than a family. No crystal ball could reveal in the morning what a family will do before night.

Mothers, on the other hand, do have special powers. Sometimes, when faced with a new calendar and a new year, they can foresee all sorts of things. For instance:

January: Meatloaf will be eaten twice as often as usual at our house, especially the week all the Christmas bills come.

February: Beth's loafers, bought in early December to last until June, will disintegrate.

March: I'll spend 4 hours cleaning out the screened porch in order to enjoy the balmy "spring." Then it will snow during the night and the snow will stay for 2 weeks.

April: I'll remember that I have a birthday, but with luck, I'll forget how old I am.

May: There will be a prom and our senior will die if she doesn't get asked; get asked, and die if she doesn't get a new dress; get a new dress, and die if she doesn't have a great time; have a great time, and actually live to tell about it all.

June: Tom and I will cry as our "first baby" graduates from high school.

July: Every precaution will be taken on the 4th, but on the 5th a sparkler wire will jam the lawn mower, again.

August: A large appliance will break down and have to be replaced the week before we take off on a vacation which we couldn't really afford even if the appliance hadn't broken down.

September: Nobody will have a decent thing to wear to school. When I get out the indecent things we do have, the boys will complain that the pants are too short, and the girls will complain that the skirts are too long.

October: Three children will fight over the witch costume. Finally, one will be a skeleton, another will be a pirate, and the third will be a gypsy. The witch costume will stay in the box.

November: The day after Thanksgiving I will start embezzling from the food money in hopes of building up the Christmas fund. Three days later, I'll rob the fund to supplement the food budget.

December: The last day of the year will come and I'll make some guesses about the year ahead. The best guess will be that there are 365 surprises, multiplied by 9, ahead for the Naybors.

1969

End of the Holidays
January 7, 1969

At last, the kids are back in school. I held my breath all weekend for fear the boiler would burst at Bailey, or the teachers would strike or the snows would come and immobilize the town.

It's not that I don't like holidays. And I think of the kids a lot. I mean I think a lot of the kids.

Anyway, the plain truth is that this year's holidays lasted so long that by the end the kids couldn't even remember why they were home, and neither could I.

I mean 16 days! Let's face it, 3 men went to the moon and back in less time than that.

I don't pretend to understand about rockets and orbits, and as for weightlessness, no woman really believes that. But I did manage to learn 2 truths in "science one."

The first is that nature abhors a vacuum. The 2nd is that certain things contract in the cold and expand in the heat. And boy, the fellow who figured that one out must have been a housewife during the holidays.

You never saw anything like it. Last summer when the mercury soared, the house seemed endless in its dimensions. Especially on hot, humid cleaning days. One child disappeared into her room and was only traced by the hum of her electric fan.

But all during the holidays the temperature dropped to new lows and you never saw such shrinkage since Alice dropped in on Wonderland.

No matter where I looked, there were crowds.

"What are you all doing in the living room?"

"Living."

"I know, but couldn't you do that somewhere else? I thought I might dust a little."

"Gosh, Mom, a few minutes ago you chased us out of the kitchen so you could sweep."

"Yeah, I know. It's a weakness I have." We have a playroom of sorts, but that seems to have shrunk along with the rest of the house.

"Mom, tell the boys to get out of the playroom."

"Why?"

"We just cleaned the whole room and set up the dollhouse and all our kitchen stuff, and they're wrecking everything."

"If you give the boys a little room for their game, then you'll all be happy. What are they playing?"

"Soccer."

You can't win.

Some people have children who are out-doorsy. Ours are more in-and-outdoorsy.

There comes a thump, thump, thump at the door.

"What do you want?"

"I wanna come in."

"You just went out."

"I don't like it out."

"What don't you like?"

"The snow."

"Unroll that muffler, unzip that hood and let me look at you. Just as I thought--you're the one who prayed for snow the whole week before Christmas."

"I only wanted it for Santa. I didn't want it for me. Kin I come in?"

"Join the club."

Just the last day of vacation I stumbled on the magic words for clearing the congestion.

I walked into the crowded room with my housecleaning tools and asked, "How about cleaning up a little in here?"

Boy, you think nature abhors a vacuum!

At our house, it's not only the vacuum but the broom, the mop, and the dust rag too.

Waiting for the Package to Come
January 21, 1969

How long is 3 weeks?

It is 21 days. Or 504 hours. Or a week less than a month. Or a smidgen more than 1/17th of a year.

It is forever, if you are anxious.

It is too soon, if you are reluctant.

But how long is it if you are a little boy who has:

--Waded through 2 boxes of Munchable Crunchables;

--saved up 25 cents;

--talked an older sister into filling out a form;

--begged an envelope and a stamp from mother;

--given the whole valuable communiqué to Dad to mail;

--only to be told that the small print says "allow 3 weeks for delivery"?

For the first 3 days his morning greeting is, "Is it 3 weeks yet?"

Mother is reassuring, "No, not yet. But 3 weeks is not a very long time."

On the 4th day Mother finds the envelope in the inner pocket of Dad's jacket, and quietly bribes an older sister to mail it surreptitiously on her way to school.

At this point Mother's attitude shifts slightly. "Don't be too anxious, you know 3 weeks is quite a while to wait."

By the end of the first week, said sad child has taken to spending the morning by the window. He is too shy to accost the mailman, but as soon as the porch is clear, he darts out to look for his booty.

He secretly expects a large rectangular package, wrapped in brown paper, tied in string and importantly marked with his name in large printed letters, which he can read.

Since that obviously is not his, he turns his attention to letters, large or small, and scans each one trying to decipher his name. He doesn't see it, but still there is a chance. He runs to Mother, hoping her superior reading skills will pronounce one of the envelopes his.

If the mail does not come before he sets off for afternoon kindergarten, his hopes rise. He is the first one home.

"Did it come? Did it come?"

It didn't, and Mother tries to soften the suspense.

"It really is too soon, you know. Let me show you on the calendar just how long 3 weeks is."

For a few days he seems to forget about the whole venture. Mother sighs with relief. Too soon. She suddenly learns his impatience has given way to anxiety.

"Does the mailman ever lose anything? His bag is pretty full."

"Do you think it will be too big for the mailbox? Maybe if we are not here he won't leave it."

"Mama, maybe they never got my letter."

Mother remembers that "no news is good news," and hope is rekindled.

Sunday brings an extended discussion on labor laws, overtime pay, civil service, man's inhumanity to man and the injustice of it all ("it" being the fact that most children don't notice until a "crisis" that there is no Sunday mail delivery).

Before long, the worst happens; the child loses faith.

"Hey, neat. Look at what you can get with 2 Shredded Hayo box tops and 40 cents," enthuses a brother.

"Don't send, it's a gyp," cautions The Waiter.

What can you say?

Finally the 3 weeks are up. Nothing has come.

"Don't be upset, it may still come. And if it doesn't come soon, Mommy will write and ask about it."

"It's a gyp."

"No, it isn't. You'll see, it will come soon."

"Gyp."

The next day, there is a letter. It reads:

"Because of the popularity of this item, our shipping department has not been able to keep up with the demand, and we are unable to fill your order immediately. However, every effort is being made to speed delivery, and you may expect your order within 10 days."

"How long is 10 days?"

"It's a very long, long time." (Mother has learned her lesson.)

"Longer than 3 weeks?"

"Much, much longer."

"Okay."

The next day a brown envelope arrives.

"Hey, 10 days is real short."

"Thank Heaven."

The envelope contains 3 pieces of gray plastic which fit together to make a submarine, 3 inches long. Two pieces of plastic, each a quarter of an inch long, are retrieved from the trash and identified as torpedoes.

They "really shoot." Nobody sees where they land.

That is the end of that.

Decisions, Decisions
January 28, 1969

It isn't the work that tires me, it's the decisions.

Cold or hot? Fish or fowl? Soup or salad? Blue or red? Drapes or curtains? Rubbers or boots? Go or stay? Work or play? Wash or wear? First or last? Now or later? Yes or no? You or me?

Solomon made fewer decisions than the average wife and mother.

Some days it starts before my eyes are open.

"Glooplishing," mutters a sleep-logged voice from the next pillow.

"Did you say something?"

"Yup."

"What did you say?"

"Glooplishing."

"Naturally. But what did you mean?" My husband has 3 academic degrees (in English, yet!), so I figure he ought to be able to express himself better than that.

"I said do you think there's enough air in here?"

"Oh, do you?"

"I don't think so. Do you think we could have that window open a bit more."

"If I say yes will you make me get up and open it just because I'm closer to it?"

"Yes."

"Then I think there's plenty of air in here."

I admire the lady on television who decides in an instant whether to "wash, bleach or Borateem." But most of my decisions are the results of weighty consideration, worthy of the city council.

"Mom, do I need snowpants?"

"I don't think so."

"If I don't wear them teacher won't let me go out to recess."

"Wear them."

"But they take too long to put on and I'm late already."

"Don't wear them."

"Okay. And don't worry, I won't be late, I'll cut through the fields."

"Wear them."

"But ..."

"Wear them."

Some decisions are easier to make,

"Kin I have a tangerine?"

"No."

"But, Mom, I'm starved and it's 2 hours 'til dinner, and you said it was all right to eat fruit after school instead of getting into the cookies and all that, and gee, Mom, why can't I have a tangerine if I promise not to spit out the seeds all over the rug like I did yesterday, and I wipe my hands when I'm through so I don't get juice all over the curtains, and stuff, and why, Mom, why can't I have just one, little tiny tangerine?"

"Because, Breathless, your brother just ate the last one."

Occasionally I need help with my decisions-making. In these rare instances, my "voices" have seldom failed me.

"Let's see, shall it be T-bone or hamburgers tonight?"

"Hamburger," pronounces a "voice."

Although it is difficult to trace this mystical aid, it seems to come from the vicinity of my wallet and speaks with unshaking authority.

Some decisions are even more tiring than others. Say it's an average morning. I've made the beds, washed the breakfast dishes, sorted the laundry, started the washer, stuffed the foam back into the green pillow, rescued a child from the clutches of a sinister folding chair and put the dog out--twice.

There is still an hour before the troops come home for lunch and the question is how to use it profitably.

Shall I pick up and rearrange, vacuum and dust, sweep and mop, or polish and buff? Or I could pick up and dust, rearrange and vacuum, sweep and polish or mop and buff. Or I could--well, you get the idea.

Usually I spend so much time deciding, that my hour runs out and the "Hungries" run in.

"What's for lunch?"

"I'm trying to decide between soup or sandwiches."

"Let's have both."

"That's my girl. You keep on making decisions like that and you'll make a fine mother."

Dr. Spock
February 15, 1969

Dr. Spock came to town recently.

The headline announcing his visit said, "War Critic, Dr. Spock to Speak."

Benjamin Spock has been outspoken in his opposition to the Vietnam War, and now is free under an appeal bond after conviction of conspiring to aid and counsel young men to evade the draft.

History will record him as a pediatrician turned war critic, and some will brand him a traitor, while others will hail him as a courageous crusader.

But my Dr. Spock is a baby doctor.

And anything he did before or after writing "The Common Sense Book of Baby and Child Care," in 1946, is only dimly relevant as far as millions of mothers like me are concerned.

I let the family in on the news.

"Guess what? Spock is coming to town."

"Spock? Oh boy, I love him on "Star Trek.""

"Star Trek? Honestly, you kids and your TV. I'm talking about Dr. Spock."

"Who's he?"

"Who's he? Your guardian angel, that's all. You just owe him your lives, that's all. Kids! Honestly, no gratitude, no loyalty, just TV."

Actually, it probably isn't fair to say that Dr. Spock saved all 7 of our kids. No matter how dumb I was when I started, the 7th one had a better chance of survival than the 6th, the 6th had more going for him than the 5th, and so on down the line.

But oh, that first baby!

A couple of months after Tom and I were married, Tom was drafted. In those days you didn't burn up your draft card, but if basic training was in Georgia and your wife was in New York, you did burn up the telephone wires with affection whenever you could scrape up the money.

"Honey, can you hear me?"

"Yes, but I think we have a bad connection. I thought you said you were pregnant."

"I did. I am."

Tom recovered. He bought Dr. Spock's book at the PX and sent it to me as a "Gee-I'm-Glad- We're-Going-to-Have-a-Baby" present.

I gave it a quick look and went about the business of being pregnant. After all, what smart, self-confident, modern-thinking, know-it-all mother-to-be needs 500 pages of advice on doing what comes naturally?

Then Ellen was born and we proudly went off to Georgia to live with Daddy.

"Tom, she's crying. Why is she crying? Tom, what's wrong with her?"

"Gosh, I don't know."

You bring home a new pencil sharpener and a 40-page booklet tells you "How to Own and Operate" your $5 equipment. You bring home a new baby and where are the operating instructions?

You call home, long distance.

"Mama, my baby's crying."

"Have you called the doctor?"

So you call the doctor.

"My baby's crying, Doctor, please come quickly."

"Have you fed, changed, burped and comforted her and checked the diaper pins?"

By the 3rd day you stop calling the doctor, out of shame for your ignorance.

"What we need is a baby book, a kind of a guide, so we will know what we're doing," says Tom.

Anyway, down under the belly bands that Grandma insisted on, but you gave up on because they got so wet every time, you find your 50-cent paperback lifesaver.

By 1957 and your 3rd child, the book is coated with strained pears, Pablum and worse, so you buy the new, revised edition. Today it is still on the shelf and still in use.

Gosh, that Spock! It's as if he knew you couldn't call the doctor every minute, but sometimes you just had to have an opinion from someone who sounded like he knew something. If he didn't write about it, it never happened. But if it happened, just look in that little book!

Turn to Page 4: "Parents are human." (Any book that starts out like that deserves a spot on history's bookshelf.)

Page 42: "Enjoy your baby. Don't be afraid of him." (Ours was a her, but we really were afraid.)

Page 57: "The easiest rule for the 2 a.m. feeding is not to wake the baby but to let him wake you if he needs to." (We quickly learned to let sleeping babies lie, without feeling guilty.)

Page 59: "Getting up the air bubble--it is a good idea to put a diaper over your shoulder in case he spits up a little." (The diaper did help, but I smelled milky around the neck for about 14 years straight.)

Page 182: "Can you spoil a baby?" (Spock and I agree that you could, and I did, in spite of all his good advice.)

Page 223: "Watching him grow: he's repeating the whole history of the human race." (When the fright was gone, it was great to have someone with whom to share the wonder.)

Page 245: "Bowel training in the first year: it's his mother who is trained." (I was too lazy for this, but we both got around to it in time.

Jealousy? Stuttering? Fears? Schools? Television? Thin children? Fat children? Little red spots? Big bad tantrums? Name your problem and look in the index; Dr. Spock had remembered to cover the subject.

Common sense was all Dr. Spock ever had to sell.

Selective Hearing
February 25, 1969

So you think it goes in one ear and out the other?

"Close the door, Shelby."

"Yeah, Ma."

The door stays open. Shelby didn't hear you? The message wasn't clear? Don't be silly; Shelby tuned you out.

Kids have a built-in selector. I don't know how it works, but it does work. Its prime function is to tune out parents.

Commercials get through: "Ask Mommy to buy Bloopo in the large, extravagant size today."

"Mommy, will you buy Bloopo? We want some Bloopo."

Disk jockeys get through: "So, if you dig the Spooners, shower us with mail, kids."

"Mommy, can I have 12 stamps?"

Hockey coaches get through: "Practice at 6:30 sharp. Anybody who is late doesn't play."

"I can't help with the dishes, I'll be late for practice."

But parents? They're automatically filtered out: "Homework first, TV afterwards."

"I can't hear you over the TV, Mom."

The selector starts to work when the baby is born. Think back to the first baby you ever talked to--remember? You said, "Coo, coo."

The question is, why "coo, coo"? Why not just "coo"? Because, even at that tender age, baby was tuning you out and you sensed it.

In later months, you followed the same pattern. You said everything twice because you knew baby didn't get it the first time.

You went from "Hi baby, hi baby," to "Say Da-da, say Da-da," and eventually on to that old standby, "No, no."

As baby's equipment became more refined, you learned to compensate: "No, no, no."

But you've been fighting a losing battle. The only time a parental voice penetrates the selector's complicated computer censor is when it shouldn't.

Try sharing a choice bit of gossip with your neighbor.

"Did you hear what I heard about Miss Kumquat?"

"Shh, the kids will hear you."

"No, they're way up on the 3rd floor. Shelby! Shelby! See, they can't hear a thing."

"Okay, if you're sure."

"I'm sure. Well, the way I heard it, she's p-r-e-g-n-a-n-t."

"Mom, can me and Arnold have a apple?"

"Sure, Shelby, help yourself."

"And, Mom, is it all right if I tell Arnold what pregnant means?"

"Shelby! What are you talking about?"

"Pregnant, Mom. Me and Arnold heard you spelling it through the radiator."

The selector has a special switch for radiator transmission.

Going to the Movies
March 11, 1969

What has going to the movies got to do with the price of bread, you might ask.

At least you might ask it if you heard me muttering in the ticket line the other day.

The thing is that bread is 5 loaves for $1.

I'll admit that at that price the product is nothing that Grandma would recognize as bread.

But if you're stoking 9 ravenous "furnaces," you compromise a little, and force yourself to forget about crispy crust and yeasty insides.

Besides, it's the only kind to use for some things, like holding peanut butter and jelly together, making French toast after someone has forgotten to close the wrapper and it has all gone stale, or "tossing on the waters" when your neighbor is hard up.

But if you've spent any time at all with kids, you know that a promise is a promise and the world will end before they will let you forget yours.

"Wah! Wah! Wah!"

"Why are you crying?"

"Daddy promised to take us to the movies today, and now he won't get out of bed. Wah! Wah! Wah!"

"But it's only 6:30 a.m., and the movie isn't until 4 this afternoon."

"I don't wanna be late."

When we got to Frandor, we discovered that the end of the ticket line was somewhere east of Okemos.

"Gosh, kids, at the rate this line is moving, we may not get in by the time the picture starts."

"Wah! Wah! Wah! I told Daddy to get up earlier."

As the line moved up a few miles, we heard the loud speaker blare out more bad news: "We have seating in the first 2 rows only."

"What do you say we come back next week?"

"It ends today."

"I know."

"You promised."

"I know. "

Finally the ticket booth came into sight.

"Let's see, Dale couldn't come, so we only need 2 adult tickets and 6 for the children."

"Tom, Ellen is 17. She's an adult."

"She doesn't vote, does she? Oh, all right, make that 3 adults and 5 children."

"Yes, Sir. That's $2 for adults, 75 cents for children. $9.75 please. Thanks. Next."

That's when I started muttering about bread.

"If $1 will buy 5 loaves, $9.75 will buy---Holyoke, Massachusetts! That's 49 loaves.

Dale didn't get to go. We brought our own bag of candy. We lied and told the kids theater popcorn is usually stale and rancid. And all we got back from a $10 bill was a quarter.

But the movie was delightful. It was Disney's "Swiss Family Robinson" and it had something for everybody in the family, from tigers for Drew to James MacArthur (swoon) for Ellen.

It was easy to tell the bad guys, and when they got theirs, everyone cheered.

It wasn't message art, unless there is still a message in love, respect, hard work, ingenuity and fun and games. But it was a full-of-fun family movie (G for Genuinely entertaining), and that kind is hard to find these days.

It was almost worth $9.75. After all, even families of 9 cannot live by bread alone.

Basketball Fever
March 18, 1969

Swoosh!

"Hey, lookit me, I 'm T.C."

"Oh, yeah? Well, lookit me, I'm Blake and I can't miss."

"You can't be Blake, you're not tall enough. Besides, you're a girl."

"I don't care if I am a girl, I can be Blake if I can make a basket. There, I made one."

When March Madness (i.e., basketball tourney time) hits East Lansing, even the small fry get basketball fever.

Little boys, who only yesterday (it seems) throbbed to the beat of "Sock it to 'em, Tigers!" and "Go, State!" suddenly turn on the fancy footwork and dribble their way around the backcourt of the neighborhood.

"I'm coming, Ma." Dribble ... dribble...stop ... pivot ... shoot! Another 2-pointer for Big Brian! "I'm coming, Ma, I'm coming!"

"Jerome, what are you doing in those shorts in this weather?"

"I'm shooting baskets, Ma."

"In shorts?"

"Gee, Ma, you're supposed to play basketball in shorts, Ma. It's real regulation. Gosh, Ma, didn't ya ever see a basketball game? The Trojans wear little tiny shorts, way up to here."

"The Trojans play INSIDE. Your basket is OUTSIDE and the temperature is 18 degrees. Go get some long pants on QUICK! And put some mittens on too."

"Aw gee, Ma, who ever heard of a basketball player with mittens?"

Mothers are a handicap, there's no getting around it. For one thing, most mothers are not very tall. Genes being what they are (capricious), a fellow's chance can be wrecked even before he's out of the cradle.

"It's a boy, Darling, are you happy?"

"Of course, Sweetheart, of course."

"You don't sound happy. What's wrong, Dearest?"

"Nothing, Dear Heart, nothing at all."

"Tell me, True Love, tell me."

"Well, Sugarplum, It's just that he's so short Who who ever heard of a 20-inch basketball player?"

"Cheer up, My Own, all babies are short the first hour or so."

Actually, being tall isn't as important as it used to be. For a long time, the ranks were firmly drawn in the backyard league: the tall kids played basketball; the short kids played marbles. But all that has changed.

"Go away, Kid, you can't play basketball. You're too short."

"Oh, yeah? That's what they used to say to Gary, too. Move over, Stringbean, and I'll show you how us short guys help win games. You be Derleth. Hey, Hey! Pass, pass, pass. Win, win, win!"

Basketball is a natural sport for girls. It's the only sport where underhand is the right way to handle the ball. Even the unathletic types get swept up in the hysteria.

"Oh, I can hardly talk. I'm so hoarse. What a game!" whispers Spectator Sal. During the regular season she is a regular, too. She yells, she cheers, she jumps, she leaps with joy.

She's big on adjectives. How was the game? "It was terrific, wonderful, positively glorious!"

She's weak on details: "What was the score?"

"Something like 98--or maybe it was 89. Does 68 sound right? Anyway, we were way ahead and it was a tremendous game."

Swoosh! The whistle blows, the crowd goes home and the little kids turn to their skateboards and bicycles. Basketball fever is over~-until next year.

Spring Is
March 25, 1969

Spring is---a smell of freshness in the air, and a feeling of gaiety in the heart.

Spring is---a small boy picking your first crocuses and bringing them to you as a gift of love.

Spring is—motorcycles and top-down convertibles.

Spring is---remembering that the light-weight coats never made it to the cleaner's last fall.

Spring is—hopscotch patterns on the sidewalk.

Spring is---navy blue, gray and yellow in the store windows.

Spring is---fresh asparagus with browned butter.

Spring is---polishing last September's dust off the car.

Spring is---roller skates left on the stairs.

Spring is---arms too long for last year's coats, legs too long for last year's pants.

Spring is---pumping up bicycle tires.

Spring is---daffodils for 89 cents a bunch.

Spring is---too late to mend the wool socks in the sewing basket.

Spring is---co-eds in bikinis reinforcing their Florida tans.

Spring is---a clean-swept garage, and 4 cartons of stuff for the Salvation Army.

Spring is---a teenager whispering and giggling into the telephone.

Spring is---a hat with a floppy brim and violets which you'll wear only once.

Spring is---when you discover 3 storm windows which never did get put up for the winter.

Spring is---wall-to-wall mud on the wall-to-wall carpet.

Spring is---a string fence to keep the kids off what you hope will soon be a lawn.

Spring is---birds trailing threads up to the crook of a strong limb.

Spring is---discarded jackets and sweatshirts dotting the yard.

Spring is---a rake, a hoe, a packet of seeds, and a lot of hope.

Spring is---when 7 children become 7 "dependents," and the income tax form makes large families seem more desirable.

Spring is---long legs sprinting on the high school track.

Spring is---garage sales in every neighborhood.

Spring is---when you miss having a baby to push around the block in a stroller.

Spring is---letting the kids stay out after supper until the street lights come on.

Spring is---time to start a diet, again.

Spring is—pussy willows in a milk bottle on a teacher's desk.

Spring is---time to put the toboggan away and vow to use it at least once next winter.

Spring is---a fresh start for the whole world.

Spring is---here.

April Fools' Day
April 1, 1969

It was just an ordinary day.

The alarm went off and Tom said, "Stay in bed a while longer. I'll get the kids started."

When I went downstairs a bit later, the children had eaten their cereal, finished all their milk, and were in the process of rinsing and stacking their dishes.

Mike brushed his teeth without having to be reminded. Meg stood patiently while I brushed out her hair and braided her pigtails.

They all left the house in plenty of time for first bell, and nobody forgot their books.

At noon, Beth was delighted to see that I was making toasted cheese sandwiches for lunch, and asked for seconds. Drew remembered to finish his sandwich before devouring his dessert cookies.

Tom called to say some business had come up at the last minute and he wouldn't be home for lunch after all. I hadn't started his anyway, so it was no trouble.

Dale found his Spanish book and brought back the $5 I had rustled up for a replacement.

When I was scrapping the lunch dishes, the disposer made a funny noise, groaned and stopped. I waited a few seconds, tried it again and it worked fine.

I had planned to vacuum and dust the living room after lunch, but when I went in to check conditions, nothing was dusty and the rug was clean. I decided to skip that chore and go shopping instead.

The refrigerator was well stocked and there was plenty of food on the shelf, so I didn't need to go to the grocery. Instead, I headed downtown to look at spring fashions.

In one of the better stores, I found a good-looking suit in my favorite color, navy. One of the buttons was loose, so the management had marked it down to half price. By coincidence that was exactly the amount I had figured I could afford to spend, so I bought it.

On the way home, I swung over to the Michigan State University campus to visit the new exhibit at the Kresge Art Center. Just as I drove up, another car pulled out, leaving me a parking place right by the entrance.

I got home just as the children arrived from school, looking bright, cheerful and learned. They all went to change into play clothes, and after asking if I needed help with supper, they found quiet games to occupy themselves.

Tom came home a little early and we found time to share a pitcher of lemonade and a discussion of the day's events before our meal.

The kids loved the casserole I had prepared and begged me to make it again soon. The whole dinner for 9 had cost me only $3.22, and had taken only 20 minutes to fix, so I promised I would.

Ellen and Dale volunteered for K. P. while Kate helped bathe the smaller children. Nobody was interested in TV, so the homework went fast.

After all the children were asleep, Tom and I opened a bottle of champagne, danced to a few of the really good old tunes, and went blissfully to bed.

And if you believe one word of that kind of a day at our house, you're a bigger April Fool than I thought.

Worries About Space
April 8, 1969

I can remember when calendars used to have little moons on them.

If you needed to know the date of the full moon, new moon, half moon or waning crescent, you could look it up.

People had various reasons for being interested, such as romancing, gardening, invading or simple werewolfing. But apparently few people bother to hug, harvest or fight by the moon anymore, and presumably there are fewer werewolves, because it's hard to come by a calendar that lists the moon's phases these days.

If you want to know what shape the moon is in, you almost have to go outside and look at it, or climb into a rocket ship and go see for yourself.

At this point, more people are going out to look than up to look, but the talk about Apollo 10 and Apollo 11 gives me the feeling that the moon is getting closer every day.

But I worry about space travel. I worry about the going up and I worry about the coming down. And I worry about all the parts in between--especially the hundreds of little movable parts.

If you can't depend on the iron or the toaster or the washer and dryer to work for 10 days in a row, how can you trust all that intricate space hardware?

Don't worry, says Tom. Hundreds of people in Houston, Cape Kennedy and Washington are paid to worry, so you don't have to worry too, he says. Get excited, but don't worry, he keeps telling me.

Excited! That's one of the parts I worry about most.

I'm worried because the little kids don't get excited about space. They take for granted all the things that seem like miracles to a mind like mine--which doesn't really even believe in electricity yet.

The dramatic moment arrives: 3..2..1...zero ... lift-off!

"Wow! Look at it go. It's a beautiful lift-off. Gosh, kids what did you think of that?"

"What?"

'That lift-off. Didn't you even watch?"

'Naw. We saw it last time."

"Shades of Buck Rogers! For centuries man has dreamed about going to the moon, and here we are within months of a landing and you don't even care."

"Oh, we care. But it's all kind of routine now. By the way, who's Buck Rogers?"

"Routine! Never mind about Buck Rogers. I guess compared to Superman and even (forgive me) Diaperman, he'd be just routine to you too."

Imagine how it must be in the astronauts' own families.

"Hey, Jimmy, ask your dad if you two can go with my dad and me. We're going to hike out to the woods and camp overnight."

"My dad's not home, Tim."

"Where is he?"

"He hadda go to the moon."

"Tough luck, Jim. Gosh, your dad shoulda been a dentist like mine. He always gets Saturdays off."

There is some compensation for the wives though. What with 24-hour television coverage, they always know where their husbands are.

"I'd give anything to know what Jack is doing now, Sally."

"Maybe you'll hear tonight."

"No, when he goes to Chicago it's as if he's in another world. How about Dick? He's traveling too, isn't he?"

"Yes, but one nice thing about space travel--if I want to check up on him, all I have to do is tune in Walter Cronkite."

In spite of the publicity and the glamour, few kids on our block care about growing up to be astronauts.

"Well, Harold, I hear you're interested in space as a career."

"Not anymore."

"Why not?"

"No future."

"No future? Why, space is the future."

"Naw. One trip, maybe 2, and you're over the hill. No future."

Little Stanley Finchley was interested in space. He figured it was the one place his mother couldn't follow him to remind him about his mittens or his muffler or his rubbers.

"Stanley, I haven't seen you jogging lately. You haven't given up on your space preparatory program, have you?"

"I gave up all right."

"What happened?"

"Aw, it's that old NASA. Imagine, 3 grown men and NASA made them postpone their space trip because they had colds. Boy, just like my mother--one little sniffle and I'm grounded."

I worry about our space program. It has all sorts of down-to-earth problems.

Fondue Flubs
April 15, 1969

The recipe made it sound so simple:

Each person spears a cube of beef on his fork and dips it into the pot until it is cooked to his taste. Various sauces may be passed. Green salad and French bread complete the meal.

It sounded so easy, I figured even 7 kids could do it.

Later, after encountering the stark realities of sharp forks, reluctant burners, tipsy pots and hot oil, I wondered how I ever came to serve beef fondue to my family in the first place.

Actually, it all started with cheese fondue, and what made me think that was a good family treat, I'll never know either.

Tom and I first ate it with a group of friends at a restaurant in Geneva, Switzerland. The restaurant was full of atmosphere--there was an air of converted dungeon about it. Cheese fondue was the specialty of the house, and our reason for being there.

The waitress brought 2 pots, atop burners, and 2 baskets of cubed crusty bread for our group of 6. In the pots was a fragrant mixture of hot white wine and melted cheese. One pot was flavored with kirsch and the other with brandy.

We soon learned the art of spearing our bread, swishing it through the cheese in a figure 8 pattern, to blend the flavors, and popping the hot tidbit into our mouth. We liked it.

The next day we bought 6 fondue forks to bring home, but it was 2 years before I got up the courage to try Fondue a la Naybor.

The first thing I had to do was buy a second pot to supplement my chafing dish, and another set of forks to accommodate our crew of 9. I saved up for awhile, and finally I was able to afford the white wine, cheese and kirsch too.

I made a salad, cubed 4 long loaves of French bread, shredded tons of cheese, stirred one pot with each hand, and finally placed my 2 pots of fondue before my eager audience.

"I don't like it," said Drew.

"You haven't tried it."

"I know. Can I have peanut butter?"

Tom instructed the family in the art of spearing the bread.

"Ouch I'm bleeding," yelled Beth. We demonstrated the figure 8 swish, and Mike lost his cube on the curves.

"Why is it so sour," protested Meg. The next time I made it, I made only one pot, and served toasted cheese sandwiches to those without Swiss tendencies.

Meanwhile, I decided we ought to get double mileage out of our equipment, and decided to try beef fondue. Everybody likes meat, so I bought enough sirloin tip for the whole crew (and served casseroles several days running to make the budget even out).

My cookbook gave me to believe that with beef fondue, the sauces are everything. So, after cubing the sirloin, I set to work to produce 7 different sauces, using mustard, mayonnaise, sour cream, parsley, capers, olives, onion, horseradish, chives, lemon juice, and assorted exotic spices in various combinations.

With both pots of oil heating on the stove, I tackled the burners. When both were coaxed to a roaring flame, I called chow.

"What are you cooking?" asked my little friends.

"I'm cooking my dinner and you're cooking yours," I replied.

"Oh oh! Mom's on strike again, you guys," warned Kate.

Dale took one look at his plate and edged away. "I'm not eating any raw meat, I've got a track meet tonight."

After one taste of browned tenderloin, however, everyone got more interested in the proceedings. That's when the fun began.

The confusion of spear-like forks, sizzling oil, leggy burners and unsteady pots was almost too much for me.

"Don't tip that pot of hot oil, Drew. Kate, your piece is done. Oh, Tom, that pot isn't hot enough. Watch out, the water in the chafing dish is boiling over. Don't burn your tongues; let the meat cool a minute before you put it in your mouth. Oops! Please watch how you wave that sharp fork around. Eat? How can I eat when you're all bent on self-destruction?"

In my alarm, I almost forgot to serve the sauces. When I presented them, only 3 out of 9 diners cared enough to taste them.

"Why spoil the taste of the meat?"

After we worked (and I worried) our way through 5 pounds of sirloin, a large salad, mounds of bread, and those 7 sauces, Dale said: "The appetizers were great. Now what's for supper?"

I may move to Switzerland.

Mother-and-Son Talk
April 22, 1969

"Mommy, do you like being a mother?"

"Some things are unalterable."

"What does that mean?"

"It means, yes, I like being a mother."

Drew, our "baby," is 5½ now, and goes to afternoon kindergarten. His mornings are his own. On warm, sunny days he disappears to find a friend, dig a hole, chase his shadow, or measure earthworms. But on April showery days, he spends his spare time with me and we talk while I work. He is past the "why?" stage and our conversation often takes unexpected turns.

"Dale has muscles all the way from here to here."

"You'll have them too, someday."

"I got one already. But it's still kind of squishy."

"I'll bet."

"My bike squeaks allatime."

"Didn't Daddy oil it?"

"I told him to, but when he went to get the oil can somebody bent the pointy thing and Daddy said ... "

"Never mind what Daddy said. Why don't you go play with Shawn for a while?"

"When do I have to come back?"

"Around 11. Wear your rubbers."

"I'm not going."

"'Why'?"

"I'm making a boat."

"Out of what?"

"You take one piece of paper and fold it like this and then, do we have any scissors?"

"Try the desk."

"Kin I use the tape?"

"Not too much."

"How many stars in the flag?"

"Fifty."

"Did you ever go to school?"

"A few times. Why?"

"I wish I was big already."

"Why?" (Mothers never outgrow the word.)

"If I was big would I still have to eat cooked carrots?"

"Yes. But then you'd like them."

"Mike rolled the bread from his sandwich up into little bullets and then he boinged them into his mouth."

"Oh, that boy!"

"When can I have jeans with pockets in the back?"

"Someday."

"Someday when?"

"When you wear out all the jeans we have that don't have pockets in the back."

"I need a haircut."

"You can say that again."

"See, right up here, I need it. I got lotsa extra hair up here. Will the barber make me bald?"

"That would be an all day job. What makes you ask that?"

"I don't wanna be bald. Pat's daddy is bald. Is our Daddy gonna be bald? I'm gonna tell Daddy not to be bald. Do I got sidebeards?"

"'Sidebeards? Oh, sideburns. Yes, you sure do. They're very fashionable now."

"Lincoln had some too. We talked about him in school a long time ago."

"What else do you talk about in school?"

"Eskimos. Eskimos don't kiss; they rub noses. Is that fun?"

"I don't know. Let's try it."

"Yipes! It tickles!"

"Do you have a job in school?"

"Yeah, I'm table wiper. Jessica is table washer and sometimes she doesn't do it good and then I have to come along and wipe where she didn't wash good. The table washer is supposed to wash good. But Jessica doesn't."

"How about washing our table? It's almost time for the others to come home for lunch and then you'll have to clean up for school."

"I gotta finish my picture. This is a cave, see. It has all those icy things hanging down. This here is a stairway. Over here is the bad place where you gotta turn, but there isn't much room and fat people can't get through. You better not go that way. And there's a big hole down here with water in it and maybe there's a crocodile in it. They have crocodiles in way down deep caves like this one. See?"

"Yes."

"Do you miss me when I go to school in the afternoon?"

"Yes."

"Next year I gotta go mornings and afternoons. Will you miss me double?"

"Yes. Especially on rainy days."

"Can we still talk when I'm all grown up?"

"I hope so. I sincerely hope so."

"Yeah. You know what I hope? I hope we have grape jelly for lunch."

Parenting Q and A
April 29, 1969

Parenthood can be baffling.

I don't claim to be an expert on parenthood, but after 7 children I do have a high rating in bafflement. And since it helps to discuss a problem with someone who has had 7 problems of her own, I plan to take time out occasionally to answer questions on parenthood--planned or unplanned.

Q. What's the most important thing to remember in raising a child?

A. Pick him up gently under both arms, and watch for his head.

Q. What's the best time for a woman to have a child?

A. Roughly 9 months after conception seems to work out best for most women.

Q. When should a baby be made to give up his bottle?

A. When it's empty.

Q. Are twins really twice as much work?

A. Yes! Yes!

Q. Can a 9-month-old baby stand a 3,000-mile trip?

A. Yes, but I don't advise it. He's too young to travel alone and no parent could take it.

Q. I am a blonde and my husband is a redhead. Whose hair will our child have?

A. His own, I hope.

Q, Do you still recommend soaking diapers?

A. I never recommended it; my children did it on their own.

Q. Is it true that most children actually need parental pushing?

A. Unless they have a motor on their pram.

Q. Should my psychiatrist see my child?

A. Everyone should see your child unless he is invisible or they need glasses.

Q. My child hits his head against the wall. Can this cause damage?

A. Yes, but a good plasterer should be able to fix it.

Q. My child likes to stand on his head when he is reading. Is this bad?

A. Not Always [this answer was printed upside down]

Q. I saw a woman leaving a busy department store dragging 5 little children behind her. Is this a good idea?

A. If she dragged 5 in, it's best to drag 5 out.

Q. When it is time for the baby to be born, who should go to the hospital?

A. The mother.

Q. If we adopt a baby, will I ever have the feeling that it is really mine?

A. Yes, when it cries at 2 in the morning, it'll be yours, all yours!

Q. Is jealousy a common family problem when a new baby arrives?

A. Yes, but give him time, your husband will get over it.

Q. Now that the baby is here, my mother-in-law feels left out. How can I make her feel that she has a supporting role in our family drama?

A. Send her the shoe bills.

Q. How should I explain to my child that biting, spitting and kicking are wrong?

A. From a distance.

Q. When will my 6th grader stop picking fights?

A. After he picks on a 7th grader.

Q. When is the best time to send a child to school?

A. If you start him off at 8, you can go back to bed and no one will be the wiser.

Q. What is the usual time for transferring a baby from his crib to a regular bed?

A. When the 2nd baby comes.

Q. I am the mother of 10 and I want to know if you approve of bunk beds?

A. Yes, but you should have thought of it sooner.

Mother-of-the-Minute Awards
May 6, 1969

I can't get excited about mother-of-the-year awards.

Motherhood is a full-time job, but motherhood worthy of commendation is a sometime thing. Few mothers would admit to being good enough a whole year at a time to win an award.

But every woman has fleeting moments of glorious triumph over formulas, budgets, appliances, teenagers or fickle fortune, and for those moments I propose a Mother-of-the-Minute award.

It could be a kind of on-the-spot acknowledgment of meritorious service, valor, courage, fortitude or just plain making do.

For that kind of recognition, even you and I could be in the running once in a while, along with:

--Mrs. A, who, when asked why she didn't scream when the oil in the fry pan flared up setting the curtain on fire, searing the dog who bumped into the feeding table, so that the baby fell out except for one foot which caught in the folding seat, said, "I didn't want to cause any confusion."

--Mrs. B, who converted her long-awaited family room into a sick room for Grandma. Grandma lived a year and a half. During that time she was helpless and needed constant attendance, but she remained alert and cheerful and a part of all the family's happy hours. When she died, Mr. B said, "Thank you from the bottom of my heart." To which Mrs. B said simply, "I loved her too."

--Mrs. C, who, on the day the school called about Little Betty and all that blood, borrowed her neighbor's car, called the sitter, took the hamburger out of the freezer and changed the baby's diaper, before remembering that she didn't have a Little Betty. But remembering that Little Betty's mother worked, she drove to the school and rushed her to the hospital emergency ward anyway.

--Mrs. D, who couldn't decide between the navy blue pumps or the black patent buckle shoes, and finally spent the money on a new blouse for Sally who is living on a tight budget at college.

--Mrs. E, who, when her mother-in-law flushed the diaper down the toilet and flooded the bathroom, hall and stairway, said, "Don't worry, Mother, it was an old diaper."

--Mrs. F, who chauffeured 10 Cub Scouts to her son's birthday party in her very small foreign car. It took 3 trips.

--Mrs. G, who has twin babies plus a girl about 9 months older than them, plus a boy about 9 months older than her, but was quick to phone a neighbor in distress to offer to take care of a couple of her little ones until the trouble blew over.

--Mrs. H, who packed 400-and-umpteen lunches for her bus-riding brood, and never gave them peanut butter 2 days in a row.

--Mrs. I, who called her husband's boss's wife to say they would be late to tomorrow night's formal dinner party because her daughter had accepted a last minute bid to the prom and she felt she and her husband should be there to greet her escort and see them off.

--Mrs. J, who lived within her husband's income this year.

--Mrs. K, who threatened her 8-year-old with hasty reprisal if he repeated that certain word again, and gave it to him when he tested her.

--Mrs. L, who loved and disciplined her only child in such excellent proportions that all his life everyone liked him, and he grew up still loving and respecting her.

--and Mrs.You, for whatever you've done that makes you special to those who call you Mother.

Clotheslines
May 13, 1969

In May I miss my clothesline.

There are times in other months when I miss it also, but those are times when the dryer is out of order, and those times have to do strictly with frustration and necessity.

In May the feeling is different. It's as if I've lost an old friend.

A lady I know still hangs her wash in her Ann Street backyard on sunny days. Watching her sheets billow, as I walked past the other day, I was almost swamped with nostalgia.

In the many years B.D. (Before Dryer), I was of the opinion that if you gave a woman enough rope, she'd hang every inch of it with wash, and demand a few feet more.

I was the living proof of that opinion. I had a thing about empty lines--whenever I saw one, I dashed in and washed a load of clothes to hang on it.

Having lived for several years in a student housing village, where lines were shared (frequently with housewives who left Monday's wash out through Thursday), I greeted my own private clotheslines with shouts of joy and miles of diapers, undergarments and bedding.

Putting the wash out was one of the least confining of household chores, and I enjoyed not only the backyard society, but the actual handling of the freshly-dried wash as well.

I knew to the minute how long it took to dry a diaper or a T-shirt. I experimented with systems of rotation, and learned to dry 3 loads of wash in an hour or less, breezes cooperating.

True, I fussed and fumed if the line broke and everything had to be re-washed. But I became an expert on rain clouds, as well as the comparative threats of small showers and sudden summer deluges.

In fall, I sought out good drying days as late as November, draping armloads of frost-stiffened laundry on the radiators to thaw and soften.

Finally, with the first snows, I moved indoors. In our student apartment days, this meant stringing intricate webs of clotheslines through the kitchen and living room late at night, and taking down the dried wash and the lines before we could breakfast in the morning.

Cellar lines, when they came later, were a true luxury which I displayed proudly to visitors.

But one muggy, off-again, on-again day between the 4th and 5th of our 7 children, Tom offered to buy a dryer. Actually, since he had been helping to hang the wash for a couple of weeks, he practically insisted we buy one.

I agreed, but pleaded for keeping the outside lines so I could hang out the sheets on "nice days." Nothing smells better than air-dried sheets, I argued.

For 4 weeks, while I was getting used to the dryer and its anytime of the day or night readiness, I hung out the sheets. The 5th week it rained every day, so I fluffed the sheets. That was the death knell for the clotheslines. We put them down in the fall, and they never went up again.

I suffered a small pang of guilt when I recognized one length binding a neighborhood Joan of Arc to a makeshift stake, but I've got to be honest: with a family of 9 and an average of 15 washer loads a week, I know I have no time and energy for carrying, bending, stretching, cloud monitoring, frost-thawing, or even billow watching.

Yet, on a May day that is perfect for drying, I remember about clotheslines and wonder if the world isn't poorer (although neater), without them.

Surely, they rivaled The Towne Courier as a neighborhood newscaster.

Embroidered tablecloth hanging? It's the Cheneys' silver wedding anniversary. A sturdy girdle on the Joneses' line? His mother is here to visit. Bright white diapers at the Clarks? The new baby has arrived. Patched undies hung inside the sheets? The Potters have fallen onto hard times. Pastel bras on the Quinns' line? Young Polly has come back with big city ways. Mattress pads airing at the Williamses? Poor old Jake must have had a bad night.

In May I enjoy looking back. Going back is something else again, and I'm glad (most days), I don't have to do it.

Community Pride Day
May 20, 1969

Community Pride Day really hit me where I live.

When I remembered that last Saturday was official city clean-up day, I grabbed Mike and Drew and dumped them right into the tub. And it was only 10 a.m.

I got so caught up in the idea, I even took down the Christmas lights from the rooftop and I burned what was left of the door wreath.

Then, to show that my heart was really in this clean-up, I took down the SOLD sign from the front of the house. After 4 years, it was beginning to be a bit of an eyesore.

I debated whether to go whole hog and scrape the Humphrey-Muskie banner off the car bumper, but at the last minute I decided there was still hope, and left it on.

Our children got into the spirit of the day too. They made "Down with Litter" signs and distributed them all over town. I understand it took 2 Brownie troops an hour and a half to pick them all up later.

The grade school sent home forms during the week asking for names of people who might need help with their clean-up.

"Why do they want names?" asked Meg.

"There may be folks in town who for reasons of poor health or old age simply cannot get their yards cleaned up by themselves," I answered.

"Old folks, huh?"

"Yes, or anyone who can't find time to do it, or even a few who just plain don't bother."

I found out later that our name turned up on 2 of the forms.

As a result, a group of college volunteers showed up on the doorstep. As I opened the door, one of them asked, "Say, Lady, where do you want us to put all this junk?"

"What junk?"

"Somebody has dumped a whole pile of rubbish out here. There's a couple of broken bikes, some old chains, some barrel staves and a lot of soggy cardboard boxes."

"Oh, that rubbish. Put it in the garage."

"In the garage? Why don't we just pile it on the curb for the trash truck?"

"Heavens! That isn't trash rubbish. That's the kids' rubbish. I mean the kids' toys!"

"Lady, you got problems."

"I know. I staged a sit-in last week to protest, but what with all the junk around here nobody noticed I was sitting in. They thought I was down on my knees scrubbing as usual."

All in all, it seemed to be a rather successful clean-up campaign. I was a bit disappointed that the mayor and the council didn't see fit to take up brooms and mops and scrub the streets like they do in Holland, Michigan. But traffic being what it is here, we might have had to pay them hazardous duty benefits if they had.

Anyway, lots of lawns were mown and raked, some of the trash bins downtown got emptied, 543 pop and beer bottles were refunded, and 10,124 assorted hamburger, French fry and pizza wrappers were picked up on one block alone.

The next day the Clean-up Award was presented to the lady who visited all the newsstands in town and pasted "Clean Up!" stickers over all the nudes in the magazines.

Backyard Rating Slumps
May 27, 1969

As frequently happens, we were the last to know. There were signs, and I know we should have suspected long ago. But it's only human to be hopeful and trusting, and when the truth finally hit us, it was as if the roof had fallen in.

I mean, how would you feel if you lost your 5-star rating among the younger set's "Best Yards to Bang Around In?"

I think our own kids were trying their best to keep the bad news from us. And we might not know yet, if it hadn't been for that kid from Red Cedar School who came over to play one day.

"Hey, you guys, let's go in your backyard and mess around," he said.
"Naw.'"
"Why not?"
"My sister planted tomatoes out there."
"The side yard, then?"
"Flowers."
"The front yard?"
"Grass."
"Gosh, you poor kids. Well, let's go next door. They got lots of good old dirt."

It set me thinking. For years all we had was good old dirt. Tom and I complained a lot, but the kids never did. I decided to speak to The Father about it.

"Tom, do you hear any kids out in the yard?"

"No, thank goodness."

"But Tom, we should hear kids in the yard."

"Why?"

'Well, for one thing, because we've got kids."

"So, be thankful it's quiet."

"But we've always had kid noises in our yard."

"Boy, I'll say."

After a good deal of soul-searching, I finally got up the nerve to broach the delicate subject to the kids.

"Where are you going, boys?"

"Over to Tim's."

"Why don't you play in our yard?"

"Gosh, Mom, we didn't do nothing! Why do we have to be punished?"

"Who said anything about punishing? I just said to play in our yard. What's so bad about that?"

"What can we do in our yard?"

"What were you going to do at Tim's?"

"Lotsa things. Maybe climb a tree. We ain't got a climbing tree in our yard. And you chased us out of the lilac bushes, remember?"

"What else can you do at Tim's that you can't do here?"

"Dig. Now that we got grass, we got no digging place anymore. Or jump from the porch railing."

We never had a porch. Or swing. Gee, we don't even have a swing anymore.

"But we've had at least 8 swings in our time."

"We got none now."

"So all of a sudden our yard's not good for anything?"

"Aw, it ain't all that bad. We got the best basketball hoop on the block. And we got a good sidewalk for skates, hop-scotch or bikes. And the fence is great."

"Well, I'm glad we've got something."

"Yeh, but we can't play baseball. The infield's too short."

Dejected, I conferred with The Father again.

"Tom, is there any way to make an infield longer?"

"What?"

"I mean, do you think we could afford a swimming pool this year?"

"No."

"How about a new swing set?"

"We've had 8 of those!"

"I know. But Tom, our yard's gone downhill. We used to be 5-star and now we're minus 2. What happened? Do you think we should have waited until the kids got a little older before putting in all that expensive grass and the flowers and the tomatoes?"

"One of the kids is 17½ now. How much older do you want?"

"But Tom, it's the little kids I'm worried about. Do you think the gang will ever mess around in our yard again?"

"Maybe. But keep your fingers crossed and pray that our luck will hold."

Handicapped Children
June 3, 1969

The list is long: 10 fingers, 10 toes, 2 elbows that bend, 2 ankles that swivel, 2 eyes that see, 2 ears that hear, a spine that is strong, lungs that breathe, blood that is pure and red, a heart that beats, a brain to make it all mesh, plus all the other working organs, tissue and muscle that go into a human being.

The list is long, but a mother fresh from the labor of childbirth, combines it all as she asks, "Is my baby normal?"

Occasionally, the doctor shakes his head sadly, and the parents know from the start that they will raise a handicapped child.

At other times, there is an uncertainty at birth, and it is only long months later that a series of suspicious little signs which have nagged at the parents' hearts, finally add up to an abnormality that is disabling and permanent.

In some cases, a child is born normal, and grows happily, until some illness or accident leaves it blind, deaf, crippled or otherwise handicapped.

When I was growing up, there was a "retarded" child who lived in a house I passed on my way to school. He sat on the porch and rocked all day.

Mother knew his family and sometimes I heard her friends talk about them: "Yes, it's the oldest girl, Jean, who is getting married. Fay is still at home and little Frank and of course, the Other One."

My mother, when I asked, said she didn't really know what was wrong with the Other One, When she talked to his mother they never mentioned him. I understood.

If your 9-month-old is already pulling vases down on her head, it is hard to know what to say to your neighbor whose baby's leg cannot hold her up.

If your teenager is big, bold and brassy, it is hard to comfort the mother of the teenager in a wheelchair.

If your children yell, fight, scold, sing, proclaim and complain in a swelling chorus of babble, it is easier to forget the quiet child whose eyes say many things, but whose voice is mute.

But today we talk about handicapped children. And we have learned to widen their horizons, lift their loneliness and improve their lives. Education, training, therapy and counseling now can mean a happy and useful life for most of them. These things, together, are called Special Education. And through them are fulfilled the beliefs that:

--Every person is important, every person has worth.

--Every person is unique; there is no other person like him.

--Every person has a right to opportunity to reach his potential.

--Every person has the right to the full benefit of education.

That's something to talk about! In our town, Special Education means that Susan who is blind goes to high school with others her age. She gets good grades and will go to college. Her future is bright.

Four-year-old Judy, with the sparkling, impish eyes and golden ringlets, has cerebral palsy, but she has learned to talk. And while therapists work with her legs which respond slowly, teachers work with her mind which leaps nimbly, and her world opens.

Tom, mentally handicapped, has learned to care for his body's needs, a painfully slow process, but a first step he would not have made without Special Education.

Jeff's long illness left him with problems which threatened to close his mind to all learning, but Special Education helped to pry open the doors and release his great capabilities.

In all, 624 children from the East Lansing School District benefit from these programs. In the Ingham Intermediate School District, 7,000 are reached.

At the moment, our sympathy, our interest and our prayers for these children are not enough. The programs which aid them need more money.

June 24 is Help the Handicapped Week. On June 9, after you have approved the millage increase for your children and mine who are in the regular schools, please pull the Special Education lever too. There are children around us who need extra help.

First Child Graduates
June 10, 1969

It was the same old problem about the presents. Finally I had to threaten the boys.

"You tell Ellen what we got her, and you'll get 2 baths a day for a month!"

"Aw, what's graduation anyway?"

"It means moving up."

"Moving up? Is Ellen going to the moon?"

"Not this trip. It just means that she's through with school."

"Through with school? Boy! For ever and ever?"

"Of course not. She's going to college in the fall. You know that. Graduation means she's ready to move up to the next step in her life."

"Gosh, Uncle Don graduated from college Sunday. And Ellen's graduating from high school on Thursday. Everybody's graduating! How come I can't graduate?"

"Well, you did in a way. You moved up from 1st grade to 2nd grade."

"Oh yeah. How come I didn't get any presents?"

"Go play, or I'll shampoo your hair!"

In spite of many similar interruptions, everything is about ready for Ellen's big day. She did her part by passing her finals and remembering to pick up her cap and gown. I put in a big supply of man-sized crying tissues and extra film.

As a matter of fact, most of the details have been attended to. So why do I feel as though something isn't ready? Can it be because something ISN'T ready, namely me?

Commencement--it means the start of a new life for Ellen. But I liked Ellen's old life and I'm not all that eager to have her graduate from it. Does everyone feel that way when the first child reaches this milestone?

Will it be different with the 5th? And when the 7th one gets there, will I yawn, "Ho hum, so you finally made it?"

I wonder.

It's a crazy, divided feeling I have right now. While one part of me wishes she could stay "our high school senior," I'm as excited as she is that next fall she'll be "our college freshman."

In many ways, Ellen has "graduated" already. Certainly, she has "moved up" from her early label, "a shy, quiet, reserved girl," to "a poised, assured, confident young lady."

Somewhere along the line, she learned the secret that kills boredom and makes structured education come alive--she forgot about herself and started to care about others.

"I hate to see the year end," she muses, all my classes are really interesting these days. And I've got some great teachers."

Her marks, certainly, are no measure of her learning. She doesn't conjugate well, but she loves people in any language.

She forgets historical dates as fast as she learns them, but cries about poverty and neglect, be it past, present, or future.

She is vague and fuzzy when it comes to math, but she sizes up human problems with no trouble at all.

She spells poorly, but she communicates better than Western Union.

She falls asleep over a textbook 5 nights a week, but she's wide awake to the world and its ways.

Her diploma will certify that she fulfilled the basic requirements. I think Drew's Sunday School certificate said it better. It reads, "This is to show that your child has grown in love of God and neighbor."

During the past 12 years, Ellen has grown in love of God and neighbor. Perhaps, after all, those are the really basic requirements for graduation or commencement.

Since she's so obviously ready, then I guess I'm ready too—as soon as I grab a tissue, that is.

Traveling with a Family
June 17, 1969

Tom has wanderlust all year around. As soon as the school doors close, it becomes acute.

"What do you say we spend a few weeks in the Adirondacks and get away from it all?" he probes.

"With the children or without?" I probe back

"With. They'll just love it. When I was a boy we spent a couple of weeks up there every summer."

Which means that if we go, he may get away from his "all," but my "all" will come along. And that's the way it has always been, except for a very few memorable trips (if you count only one hand you can skip Tall Man).

Now that we don't have to carry the diaper pail, sterilizer, playpen, fold-a-bed and paperback Dr. Spock, traveling with the children isn't quite the expedition it used to be. We are still crowded, with 9 plus luggage, in one car, but compared to Pilgrim's plodding Progress we make pretty good time.

Frequently, the children actually spur us forward:

"Daddy, please find a gas station SOOOOON!"

With courage born of our combined ignorance, Tom and I traveled thousands of sticky miles with our first baby. She slept in a florist's box in Rhode Island, in a gigantic dresser drawer in Tennessee, and on the back shelf of our old Chevy coupe in about a dozen other states.

Before starting on one trip from Atlanta to Washington, we got the bright idea of feeding her before we set out: at 4 a.m. thinking she would then sleep the first few hours of the trip. She fussed and fumed and made it plain that Pablum at 4 in the morning was not exactly her dish, but finally she downed most of it, and we set out.

Then she really woke up. And howled. I picked her up to sooth her, and up came breakfast. All over me. I still shiver when I remember standing by the side road and changing my clothes in the cold chill of a Georgia mountain morning.

My dirty clothes went into the trunk and Lincoln held his nose as we drove by.

One year we rented a cottage in the Petoskey area for a month. That year's baby arrived so much later than expected that we ended up traveling north with a 9-day-old infant. Since he was No. 6, and Nos. 5 and 4 were also still babies, it was a long, hot, milky trip.

To make matters worse, when we arrived at the cottage, we deposited Baby No. 5, then barely 11 months old, on the floor, only to watch her get up and walk away--her first steps. Good-bye playpen, hello trouble!

To add to her achievements she decided that same day to go on a hunger strike. She lived on Cheerios and peaches for the rest of the month.

If traveling with babies was difficult, traveling with 2 teenagers, one sub-teen, 2 sub-sub-teens, and 2 natural-born wigglers, is an experience. For one thing, they take up more room than babies. For another, they talk.

Girl Teenager: "Arizona sunsets are the most beautiful in all the world!" (The night before it was Colorado sunsets.)

Boy Teenager: "Wake me when we get there." ("There" being a place to sleep.)

Girl Sub-teen: "Open the windows, the car smells." (The smell was dead skunk and it was on the outside until we opened the windows.)

Two Sub-sub-teens: "Why do I always have to sit in the worst place in the whole trip?" (In unison.)

Two natural-born Wigglers: "I AM sitting still!" (They're not, but probably they don't know the meaning of the words.)

The Father: "Whose idea was this trip anyway?" (His, but I'm not going to remind him now.)

The Long-suffering Mother: "It's a good thing I'm a long-suffering mother." (I suffer long, but not silently.)

Interested Friend: "I hear you're planning a trip or 2 this summer to get away from it all."

All: "You bet your sweet roadmap we are!" (Some people never learn.)

Old-Fashioned Fourth of July
July 1, 1969

"Going away for the holiday, Tom?"

"No, we always stay in town, Jack. A picnic if the day is good, the ballgame or a nap in the afternoon, fireworks at night--that's about all."

"Oh, an old-fashioned 4th of July!"

"Sure, that's still the best kind."

Old-fashioned is a magic carpet sort of word. People talk about old-fashioned Christmases, old-fashioned Thanksgivings, and old-fashioned 4ths with a bright gleam in their rose-colored Polaroids.

It's the kind of word that makes strong men weep and frail women coo. The women recover first. Along with thoughts of Gibson Girl blouses, parasols, rosewood spinets, and lavender-scented sheets, they soon remember tales of lye soap, wash boilers, itchy wool bathing stockings, and distant outhouses.

But men have short, selective memories and lousy imaginations. Most of them recall vividly Grandfather's glowing account of the holiday fun of his boyhood, and forget completely Grandmother's parenthetical version of the same occasion.

"Yes, Sir, we always had a parade in our day. Marched the whole length of Main Street," recalls Grandfather. ("Main Street was 4 blocks long and the parade took 2 hot, dusty hours to organize and lasted 4 minutes," adds Grandmother.)

"Lots of patriotism, too. You should hear how we clapped after Judge Wilson gave his stirring speech on the Birth of Our Nation." ("Judge Wilson gave the same stirring speech every year, and the citizens clapped because they were glad it was over.")

"And picnics! You never saw such goodies as Mama packed into our picnic basket." ("Even Mama never saw some of the 'goodies' that went into the basket in those pre-refrigeration days, but food poisoning was one of the known hazards of any picnic.")

"Ah, that chicken! Mama sure could fry chicken!" (Mama fried it over her old wood stove, and if the temperature was 89 in the sun, it was 109 in the kitchen. Mama and the chicken fried!")

"Homemade ice cream--now that was ice cream!" ("It was ice cream if the cream was rich enough, and if there was enough rock salt to last through the cranking, and if there was enough young muscle around to crank the freezer long enough.")

"We lathered up our giant ears of corn with butter, and we ate til we'd like to burst." ("Michigan corn doesn't come in until August, but sometimes Grandfather gets carried away when he's remembering the good old days.")

"Had us some real ballgames, too. Old Jake Miller hit one so hard, he collapsed on the spot from the effort." ("Jake came to bat in his high, starched collar, tie, sleeve garters, suspenders and blue serge trousers. What he collapsed from was discomfort!")

"And the kids, what a time they had!" ("That naughty Tommy Jenks threw a firecracker right into the path of the Hill's carriage, and the horse reared and Little Jenny fell from her mother's lap and broke her arm. Later, Jody Thomas lost three fingers when he forgot to let go of a cherry bomb.")

"Maybe the band concert at night was the best part of the day." ("It probably was for poor old Mama; it was the only time all day she got to sit down.")

"Such a pile of memories as we took home!" ("And such a pile of dirty dishes too--give me paper plates any day.")

All in all, I thought it best to double check on Tom's intentions.

"I heard you longing for an old-fashioned 4th. Are you serious?"

"Sure, sounds great."

"Right. If you'll kill the chickens, chop the wood, light the stove at 4 a.m., milk the cow, separate the cream, put the melons in the well to chill, and harness the horses, I'll pluck the chickens, bake the bread, make the butter, cook up some mayonnaise, render a bit of lard, and freshen up the fringe on the surrey."

"Oh, when I said old-fashioned, I didn't mean all that. "

"What did you mean?"

"I meant, let's have some root beer with our lunch."

Unscheduled Vacation Days
July 8, 1969

Summertime—but who said the living is easy? It couldn't have been a mother. You can bet on it, the more easy-going the living, the harder the mother is working.

The trouble is that everybody in the family thinks that easy-going really means unscheduled.

Now I'm not a laundry-on-Monday-bathrooms-on-Tuesday-kitchen-on-Wednesday kind of housekeeper. I'm more of an if-the-carpet-can-wait-until-Friday-I'll-probably-get-to-it-by-Monday sort.

But even to my sort, unscheduled is unsettled, and unsettled is chaos. I try to be easy-going about the start of the day.

"It's vacation time, so you can get up whenever you want to," I say, remembering the painful struggles on a typical school day.

In the middle of the night I wake up to find Drew by my bedside, fully dressed.

"What are you doing out of bed? Why are you dressed? What time is it? 4 o'clock? In the morning? Why are you crying?"

"I want my breakfast."

"Drew, it's still nighttime. The sun isn't up yet. Why did you get up at this awful hour, anyway?"

"You said it's vacation time, and you said we could get up whenever we wanted to. I wanted to get up now. And I want my breakfast."

Breakfast is something else I try to be easy-going about.

"Juice, cereal and toast, that's what's on the menu---up until 10. Anyone who gets up after 10 has to wait for lunch," I decree.

At 11, the din of a parade draws me to the kitchen.

"We're hungry," shout the marchers.

"Ha! You're too late. I told you that anyone who doesn't have breakfast by 10 has to wait until lunch."

"We had breakfast. We want lunch now."

For some reason, the easy-going life is a dirty one. The laundry piles up. And up. In my easy-going way, I toss a load into the washer whenever I pass it, which isn't often since it's in the basement.

It is always the wrong time.

"Hey, down there! I'm trying to take a shower. Can't you wash some other time?"

"Okay, some other time it is. But if you're the one who has been wearing the same underwear for the last 3 days, maybe you'd better leave it on while you shower."

An unscheduled day seems to drag on longer than the Vietnamese war.

"What is it time to do now?" asks one of the troops.

"Nothing. It's not time for anything. Isn't that wonderful?"

"It's no fun to do nothing. Tell me what to do."

"Don't tempt me."

Once in a while I try to liven things up by springing an impromptu treat.

"If you can be ready in 5 minutes, I'll take you all to the park."

The response is immediate, but negative.

"I can't go now, I'm washing my hair."

"Gee, you pick the worst times. I'm waiting for Marilyn to call me back."

"If I don't finish helping with the tunnel, the guys won't let me go in it all summer."

"Why dincha tell us before we started this game. We're at the best part."

At bedtime, whenever that is, I hear one of the kids voicing an unscheduled worry:

"Gee, Dad, I think Mom's flipped. She goes around muttering about school starting, and heck, it's only just ended."

Sales
July 15, 1969

"Kaye, why do you have your hand over that child's mouth?"

"She just said a 4-letter word."

"Oh. But I thought you and Tom agreed that the best reaction to that was no reaction at all?"

"We did, but this is different."

"A 4-letter word is a 4-letter word. What do you mean it's different?"

"This is the kind of word that strikes terror in a mother's heart."

"Tell me! Is it one of the words in Jacobson's construction walkway?"

"No!"

"Spell it. Or whisper it. What was the word?"

"Sale."

"Sale? Oh, Kaye! Sale? SALE! Kaye get your hand off that poor child's mouth. Are you all right, Little One? Come tell Aunt Josie, what kind of a sale? Half price? Closing Out?"

"Sidewalk."

"SIDEWALK? That's the best kind! Grab your purse and let's go, Kaye."

"I'm coming."

"By the way, since when is sale a 4-letter word?"

"It isn't to most people. I'm just trying to protect my children."

"Against what, for goodness sake?"

"Against my addiction."

It is said that once you can face up to a problem and admit to it, you've got it half licked. Therefore, I hereby admit that I am addicted to sales, that I am a compulsive marked-down buyer, and that I have not willingly paid the full price for anything since $5 first went on the tag as $4.98.

It all began long ago when I was first learning to stretch a monthly salary to cover 31 days, except in September, April, June and November, when I made whooppee with what I saved on that missing day.

The first month we made it through the whole month. The 2nd month we got through the 20th. The 3rd month, well, things were fine right through the first week. Sales, obviously, were the only solution to my woes.

Soon sales had me in their grip. Clearance sales, fire sales, one-cent sales, F.O.M. sales. I just learned that means First of the Month. I used to think it meant For Overdrawn Mothers, manager's sales, come-in sales....

Certain words automatically touched off my need. Did you say marked down, seconds, discount or new, low price? I heard you and was off and shopping. I was spending less and liking it more. In short, I was hooked by a dollar sign, less 10 per cent off.

I worried about it. I mean, anyone who starts to shake her purse at the first ding of a cash register bell knows she's playing with hot coals (89 cents a bag, reduced from 95).

My mother came to visit. I tried confiding in her.

"Rest with your feet up a couple of times a day," she advised. "By the way, did you notice that round steak is down to $1.09 at the Y & Z, today only? Grab your coat."

"Mother!" I cried, "you too? Then there's no hope for all my little ones--the weakness obviously is inherited."

For years I watched my babes push, grab and run to pay up at the annual school Junke Shoppee, but I laughingly called it "Fun Night" hysteria. I never let them loose in a real store; I was afraid to learn the worst.

One day last month we faced the moment of truth; the children broke out in a rash of salesmanship.

"Mom, guess what? There's a garage sale. And they got lotsa real neat junk. And it's CHEAP!"

"You can't go. You're not allowed off the block."

"It's right on our own block. We don't have to cross any streets. Kin we go, huh, Mom, kin we?"

You have to face facts. I decided the day had come to find out whether the curse had really won over yet another generation.

"Okay, you may each have a quarter. Go spend it."

In 10 minutes the first child was back, a self-satisfied smirk on his face and 9 cents still clutched firmly in his sweaty hand.

"I got a teddy bear, a fire engine, some pinochle cards, a flashlight that works, 2 window shades, a bottle cap collection and..."

"STOP! I've heard enough. Either you're the world's best sales shopper, or (perish the thought), those people really mean to clear out their garage before noon."

The best cure, I'm told, is 6 months on a desert island. Even then, there is always the danger of backsliding.

An alternate cure, still in the testing stage, is to go to a sidewalk sale. They say there will be so many super bargains, you'll spend all the money you can spare, and be free of the curse—at least until the next payday.

"Oh, Josie, look! Christmas cards, 33 per cent off!"

On Not Painting
July 29, 1969

There are certain things I don't do.

I don't smoke, I don't cuss, I don't steal, I don't tell tales and I don't paint.

If you don't smoke, you are admired. If you don't steal, nobody expects you to make excuses. But if an East Lansing housewife doesn't paint, she'd better have a visible physical deformity.

The tiny blonde across the street came out one day with a ladder and proceeded to paint the garage, the breezeway and finally the whole house.

Two months later, we moved away. Wouldn't you?

My new neighbors were most cordial.

"House is really peeling, isn't it?"

"Oh?"

"Your husband is the one who messes around with innovative education, isn't he? Pity. Well, when you decide to start scraping, be sure to come over; we've got all the tools you'll need.

"I'm not planning to paint the house."

"Pregnant again, huh?"

"No, I simply don't paint."

"Gonna hire a professional?"

"No."

"Well, dearie, if you're planning to wait for your husband..."

The girl down the street confided that she was doing only the low parts of their house.

"I just can't climb ladders. You too?"

"No, I just don't paint."

"You mean you do the inside."

"No."

"The trim?"

"No."

"Refinishing? That' s it, you refinish things."

"No."

"No?"

"Sometimes I steady the ladder for Tom," I said. She looked so worried, I had to say it.

"Men are good painters," she conceded, "but it's the waiting I mind."

I waited. It took 4 years, but I waited. People took to pointing our house out to tourists and Notre Dame football fans:

"The woman who lives in that eyesore on the corner doesn't paint," they explained.

Meanwhile, I fed my first son milk shakes and prime beef and told him what fun it would be when he was big enough to help Daddy paint the house. He got big enough.

Luckily, while my husband was finding the time, and my son was developing himself, someone developed latex. Now I'm glad I waited. The "hired" help is reluctant, unskilled and slow, but the paint is great.

"When do you want to stop to eat?"

"Is it ready? I can come whenever it's ready."

"But don't you want to finish that board. My father always had to finish the board."

"Naw, with latex you can start and pick up anytime and anywhere."

My husband and my son start and pick up anytime and anywhere.

"Aren't you going to paint today?"

"Naw, too sunny."

173

"But you've started all four sides. Can't you just finish one side so it won't look so patchy?"

"What's the difference, it'll all get done in the end."

So it will.

Women who don't paint learn to wait.

Camping Lingo
August 5, 1969

Everybody's going places, and whether it's to the moon, Traverse City or Colorado Springs, they seem to be taking their beds along.

Apollo 11 may not exactly qualify as a camping rig, but if you spend one day on the road, you get the impression that everything else does too. Pick-up campers, trailers, motor homes, fold-outs, pop-tops, and even houseboats whiz by, bumper-to-back porch, with such frequency that the unadorned car is the rarity.

The variety of bed and bedding on wheels has inspired a new term of description--recreational vehicle--to include them all.

Meanwhile, new campgrounds have sprung up and old ones have been expanded all over the nation to accommodate the boom. The facilities vary almost as much as the recreational vehicles themselves. Federal, state or privately owned, they range from primitive forests to elite stop-overs offering more comforts than home.

So, in every "reeveh," the navigator (that's also spelled Mom), sits armed with a state map, a road atlas and most important, a 600-page campground and trailer park guide. Once the fight in the backseat is broken up, and Dad is headed in the right direction on the interstate, Mom sets to work picking the nesting place for the night.

Everything in the guide is in abbreviated code, but after a while on the road, the code is a cinch to break. "Fp" translates into fireplaces; "rw" becomes running water; "snbr" is obviously snackbar; and "ice" always comes out ice.

After several seasons of camping or trailering, Mom finds herself not only breaking the code, but reading between the lines.

"Groc," for instance, looks like grocery and that's what it means. When you get there, wondering whether it will be an A & P or a Kroger supermarket, you find 2 counters behind the cash register of a gas station.

There is a choice of white, sliced bread, or no white, sliced bread; bologna, or no bologna; and 1/2 gallon of milk at 69 cents, or no milk.

"PiTlt," of course, means pit toilet, and pit toilets by any abbreviation smell the same.

"Plgd" means playground, a place the children will avoid like the "plag," (plague).

"ScClfs" means scenic cliffs, a place the kids will like better than the "Plgd," much to their parents' dismay.

"Dkwt" is short for drinking water. Frequently it is pure spring water, and the kids, bred on East Lansing's rich "nectar," refuse to drink it.

"HdPls" are offered at private grounds, meaning heated pools, and $1.50 extra a night. At that, it's a cheap family bath.

"SaNa" is an interesting abbreviation which turns out to mean sauna bath. To Mom it automatically means "push on, this place is too expensive for a family of 9."

The navigator soon begins to add a few abbreviations of her own to those in the book, which makes it a more valuable reference. Should the family come this way again, they'll know that:

"Ftpnck," penciled in by Mom, means the terrain is as flat as a pancake, and the stop is strictly for convenience, not beauty.

"Bthtkg," on the other hand, means the area is breathtakingly beautiful and it's a great place for a 3-day stop-over.

"Tmwch" means Tom's watch, and indicates that this is the place where Tom lost his watch last year, and everybody should be on the lookout while they're out hiking.

"No No" means No, No, and that means this is the place where the baby vomited in the heated pool, and it would be best not to stop here, in case the manager remembers.

"HCTYA" is my own notation, and means Happy Camping To You All.

Blimp Ride
August 12, 1969

"Did you see me? Did you see me up there?"

"Sure. Gee, Mom, you were hard to miss!"

If you looked up in the air last Tuesday between 1 and 1:30 p.m., and saw a big sausage-shaped balloon full of air floating over town, then you saw me too.

Actually, the sausage wasn't me. It was the Goodyear Tire and Rubber Company's blimp, the Columbia. But I was riding in it, and so were Mike and Meg. And talk about being up in the air! We haven't hit ground yet.

It all started with a telephone call:

"Mrs. Naybor, would you care to ride in the Goodyear blimp?"

"Would I. Gosh, I grew up with that blimp."

"What?"

"I mean, I always thought things like that were way over my head."

"What?"

"Imagine, a chance to be lighter than air!"

"What?"

"Yes!"

"Great. And bring along a couple of kids if you want to."

Everybody knows you can't just draw straws for anything as important as that; you have to consider, and make a reasonable selection. So I reasoned that the 2 oldest kids should go. After all, I reasoned, if I got invited once, I might get invited again, and then the next 2 would get a turn, and so on.

Which was good reasoning, until I found out about the weight limit.

"Are the children little, Mrs. Naybor?" asked the voice on the phone.

"Well, no, they're teenagers. You know, healthy, well-fed, tall-type American teenagers. And one of them is growing his first chin hairs. He likes to think it's a beard, but little Drew says you can only see them if you stand away from the sun...oh, I see, the weight limit is 700 pounds. No, I'm not what you'd call tiny. Medium? No, more like economy-sized. I'll tell you what, the heck with reason, I'll weigh them all and pick a couple of 50-pounders. Okay?"

"Swell."

And it's a good thing I did because The Towne Courier sent along a photographer with a 50-pound camera (at least!), and an adman who looked as if he might be a heavy thinker.

Now, what do you wear to go blimping? A worried look and your running shoes, that's what.

The blimp doesn't really land. It sort of floats down and a swarm of men grab for the guy lines, and if they're lucky they catch them.

It bounces around in the air and you run to where you think it will stop, but it doesn't quite stop, so you run some more to where it hovers.

Then they suspend a ladder from the door and another swarm of men lift you up. The door closes and another bunch of men give the whole rig a skyward shove ("All together now!"). The pilot guns a couple of noisy 210 horsepower engines, and boy, away we go!

What do you say when you go blimping? Nothing, it's too noisy to talk. But everybody does a lot of smiling and pointing.

What do you see when you go blimping? Everything. It hovers beneath the clouds at a nice, lazy 35-miles per hour, and you can see everything:

the toy cars in the parking lots at Oldsmobile, the flag over the Capitol, the lucky people in their backyard pools, and even the rusty radiator grills in the junkyards. Jet travel was never like this.

How did the kids like it? Meg pointed and craned and exclaimed and had a ball. Mike (the terror of Bailey School, remember?), turned white, grabbed tight to his knees, and wondered why there weren't any seat belts.

Later, he told the neighborhood kids all about it in glowing superlatives, "but they didn't believe me, and now they won't play with me."

But Tom got it all on film, so when the kids see the pictures, Mike should have friends again--jealous friends, maybe, but believing friends.

Which reminds me of another nice thing about that blimp. You have your picture taken in front of it and nobody, but nobody, asks, "Which one is you?"

No matter how round and firmly packed a gal may be, Miss Columbia has her outclassed. She's 160-58-51, and that's in feet, not inches!

Clothes for School
August 19, 1969

"Meg, did you count Mike's socks?"

"He's got 11."

"Eleven pairs?"

"No, 11 socks."

"You mean 5 pairs and one left over."

"No, 3 pairs. The other 5 socks don't match."

"Groan. Well, add socks for Mike to the shopping list."

"Okay. But I'll need another sheet of paper."

"And I'll need another checkbook, preferably J. Paul Getty's."

There are some times when I am all sweetness and light, but the day we check the closets and make up the back-to-school clothing list is not one of them.

When this year's list is revised, Mike's socks will be listed under L.P., meaning low priority. With 7 scholars to prepare for school, it's strictly first things first.

This year's first things will be what Ellen needs for college. Second will be Dale's needs for high school. Third will be Kate's needs for middle school, and the 4 grade-schoolers will get patch-up and hand-me-downs.

At that rate, 3 pairs of socks and 5 unmatched spares may well have to see Mike into November.

When a college-bound girl looks into her closet and exclaims, "Mother, I don't have a thing to wear!" nobody pays much attention.

But when the mother of that college-bound girl looks into that closet and exclaims, "You don't have a thing to wear!" things are serious.

"What did you do with all your clothes?"

"They're right there in the closet."

"I don't see anything but faded blouses, beat-up old sweaters and out-of-date dresses which probably don't even fit you anymore. What happened to all your high school clothes?"

"See those faded blouses, beat-up sweaters and..."

"Oh, no!"

I promise her the basic necessities, and we both secretly hope there will be enough left over to add a vest, a tunic and some wide, wild pants, for spice.

Things are almost as bad in Dale's closet.

"How many pairs of good school slacks do you have left?" I ask hopefully.

"If you count these black ones with the paint, and the gray ones with the patch, I have 2."

"Who do those other 6 pairs belong to?'"

"They're mine, but I can't wear them."

"Too proud, eh? Well, I'll have none of that in this house. Try these brown ones on right now."

"Okay, but when I had them on the other night you made me take them off. You said they looked like I had my little brother's jeans on."

"You mean those are the ones that were 9 inches above your ankles? How did you grow so tall so fast?"

I tried to be extra patient with Kate. Middle school and 7th grade are 2 giant steps in a young girl's life, and it's a mother's obligation not to complicate things.

"If we buy you a new jumper and a couple of blouses, and I shorten these 2 skirts and make you 3 new ones, do you think you can manage?" I ask generously.

"Maybe," she answers cautiously.

It is hard to believe that this is the same pubescent female who, on our last camping trip, spent 11 days straight in a pair of ratty, old levis which the trash collector later sealed off in an airtight cylinder and carried off for decontamination before destruction.

In Meg and Beth's closets, things are a bit cheerier. Last year's skirts look like minis now, and the girls are tickled pink.

"I always hated this gray skirt. It was so long I looked like Mother Hubbard. Now it's just right," gloats Meg.

"Just right" is half an inch shorter than her jacket, but when you are 8 and your knees are pink and dimpled, that's not all bad.

Mike is indifferent about clothes, at the moment, but concedes that he'd be more comfortable if his shirts were big enough in the neck so that he could still breathe with the buttons fastened.

Drew, on the other hand, has very definite views.

"Don't you dare buy me any new pants for school. I hate new pants. They scratch and they don't bend. And besides, I can't even pull up the dumb zipper!"

"Yeh," chimes in Mike, "why can't we wear our old clothes to school? Everybody else does."

Now I know "everybody else's" mother, and I don't swallow that line. But priorities being what they are this year, I'm tempted to give a little and let everybody wear their old clothes.

If only anybody had any old clothes.

Gift for Grandmother
August 26, 1969

"Well, why didn't you get anything?"

"They didn't have anything your mother needs."

"Needs? Why didn't you get something she doesn't need, but wants?"

"They didn't have any of those either."

"I know. That's what happened when I looked, too. Say, how about sending some flowers?"

"She has a garden full at this time of year."

"Candy?"

"She counts calories, remember?"

"A wallet?"

"We sent her one for Christmas."

"A robe?"

"She had a new one when she came last time."

"Earrings?"

"That would make the 13th pair we've sent her."

"Something for the house? How about china or silver or knickknacks?"

"After 49 years of marriage, there isn't much she doesn't have. Besides, she's started to give away her nice things. She says it simplifies her housekeeping."

"Ask the kids. Maybe they can come up with some ideas."

Normally I don't ask kids for advice. If they give you bad advice, it breaks their hearts it you don't follow it. If they give you good advice, and you do use it, they never let you forget it.

But they are specialists when it comes to birthdays and presents.

"Can anybody think of something we can send Grandma Naybor for her birthday next week?"

Ellen: "A trip to Australia! When she was here she said that's what she dreams about."

"I wasn't planning to spend that much. Can you remember any of her cheaper dreams?"

Dale: "How about a bike? Everybody can use a new bike now and then."

"She's going to be 70. 1 think it would tire her to unwrap a bike, much less ride one!"

Kate: "How about a family portrait?"

"I'm not going through that sitting business with you 7 worms again!"

Beth: "Do you know where to buy gumption? I heard her say she was just about outta that."

"If I knew where to buy that, I'd lay in a supply for myself."

Meg: "Does she have enough crayons? I never have enough crayons."

"I'm sure she has enough to fill her needs."

Mike: "You know what Grandma needs? Some toys. When we were there last time she didn't have hardly any."

"If you're still harping on why did I forget to pack your ball and mitt last time, maybe next time you'll remember to pack it yourself."

Drew: "Lotsa hugs and kisses."

"Oh, we'd have to go there to give her those."

"Okay."

"What do you mean okay?"

"Okay, let's go to Grandma's and give her lotsa hugs and kisses for her birthday."

"But she lives 500 miles away."

"Oh."

"Still, we did think about taking another trip before school starts...Say, Tom, I thought of an idea for your mother's birthday!"

"Great! Are you sure she'll like it?"

"I'm positive!"

School Year Begins
September 9, 1969

Monday morning was pretty rough.

"Mom, you put Mike's name in my sneakers," wailed Meg.

"Indelibly," I lamented, as I passed out pencils, paper and crayons.

"Beth, please eat that cereal," I ordered irritably.

"But Mom..."

"Just eat it!"

"Has anybody seen my brown belt?" shouted Dale, clutching his permanent press, ultra-slim, tapered leg, cuffless slacks which couldn't fall if they were pushed.

"When did you have it last?"

"Just the other day. I remember it was that day that old lady, Mrs. Coldwater, came to visit."

"Mrs. Coldwater is MY age. And that day she came to visit was last May. And if you haven't seen it since then, you might as well forget..."

"Never mind. I found it."

Last year we returned from a long trip at midnight the night before school started. Under those circumstances, I expected a bit of confusion on the first day of school. And the 2nd. And the 3rd, 4th, 5th, 6th, and well into October.

But this year I thought things would be different. After all, we got home half a week early. There was plenty of time for last-minute jobs like booster shots ("You mean all we're having for supper tonight is scrambled eggs?"); haircuts ("What? Canned soup again?"); shampoos ("Leftovers?"); and converting old shirts into painting smocks ("I know you were busy, but I'm hungry for more than just a toasted cheese sandwich").

"Beth, eat!"

"But, Mom..."

"Eat!"

Perhaps there was too much time. The girls laid out lightweight outfits on Saturday, switched to heavier ones on Sunday, and then got up 2 hours early on Monday morning to work out suitable compromises.

I got up 2 hours early too. But it wasn't early enough. At the last minute, there I was with 2 pigtails still to be braided, one sleepy first-grader still to be reassured, and the check for Kate's middle school fees missing. (Was it that strange sound from the disposal when I ground up the banana peels? Could be.)

"Beth!"

"But..."

"Eat..."

I was fervently thankful that at least I am spared the lunchbox routine. My friend packs for 8. Sometimes her husband wakes in the night to hear strange sounds coming from the other pillow.

"Two salami, but no butter for John (Watch for the bus, Arthur!); ...one peanut butter with gooseberry jam for Clarice (See it yet?); ...3 bologna with horseradish mustard for Leonard (Is it on the block?); ...crusts off, chopped carrot with diet dressing for Alicia (Run out and ask him to wait!) ..."

By the end of last semester she had used up 5,347 plastic baggies, one breadboard, 2 carrot peelers, and 12 gallons of gas--the gas was for the 4 times a week one of the 8 went off without his sack, and she had to chase after the school bus in her station wagon, curlers and robe.

"Beth, for the last time, eat that cereal!"

"All right, but Drew's gonna be awful hungry by lunch."

"Why?"

"I've been trying to tell you. I already ate my cereal. That's Drew's you keep pushing in front of me."

The school year is long. Monday mornings should improve.

Mother Alone
September 16, 1969

Young mothers, do you feel like barges nudged by tiny "tugs" whenever you move?

Have you never in your motherhood taken a walk that didn't resemble the Pied Piper's march?

Have you even started anything, a cake, a bath, or a sandwich, when you haven't been interrupted by cries of "I gotta go potty, NOW!"?

In short, are you a prisoner of mother-love?

Relax, even if you've been careless enough to have as many as 7 kids (it happens!), I can promise you that your day of freedom is coming.

Your emancipator? School, glorious school! Elementary schools, middle schools, high schools and colleges--all are waiting with open arms to receive your brood.

There were times, I confess, when I thought it would never happen. But at last the day has come--all my charges are in school and I am a FREE WOMAN.

At last my time is my own! After I plan, shop, cook, wash, iron, scrub, dust, vacuum, wax, polish and scour; and after I scold, correct, cajole, encourage and love; and after I find rubbers, separate fighters and hear prayers; and after I do a few dozen other little jobs--I am free to do as I please.

But you know what? Emancipation is a mixed blessing. I know you think I'm putting you on, but already there have been times when I actually missed having a child or 2 around during the day.

True, when the phone rings between 8:30 a.m. and 3 it's fun to answer because now chances are good that it's actually for me. And while I am talking on the phone nobody lifts the upstairs extension and says, "Mama, Mama, me talk too," or "Gosh, Mom, are you gonna be long? I gotta important call to make."

But, on the other hand, I have to run every time it rings, and frequently when I come gasping up from the basement I am too late.

Also, it's great to know that if I decide to sweep the kitchen, I don't have to wait until someone moves their castle, toothpick by toothpick.

But, there is no one to hold the dustpan.

No apple cores appear mysteriously in ashtrays I have just dusted.

But there is no one home who is just the right height to reach all the low spots on the table legs, and I have to dust them myself.

No one falls off their bike and comes screaming to the door, nose bleeding, while I am in the shower.

But, if I forget my towel, there is no one to hand it to me and I have to walk, dripping, out to the linen closet.

If I am invited to a coffee in mid-morning, I can go without having to find a sitter, and you know how impossible they are to find in mid-morning.

But when Mrs. Persistent Clubwoman calls to nail me with a job, I can't plead pre-schoolers and beg off.

If I have a headache, I can take a pill and curl up on the sofa in peace and quiet.

But if I am blue, the quiet is deafening, and no childish prattle distracts my gloom.

It's possible to start a job which requires concentration, or persistence, and finish it without interruption.

But some such jobs are dull and tedious, and I remember wistfully the "rocking chair breaks" of earlier days.

I shop now without an entourage, and buy only what I came for.

But sometimes I find myself talking to myself as I try to remember which cereal we have 2 started boxes of, and which one we ran out of this morning.

I can leave the house whenever I please; no one is napping, no one has the sniffles, no one is cranky, no one screams in fear of abandonment if I so much as peak out at the mailbox.

But for 18 years I have had a stroller to push, a sticky hand to hold, or a trike to carry home, and a walk around the block is not the same anymore.

So, how does it feel to be free of my motherly duties for some 4½ hours each day?

It feels great, girls, just great!

But once in a while I am a little bit lonely.

"Where Did You Put It Down?"
September 23, 1969

Nobody ever puts anything down permanently in our house. At least that's what they would have me believe.

Schoolbooks on the dining room table?

"I just left them there for a second."

Forty feet of green garden hose on the kitchen stove?

"Just for a minute--I'm on my way out with it."

A football helmet on top of the toaster?

"Sure it's mine, but I wasn't gonna leave it there."

A raincoat on the newel post?

"Let me catch my breath, and then I'll hang it."

Four grasshoppers (3 dead, 1 gasping) in the empty sugar canister?

"I put them there yesterday, but just until I find an empty coffee can."

Drumsticks in the Limoges vase?

"I wondered where I set them down."

A ruptured inner tube on the bedspread?

"The phone rang as I was passing through."

Half a melting chocolate bar on the brand new couch?

"Well, where is a fella supposed to put stuff when he has to sneeze or something?"

Where indeed!

No builder's blueprint ever showed an area marked "Space for temporary put-downs." No interior decorator ever eyed the style and symmetry of a table and advised, "Now that's just perfect for a family drop-off spot."

As a result of this gross neglect, families find their own "Just for a second" storage spots. In some households it is any nook discreetly hidden behind the ironing board.

"Why don't you put whatever you're carrying in the storage area?"

"I don't think my alligator would be happy back there."

In many homes, the living room mantle becomes the catch-all.

"I can't find my track shoes."

"Have you looked on the mantle?"

"Aw come on, I wouldn't put them there! Would I? Sure enough, there they are! Gosh, how'd you know, Mom?"

In our house the spot most often selected for "temporary" resting is the dining room table.

"Get this guitar, those water glasses, and whatever that dishful of floating green things is, off this table, please."

"Why? It isn't Sunday or a holiday, is it? Are we gonna eat in the dining room on just a plain old Tuesday?"

When Sunday or a holiday does come around, it takes a wheelbarrow to cart away the accumulation.

On Monday I hear the repercussions.

"I've looked all over this house for my speech notes and they've simply disappeared. I just put them on the dining room table for one-sixteenth of a half a second, and somebody managed to lose them for me. Wouldn't you think that just once I could put something down for an infinitesimal period of time and find it there the next minute?"

"When did you put it down, exactly?"

"Let's see, I guess it was last Tuesday. But it was only for half a mo…"

As soon as I can find a man who is handy (do they make that kind anymore?), I'm going to remedy the situation. I'm going to have him build me a special "temporary deposit" shelf.

What's going to be so special about it? This: as soon as the depositor's back is turned, the shelf will flip over, sending the jump rope, electric drill, or stone cold scrambled eggs sliding down a chute to a bin in the basement.

And there the family treasures will sit until "just a second" is over and the anxious owners remember to descend into the bin to reclaim their loot.

Just one problem--once a year I'll have to hire a tractor trailer to haul away all the forgotten "temporaries" that threaten to become permanent.

Letter to a Freshman
September 30, 1969

Dear Ellen,

The strike is over, your fees have been paid, you've moved into the dorm, and you are now officially a student at Michigan State University.

It may seem silly to you to get a letter from your family when you are only 5 blocks away. And we know that the last thing you need this busy first week of college is advice from home.

But you are the first of our 7 children to leave home, and we miss you already. Part of missing you is the need to tell you some of the things that are in our hearts.

Don't be alarmed! We promise you this won't be a letter full of "Thou Shalt Nots." You've heard enough of those to last you a lifetime. We'll admit there are a few "Please don'ts!" which we'd like to add, but we feel you've already heard them in your heart although we have never spoken them.

No, this letter is about other things. Principally it's about MSU. Your father has been a part of that academic community for the past 11 years. During that time our family has lived in the shadows of its towers, Beaumont and Ivory.

Like any loving family, we have been loyal to our breadwinner's employer. We wear green and white whenever possible, cheer for Duffy's boys on fall Saturdays, bypass Ann Arbor on the highway, and take our dog to the campus vet clinic for shots.

At times the university's problems have been ours. With it we have weathered slings and arrows, student revolts, staff strikes, legislative snubs, parking crises, unisex, and even demotions to No.1½. Its growing pains have often left us aching.

At the same time, we have shared the glory of its successes, its growth, its progress and its excellence.

We hope that the fact that so much of MSU is familiar to you will not diminish its excitement for you. Let it rather be a measure of security on which to build the self reliance necessary for your growth.

Since you were accepted as a student, the university has written you a ream of letters telling you what to expect, as well as what it expects from you. We think you should know also what your parents expect from the university and you in return for the $6,000 more or less that we will be paying out in the next 4 years.

If you go back and read the fine print in all those letters, you'll find that all MSU has really promised you are 3 things: food, shelter, and the opportunity for an education.

Barring tornados, sit-ins, or more strikes, we expect MSU will keep those promises.

From you, meanwhile, we expect the willingness to take what is offered.

We do not expect MSU to be your parent or guardian. You have 2 parents who love you, and you know by now better than any institution ever can, what pleases or displeases us. And if we did not think you were old enough and wise enough to be your own guardian, we would not have allowed you to leave home.

Also, we don't expect that the university will actually train you for a particular job. It is equipped to offer you such training if you should decide that is what you want.

But while you are undecided, we expect it to offer you the opportunity to think, to question, to reason, and to grow in self-knowledge. And we expect you to take full advantage of that opportunity.

We expect MSU to offer you teachers who consider teaching a high order, and the young mind a sacred trust. We hope they will spark your creativity, stimulate your awareness, and enrich your being.

We expect you to seek out those who are able to so enrich you, and respond. And blossom.

In short, we expect that in the next 4 years you will ask, "Who am I? Where am I? Why am I?" If the university helps you to find some honest answers to these questions, we will know that you have indeed received the education we sought for you--preparation for life.

Love from all,
Mother and Dad

P.S. Come home once in a while--if only to ask for money or to drop off your laundry.

Marriage Proposals in the Sky
October 7, 1969

I can hardly wait until the next Michigan State University home game to see if Jan accepts Bill's proposal.

All the people in my section of the stadium got so worked up over the matter that we missed most of the SMU game, and some of us didn't find out until we saw Duffy's Sunday night TV show that State won.

Naturally, most of the ladies in the crowd got romantic and thought Jan ought to marry Bill right away.

"Imagine, a sky-written proposal," one of them (an old maid I'm sure) sighed.

"Boy, he's up in the air over her, for sure," agreed another.

"Man, that's putting it 'plane,'" howled a nut in a striped muffler and plaid jacket (no taste at all).

And I've got to admit that "Marry me, Jan—Bill" was more direct and to the point than some of the passes that filled the air that afternoon.

For a few days I waited eagerly to see if the couple would elope to South Bend and have a sky-diving wedding with Father Hesburgh reading the rites from a helicopter. But that day progressed with only the normal Notre Dame game madness.

I was relieved because I don't think Jan ought to do it.

To begin with, when the plan first went up, the message read, "Marry me, Fan--Bill." Now, no girl should marry a fellow who (1) doesn't know her name, or (2) can't spell her name, or (3) can't make himself understood when he orders a sky sign made.

No matter how you look at it, that guy has troubles.

Then you've got to wonder about a guy who pops THE question before (or above, if you like) 70,000 people. If you ask me, he's the sort who would take his whole fraternity on his honeymoon. Or worse yet, his mother.

"Drop Bill, Jan -- soon!"

But, you're saying, maybe he's just shy and couldn't bring himself to propose on a sofa in the Phillips lounge. Then, I say, no, Jan, no! If communications are that bad between you now, just think what things will be like in 18 years or so.

Take it from an old married--18 and three-quarters years, actually--the communications gap gets worse. In no time at all, Bill will decide that plane-talk is too high (financially, I mean), and you'll be reduced to cryptic messages etched on old shirt cardboards.

And remember, Jan, he's nothing but a 4-word letter. Man. You'll be doomed to a lifetime of short, snappy conversations.

Sure, they'll be romantic messages at first, like "Kiss me, Jan--Bill." But soon they'll degenerate to "Mop floors, Jan—Bill," or "Stop spending, Jan--Bill," or even, on occasion, "Shut up, Jan—Bill."

All things considered, my advice to you is "Drop Bill, Jan—SOON!"

Tales in the Trash
October 14, 1969

We're all in the same boat.

Not the Christina, exactly; we're not all Greek goddesses. But on the barge of life, we're all at the mercy of the quick route to fame and fortune which is the exposé typewriter.

Sure, you and I don't have private secretaries who can tell that we bought day-old raisin bread to save for mink brown pantyhose. And we don't have Scandinavian cooks who know all about the spice in our lives. As for that girl we hired last year to scrub the woodwork, she couldn't read, much less write.

But suppose the milkman suddenly decided to butter his bread with our knife? Or suppose the cleaners emptied our pockets for all the world to see? Or suppose the hairdresser (only she knows for sure!) really let her hair down? Or suppose Father Faithful suddenly turned into author and wrote his own Book of Revelations?

Which one of us could stand tall in the glare of public scrutiny? Not me, that's for sure. Take the garbage man. Boy, what he could make of the crumbs from our table and the wrappers from our daily bread!

I can see it now in cold, black print, "Memoirs of a Tuesday Morning Pick-up!"

The sub-title could read, 114 Cans, 2 Bushels and a Yard Cart Full of Life Among East Lansing's Middle Class."

The story could start with a fat dose of trash--it sells so well in literary circles these days:

"I first met Mrs. N. on a brisk fall morning. The truck was late that morning, but as we got to her driveway, the boys and I realized that only part of her trash was out. She called to us from the garage in a husky, still-in-her-curlers-and-robe voice, 'Could you wait just a minute? Would you believe that husband of mine forgot again?"

"It was just an off-hand kind of remark, but I looked deep into her contact lenses and read the truth--the famous made-in-Heaven match was definitely flickering!"

"She made a second trip into the garage and returned dragging a beat-up, overloaded can, minus its lid. She smiled to hide her grief, and murmured, 'My husband says I'm the trashiest woman in town."

"There was no doubt in my mind now. All I suspected was true--this family was having problems!"

"Of course all the fellows on the truck felt the same way about the incident. None of us would think of writing about it to make money. But history! That's something else again. Who but a garbage man knows those endearing little things about a family that all the world waits eagerly to hear? Why every little bleach bottle in that trash can was throbbing with the desire to tell its small part about the family's dirty linen.

"I did sell this story to a magazine (21 thrilling installments!), and the book will be out next month (only $6.98) but I'd never think of taking a penny for my historic revelations --except that they keep forcing it on me, you understand."

It's a fact, we're all in the same boat, and "sales" control our destiny.

Waiting for the Repairman
October 21, 1969

Will he come? Will he call? Has he forgotten all about me?

Why are men always so vague? He said this afternoon. But it's 3 already. Should I call? No, better not to be too anxious.

Maybe he has forgotten the address. Did I remember to say East Lansing instead of Lansing? Of course, I always do. Did he understand I meant today? I'm sure he did.

I think I'll call. No, I'll wait awhile. But if I wait too long, there may be no one there.

Oh, the uncertainty of it all!

I'm as nervous as a 16-year-old waiting for her first date, and twice as worried. After all, she's waiting for an admirer--I'm waiting for the repairman.

My idea of Utopia is a place where the moment an appliance goes out of order, it self-destructs.

And you reach up on a roll and tear off a new one to replace it.

Meanwhile, I'm stuck with a repairman--or rather without one.

Saturday night the washer coughs a little, shudders a lot, and dies.

Out of courtesy, I offer the man of the house first chance at the remains.

"Call a repairman," he advises, "it appears to be something rather complex."

This means he has checked to see if the plug is in the socket.

"It's Saturday night," I groan.

"Some are marked 24-hour service. Try them," he encourages.

I try. On Sunday I try again. On Monday morning I get an answer. Or rather a question.

"What's the trouble with your washer, Lady?"

"I was hoping you could tell me."

"What kind is it? Neverfail? Boy, what made you buy that lemon? Doncha know nobody can fix those babies."

I try another number.

"How old a machine is this, Madam? I see. Well, I must warn you that your company is out of business and some of the parts are no longer available. But if you like, I'll come look at it. How about the 3rd? Yes, of course, I mean November 3rd!"

I try another number.

"Could you look at a washer today? It's only broken a little, I think. Did you say you could? You mean today? You mean you'll come right this afternoon?"

"Yep."

Then the vigil begins. I tidy up the corpse, and collar the dog. Then I wait.

12 p.m. "Hurry with your lunch, kids; I'm waiting for the repairman."

1 p.m. "Mary, sorry about bridge; I'm waiting for the repairman."

2 p.m. "I wonder what time this afternoon he meant."

3 p.m. "It's still early. I'm sure they work until 6."

4. p.m. "I could call, of course, but it's probably better not to bother them."

5 p.m. "Yes, all we've got is sandwiches for supper. I was waiting for the repairman."

6 p.m. "He must be coming. He said he would."

7 p.m. "Did you get all the towels? Yes, try to get 5 washers, that's 3 days' laundry. And bring them home to dry. The dryer still works--I hope."

Halloween Dress-Up Box
October 28, 1969

My philosophy concerning Halloween costumes has always been, "If there is room in the box, keep it."

Which is why there are now 3 boxes full of put-ons.

Even discarding wilting wigs, molting mustaches and corroding coronets, we could field simultaneously two clowns, Captain Hook, and two nefarious pirate crew, Red Riding Hood, Bo Peep, Sleeping Beauty, Zorro, a scarecrow, an angel, the devil, a skeleton, a nurse, a cow, a dragon, 2 gypsies, a baby bunny, a Playboy Bunny, Bart Starr, Peggy Fleming, Matt Dillon, Lassie, Joan of Arc, Scarlet O'Hara, and, if I can fake a halo, the Blessed Virgin Mary.

Viewing this obvious bounty, I sigh with relief. There'll be no last minute sewing or shopping this year. Ellen, Dale and Kate make it clear that they are too old for dressing up. My theory is that with today's teenage fashions leaning toward Edwardian lapels, Elizabethan tunics, floor sweeping coats, and high-buttoned shoes, every day is Halloween in their world.

Anyway, that leaves all 3 boxes of goodies for Mike, Drew, Beth and Meg. They empty all 3 boxes ("Is there a suit that goes with this gorilla mask?"), try on everything (except the devil—his zipper is stuck), and announce, "There's nothing good in there!"

Being a wise, understanding, loving and patient mother, I explode: "WHO SAID THAT?"

"We all did. None of us found anything to wear," volunteers Beth, while the others hide behind her.

"How can you say that?" I shout again, remembering to smile, so they will remember how wise, understanding, loving and patient I am.

"I sure didn't find what I want," ventures Mike, gaining enough confidence to speak up, but not enough to move out from behind Beth.

"Just what was it you wanted to be," I ask, smiling wisely, understandingly, and the rest of the bit.

"A computer. Can't I be a computer, please, Mom?"

"I wanna be a lighthouse," says Meg, adding, as I scowl, "but not a very big one."

Beth and Drew opt for a 12-string guitar and Walton B. McCluskey, respectively.

"What in the world is a Walton B. McCluskey?"

"It's a janitor, like at school."

"Walton I can maybe handle," I relent. "But a computer, a lighthouse and a guitar—I don't know. With ideas like that you should have picked another mother."

I wonder if I should confess that I have a very uncreative background for this sort of thing. When I was little I was Sitting Bull for 3 years in a row, using my father's sleeve garter for a headband, a feather from the stuffed pheasant in the living room, and the imitation Navaho blanket from the back seat of the car.

But they give me "the look," and I decide to compromise.

"Okay, we'll give it a whirl. If it can be made out of cardboard and scotch tape, you can have it."

We pack up the three boxes. Who knows, maybe next year.

Kids' Thank You Notes
November 4, 1969

The Aztecs called it "cacahoatl," the Spaniards made it "cocao," and the kids call it "great!"

But I think the chocolate bar ought to be called the friend-maker.

"My teacher is reading 'Charlie and the Chocolate Factory' to us," reported Meg.

"Sounds like fun. You want to take some chocolate bars to pass out in class after the last chapter?" I offered.

"Oh, boy! I'll tell my teacher!"

And that's how it happened that I gave out 26 chocolate bars and made 26 friends. As an extra bonus, I got 26 thank you notes, each one sweeter than the confection it acknowledges.

Third graders, I learned, are still a bit weak on spelling, capitalization, punctuation and form, but they are already masters at the art of getting to the point.

Erik, among several others, wasted no time beating around the bush. His letter, a model of brevity, said:

Dear Mrs. Naybor,

Thank you for the candy bar.

Sincerely,

Erik

Steve used only one word more, but added a brand new idea:

Dear Mrs. Naybor,

We enjoyed the candy bars. Thank you.

Sincerely,

Steve

Jerry felt he had been appointed a kind of spokesman. He wrote:

Thanck you very much for the candy bars. The rest of the class liked them, and i liked them to!

Sencirely,

Jerry

John had a different approach to the problem at hand, and to capitalization:

i liked the candy Party it Was a good Party that candy Was good

Love Sincerely

John

Philip caught the true spirit of the thing:

Thank you for the nice Sirprize you have gave us I enjoyed the candy bars So did the class

Sincerelly

Philip

Betsy's letter had a confidential tone:

Thank you for the candy bar. It was good and I likd it becawse I have not had choclet in a long time.

Betsy

Linda wrote this:

Thank you. For the candy bars. Our class liked them vary much. It was vary nice of you to think of it.

Scincerely

Linda

Jane said:

The candy was good. Thank you. I ingoyed it. And so did the class.

Love

Sincirely

Jane

Tim confessed true rapture:

I in turn enjoyed the candy bar so much that I kood hordlee eet it. it was d-l-i-shis

Tim

I, in turn, "ingoyed" all the notes, and "sencirely" thought that most of them were absolutely "d-l-i-shis"!

November Birthdays
November 11, 1969

Every time November rolls around, I remember another way I slipped up in my family planning.

In this penultimate month, when saner heads are already half-way down on their Christmas gift list, I am spending my money on birthday presents.

Not for one birthday, but for 2, and for teenagers! Teenagers--that's another word for expensive.

"Any ideas for the birthday presents?" I ask the breadwinner, who says he sees lots of bread, but not much else of the bacon he brings home.

"My gosh, in November. What a lousy time for birthdays!"

The kids are going on 15 and 16, and he's made that same remark every year.

"Something they really need--that's all we can afford at this expensive time of the year. What do they need?"

"Clothes."

"Okay, that's it. Buy whatever clothes they need. And don't spend very much."

"Make yourself clear; shall I buy them the clothes they need, or not spend very much. You can't have it both ways."

It's better you don't hear his answer.

One year I suggested to the kids that we move their birthdays to a more affluent time of the year. After all, Elizabeth of England was born in April, but Britain celebrates the Queen's Birthday in June. I understand the problem wasn't so much monetary, but something about June being slightly less cold, damp, foggy and wet than April.

"I'll agree to June, like the queen," said Ellen, royally.

"June tends to be full of graduations and weddings, and Mike has a birthday. Pick another month," I suggested.

"April?"

"Mom and Dad have birthdays that month," said Dale.

"And it's income tax time, too," I added.

"July or August?"

"Drew and Kate in July, Meg in August, and vacation trips both months."

"How about January?"

"Christmas bills."

"February?"

"Beth."

"Just when is the right time to be born?" they chorused.

Which is a real good question, the only good answer to which probably is, "Around the 9th month."

A long time ago, some methodical friends of ours tried to convince us that the right time to be born was December 15. By then, I was already 4 months along and shooting for November 21, so it was purely a rhetorical question for us. But they figured it all out and set out to meet their deadline.

They reasoned that December 15 was good because by then you could have all your Christmas shopping done (you see right there how queer they were!), and you could be back from the hospital--baby, potted poinsettia, and all--in time to enjoy a family Christmas.

The economic reason was even more interesting. A baby born in December was entitled to a full income tax deduction, although you would actually have had its support for only a couple of short weeks (except for the mother who "supported" it for longer than that).

Our firstborn came on November 21, just as unplanned. Meanwhile, our friends were busily finishing up their shopping and writing out Christmas cards, leaving a space for the baby's name.

At last December15 came. Then the 16th, and the 17th, and the 18th. When the 25th came (there sat the Christmas-announcement cards, all stamped), they began to get panicky.

"Doc, it's got to come before the first. It will, won't it?" they pleaded.

"Weeeell," said the doctor.

The baby came on December 27, in plenty of time, deduction-wise.

But that poor kid! Imagine having a birthday 2 days after Christmas. That's even worse than 2 birthdays in November.

Remembering Pregnancy
November 18, 1969

My friend Carol tried on her winter coat the other day and discovered that it only covered about 4 months' worth of her 6-months pregnant figure.

"I just got it last January and I hardly got to wear it at all," she moaned. "What will I do? I've still got 3 cold months to go!"

It looked to me as if she had 2 unhappy choices: wear a sweater under her already stretched out raincoat, or buy another winter coat.

"I don't even think they make coats that big," she wailed. "And even if I do find a tent that will fit this baby elephant, what will I do with it next year?"

I was about to suggest that just to get her money's worth, she could arrange to be pregnant again next winter when she came up with a 3rd choice.

"I'll hibernate! For the next 3 months, I'll simply stay home. I won't go anywhere."

But the thought of that kind of existence brought up another choice.

"I'll die!"

Which is when we both took one more look at that gorgeous fur-ringed beauty with its svelte Russian lines, and laughed until she was holding her sides and groaning.

The distance between the buttons and the buttonholes was as wide as E. Grand River, and just as impossible to breach.

"How can you laugh?" she asked, still weak from her own mirth. "You're absolutely heartless. And I know why--you don't remember what it feels like to be 6 months pregnant!"

Carol is younger than I am, and this is "only" her 3rd baby, but even she must know that any woman who has had 7 children and has been pregnant for at least (let's see, 7 times 9 is 63), I think 63 months, will NEVER forget what it feels like to be 6 months pregnant.

Oh boy, do I remember. I remember so well that every time I hang out the Indian corn or put some wheat in an arrangement, I look up humbly, and I say, Remember, that's for the crops, not for me.

Then I run and put some more moth balls in my maternity clothes.

But if I'm never pregnant again (and you understand that's the preferred choice), I'll always remember how it feels to be pregnant.

How can I forget the joy of waking those first 5 or 6 weeks?

"'Hi. Feel all right?"

"Yep, I think I'm over it now. Boy, won't it be a great morning when I can count on getting up without having to run---whoops!"

'This isn't that great morning, huh?"

"This isn't it."

The middle months usually were kind of fun. Especially the guessing games.

"What a pretty dress. Kind of an A-line, isn't it?"

"Actually, it's a maternity dress."

"You mean--oh, you couldn't be pregnant again?"

"Oh couldn't I!"

But the last couple of months were the most memorable.

Listen to one of the little ones talking to the mailman:

"Mama used to tie my shoes because I didn't know how. But now I tie her shoes because she can't even see them."

Your best friend tries to take your mind off yourself.

"Let's run down to Knapp's and look at bedspreads."

"'Knapp's? Okay, I know where their Ladies is."

Your mother is kind and thoughtful:

"Are you more comfortable now that you've taken your girdle off?"

"What makes you think I have my girdle off?"

Your mother-in-law is political too:

"Did you say you're sure there haven't been any multiple births on your side of the family?"

"Not unless you consider the poodle my side of the family."

Your husband, of course, is a real doll.

Besides doing all the lifting, stretching, bending and squatting, he looks as if he would offer to do the carrying, if that were humanly possible.

Later when a new mother-to-be wonders about "all those pregnancies," you admit that in all you had an easy time of it.

But, you add, it was memorable.

The Snows of Yesteryear
November 25, 1969

At our house the thing that separates the men from the boys is snow.

At the fall of the first flake, the boys run eagerly outdoors, and the man--it turns out there is only one--heads hurriedly in to watch the football game on TV.

If the first flake is followed by many, many more, the separation continues, but in reverse. The man goes out to shovel, and the boys stumble over each other in their rush to get in where it is warm.

The boys, backed up by a few girls, think the separation would end if the family had a snowmobile.

"Gee, if our snowmobile would only come, we could all go out and have fun."

"OUR snowmobile? What snowmobile?"

"Gosh, you did buy those raffle tickets, didn't you?"

"Sure, but we didn't win."

"We didn't win? Boy, of all the bad breaks. Now we'll have to wait until Christmas to get a snowmobile."

"Don't hold your breath."

"What does that mean?"

"It means, why don't you get out the toboggan and go find the nearest hill."

"But the nearest hill is in Okemos."

"I know."

All of which leads the kids to believe that mommy and daddy dislike snow. And that just isn't true. We think it's great stuff for looking at, playing in, and gliding over. What we don't like is driving in it, shoveling it up, and skidding on it when it turns to ice.

Actually, both of us were brought up in the snow belt of New York State, and we often find ourselves telling the kids all about the "real stuff" we had when we were kids.

For some reason, we don't make much of an impression.

Parent: "Snow comes and goes around here. But when I was a boy the snow came early in November and we never saw pavement again until Easter."

Child: "What does this ski-mobile ad mean when it says, 'At $1850, it's not for everyone'?"

Parent: "Why I never remember a Thanksgiving when it wasn't at least up to the windowsills."

Child: "The Richardsons are going up to Boyne for the whole weekend, the lucks!"

Parent: "Our house was on top of the hill--all you had to do was miss the last step and you'd coast clear into town."

Child: "Have you seen that new thing called a Sitz-ski? Boy, whatta way to go!"

Parent: "Have I ever told you about the sleigh rides we used to have? We'd put bells on the mares and everyone would run to their windows to see us go gliding by."

Child: "Johnny's new skis are made of aluminum and neophrene and polyethylene. They come from Austria."

Parent: "Barrel staves--yes, sir, you guys won't know what real fun is until you get out there on a pair of barrel staves held on with jar rubbers."

Child: "Some day could we go ice fishing? Or how about ice sailing? And bob-sledding?"

Parent: "Sure, sure. But right now, how about another log for that fire."

The Hinting Season
December 2, 1969

They've finally gone and done it; they've moved Christmas!

I was just sitting there without a thing on my mind except:

1. The possibility of sneaking another turkey casserole past my increasingly less thankful family, and

2. The question of whether it was time to take the Halloween witch down off the porch, and

3. The problem of where to put that one last box of 4th of July sparklers so we'll find it next year, when,

"Now that Christmas is here..." went the commercial.

I was so stunned by those first 5 words, that I never heard the rest of the pitch.

Now that Christmas is here? Not now that Christmas is coming?

Putting my finger aside of my nose, up from my chair I hastily rose, and hurried to check my calendar, wondering all the while if I'd pulled a Rip Van Winkle and slept a month or so by accident.

But no, it's still on the first week in December. In spite of all the store decorations, and even in spite of that "memorable" commercial, there is still time for my favorite time of the year, the "hinting season."

Our kids have hinting down to a fine science now. For one thing, they have all learned that hinting should be aimed directly at Mother, not only because she obviously has a hot line to Santa, but because Daddy seldom gets the hint.

They know that if they say, "Boy, look at the great ice on the driveway, it's just like a rink!" Daddy will think, "Wonder if there is any rock salt left in the garage."

Mother, on the other hand, says, "How many of you have outgrown your ice skates and want new ones for Christmas this year?"

Even Mother knows that Daddy is immune to hinting, and has given up on such things as, "If there is anything I like on a woman it's the soft, cuddly look," when she really means "Think mink," "Sable's stable," or "'Let him sell ya chinchilla."

So Mother is the target during the "hinting season," and like the Michigan deer in hunting season, she gets it from all sides:

Miss College Freshman: Everything is going great, but, you know, I've been late to class about 500 times. (She wants a watch for Christmas.)

Mr. High School Junior: Boy, that really got me. Good thing I can come home and let off steam. (He wants a new cymbal for his drum set.)

Miss Middle School: Do you suppose my legs are going to be as long as Daddy's? (All her slacks are hitting her mid-shin, and she's desperate for some new ones.)

Miss 4th Grade: Boy, is the floor ever cold up in our room! (She wants new slippers.)

Miss 3rd Grade: Save me lots of cartons because Jan and I are going to play store all during vacation. (She wants a cash register.)

Mr. 2nd Grade: I found 2 batteries in my toy box and they're still brand new! (He'll settle for any toy that takes batteries.)

Mr. 1st Grade: I did look around, but I still don't have anything to do. (He'll settle for any toy!)

Mother Power at Christmas
December 9, 1969

A mother gets heady with power this time of the year.

After all, it is she whom Santa depends on for the inside story when it comes time to make his list and check it twice to find out who is naughty or nice.

"I don't wanna go to bed now," asserts Mr. Six, fully prepared to stand his ground until midnight.

"Okay by me. Hmm, I wonder, is that one black mark or 2?"

"I'm going. I'm going!"

Some mothers really take advantage of their new whip.

"I need help. Who is going to volunteer to sweep the cellar stairs? No takers? It's worth 2 points towards nice."

There is a general enlistment on the side of good at that point, and in addition to the stairs, I get help with the dusting and the scrubbing and I finally find time to sort out the bathing suits and put them away (all except that moldy one wrapped up in my best company towel).

But even while she is glorying in her newfound authority, a wise mother remembers that this is the time to give up one important power--the power to probe.

"I need tape and glue and a small box," says a 7-year-old.

"What for?" asks mother, simply because that's what she always asks after a request like that.

But immediately she catches herself.

"Never mind what for. Here's the tape. I'll buy you some glue this afternoon. Is this coat box going to be big enough?"

"Naw, that's too big. I'll take this little tiny one."

"That's not big enough for anything."

It's plenty big enough for the. . ."

"Never mind! Don't tell me. Just take it."

It's bad enough to be expecting a present made mostly of tape and glue and small enough to fit in a pillbox, without having to know in advance what it is.

Actually, there is a possibility that in addition to tape and glue, the mysterious something may also be made of foil, beads, burlap, cork, artificial flowers, lace scraps, sequins, rickrack and other such "art" materials.

The reason I say this is because several weeks ago, the teachers sent out a plea for contributions of such "Trash Can Treasures," as they called them.

Bailey School parents are always too quick to comply, so I'm sure they got a good stock.

As a matter of fact, that's what worries me a bit. I just hope they didn't cooperate too much.

For instance, did they also send "buttons, buckles, cellophane, pine cones, thread, yarn, felt, feathers, wrapping paper, ribbons, seashells, veiling and velvet?"

Perfectly harmless? Of course. But read on:

"Cheese boxes, leather scraps, old jewelry, drinking straws, spools, juice cans, dried peas and onion bags."

Even I have to agree that to some there may well be artistic value of a sort in those items. Even onion bags.

I can even see an esthetic use for linoleum scraps, toothpicks, popsicle sticks, and tongue depressors if I really try.

What has me worried are the following:

"Emery boards"--I'll admit I may have missed something. I daydreamed a lot in school.

"Inner tubes?"--I must have been out sick that day.

"Core discard from foundries"--There, now you've lost me completely.

"Pencil shavings"--Not on your life. I don't know how you planned to use them, but you'd better plan something else. I'm not sending any.

I may have given up the power to probe, but my power of suggestion is still intact--and if any of those last four items shows up in my pillbox, stuck on with my glue, and sealed with my tape--well, just watch out, teacher, you may just get it all back next Christmas!

I Like the Christmas Bustle
December 16, 1969

If you are smiling this morning, you'd better stop quick before someone sees you. It just isn't fashionable to enjoy the last week before Christmas.

You're walking down the street, tickled pink with purple shirt and tie set you just bought at Jake's when all of a sudden you meet a friend. She's carrying a mammoth coat box, and she's on Cloud 9 because her husband agreed that they could afford that yummy fake fur for daughter Suzie.

"Got all your shopping done?" scowls the friend.

"No, and I never will!" you groan.

"Don't you hate it all?" she asks.

"Every minute of it," you agree.

On Saturday you have your hair done, buy some scandalous silver pumps, and attend a party where you dance a bit, drink a bit and sing a lot. When it is over, and everyone leaves, all aglow, it is just the same:

"Boy, parties!"

"Yeah, isn't it awful?"

"And there's another one Tuesday."

"Oh, no!"

That's the way it is.

But someplace in this town there must be another woman who will admit that she bought gifts with all the Christmas money, spent half of the month's food budget on a party, and even made a dent in that special check from Uncle Arthur--and loved every minute of it!

My secret is out--I like the hustle and bustle of Christmas.

I even get a kick out of that breathless feeling of being so far behind that I'll never get everything done by the 25th. (Some years I don't, but so far nobody has noticed.)

The busy business I like best of all has to do with cards. I love to get them and I even like sending them.

I start by dividing my list into Groups A and B. Then I let out a loud groan and a soft sniffle.

"What's the trouble? I thought you enjoyed writing out the Christmas cards?"

"I do. It's a nice sitting-down job and it brings back so many happy memories."

"So, why the long face?"

"Do you realize that Group B is getting longer and longer? I could just weep."

"What's a Group B? And I know I'll hate myself for asking."

(Husbands talk like that because of some hormone or other.)

"Group B is all those people we really shouldn't send cards to at all, only we just have to."

(My husband says wives talk like THAT because of some hormone or other.)

It's very simple. About Groups A and B, I mean (not hormones, they're sticky business).

Group A people send cards with notes on them. Group B people don't write notes. Sometimes they don't even sign their cards; they have their names imprinted on them.

(Every Year I ponder over that one. Imagine buying all those lovely cards, addressing them, and spending 6 cents to mail each one, and not caring enough to write a note, or even to sign the card. Talk about hormones!)

The dear old A's, bless 'em, write about their children, their grandchildren, their joys, their sorrows, their hopes, their disappointments--and we know they are real people who are glad to relive the miracle of Christmas.

It warms us to hear from them, and it is fun to write to them.

Group B, unhappily, grows longer every year. But after a while, they are just names on a list.

Memorable Christmases
December 23, 1969

Christmas is memory-making time.

Where were you on Oct. 15, the year you were 11?

Aha! Of course, you don't remember.

Where were you on Dec. 25, the year you were 11?

You could probably go on for hours with memories of it.

Great-Aunt Jane's big, rambling farmhouse, the special almond cookies she made because she knew they were your favorites, the skates you got from Uncle Ted, and the glow you still feel when you think back to that warm gathering of relatives and friends.

Some mothers get a bit uptight when they realize that today's Christmas is tomorrow's memory. They want everything to be perfect. And some years, for some mothers, it happens that way.

Their cards are distinguished, their gifts are appropriate, their goodies are good, their families are happy, and even their spirits are holy.

But don't expect it to happen that way for you this year, if, as of today, you still have 32 cards to address, the fruit for the cake you always bake Thanksgiving week is still on the shelf, and you forgot to light the last candle on the Advent wreath during Sunday's dinner.

There was one fleeting moment (between my 5-day bout with something flu-ish, and the postmaster's announcement that Grandma's box was 6 inches too big for mailing), when I thought this might be one of the rare years.

It was the kind of a thought you get after you've had a high fever, I discovered as the week wore on.

But that doesn't mean this won't be a memorable Christmas. On the contrary, it may be exactly the kind of Christmas that memories are made of. For one thing, the kitchen is being painted, and already I am saying memorable things as I hunt for the thyme in the bottom of a grocery carton, stacked under a box of plates, piled on a card table, squeezed between a lamp, a chair and the Christmas tree in the living room.

Just ask your children about their Christmas memories and notice how often a grown-up "disaster" is a child's joy.

--"I remember last year when you made these cookies the phone rang and you burned 2 dozen. Mike and I got to eat every one. Are you gonna burn any today?"

--"How about that year Grandma and Grandpa came by plane, but sent the gifts ahead, only the box went to Lansing, Kansas, by mistake, and when they finally got here in February it was like having Christmas all over again."

--"I wonder if Santa's elves are checking their work this year. Last year when my best toy didn't work on Christmas morning, Daddy took it back to the store the next day and I got to pick out 3 toys to make up for it. That was neat!"

--"Remember when Aunt Sarah forgot to mail Mama a Christmas check, and then at the last minute she sent it and Mama didn't have time to buy socks and pajamas and that kind of junk, and we each got to spend our $5 on toys?"

--"I like it when Daddy forgot to mail the invitations and nobody came to the open house. We helped eat up all the good stuff so it wouldn't spoil."

--"Santa sure does get mixed up sometimes. One year I got 3 Almond Joys in my stocking and Beth and Meg didn't get any."

--"Mama, are you still upset about the time you forgot to set the oven timer for the turkey, and when we came back it was still raw, and we had to have hot dogs for Christmas dinner? I like hot dogs."

--"Like, man, I sure protested when we all had to get dressed up to go to Mass at 6 o'clock in the evening, but it turned out there were only a few people there and everyone smiled at each other, and I just never felt so close to God before. Man!"

--Merry Memorable Christmas from all your Naybors, Tom, Kaye, Ellen, Dale, Kate, Beth, Meg, Mike and Drew!

New Year's Resolutions
December 30, 1969

It's too late, much too late. And that's great, that's just great.

There is something relaxing about the last week of the year. For 12 months we set ourselves impossible goals, and suddenly, time runs out and the pressure is off.

For me, it's a relief to tune out the nagging voices and admit, finally, that this is not the year that I will.

1. Make a million dollars. (Instead, I added to the national debt.)
2. Be the perfect mother. (Actually, I'm on probation from adequate.)
3. Unify the nation. (I thought I was making headway until Spiro started spilling over.)
4. Lose 50 pounds. (I lost 5--twice.)
5. Talk less and say more. (Enough said.)

Having admitted defeat, I can forget about this year and set myself some goals for 1970.

Out of conscience I will start this year's list with last year's list. After that, however, anything goes. And since goal-setting is so much easier and faster than goal-meeting, my list grows faster than Jack's beanstalk.

In short, but rather at length, I'd like to be the kind of woman

WHO lets her children go barefoot without worrying about rusty nails and runny noses.

WHO knits Norwegian ski sweaters.

WHO works gastronomical miracles with ground beef.

WHO smells of lavender.

WHO never raises her voice but manages to keep her children from raising the roof.

WHO always remembers to have the gas tank filled when it gets down to half.

WHO can kick her foot above her head.

WHO grows forget-me-nots, bleeding hearts and lemon verbena.

WHO can wear her hair parted in the middle and piled softly in the back.

WHO sews her own suits.

WHO paints woodwork, does a good job, and loves it.

WHO resists the temptation to say "Be careful!" when her teenagers take the car.

WHO always has an extra can of mushroom soup on the shelf.

WHO wears the same dress size as her high school daughter.

WHO troubled to learn the language of her forefathers.

WHO may know her husband isn't perfect, but has never let him know she knows.

WHO likes other women, even smarter and prettier ones.

WHO treats her children's friends like people.

WHO plays the harp, or at least the piano.

WHO bakes light, fragrant yeasty things.

WHO remembers the names that go with the faces of the people she has met before.

WHO started a quilt (or a rug, afghan or bedspread) and finished it.

WHO can quote the parts of Robert Frost that move her so.

WHO means it when she says "Thy will be done."

WHO knows that next year at this time she will be no closer to these goals than she is today, but will be able to say, "I did my best," and Happy New Year to you, too.

1970

A New Decade
January 6, 1970

It just goes to show you what can happen when you start celebrating.

There I was saying good riddance to the old year, and I hope things look up, to the new year, and they slipped another decade past me.

I might never have noticed at all except that I heard some friends discussing possible titles for the new decade.

"How about the Sensible '70s?" someone suggested.

"That's what we need after the Sick '60s, that's for sure," said another.

And suddenly I realized that no matter what they call it, I'll never see those 10 years again.

The older you get, the more you shudder at the end of an old decade and the dawn of a new one.

Four of our children are not 10 yet, and they can't understand what all the fuss is all about. As a matter of fact, they couldn't really get into the spirit of any of the New Year business.

"Does Father Time bring presents like Santa?" asked one.

"No."

"Eggs like the Easter bunny?"

"No."

"Valentines? Fireworks? Turkey and dressing?"

"No. Try football games."

"Boy, I can't understand why grown-ups bother to stay up for a nothing holiday like that!"

Two of our 3 teenagers remember the start of the '60s, and they are a bit more interested in decade changing.

Our firstborn, who turned 18 this year, was aghast at the way the past 10 years "flew" past her.

"We just started the '60s, it seems," she moans.

Her brother, 16, is preoccupied with the sound of the new decade.

"1970! It sure sounds strange! And just think, pretty soon 1980, then 1990, and then 2000! Wow, 2000 is really way out!"

The kids get into a long discussion over whether people will say "in the year 2000," or just "in 2000," which they think sounds kind of flat after the mouthful of 1999.

Listening to them talk, I see another gap between our generations. They can talk about the year 2000 with some certainty--they are almost sure to live to see it. But if you were weaned in the 1930s, schooled in the 1940s, married in the 1950s, and wearied in the 1960s, you are more likely to look backward than forward.

"Which decade would you choose to live over again?" I ask my husband, who weaned, schooled, married and wearied at just about the same pace as I did, although he shows it less.

"How about the first one? You know, no cares, no worries, someone to cater to your slightest whim or whine."

"I don't know about that. It means cutting all those teeth, eating pablum, learning to button and zip, and that awful first day of school all over again."

"Yeah, I forgot about all that. Well, maybe the 2nd decade. That had high school, and sports and proms and a few other appealing things."

"Well, that might give you a chance to raise your algebra mark, but you'd have all the agony of that first date again, and your first piano recital, and probably at the rate you grew, your slacks and sleeves were always too short."

"Boy, you can say that again. But in the next decade I had my army service and I got married and..."

"Watch what you're lumping there, fellow."

"Well, I mean those were great years, but they were hard too. Remember living on that starvation allotment, and then the babies coming and living in that old barracks at graduate school, and your operation, and getting my first teaching job? Wow, that was an eventful decade!"

"Probably the best years of our lives. But you are right, we'd just never have the stamina to live all that over again."

"That brings us to the Sick '60s again. The family has been fun these past 10 years, and my job has been stimulating, but it was a disturbing decade. There was Jack Kennedy and Bob, and King, and all that civil rights turmoil, and the horror in Vietnam. Nobody would want to relive those years."

And I agree with him.

So we bridge the generation gap a bit and decide to look forward instead of backward.

Maybe we won't make it to the year 2000. But meanwhile, it should be fun seeing what the 1970s hold. And the 1980s. And the 1990s. And do you realize that the year 2000 will be the 21st century?

Hmmm, I wonder what my chances are.

Heroes Taking Shots
January 13, 1970

Everybody knows about heroes.

A sports hero is big and brawny

A space hero is well-disciplined, learned and brave.

A national hero is honest, trustworthy and self-sacrificing.

A war hero is fearless, dutiful, and courageous.

A TV cartoon hero is tall, dark, handsome, tough, brainy, wise, true of heart and utterly unbelievable

But what is a rubella hero? Deep down in his heart he is a bit of all of these wonderful things. But on the surface he is small, young, apprehensive and (pretend you don't notice) reluctant.

Last week hundreds of East Lansing's younger citizens rolled up the sleeves of their assorted school dresses, blouses, shirts, striped jerseys and baggy sweaters, and lined up on the side of modern medicine in the war against rubella, that rampaging, "measley" perpetrator of birth defects.

Heroism in order.

Heroism was the order of the day at Bailey and Central schools where we joined other mothers and a "corps" of Board of Education, county health department and volunteer nurses, who administered the vaccine free to hundreds of children in kindergarten through the 3rd grade.

Matthew, a Bailey kindergartner and the first child in all of East Lansing to receive his "shot," was a true pioneer. He raced back to his classroom to inform the others that he had not cried, but "I eeked just a little."

The vaccination had obviously been the topic at breakfast for many of the children and some of them walked in the building already pale and shaky. But those up front in the line, who had very little time to think the whole thing over before bing-bang-bong, it was done, were quick to reassure the others.

"Hey, Charlie, guess what? I didn't feel nuthin!" shouted one veteran.

Whereas some of the children grew very quiet when their moment of truth arrived, little Christina at Central suddenly spouted a flow of anxious questions:

"Will I hurt? Can I squeeze my arm up there so it won't hurt so much? Does it take long? Will it hurt tomorrow? Is it ready?"

Suddenly, the fountain of words stopped.

"Oh," sighed Christina and not a word more.

One little fellow, his eyes smarting, insisted to his colleagues, "I didn't feel a thing."

There were a few small quiet tears, but mostly shouts of bravado and reassurance echoed through the corridors as the battle-scarred met the new recruits.

"Hey, Tom, it was just a little sting--kinda like my wart medicine!"

Only one little girl out of the classes at both schools balked altogether. She clenched her permission slip (clearly stating her mother's wish for her to have the shot), and yelled, defiantly, "My mother says I don't have to have it."

Mother, summoned to school by the principal, disagreed with daughter, and to the tune of much weeping and protestation, the needle went in.

When it was all over, and 6 volunteer aides, their nerves shattered by the experience, collapsed, little Debbie declared, "Ha! It didn't even hurt."

A spot of blood appeared on the arms of a few of the children and these few won the special honor of a bandaid to keep their sleeves clean. The sight of his blood fascinated one young man.

Pleasant experience for most.

"Lookit, it's dripping right down my arm," he proclaimed proudly and without a trace of fear.

For most children, the experience was pleasant. The work was efficient and swift, and to make it all worth while, there was that beautiful badge showing a conked out rubella germ (all green and dragon-ish with red spots, yet), which each child received to mark him an official Rubella Hero.

A few children apparently had been interested enough to ask questions and seemed to understand that the greatest beneficiaries of their act of heroism were the unborn.

One child seemed to understand it without reservation. Her comment: "I don't know why I have to have a shot. My mother says she's NEVER gonna be pregnant again."

Having Older Brothers and Sisters
January 20, 1970

I never had a baby sister or baby brother, and I don't remember ever wanting one.

It wasn't that I was selfish. As an only child I was often lonesome and there were times when I wanted a brother or sister more than anything else in the world.

My problem was that I wanted the brother or sister to be older than I.

I didn't get my wish.

And only now, as I watch my own brood of 7 grow, do I realize how much I missed in not having that older brother or sister.

My firstborn and I agree that if you have an older brother or sister life is better for you because:

--Your mother and father tried out all the new theories on their first child, and they are relaxed enough by the time you come along to let you thrive without interfering.

--Your older brother or sister has tried and tested your parents on every conceivable matter, and you can do almost anything you want to, as long as you don't make waves.

--You get a pretty name because your parents fulfilled their obligations to their parents when the first child came along.

--You don't have to be careful of your clothes--most of them are hand-me-downs--and your mother is grateful for every day they last.

--You get a bikini 2 years (and no tears), before your older sister did because her old one is there for you whenever you are big enough to hold it up.

--You don't have to beg for a basketball (football, hockey stick, croquet set, hair dryer, eyelash curler, or leg shaver); you just "borrow" from you-know-who.

--You never have to be afraid of that bully on the next block--he's seen your big brother's muscles.

--By the time your parents decide it's time they spoke to you about the birds and the bees, you have overheard enough from your older siblings to understand what your parents are trying to tell you,

--You don't have to cry for a dog because somebody else did and hair on the carpet is already a way of life in your house.

--You don't have to eat eggplant, artichokes, cauliflower or rutabaga--your folks gave up on that bit a long time ago.

--You get to ride a 2-wheeler 3 years before the older kids did because there is one sitting out in the garage and your parents are glad to see someone get some use out of it.

--You are allowed to cross Albert St. at the busy time (which is any time), when you are only 8, because your mother has gotten used to having someone who can dash to the store for her when she forgets part of the supper.

--You can wear your hair any style or length you wish; your parents have gotten used to hair and don't notice.

--You get to go to band concerts and plays ("Marat-Sade"?) at the high school because your older brother or sister is performing.

--Kids without older brothers or sisters don't even know where the high school is, but you know all the fight songs and yells already. (You inherited your sister's blue and white pom-pom), and by the time you get to MSU you know your way around most of the buildings on campus and whose anthropology section you should avoid.

--You know just how much your parents will allow when it comes to cutting classes, skipping school or failing courses, but to your great surprise they haven't mellowed on this one.

--You know which phrases to avoid in an argument, ("Everyone else does it"), and which phrases will swing them over to your side, ("I did what I thought was right and I'm willing to take the consequences.").

--Best of all, you're someone's baby brother or sister and all your life you'll bask in the warmth of their love.

How Kids See Their Parents
January 27, 1970

Who needs a mirror? If you have children you know what you look like.

Right from the start, Mother and Dad are their favorite models, and from the day they stop eating the crayons and start drawing with them you loom large in their picture of life.

"Da-Da, Da-Da," chants the baby, joyfully showing you a trapezoidal object and a pear-shaped blob newly embossed in graham cracker on the living room wall. "The resemblance is remarkable," mutters Mother. "I warned you to keep his playpen pulled away from the wall."

In later drawings, Father becomes a tall, good-looking giant with many muscles and a benevolent smile. When the child goes to Sunday School, he uses this same figure of God, only he dresses it in flowing robes instead of trousers.

Mother is always easy to find in a family drawing.

She has a square head, a built-in bustle, stilt-like heels, and her mouth is open.

Getting a true verbal picture of how your children see you is a bit more difficult. Questioned outright they will stammer, "Aw, Dad's all right, but Mom yells a lot."

On paper they will write all the things teacher expect like:

"My father is tall and honest and good."

"My mother cleans the house, except when she is tired, and then she yells a lot."

A group of mothers I discuss food prices and tornadoes with, decided to find out how the children really see them by holding a watch-in. For a whole week it was life as usual at our homes, except that mother was tuned in every minute of the time.

One mother didn't last the week. On Thursday she packed a bag and went home to her mother.

"I watched them from Sunday to Thursday and the only time any one of them saw or heard me was on Wednesday night when I tripped over the dog and she yelped and they all looked at me as if I were a Chinese torturer," she wailed.

Mother No. 2 discovered her family saw her as a driving woman.

"I dropped off Fred and picked up Sally and carted the Scout troop and when I went in to cover the baby at night she mumbled, 'Go bye-bye car' right in his sleep."

A mother with toddlers decided they saw her as a chair.

"Every time I went near them they climbed up and sat on me," she said.

Another mother decided her 5-year-old saw her as a kind of wizard.

"How come the bread doesn't break when you spread the peanut butter?" he asked auspiciously.

"I'm a wailing wall, not a woman," said another mom. "All week long it was 'Johnny hit me,' 'The TV won't work,' 'I need some now bell bottoms.' Nobody saw me as a person. Even in the mirror I look blurred."

At our house nothing quite so traumatic happened. I cooked, laundered, scoured and watched. By the end of the week I had learned 2 things:

1. My children see their father as a tall, good-looking giant, with many muscles and a benevolent smile, and

2. My children see me as a square head with a built-in bustle and stilt-like heels. And they think I yell a lot.

Poor Richard for Families
February 3, 1970

Some of the most often quoted maxims or proverbs in the English language can be traced back to Benjamin Franklin's annual of dates, weather and advice called Poor Richard's Almanac.

Franklin was big on what country folk call horse sense. A remarkable self-made man, he was a Jack-of-all-trades, and truly the master of many.

He got a big jolt when he flew his kite in a lightning storm but he managed to put even that shock to good use.

Later his home was saved from destructive fire by his invention called the lightning rod.

And the way I figure it, Ben learned a lot from having kids. He was the father of 4, and when he wrote in the Almanac that "Little strokes fell great oaks," he probably was warning all parents not to let the kids get you down.

I'm certain he had his children in mind when he said, "Vessels large may venture more, but little boats should keep near the shore." In today's language that comes out, "All right, but don't cross Ann Street."

He obviously learned early that children are expensive--and fathers seldom have as much money as bachelors for wine, women or song. As he put it, "What maintains one vice, would bring up 2 children."

He doesn't admit it, but I know it was teenagers he had in mind when he said, "Savages we call them because their manners differ from ours." (Apparently there was a generation gap way back then, too.)

Franklin had the answer to the peace-on-the-block-in-spite-of-the-kids problem. He wrote, "Love your neighbor, yet don't pull down your hedge."

On the matter of frustration from jigsaw puzzles on the floor, banana peels on the couch and soft chewing gum on the chair where father sits wearing his brand new one pants suit, he advised father to pretend not to notice.

Actually what he said was, "Keep your eyes wide open before marriage, but half-shut afterwards."

My husband says I've got it all wrong on that maxim. He claims Franklin was bemoaning the fact that he couldn't take a nap on the couch without being shocked back to reality every few seconds by either a bouncing ball or baby.

Even though Franklin lived before the telephone was invented, he knew the trials it would bring to parents. His answer was simple, "Teach your child to hold his tongue; he will learn fast enough to speak."

In spite of the trials of parenthood, he was all for family unity. As he put it, "We must all hang together or assuredly we shall all hang separately."

Keeping up with birthdays was a strain on his budget, apparently, for he said, "He has paid dear, very dear, for his whistle."

He knew all about those long school vacations when the kids do nothing but fight and yell. He wrote, "When men are employed, they are best contented, for on the days they worked, they were good-natured and cheerful. And they spent the evening jollily; but on idle days they were mutinous and quarrelsome."

That he knew the joys of parenthood, in addition to the tribulations, is evident in his remark that, "The sun [he meant son, I'm sure] gives light as soon as he rises."

We can picture him bouncing his little, drooling Susie on his knee when we read, "She laughs at everything you say. Why? Because she has fine teeth."

He probably heard, "I'll do it later," until he could stand it no longer and finally cautioned, "Never leave that till tomorrow which you can do today."

To the little guy who waited for Mama to buckle his boots, he said, "God helps those who help themselves."

And to the fellow who wants to watch "just one more TV show," he said, "Early to bed and early to rise, makes a man healthy, wealthy and wise."

He even had a word for me. He said, "Strange that a man who has wit enough to write a satire should have folly enough to publish it."

Valentines
February 10, 1970

Happiness is giving out 24 Valentines and getting back 25.

What? You thought most people only sent one Valentine to Miss Right, Mr. One and Only? That may be true in most circles, but among my square (the under-12 crowd), things are different.

As February 14 approaches, nay as the month of January dies, the order goes out:

"I need 24 Valentines for my class and one for my teacher."

"Okay, Meg. How about you, Mike?"

"We got 26 in our class. Do I gotta give one to all the girls too?"

'Sorry, fella, but you do."

"That's the way it's done in grade school. You give a card to each child, and each one will give a card to you."

"I hate girls."

"I know. How many do you need, Beth?"

"Twenty-six, and please don't get such baby ones this year!"

"Okay, 26 sophisticated cards for the 4th grade. How about you, Drew?"

"I need 50."

"Fifty! What are you going to do with 50? There are only 23 or 24 in your class.

"There's 23, but I'm not gonna give them my Valentines. I'm gonna keep them myself."

"But Drew, you'll get a whole pile back."

"I got a whole pile last year, but I liked the ones I gave out better."

Six-year-old boys understand pockets, string, and ballistic missiles, marbles, grape jelly, the Holy Trinity, fence-walking, space modules, cartoons, rubber bands, wild strawberries, and a few other things. But they don't really understand about Valentines.

Little girls catch on sooner than boys that it is quality, not quantity, that counts in Valentines.

"I got 25 Valentines, and guess what?" enthuses Beth, "One was a 10-center."

Now if when I say Valentines, you are thinking in terms of roses and violets, ribbon and lace, sweetness and light, well, forget it.

It is true that a small number of such cards may come into the house (probably from Grandma), but the school cards are something else.

"Mike, can you spare a card for Drew? He's short one."

"Sure. But don't take that monster one. I'm saving it."

"What are you saving it for?"

"My best friend, Paul."

"Let me see it. Why, Mike. That card is horrible."

"Yeah, I know. It's the first best one, all right."

"The first best one?"

"Yeah, the 2nd best one has a werewolf and some bats on it, and there's blood dripping all over everything,"

218

"Oh, Mike, it's just plain awful!"

"Well, I like it. Besides, it has good words on it."

The "good words" are:

"I live by the cliff, Drop over some time."

"Isn't that great?"

"Great."

Also great is the "happiness" card, the 25th when you only gave out 24, or the 28th when you gave out only 27. Who did it come from? Oh, joy! Nobody knows, and that's what makes it fun.

Adding to the joy is the verse on the card.

"Absence makes the heart grow fonder, so get lost."

It's obviously a case of true love.

Getting To Go with Husbands
February 17, 1970

Wives can't organize because they already belong to a union.

But that doesn't stop them from sticking together. And when they stick together, they can move mountains, and even, on occasion, husbands.

And that's how my friend, Tillie, got to go to Chicago for the weekend with her husband, Edgar.

To tell you the truth, Tillie wouldn't have made it to Howell without the help of Go-Go Anonymous, which is just a group of wives who stick together and give each other courage.

For years Edgar has been getting on buses, trains, and planes and saying, "Wish you could come along."

And Tillie has been waving back, "So do I."

But nothing ever came of it.

Then suddenly it occurred to Tillie that the last time she and Edgar had been alone (that means without the kids), was on the 13th of May the 3rd year of their marriage. It might never have occurred to Tillie at all except that one day her oldest kid asked, "Hey, Ma, what's your first name? I need it to fill out a form for school."

"You know my first name," she said.

"No, I don't, Ma, honest. Grandma calls you Baby, and Pa always calls you Mom. I don't know what your name is."

When it dawned on Tillie that Edgar really had called her Mom for the past 15 years, she decided it was time she went with him on one of those weekend trips.

But except for Go-Go Anonymous she'd still be waving at trains.

"I can think of a million reasons why I shouldn't go," worried Tillie.

But Go-Go Anonymous has dealt with Worried Wives before and they were ready when Tillie dialed for courage.

Worried Wife: Should I go to Chicago with my husband for the weekend?

Go-Go Anonymous: Go! Go!

W.W.: My husband didn't invite me to go.

G.G.A.: Hint around until he thinks he did.

W.W.: Suppose he says we can't afford it?

G.G.A.: Wrap a handkerchief around your brow, squint a little, and let it drop that the tranquilizers your neighbor takes cost $18.50 a week.

W.W.: Maybe I shouldn't go. After all, I have a very small baby.

G.G.A.: Good, he will never notice you are gone.

W.W.: But what about the teenagers?

G.G.A.: Boy, are you lucky--built-in babysitters.

W.W.: I'd feel better if there were an older person to take care of things.

G.G.A.: Call your mother-in-law; she'd been dying to run your house for years.

W.W.: Edgar says this is a business trip. Do you think I'll be in the way?

G.G.A.: Make it your business to be.

W.W.: I haven't a thing to wear.

G.G.A.: That's in style this year.

W W.: Chicago's a long way from home.

G. G.A.: Yeah, isn't that great?

W.W.: I just can't go. I keep worrying about the diapers and the lunches and the swimming lessons and the dentist and Sunday School and...

G.G.A.: Are you listening? Your husband calls you MOM!

W.W.: You definitely think I should go?

G.G.A.: Are you still here?

So Tillie went to Chicago with Edgar and for 2 days and 2 nights and they were alone together (that means without the kids). Edgar even remembered her name.

"That was a great weekend, Mathilda. Let's do it again soon," he said.

"Oh, Edgar," purred Tillie, "call me Mom."

(Kaye's Note: If there is no chapter of Go Go Anonymous listed in your local directory, why don't you start one? All it takes is a few wives, a little courage and a lot of glue.)

How Kids Talk Today
February 24, 1970

The experts say that if we would understand today's youth, we must listen to them.

So I listen. But sometimes I think we don't speak the same language.

It used to be that if you wanted to stay up on all the latest "in talk," all you had to do was watch TV or go to the latest movies. But have you noticed how quiet the heroes of today's "with it" movies are? They don't talk much, and that's a fact.

Remember that Benjamin kid in "The Graduate"? Boy, he did a lot of things, but talk wasn't one of them. And in "Easy Rider," hardly a word breaks the silence in the first half hour of the film.

I realize it must be almost impossible to carry on a conversation on a roaring motorcycle. Maybe that fact accounts for TV's monosyllabic hero, Bronson. Maybe he just can't be heard over that cycle, so he goes around speaking volumes with his eyes. (Well, not volumes exactly, it's more like he's mumbling a word or 2 between blinks.)

I figured there must be a reason for all this silence besides the cycles and simply not having very much to say, and sure enough, after a bit of probing, I think I've found the answer: timeliness.

If you want to make a NOW movie, you can't afford to have people doing much talking in it because nothing dates you like your language. And language these days changes so fast that even a picture studded with Today Talk would be strictly From Yesterday by the time it hit the screen.

If you don't think language changes all that fast, read the following and then let's talk it over if you can find the right words!

Psychodelirium Tremens.

Remember when HIPPIE meant big in the hips,
And a TRIP involved travel by cars, planes and ships?
When POT was a vessel for cooking things in,
And HOOKED was what Grandmother's rug might have been?
When FIX was a verb that meant mend or repair,
And BE-IN meant simply existing somewhere?
When NEAT meant well-organized, tidy and clean,
And GRASS was ground-cover, normally green?
When lights and not people were SWITCHED ON and OFF.
And the PILL might have been what you took for a cough?
When CAMP meant to quarter outdoors in a tent,
And POP was what the weasel went?

When GROOVY meant furrowed with channels and hollows,
And BIRDS were winged creatures, like robins and swallows?
When FUZZ was a substance that's fluffy like lint,
And BREAD came from bakeries, not from the mint?
When SQUARE meant a 90-degree angled form,
And COOL was a temperature not quite warm?
When ROLL meant a bun, and ROCK was a stone,
And HANG-UP was something you did to a phone?
When CHICKEN meant poultry,
And BAG meant a sack?
And JUNK trashy castoffs and old bric-a-brac?
When JAM meant preserves that you spread on your bread,
And CRAZY meant balmy, not right in the head?
When CAT was a feline, a kitten grown up,
And TEA was a liquid you drank from a cup?
When SWINGER was someone who swung in a swing,
And a PAD was a soft sort of cushiony thing?
When DIG meant to shovel and spade in the dirt,
And PUT-ON was what you would do with a shirt?
When TOUGH described meat too unyielding to chew,
And MAKING A SCENE was a rude thing to do?
Words once so sensible, sober and serious,
Are making the FREAK SCENE like PSYCHODELIRIOUS. It's
GROOVY, MAN, GROOVY, but English it's not. Methinks that the
language has gone straight to POT.
Author Unknown.

"I Am Sick"
March 3, 1970

Call it the flu. Call it a bad cold. Call it the misery. Call it anything you like--you won't like it.

As a matter of fact, if you haven't had it yet, take my advice and call it off.

But if you are committed to catching whatever is in the wind, be positive about it. Admit you are sick. Say it. Say, "Oh boy, am I sick!"

Some people make the mistake of denying their illness in the hope that denial will be enough to cancel it. It doesn't work. People have been known to deny that they are sick with their dying breath, but they have seldom managed to convince anybody.

Mainly there are two kinds of sick people--sick men and sick women.

It is the men who are least likely to admit they are sick. They sniffle, sneeze and harrrrrrrrup their way through the day, scattering germs and gloom along the way, but will admit only to being "a little out of sorts."

They may be dripping, coughing, and ablaze with fever, but as long as they are able to drag themselves to the office, they are not sick, and what's more, they have absolutely no intention of being sick.

They do not lie down until they fall down. Then everything changes. Suddenly they are SICK. They are SICK! SICK! SICK! every second of every minute of the time until they're back in the office.

With women it is different. Women admit they are sick right away. They say it, "I am sick." The difficulty is, nobody hears them.

In the office nobody hears them.

"I am sick."

"Yes. And after you bring that account up to date, retype this 30-page report, I need it in an hour."

In the store nobody hears them.

"I am sick."

"Yes. And after you wash all the crystal and china on this shelf, you can start the inventory of the small gifts department. Get it done before you leave for lunch."

In the home nobody hears them--especially in the home nobody hears them.

"I am sick."

"I'm supposed to bring the treat for Brownies, but I forgot to tell you. Can you make 3 dozen cookies this afternoon?"

"I am sick."

"I need that book from the state library by second period. Can you drive down and get it right after breakfast?"

"I am sick."

"Now about these people from the conference--no need to do anything fancy, just a small buffet and some punch. Figure on 22 people. Is 6 too early?"

"I am sick."

Even after a woman finally collapses altogether and takes to her bed nobody wants to admit that she is sick.

"What had you planned for lunch?"

"Nothing."

"Oh come on. You must have had something in mind."

"No."

"Well, what do you suggest?"

"Skip it."

"You're kidding."

"No."

"Oh. Have you shopped for supper?"

"No."

"Say, are you sick?"

"Yes."

"Gosh, if you're sick, why don't you say so?"

"I am sick."

"Sure. And after you fix lunch, you probably ought to lie down for a while."

"I am sick."

"And if that doesn't kick it, you might even take an aspirin before you fix supper."

Timing is All
March 10, 1970

A sense of timing is important to comedians, auto racers, hurdle jumpers, orchestra leaders, dynamiters, and among a few others, mothers.

A woman frequently becomes aware of this need right at the start of her motherhood.

"How often are the pains, Mrs. Jones? Umm, yes, I see. Well, hurry right down to the hospital. The doctor just left for lunch, but I'll see if I can find--I mean, I'll get him right away."

After baby comes home from the hospital, Mother learns that the secret in getting any sleep at all is to develop a sense of timing about it. The trick is to fall asleep the minute the baby does--whether it is night or day.

Timing is important later, too, when baby learns to eat from a spoon. The rhythm goes something like this: scoop, pop, duck, slop, and all over again until the end, when you scoop up what hit the floor, the wall and your chin, and give baby a piece of zwiebak to finish up on.

Mother's sense of timing is put to its severest test when the child is ready for toilet training. Part of the trouble is that Mother is always ready for the training long before the child is. In spite of this, timing insures some success (beginner's luck), which makes the failures doubly disappointing. (Wise Man says disappointment in training pants is twice as messy as disappointment in diapers.)

To make matters unfair, children appear to be born with special timing equipment which makes it possible for them to make life miserable for their parents with perfect regularity.

---In infanthood they lie meekly still until the moment the pin point is directly adjacent to Daddy's thumb. Then they kick.

--As his parents watch enraptured, a toddler will waddle one step, 2 steps, 3 steps. They are still spellbound when he reaches the table and yanks down the tablecloth sending coffee and dessert down with a clatter.

--On trips a whole carload of children will sleep soundly through the gas-up only to waken with urgent needs the moment you are on the 30-mile no-exit stretch of the expressway.

--After an 8-year-old has talked you into riding the triple whipper, neck breaker, carnival torture machine, he will wait until it starts, to tell you that yesterday one of the seats broke during the whirlspin-lift-and-tilt part of the ride and now somebody's mother is in a cast from the nose down.

--At a church supper, your 10-year-old will wait until the visiting preacher pats him on the back before heaving his supper back up squarely onto his plate, with the polite understatement, "I feel sick."

--Your teenager will wait until Grandma is visiting to bring home her friend who never, ever wears shoes, but wraps his feet in dormitory towels during the really bad weather.

--If there is a bug in the air, all 7 of your children (7! Talk about timing!)will catch it the morning you are to leave on your already thrice-postponed trip to Mexico.

--A 6-year-old will let you deliver all 4 minutes of a wilting, down-and-out, rip-roaring, dressing down before handing you the bouquet of dandelions he is holding behind his back.

--A lanky 16-year-old who manages to grow an inch every time he yawns, will tell you the morning of The Big Dance that he has invited a girl to go, and is there anything you can do to make his only suit 3 or 4 inches longer and a couple of sizes bigger through the shoulders.

--The day your husband gets the raise that will finally make it possible for you to come out only $50 short in your monthly budget, your daughter finds out she needs $750 worth of braces.

--The day you convince yourself that you are NOT too old for a glamorous blonde wig, your daughter-in-law tells you that you are soon to be a grandmother.

But the age of miracles is not entirely gone, and occasionally a child's timing and yours will come together in perfect harmony.

It happens when one pair of eyes says "I need you" at the same time that the other pair of eyes is saying, "I love you."

St. Patrick's Day
March 17, 1970

Oh, to be Irish on St. Patrick's Day!

On 364 days of the year I am content to be just what I am, but come the 17th of March, and 'tis yearning to be a son of the old sod that I'm after.

It all goes back to my childhood. I grew up in an Eastern, knitting mill town. The mills were manned and womaned ("soft" industry hires mostly females), by immigrants. The schools were mostly an integrated mixture of Irish, Italian, Polish and German children, with a sprinkling of Lebanese, Greeks and Blacks.

But the churches were something else. St. Agnes was strictly Irish, St. Anthony's was Italian, St. Stanislaus was Polish, and Sacred Heart belonged to the Germans. The Methodist church down the block was known to most of the immigrants as the "American" church.

When a teacher called the roll, O'Dwyers, Polanskis, Romanellis and Schwenders answered.

When a belligerent kid asked you, "What kind of a name do you call that?" you answered with pride in your heart and fire in your eye, "I'm an American of (whatever) descent!"

My own particular "descent" was Italian and most days it was a happy enough thing to be. Our families were affectionate and closely knit, the neighborhood grocery smelled of oregano and dried figs, the pastry was great, and when the old priest said the Mass in Italian, it was so close to Latin that you could follow right along with your finger in the Missal.

It was a most secure kind of childhood. But once a year, it just wasn't good enough. On St. Paddy's Day, my heart turned Shamrock green with envy and I re-suffered each year the pain of not being Irish.

Nowadays anyone can wear a bit of the green to help the Emerald Islanders celebrate, but back then there was an unwritten law in the school I went to: only sons and daughters of Erin got to wear green on March 17. The rest of us knew beyond a doubt that we did not BELONG. And we hated it.

Not that the Irish had any quarter on feast days. Why, when the Italians celebrated the feast of Saints Cosmo and Damian, the festival went on for the whole weekend. There was a procession through the streets with 2 bands, and 3 whole city blocks were roped off for the fun booths.

The smell of sausage, peppers and onions formed a canopy over the area, and lingered for a week after the doings were over.

The biggest treat of all for me was going to the pastry shop and sitting at small cafe tables on wire-back chairs, and making the agonizing decision between those 2 frozen delicacies, gelati and spumoni. I never could decide which I liked better, and for years only my shyness kept me from demanding, "One of each, please."

But for all their excitement, none of our feasts ever seemed to take over the world, or the school (which was my world), the way the Irish patron's day did.

Even the textbook was with the Irish, and if the teacher planned it right, we read that week about the potato famine, or the Blarney Stone, or the legend of the leprechauns. And when the music teacher came, we sang "Danny Boy" or "When Irish Eyes are Smiling." The radio played such ballads by the hour. And if, by chance, the mayor was Irish, beer ran green (I heard tell) in all the local taps.

My best girlfriend was Irish, and for a while I flirted with the idea (her name was Mulligan) of marrying my way into the clan, but it was just a passing fancy.

But things change as you grow up. For one thing, my Irish girlfriend married a Kowalsky, and not even Hallmark has heard of St. Stanislaus Day.

For another thing, you find out that the important thing in life is not what you are, but how well you know who you are.

And if you decide to be a wee bit Hibernian on a certain day in March, sure and not even St. Pat himself is likely to challenge you--begorrah.

How a Mother Prays
March 24, 1970
[Editor's Note: Pam's son David read this column at her funeral]

Holy Week, already?

Dear Lord, I am going to make this a real Lent this year. I thought that with the children all in school I'd have time to do so many special things to show my love.

But the "busyness" that rules my life all year continued right into Lent, and my promises to serve you better are buried under a mountain of laundry, a stack of egg salad sandwiches, and a checkbook that stubbornly comes up $1.37 short.

Here I am washing lettuce for a salad. I should drop everything and go off into a corner of quiet and talk to you right now. But there are few corners of quiet in my day, Dear Lord.

Right now the TV is on too loud—come to think of it, it shouldn't be on at all until 5, almost half an hour to go. But if I ask the children to turn it off, they'll beg to leave it on "just this once." Then I'll be angry with them for disobeying such a simple rule, and it will be a long time, Dear Lord, before I even think of you again.

Some people, I think, do pray on their knees with all the world blotted out from their minds. But somehow, I never learned how. Even in your church, if I recite the formal prayers I learned as a child, my mind wanders to a wiggly boy who is kicking the kneeler, or to the woman in front of me whose back buttons are done up wrong, with one empty loop sticking out at the top.

I often wonder if, in fact, I pray at all. I talk to you silently as I am doing now, but is that prayer?

Do you hear me when I talk to you over my salad making? Are you upset when I forget you entirely as I slice my finger with the radishes, or the potatoes boil over behind me?

It is true that I often forget you when my heart is at peace, and turn to you most often when I am fearful. How hard I pray when we drive in fog, or when I am forced to step onto one of those down escalators which unnerve me so. And how often I have closed my eyes as my loved ones have taken off in a plane, and begged you to give the pilot a hand, and to do whatever it is you do that makes planes stay up where they should.

But I do remember to tell you that I am thankful, not often, that's true. I say to the children, "Thank God for all His goodness," but I forget to do so myself as I get caught up in their arguments of who pushed whom and who ripped whose special picture.

I remember thinking once that since my children took up so much of my time, perhaps they could be the evidence of my love for you. I imagined that I could raise them with such gentleness, kindness, and justice, that they would be perfect Christians and living tributes of my love. Dreamer! I am more frequently not gentle, nor kind, nor just. And they are not monuments. They are normal human beings, given sometimes to sudden bursts of selfishness, and at other times to unexpected blooms of love.

Looking back some day, they will not even remember me as a religious person. If they walked in now, I would not say, "Come back later; I am praying," and they would see only that I am making a salad.

"Do you have a prayer corner," asks Mike, who came home from Sunday School to make one of his own, adorned with candle, statuette and prayer book. He placed it on the toy shelf, next to his china Pooh Bear and the double decker bus Tom brought back from England.

"No special corner," I tell him, and I move the Indian totem pole to the other end of the shelf. "I pray in whatever corner I happen to find myself."

"Sister says a prayer corner is good for praying," he replies, "so I am going to pray here, okay?"

"Okay, but do me a favor and pray when you come down the slide at Bailey School, too, will you?"

"On the slide? Why?"

"Because it's such fun to slide—you ought to share the good feeling with God right then and there."

"How do I do that?"

"You say, all quiet in your heart, 'Whee! This is fun, God, and I love you.'"

"Aw, Mom, that's not praying—is it?"

"Yes it is," I tell him. "Any time you think of God and talk to Him from your heart, you are praying."

You understand, Dear Lord, that I have to believe that you hear that kind of prayer, and that it pleases you.

"What are you doing, Mama?"

"I've just finished the salad. It's time for Beth to set the table. Will you call her?"

"Sure, but first can I taste a radish?"

"Yes."

Amen.

"Daddy's Home!"
March 31, 1970

"Daddy's home!"

Any day of the week, that cry is enough to cause a spot of excitement at our house. Everyone runs to the door and starts to blare his own piece of "good" news.

"Daddy, my tooth came out today. It was a really big one," yells Child One. "Will the tooth fairy leave me a quarter instead of a dime because it was a big one?"

Child 2 chimes in at the end of the first phrase, just like in Row, Row, Row Your Boat:

"I fell in gym and I had to go to the office and get 3 bandaids on my arm."

The others wait for their "beat," and pretty soon the air rings with a mixed chorus of childish babble. This is Daddy's welcome home, and he loves it. We know, because he keeps coming home.

When Daddy has been gone for 3 long weeks, his welcome is SOMETHING ELSE.

First there is a major stampede.

"Help!" he shouts, "Who opened the gate to the harem nursery? Are all these kids really ours?"

Everyone wants to be the first to kiss him, or hug him, or at least touch him. And the noise is like V-E Day all over again. The children are sure that he needs to know, in the first 10 seconds, that

--Ellen is home from college;

--Dale scored 2 goals in hockey, and missed making the hat trick by 2 inches;

--Kate has a new dress with a yellow sash;

--Beth got her bangs cut and we can see her eyes now;

--Meg's new shoes had to be special-ordered because of her narrow feet;

--Mike went to the Kellogg factory in Battle Creek with his class, a sack lunch, and 50 cents for spending money;

--Drew got diarrhea and couldn't go to his pal's party;

--Mama bought chicken, lobster tails, shrimp and saffron to try a new paella recipe;

--5 out of 7 of them are sure they don't like paella, whatever that is;

--They took all his post cards to Show and Tell;

--They prayed for him (when Mama reminded them);

--They missed him and are glad he is home.

After all this important information has been imparted, they suddenly grow strangely silent. They listen politely as he tells of the exotic lands he has visited, of the abject poverty or sublime beauty he has seen, and of his loneliness for them all the while he was gone.

But as he talks, their eyes wander to the 2 suitcases he carries, and their minds follow. Is there another bag to come? Do these 2 look heavier than they did when he left? Could that striped bag in his pocket possibly hold anything more exciting than foot powder?

Finally, the youngest forgets his good manners and voices everyone's true concern:

"Daddy, did you bring me anything?"

It turns out that the 2 suitcases and the package in his pocket are all he has, but the bags are indeed heavier than they were when he left. At home at last, they hint, suggest, recommend, and finally beg, that he unpack immediately.

Slowly and deliberately, he teasingly unlocks and opens the first case.

Dirty underwear! Dirty pajamas. A crumpled sweater!

"These are presents for Mama," Daddy jokes, while the older children pretend nonchalance, and the younger ones sigh audibly.

And then, under the laundry, between the layered suit, behind the shaving kit, and in every possible corner, Daddy finds something special for each lucky child, and Mama too.

Surely no other 2 suitcases in the world hold so much treasure crammed into such a small space. Surely no other world traveler had so little spending money for trinkets, yet pleased so many homefolks.

Geisha dolls from Japan, jewelry from Thailand, and embroideries from Pakistan delight the little girls. Chopsticks from Hong Kong, carved elephants from India, and matchbox cars from Britain, charm the small boys. In addition, there are Thai ties, bracelets from Afghanistan, exotic recorders from the floating markets of Hong Kong, silver earrings, inlaid marble boxes from the Taj Mahal, Indian brass, Japanese scrolls, rice paper hangings, souvenir spoons from everywhere, hundreds of slides, and dozens of other inexpensive items that give, along with Daddy's stories, a small peek into the faraway and intriguing Orient.

As the excitement dies down, there is a precious "gift" for Daddy, as a small voice says, "I like my presents, but I like having you home best of all."

Spring Is Late
April 7, 1970

Memo to spring (wherever you are):

You're late, you're late, for a very important date!

You expect certain things to be late, like women, babies, mail, trains, planes, the morning paper, the trash pickup, the milkman, your dentist appointment, the first act curtain, and the guests for whom you prepared the souffle which is threatening to fall any minute.

But certain other things should never, never be late. Among these are bridegrooms, paychecks, obstetricians, the throw to first base, the lift of the drawbridge, the good guy's draw, the governor's pardon, and the arrival of spring.

The human race is strange and fickle. It forgives Nature's oversight if fall is late, it even rejoices if winter is tardy by a month or so. But if spring is delayed, (skiing in April?), the whole world is out of sorts.

Children chafe to shed their snowsuits and boots; golfers s-putt-er; cooks stew; farmers fret; builders blast; lovers languish; buds bruise; painters pout; students strike; cars cough; willows wallow; rivers roil; robins renege and crocuses cringe.

As for our back room, what happens to that when spring is late is enough to make any woman wail and any man stay out.

Our back room is more of a hall than a room, but we always call it the back room, except when spring is late, when we call it a mess. Our back room is what some people call a mud room, except that you have to cross the kitchen to get to it from the back door which really makes the kitchen the mud room.

Our back room is very small, but it has hooks for the children's jackets, shelves for their books, drawers for mittens, hats and scarves, a closet for whatever will fit, and under the boots, rubbers and roller skates, I think there is still a floor.

On a good day, say like the 32nd of July, any year, everything is hung, shelved, drawered and picked up. Most days, however, things are a bit crowded and messy, and on a day when spring is already about a month overdue, things are chaotic.

When winter overlaps into spring, boots overlap into rubbers, parkas overlap into raincoats, mittens overlap into umbrellas, and so on, until one fine wintry, spring day, you can't get into the back room at all.

A reasonable mother tries to restore order.

"Let's put away all the winter things since it's so nice and warm now, and get out some lighter jackets for spring," she says the night before the 5-inch snowfall.

A week or so later, she tries again.

"Take all the boots to the basement and line them up. I think we're through with them for this year." (Which goes to show you that mothers don't know everything.)

Unable to win on that score, she tries another route to sanity.

"How about installing a few more hooks in this room?" she asks hubby.

"Sky hooks?"

Well, you can't win them all.

At this point, she decides to take direct action and make the kids sort out the mess.

"Get rid of every single thing that doesn't absolutely HAVE to be here," she orders.

They sort manfully and get rid of a broken yo-yo, a Barbie shoe, Mother's No. 9 knitting needle that has been missing since Christmas, and 2 sweatshirts which belong to the boys next door.

"Everybody out!" yells Mother. "I'll find something we can put away, give away or throw away--because if I don't, we'll have to move away!"

The children are very quiet; they are praying for spring.

Canisters
April 14, 1970

"Nobody understands me!"

I make the above remark occasionally, and when I do, my whole family springs into action, proving that after several years of communal living, they understand me very well indeed.

"I'll pick it up, I'll pick it up," mutters one son, heading for his room.

"Gosh, I only used this much," argues a daughter as she replaces the cap on the shampoo.

"Honey, I meant to call, I really did. But I got tied up," says my husband.

"I'm sorry, Mama," chant the little kids, who are not exactly sure what it is I've caught them at this time.

I must admit the response is gratifying. Even Lucy (The Psychiatrist Is In--Fee 5 cents) knows that what the world needs most is to be heard and understood.

But in some circles, asking to be heard and understood is like asking for the moon on a platter. There is no way, for instance, of getting manufacturers of household equipment to understand the women who use their products. For hundreds of years they have ignored the size, shape, strength, needs and habits of the homemaker, and it looks as if they always will.

Which brings me to canisters. You know what a canister is--a covered can or box for storing kitchen staples, right?

If you shop for canisters, you will find that they come round, square, bin-like, or wedge-shaped. They come in tin, aluminum, copper, pottery, wood or plastic. They come striped, plaid, beflowered, multicolored, dotted, speckled, grained, or even plain.

One more thing about canisters: they come in sets of 4. I think they have come in sets of 4 ever since early man placated early woman (who said, "Nobody understands me! "), by carving out the first stoneware canisters.

When my mother bought her first set some 45 years ago, they came in sets of 4: 2 large and 2 small. When I bought my first set, some 19 years ago, they came in sets of 4: 2 large and 2 small. Probably when my great grand-daughter buys her first set, they will come in sets of 4: 2 large and 2 small.

Now, the question I'm asking, that nobody is hearing or understanding, is "Why 4?" And why 2 large and 2 small? Why not 6? Or 5? Or 3? And why not all large, or all small, or 3 of one and one of the other? Or, better still, why not open stock so you can choose just what suits your needs?

I'll tell you why not. The reason canisters come in sets of 4 is because somebody a long time ago (probably that guy who carved out the first wheel), decided that canisters should hold flour, sugar, coffee and tea, in that order. To make sure we got his message, he plastered his cans with the biggest labels he could find--flour, sugar, coffee and tea, in that order.

But I DON'T WANT TO KEEP MY COFFEE IN A CANISTER! I think it stays fresher in its own tightly-lidded can.

And what I'd really like is 2 CANISTERS FOR FLOUR, because I now regularly usc 2 kinds, an all-purpose variety for baking and the new kind that gives me lumpless gravy in spite of my bungling.

And TEA BAGS TAKE MORE ROOM THAN LOOSE TEA, so my tea bags get all squished in that little box marked tea.

What's more, I AM SICK AND TIRED OF A SUGAR CANISTER THAT HOLDS ONLY 70/80ths of my 5-pound bag of sugar.

While I'm raising my voice, I might as well add that I think canisters should have lids you can remove with one hand; they should be easily grip-able even with floury, buttery or clumsy hands; they should have rust-proof liners; the bottoms should not leave rings on the counter tops; they shouldn't come in sets; and they should NEVER, NEVER be labeled.

I mean a homemaker should feel free to put matches, green stamps, socks that need mending, canceled checks, the change from a $5 bill, the valve that blows up the football, her neighbor's house keys, the milk bill, her wedding ring, the badminton birdies, some root beer barrels, or even coffee in her coffee canister.

Understand?

Eating Over
April 21, 1970

"Sally is eating over at Penny's. And yesterday Becky ate over at Mary Lou's. One day Mary Lou had 2 people over."

"Are you the new social reporter for The Towne Courier, or are you trying to tell me something?"

"How come I can't ever have someone to eat over?"

"Who said you can't?"

"You mean I can? Can I have someone tomorrow?"

"Yes. Who do you want to ask?"

"Betsy Pringle."

"I don't remember you mentioning her very often; is she in your class?"

"Yes, she just came this year."

"So you're good friends already. That's nice."

"We're not really good friends."

"You're not? Then how come you want to invite her to lunch?"

"I heard her telling Sally that hot dogs are her favorites. They're my favorites too."

--Social Note: Miss Betsy Pringle was a guest at lunch in the home of Miss Beth Naybor at noon Wednesday. Also present were Miss Naybor's sister, Meg, and her brothers, Mike and Drew. On the menu were hot dogs in rolls, potato chips, carrot sticks, sweet pickles, milk and assorted cookies.

--Mother's Note: Miss Pringle, whose favorite food is rumored to be hot dogs, ate 4 of them, but resisted the potato chips, carrot sticks, sweet pickles, milk and assorted cookies. She especially resisted the milk. Mr. Naybor, also invited, resisted the invitation ("Thanks for warning me--I'll eat at the cafeteria").

One week later:

"How come Beth got to have someone eat over?"

"She thought it was a nice idea."

"How come I can't have someone eat over?"

"How about tomorrow? Who do you want to ask?"

"Jinx. Can I really ask him, Mom?"

"Go ahead. But be sure he asks his mother. And ask him if he likes soup and sandwiches."

"He likes noodle soup and peanut butter and marmalade sandwiches."

"How do you know?"

"I told him that he could come to lunch if he liked what I like and I like noodle soup and peanut butter and marmalade sandwiches."

--Social Note: Master Jinx Winslow was invited to lunch by Master Mike Naybor recently-- Home-made chicken-noodle soup was served, along with "moon sandwiches" (really peanut butter and marmalade sandwiches cleverly cut by the hostess to resemble fall and half moons with a biscuit cutter). Dessert was chocolate chip cookies.

--Mother's Note: Upon being served, Master Jinx confessed that he is "kinda allergic" to soup. It also developed that he is "kinda allergic" to peanut butter, marmalade and bread. He was delighted to report he was not allergic to chocolate chip cookies and lunched on 10 cookies and 2 glasses of milk.

One week later:

"How come Beth and Mike got to invite someone to eat over? Can we invite someone to eat over too?"

"Invite anyone you like--just tell them to bring their own sack lunches."

--Social Note: Drew and Meg Naybor were hosts at a novel luncheon party last week. Each guest brought his own sack lunch. After lunch, the children played kickball on the side lawn until it was time to return to school.

--Mother's Note: The side lawn later yielded 2 bushel baskets full of trash, including half a banana, 2 apples, a stick of licorice, an empty soup thermos, 2 sweaters, a shoe and 2 complete and unopened sack lunches.

--Mother's Conclusion: Kids like to "eat over," but the "over" is more important than the "eat."

Helping the Environment
April 28, 1970

I have to tell you that I've been a pessimist about this whole environmental disaster right from the first minute someone noticed that on a clear day you no longer can see forever.

Clear days are mighty few and far between, and even then all one can see is smog in the sky, trash on the ground, and detergent foam on the waters.

Ever since I realized the severity of our resource loss, I've done my best to compensate for helping to overpopulate the country by telling anyone I can buttonhole (especially newlyweds), that parenthood isn't all it's cracked up to be. Believe me, if any of my friends have 7 kids, it won't be because I made it look easy!

But somehow I still feel I'm not doing enough. I did say "No!" loudly and firmly when my son wanted a ride to his track meet. (I told him the 4-block run would limber him up.) And when he gets his license, I plan to make the car consistently unavailable so he won't bear the guilt of helping to pollute the air.

Also, I let out the seat of my husband's favorite relaxing slacks. If he wears them another year, they will disintegrate and won't add to the throwaway problem.

In addition, I'm buying lots of yellow sheets--which is the color my white ones turn if I don't use enzymes---so I can go back to using laundry aids that don't try so hard to be great at the expense of our rivers.

Yet all that seems a mere drop in the bucket when you think of how the waste is piling and the elements are being used up.

I am slightly heartened by the fact that as an Earth Day observation last week, my children joined their classmates in picking up debris in the Ann, Bailey, Haslett and Linden Streets area. When you realize that most of these children (especially mine) have not willingly picked up anything other than their forks and spoons since birth, you will understand how important a beginning we have made.

Another ray of hope hits me when I realize that not only has this issue brought together government, industry, labor and science, but even the young and the old are united in studying the inherent flaws of our technology which have brought us to the brink of environmental saturation. (And, like man, they haven't seen eye to eye on anything in like half a century.)

What still worries me, in spite of all this progress, is the "Who, me?" problem. "Who-me-ism" is easy to understand if you've ever spent anytime living in a house crowded with children. It goes like this:

Mother: "I hate to be picky but you left the faucet running in the bathroom, the light on in your room, and you dropped a gum wrapper on the floor in your haste to get to the litter rally yesterday."

Child: "Who, me?"

Adults do it too.

"No family in this town needs 2 cars. Take my neighbor, Smith. He lives and works right on the bus route. If he and hundreds of others like him left their cars home and rode the buses, it'd be a heck of a lot easier for me to drive to work," says Joe.

"Why don't you take the bus, too, Joe?"

"Who, me?"

"Wow, look at that campground! There'll be no woods left at all if so many people keep crowding into the wilds each weekend. You'd think they'd stay home once in a while," says Pete.

"Aren't you the guy who demanded a spot in the overflow area when the campground was full last weekend?"

"Who, me?"

"Another air-conditioner! Boy, that Lucy is putting on airs. Running 2 units for just one old maid is squandering the nation's power, I'd say," says Ethel.

"Running an aluminum factory takes more power per week than Lucy can use in a lifetime. Say, aren't you the lady who won't buy pop except in throwaway cans?"

"Who, me?"

The experts warn that we may have to change our whole way of living if we want to save this world. Every man may have to go backwards to go forward. Are you willing?

The answer to "Who, me?" is "Yes, you and you and you and you. . ."

Mothers Are Here To Stay
May 5, 1970

Mother's Day has fallen on hard times.

The recent concern over the world's over-population makes it clear that to some, motherhood is no longer cause for celebration or veneration.

As I understand it, it's not so bad to HAVE a mother; it's BEING a mother that has lost favor. If you have a mother, I guess it's still all right to be nice to her now and then. But if you are a mother, or worse yet, are thinking of becoming one, your desirability has dropped from next to apple pie, to somewhere lower than cyclamates.

This comes as somewhat of a blow to women (and there are a large number of them), who have been mothers for a long time, and in truth have no other claim to fame. Up until now they have held places of respect and honor in society, based in some cases solely on their motherhood.

It is even possible that soon, instead of being acclaimed loudly as perpetuators of the human race, they may have to skulk down back alleys to avoid public shame for having added to the world's burden.

Now, if like me, you find yourself with half a lifetime invested in the birth, care and feeding of several children (from now on it may be better not to admit publicly to the exact number), you may be a bit worried. With some people yelling "ZPG" (zero population growth), and others pushing pills, abortion and sterilization, you may well feel superfluous and maybe even a bit guilty over having done what came naturally.

You may even be raising your voice in that age-old lament, "What's a mother to do?"

My advice to you is one word: relax. That's right, relax. Frankly, I think mothers can survive this period of censure and condemnation. Another war, a few more riots, another cut in the poverty program, and the balance may shift again--and then won't there be a clamor for mothers!

Meanwhile, the world still needs us, if not to bear more children, at least to continue caring for the ones we already have. As a matter of fact, I think it still will be a crime if we don't. The world needs us to support industry too. If we were not here to accept with tearful gratitude the millions of Mother's Day cards, pink carnations and heart-shaped boxes of candy which industry has produced, thousands of people would lose their jobs and the economy would collapse.

In some intellectual circles where the sting of looks and comments may become unbearable, it may be wise for young mothers with new babies on the way to go underground for a period of time. Organizations can be set up to buy up canned formula and cotton balls and diapers for distribution to those mothers too sensitive to brave the disapproval of crusading clerks or ZPG picket lines.

For those women who are not now pregnant, such drastic measures may not be necessary. Instead of going underground, they might find protective cover by assuming new titles for the duration. Instead of mothers, they could call themselves by less reprehensible appellations.

For instance, one mother I know plans to take the title Dispatcher until things cool down.

"It's what I really do anyway," she says. "All day long I dispatch people--Jimmy and Carol to Donley School, Faith and Charley to MacDonald, Joe to the high school, and Pete to work. After school, it's more of the same--Carol to Brownies, Jimmy to Scouts, Faith to piano lessons, Charley to the dentist, Joe to the supermarket where he works, and Pete to another meeting."

Another mother decided on the title Receptionist.

"I say Hello, I say Good-by," she says. "I answer the phone and take messages. I carry petitions to the Top Brass (Dad), and I relay his orders back to the children. I spend all my time arranging common times for meals and meetings."

Others are thinking of passing themselves off as cooks, drivers, domestic managers, personal shoppers, laundry aides, or teachers.

If you know a mother, you can help by keeping her secret during these dark days. If you are a mother, cook that meal, change that diaper, love that baby, and keep your head high.

I have an idea motherhood is here to stay. After all, look at all the nasty things Ralph Nader said about cars, and do you see anyone walking?

Child Study Club
May 12, 1970
[Editor's Note: This is a feature article and not a Family in Towne column.]

CHILD Study Club? Child STUDY Club?

There I was, my whole day and half the night wrapped up in formula, diapers, cracker crumbs, school dresses, smelly gym shoes, and the rest of the never-ending work that goes with a houseful of children, and there was Marge Williams saying that she and Lucille Patriarche wondered if I might enjoy joining their child study club.

I thought they were nuts. But you can't say that when you're new in the neighborhood and these people seem to mean well. So I said I wasn't much of a joiner. I said it was very hard for me to get sitters. I said that most nights I was usually too tired to go out. And besides, I said, I wasn't really too interested in studying children, under the circumstances.

But those women persevered. They didn't really study children, they said, although they sometimes heard speakers who talked about children's problems, or parental problems, or both. Actually, said Marge, it was a good way to get away from children--a night out once a month was probably just what I needed.

Boy, she had something there. So I promised to go with her as a guest to the next meeting.

That's all it took. I was hooked. I was hooked on a warm welcome, new friendships, good speakers, lively discussions, and interesting civic projects.

And this year, while the club celebrates its 50th anniversary, I celebrate my 10th anniversary of membership. Some years I did a lot, some years I did a little. The club was pleased when I pitched in, sympathetic when I couldn't.

"What do you do at Child Study Club?" the children ask. We help people, we keep informed, we enjoy each other's company, I tell them.

But what do you do, exactly, they demand to know.

Over the years I once made a centerpiece out of cabbage and peppers, I once introduced a state senator, I once helped to write a unit for the state syllabus, I worked on several rummage sales, baked for umpteen bake sales, directed a fashion show, helped plan programs, helped pick a worthy project, led a couple of discussions, participated in several others, shocked a few members with my liberal views, extended sympathy to two widows, bought Christmas gifts for needy children, listened to many speakers, informed myself on many issues.

Child Study Club--let me spell out for you what it's all about:

C is for Children, in whom it's necessary to be interested and about whom it's permissible to talk without danger of being typed as a woman who talks about children because that's all she knows about.

H is for Home, which always looks better if you've been able to leave it behind for 2 or 3 hours.

I is for Ideas, which you discover other women have lots of.

L is for Learning, about our town, our schools, our children and ourselves.

D is for Duty, which you assume periodically and perform admirably, even if you didn't know you had it in you.

S is for Service which the club has offered our city for 50 years, and in which you proudly share.

T is for Thoughts, Talents, and Time. You may have only a small amount of each, but when you combine them with that of others, it is possible to do something BIG.

U is for Understanding which you gain by hearing about how others have faced the same problems you may face.

D is for Determination, which is what you're glad you had after you force yourself to pull yourself together, put on a new face, and get yourself to the meeting (although at 7:45 you felt more like limping than primping, more like drooping than grouping, and more like balking than talking).

Y is for You, the new one you discover when you break out of your own small world and take time to notice what's going on around you.

C is for Columbine Drive, Center Street, Cowley Avenue, Curtis Road and Colorado Drive. Suddenly you've expanded the small circle of your own neighborhood, your school area, your husband's department, and even your church parish, and you know interesting people in all areas of town, great variety of positions, and different beliefs.

L is for Lingering which you find yourself doing long after the program is over because the company is good and the discussion is interesting.

U is for Useful, which is what you feel when the year's project has been particularly worthy.

B is for Belonging, which has been fun..

Antique Collecting
May 19, 1970

CRASH!!!

"Oops, I'm sorry. It must have slipped. I'm sorry. I'll replace it for you."

"Oh it was old. Don't bother to replace it. It's worthless."

(Both friends laugh.)

CRASH!!!

"'Oops, I'm sorry. It just slipped. I'm so sorry. I'll replace it for you."

"Oh, it was OLD. It can't be replaced. It was priceless."

(Both women, no longer friends, cry.)

Moral: If you have butterfingers, don't visit friends who collect antiques, especially glass and china.

More and more I seem to be visiting friends who collect antiques. No, I haven't broken anything yet, but something else does seem to be happening--I'm catching the bug.

Like many other afflictions, antique collecting is not hereditary, but the tendency may be passed on. One reason I'm so susceptible is because my mother was a collector. Not of priceless antiques exactly, but she never threw anything out, and after a while some of the things she saved just naturally became old and even slightly valuable.

After you have lived with old things (old sofas, old dressers, old curtains), for a while you begin to long for some genuine antiques. The difference is more than a matter of years; it is also a matter of inflection.

Instead of "THAT old thing," one says, "that OLD thing," and if "that OLD thing" is yours, it is permissible to purr a bit.

It is hard to know how to start collecting antiques. Some people inherit most of their cherished possessions. Others buy them. Which leads me to believe that one could start antiquing in one of two ways--either have a grandmother and mother who never, ever broke anything, or marry a rich husband and go out and buy what someone else's grandmother and mother never, ever broke.

Every would-be collector, early in her career (men collect too, but that's another story), is convinced that just around the next bend in the road a fortune in antiques sits in a barn waiting only for her discerning eye to seek them out.

Her dream goes something like this:

Farmer: "I'm fresh out of strawberry baskets, do you mind taking them in this old dish?"

242

Discerning Collector: "Of course not. Say, that's a lovely dish. Umm, I wonder--is there a mark on the bottom?"

Farmer: "Yep, looks like Wedgwood."

D.C.: "Wedgwood! Let me look in my book. Why, here it is, it's one of the very first ones made. Oh, it's terribly valuable. Could I...that is, would you...I mean, would you let me buy it from you?"

Farmer: "Yep, cost you a dollar though. Hettie always liked that one for dandelion salad. Now, let me get up off this old chair and get you some change."

D.C.: "Your chair! Is that for sale too? I don't want to cheat you, but I can tell it's a genuine piece of Americana."

Farmer: "Take it. Durn thing gives me a pain in my sciatica. And don't forget your strawberries."

My own experience with such dreams is that you wake up empty-handed.

Many collectors specialize. Some collect only spoons, or bisque dolls, or Chippendale furniture, or Northwood custard glass, or cameos, or grandfather clocks, or buttonhooks, or Model T Fords, or Meissen porcelain, or Shaker chairs, or lard oil lamps, or paperweights or thimbles.

My own collection is more of a mixture. In addition to a few old fruit jars, insulators, and whiskey bottles, I also proudly own an old flat iron, a dented tea tin and a chipped china cruet, and a brick from MSU's old Wells Hall.

My children, should any of them be interested in old things, will be lucky indeed, because anything that comes into our house ages quicker than you can say "genuine certified Hepplewhite."

I bought a brand new Heywood-Wakefield tea cart a couple years ago which my family has since distressed and antiqued for me. Everyone who sees it says, "What a lovely old tea cart. Has it been in your family for a very long time?"

"I guess you could say that," I answer.

After all, for our family, a couple of years is a very long time.

What Does It Mean To Be Rich?
May 26, 1970

"Are we rich?" asks a small son.

"Gracious no," answers Mother.

"Well, are we poor," he persists.

"Of course not," says Mother, indignantly.

"If we aren't rich, and we aren't poor, what are we?" he asks.

"We're—there isn't any word for it—we're sort of in between. And did you clean your room like you were supposed to?"

"Does that mean you don't know, or you don't want to talk about it?"

"It means I'm busy right now, and you should be. Come back later and we'll talk about it," concedes Mother.

By the time "later" comes, Mother has had a chance to gather her thoughts and takes the initiative.

"The first thing you need to understand is that rich is relative," begins Mother.

"Which relative?" the son asks eagerly.

"Not any relative. I simply mean that if everyone had the same amount of money and goods, nobody would be rich and nobody would be poor. The difference makes the difference. Do you follow me? Let me put it this way. How much money do you have in your piggy bank?"

"Seventy three cents."

"How much does your brother have?"

"He has $8.21."

"There, you see. That means that compared to you, he is rich, but compared to a Ford or a Rockefeller, he is poor," explains Mother.

"Naw, it means he's a miser, that's what it means. I bought him a great, expensive present for his birthday and he gave me a stack of old beat-up baseball cards for mine. Boy, what a tightwad!"

"I can't think I'm explaining it right," mumbles Mother. "Let's try another angle. You tell me what you think it means to be rich."

"That's easy. Rich is when you lose your brand new jacket and nobody even cares because you got 2 more just like it at home."

Mother: "That's not rich, that's careless."

Son: "Rich is when you hit your ball into crabby old Mr. Miller's yard, and you don't have to go to his front door to ask for it because you got another one in your pocket."

Mother: "That's not rich, that's cowardly."

Son: "Rich is ordering 2 banana splits instead of one measly little single dipper."

Mother: "That's not rich, that's foolish."

Son: "Rich is owning a Harley-Davidson when you're only 10."

Mother: "That's not rich, that's deadly."

Son: "Rich is spending the whole summer just lying on the beach."

Mother: "That's not rich. That's lazy."

Son: "Rich is flying to San Francisco on Monday, to Australia on Tuesday, to Spain on Wednesday, to Istanbul on Thursday, and to Alaska on Friday."

Mother: "That's not rich, that's exhausting."

Son: "Rich is having 20 bedrooms, 15 bathrooms, and 8 Rolls Royces."

Mother: "That's not rich, that's ostentatious."

Son: "Rich is owning New York City."

Mother: "That's not rich, that's having problems."

Son: "Rich is bringing your mother 20 gorgeous red roses on her birthday."

Mother: "That's not rich, and that's not fair. That's bribery."

Son: "I know. But what have you got against being rich?"

Mother: "Not a thing. If you make it, invite me along. By the way, why did you ask if we were rich in the first place?"

Son: "Oh, yeah—I lost my brand new jacket, but I'll find it, I'll find it!"

Mother: "Poor boy!"

Cookouts
June 2, 1970

Where there is smoke there is fire. And in our neighborhood, where there is fire, there is usually a cookout.

The backyard picnic season has officially started. Almost every family in town cooked at least one of its Memorial Day weekend meals over the coals.

Most of them, filled with memories of saucy ribs, sizzling steaks, or juicy hamburgers, will try it again. A few, those who had to dash to the chicken take-out when their 2-inch sirloin charred to within a half-inch of its digestibility, probably will not.

Outdoor cooking, except on the occasions when you spear a hot dog on a green twig and hold it over the campfire, requires skill, patience and good planning.

Most people planning a cookout are careful to assemble good equipment, good materials, good ingredients, and careful attention. Their results are perfect.

Most people planning a cookout also take time to chart an alternate plan of action--which means that they are prepared to toss their meat in the oven if it rains. Some, however, are so addicted to the taste and smell of charcoal broiling that the roast goes on despite rain, sleet, snow or dark of tornado warnings.

For the most part, outdoor cooking is a male specialty. Something about the fire and smoke brings out the bold explorer, or the rugged pioneer, or the nomadic cowboy in them. In some, it even brings out a bit of culinary ability.

A few husbands, however (his name is Tom), regard the grill or brazier as inventions of feminine cunning, designed to trap husbands into worrying the main course to perfect succulence, while their wives relax over a salad bowl.

These few husbands are likely to trace their woes back to humanity's very beginnings, when early man first discovered that fire was good for more than just scaring off wild beasts and warming the chill of night.

Their theory, loudly proclaimed through choking smoke, is that ever since man first discovered that cooking improved his catch, woman has contrived to push the job over on him.

The scene, as they see it, went like this:

Early Man: "Hey Beulah, the baby's crying."

Early Woman: "I know, but if I don't turn this meat, it will burn."

E.M.: "You go in and rock the baby, and I'll stay out and watch the meat."

E.W.: "Okay, but remember, I like it brown, not black."

E.M.: "Just leave it to me, I know what I'm doing."

My version of the same scene, based on the premise that since the beginning of time, woman actually has been trying to keep the cooking in the cave, goes like this:

Early Man: "Hey, Beulah, the baby's crying."

Early Woman: "I know, but if I don't turn this meat, it will burn."

This is where our stories differ:

E.M.: "I'd like to help, but I've got this wheel I'm working on and I can't leave until I get all 4 corners done."

E.W.: "Cooking and baby-tending are my jobs; I don't mind doing both--but I wish there were some way to do the cooking where the babies are."

E.M.: "Gosh, Beulah, you can't cook bear inside--it just won't taste the same."

E.W.: "I suppose you're right, but--oh, oh, there goes the baby again."

E.M.: "Keep your chins up; as soon as I get this wheel squared away, I'll invent a chimney and then maybe we can bring that fire inside."

E.W.: "A chimney! Oh, you're so good to me. While you're at it, do you suppose you could also invent a stove?"

E.M.: "A stove: I wonder what I'm doing wrong on this wheel. By the way, the baby is crying again, and don't I smell something burning?"

Women, of course, are endlessly adaptable. If they absolutely have to cook outdoors, with cinders flying and flies landing, they can do it. Often on weekdays, when hubby is still at work they will start the coals, season the meat and have the whole meal at the peak of delicious readiness when their Highness appears.

On weekends or holidays, however, they can't do anything right. They know this because you-know-who keeps telling them.

"Mabel, what are you doing to those coals? Honestly, you can't do anything right! Here, let me at that grill. How come you can't ever start the coals right?"

"I do it when you're not here," mumbles Mabel.

"Look at that smoke. (Choke, cough, choke.) Boy, you really fixed things. What did you say?"

"I said, 'I'll go in and toss a salad.'"

"Okay, but you better let me mix the dressing; you never mince the garlic fine enough."

When School Ends
June 9, 1970

School ends this week, and I feel guilty.

This was the first year since I began motherhood almost 19 years ago that all the children went to school all day. True, they came home for lunch, and dismissal came very early in the afternoon, but they were gone between 8:30 and 11, and between 12:30 and 3 every day.

It's the "betweens" that I feel guilty about; I learned to like them.

For the first couple of weeks after school started, my whole life seemed to fall apart. I missed having my little ones around. The house was empty, and my footsteps echoed as I walked from room to empty room.

But I got used to the empty, quiet, clean, picked-up house, and I got positively hooked on the "betweens."

The time between 8:30 and 11 only adds up to 2 ½ hours, but it is amazing what a woman without children to distract her can do in that period. On an industrious day, she can make all the beds, clean the baths, collect and wash the dirty laundry, fold and distribute the clean laundry, vacuum and dust the downstairs, make dessert for supper, and discuss Cambodia, the rip in her new dress, and Sally's new hairdo, with her friend Elaine on the phone.

On a lazy day, she can make all the beds and sort out the magazine rack. And if she pokes her way through her morning "between," there is always the afternoon "between" when she can catch up.

Many a Sunday night I found myself surveying the wreckage of a normal weekend and consoling myself with the knowledge that most of it could be righted in a couple of child-free hours, say between 9 and 11, on Monday.

But that bliss is over, and I don't even have naptime to fall back on. School age children on vacation don't nap. What's more, they go to bed late, and get up even later. They are seldom hungry at mealtimes, but they are starving all the rest of their waking hours.

During those waking hours, and between bites, they complain loudly that there isn't anything interesting to do. Between the bites and the complaining they manage to leave the house looking like Sunday night, on a Thursday morning yet.

My neighbor, who is suffering the same trauma, says we must grab our bulls by their horns and set up RULES right at the start of this vacation. For a starter, she suggests, "Disappear from view between 8:30 and 11, and 12:30 and 3."

With my luck, they would disappear all right, and I'd spend the whole "between" time trying to find them.

My other neighbor, whose children are married and live 2,500 miles away, suggests I use this vacation time to get reacquainted with my children.

I give this a stab, but it is difficult to re-establish an all-day relationship without the grace periods of my "betweens."

"Children," I begin, "let's sit and talk for a few minutes this morning."

"What did we do?" they wail.

"Nothing," I assure them.

"So we didn't do nothing! Well, give us time. Gee, do you have to pick on us about it the first day of vacation?" they protest.

At this point, I go off and have a small talk with myself.

"These are your children," I remind myself. "They live in this house. You love them, remember?"

I give myself a little shake, and then I talk some more.

"So the children are home all day now--does that mean you have to fall apart?" I ask myself. "So what if the house looks a little messy now and then, or even all the time? Is it a showplace or a home? Even if you worked 24 hours a day and no one ever came home, it wouldn't be a showplace.

But if you let up a little these first few days, there is a chance it could be a happy home," I assure myself.

"These are good kids you've said so yourself many times," I say to myself. "If it makes you nervous to hear the refrigerator door swinging open every 15 seconds, tape it shut. Leave a loaf of bread and a stick of butter on the table and just pretend you don't see it vanish. Be firm about brushing teeth, but let up on the knees and elbows. If things get too bad, you can always turn the garden hose on them. They think that's a treat and it means no bathtub ring," I remind myself.

"You used to think it was fun having a houseful of children," I say to myself. "Give it a chance, maybe it can be fun again. When they get you down, go off and read some more Agatha Christie. It's their vacation, let it be yours, too," I say to myself.

Myself thinks I am talking sense. We decide to give it a try.

Swimming Season
June 16, 1970

The wrinkled skin season has arrived.

Kids who scream, kick and bite when dragged toward water in the winter, suddenly can't breathe unless they are riding the waves into shore, diving into an Olympic-sized pool, or wading in a mountain brook. Lacking these desirable options, they will settle for running through the backyard sprinkler. The object is to stay as wet and puckered as possible from now until September, even if it means sitting in a rain puddle--or should I say, especially if it means sitting in a rain puddle.

"I wish we had a pool," moans one soggy specimen.

"We do."

"Aw, that's not a pool, that's a baby's bathtub. I'd like a real pool, say 10 feet of water and a double action diving board."

"You don't even start swimming lessons until next week. What do you want with a 10-foot pool?"

"I bet I learn to swim the first day."

And you know, he just might.

When our first child started swimming, lessons No.1 through 6 were on.

"Of course our ears are wash and wearable; just hold your breath and put your head under."

About the time she caught on, child No. 2 announced firmly that there was No Way we could make him take swimming lessons. We found a way. We dragged him to class, announced loudly that he would love it, and prayed silently and fervently that he would neither drown, nor hate us for the rest of his life.

He not only learned to swim, he nearly broke us begging for quarters for extra time in the water. Child 3 took beginners lessons twice without protest but likes sun bathing more than water bathing.

For some reason, known only to Neptune, our 4 younger children are water babies. At any lake, pool or rain barrel, they splash until they are water logged and three pounds heavier than when they went in.

They hold their breath and dunk their heads, each eager to beat the other's record for staying under. They kick their feet, wave their arms, and flail wildly--especially when it is time to come out of the water.

They are signed up for 2 weeks of beginner's lessons at Hannah Middle School, and by the end of that period it is probable that 3 out of 4 of them (Meg likes sand castles better), will be swimming.

But they sure don't get it from me. I could learn to swim, I am sure of it, if only I didn't have to go into the water to do it. It's not that I don't like water. I value it highly for drinking, cooking, laundering and bathing--anything I can do with my feet planted flatly and firmly on the ground.

I have tried letting myself go, but my feet don't get the message and they refuse to come up. On the few short occasions when they have relented a bit, it was my head that swam, not me. I even get nervous walking on a boardwalk; all that swaying motion down below makes me woozy.

If the water is clear (dreamer!), and the sand is white and rockless, I am tempted to inch myself step by cautious step into the water. Right up to my knees. Then I start to lose my nerve.

If a hearty splasher splashes by, I am completely disoriented and there is nothing I can do but sit down. With 2 feet and one seat touching bottom, I am fairly secure. I can actually smile a bit, move my arms in graceful arches and pretend I am a mermaid born to the sea.

I sway and glide and mentally revel in the swirling deep. Keeping my chin carefully up above water, I close my eyes and imagine I am skimming the waves. Floating, floating, floating...

"Mommy, why are you just sitting there in the shallow part?" asks my 6-year-old, towering over me with his knobby knees staring me in the eyes.

"Go away, you fresh kid. And don't you dare splash!"

250

Old-Fashioned Cookbook
June 30, 1970

At our house, the cook loses interest in food in the summer.

She doesn't lose interest in eating, you understand, only in cooking. She dreams of a whole poached fish, delicately sauced, and eaten in the shade of a century-old fig tree in a Spanish garden 2 summers ago. She remembers an English trifle, cool and creamy, and pungent with Madeira. She longs for a plate of succulent sausages as served in Zermatt in the shadow of the Matterhorn.

But it is hot and humid and she is lazy and listless, so she settles for thoughts of gazpacho, made in the blender and served on the porch, and wishes someone would make it for her. While she is wishing, she also wishes someone would take over all the cooking for a couple of months. Weeks? Days?

There are no offers, so she gets out the cookbooks in hopes that her usual interest in new recipes will rekindle her culinary joy. One of her books, an encyclopedia of cookery (from abalone to zythum--an ancient beer-like beverage made from malt and wheat), never fails to entertain her. Published in the '40s, its tone is even more old-fashioned than that date would indicate. Not only do its recipes still advise you to "sift flour, measure and resift 3 times with soda and salt," but in the case of pheasant, it even includes an essay on the joy of "bagging" the bird.

It recommends also that the pheasant must be allowed to hang and ripen in order to arrive at the moment of perfect tastiness. "The right moment," the book says, "reveals itself to the uninitiated by a slight odor and a change in the color of the belly of the bird, but the gourmet divines it by instinct." It then proceeds to give a recipe for stuffing the pheasant with duck liver and chopped black truffles which have been sautéed in port wine. Our cook flips the pages. She has neither the nose, stomach, nor purse for pheasant, she decides.

Our cook begins to realize how easy life is for her (even in the summer), when she comes to the section on rabbit. Here, half a page is given over to 8 quick steps for skinning and cleaning the hare. Step 6, which describes how to cut the eyelids free without damaging the pelt, threatens to make her a vegetarian for life.

One of the fascinating things about this book is that it does not mince words. Dealing, for instance, with the Dagwood, it says it is "a sandwich of comic strip origin, put together so as to finally attain such a tremendous size and infinite variety of contents as to stun the imagination, sight and stomach of all but the original maker." Ugh.

There is no food or drink so obscure as to escape at least definition in this volume. There are recipes for frittering, scalloping, or stuffing dasheens, a "starchy tuber." It lists and describes 9 Biblical wines, and gives chapter and verse and the number of times it is mentioned. It lists the nutritive value of acorns.

It gives hints on buying limes ("deep yellow-colored ones do not have the desired acidity") and tells how to capture frogs, "the hind legs of which are the only parts used for the table."

There is a recipe for parsley jelly, which the book says is a delicious change from other jellies. It also says that should you wish to make 5 gallons of dandelion wine, you must have 15 quarts of dandelion blossoms, 3 gallons of cold water, 15 pounds of sugar, 1 yeast cake, juice of one dozen oranges and 1/2 dozen lemons, and 2½ pounds of raisins.

Our cook, who not too many years ago was a non-cook, is grateful for the many elementary steps given in this book. The 10 pages on potatoes, which include several paragraphs on buying ("pick sound, smooth skins and shallow eyes") and preparing ("rapidly boiling salted water"), have been of more use to her than the page and a half on eels (" never choose a sluggish one"), but that is a matter of family appetites.

Speaking of family appetites, which are never sluggish, our cook usually manages to satisfy them, come hot weather or cold. That great cookbook helps, but the real reason is this: our cook is me and I'm always hungry too.

Kids' Memories
July 7, 1970

"Say something, Mike."

"What do you want me to say?" asks our 8-year-old in surprise.

"How does the place look to you?"

"It looks awright. Can we go swim now?"

"Swim! This is the cottage we spent a whole month in when you were 9 days old, and you want to swim?"

"It's nice, I guess, but I don't remember it," says Mike, truthfully.

"I don't remember it either," says Drew.

"I don't expect you to remember it, Drew, you weren't even born then."

"Oh yeah. Can we go swim now?"

"Swim, swim swim! Do you think we came 200 miles just to swim? This cottage is a piece of your family past. Aren't you interested? Don't you care to know all about it, to refresh your memories of those great times we had here? Doesn't anyone have any feelings for this place?"

"Ellen and Dale probably do, but the rest of us aren't old enough to remember back 8 years, Mom," says Kate, with 12-year-old practicality.

Ellen and Dale are working this summer and didn't make this "pilgrimage" to Petoskey. Tom and I begin to wonder why we bothered to bring the other 5 kids along. We should have known better. Our children display a lot of interest in our collective family past, but it's mostly at night when they are trying to stall bedtime.

"Tell us again about the house we stayed in at Old Mission," begs Beth.

"Yeah, remember that time we went to that cabin in Pennsylvania?" urges Meg.

Sometimes we will talk for half an hour before we realize that we are doing all the remembering, and all the kids are doing is urging us on. What they do remember seems to run together in their minds. Drew, the youngest, thinks he remembers a small lake where we stayed in a huge house full of antiques, and where we rowed in a yellow boat to an island where we had a picnic and ate chicken and brownies.

When we sort all this out, Tom and I discover the lake was one we stayed at in 1964; the house was 1963; the yellow boat was 1965; the island was 1966; and the picnic was last week at Alton Road park. Since he was born in 1963, the only way Drew could possibly remember anything, except the picnic, is by hearing the older kids tell about it.

Something else kids don't remember is the house where Dad was born, the street where he used to deliver papers, the school which he walked 2 miles to get to, and the fire station that was next door to his grandmother's house. But every year, Dad takes them on a drive past all these unfamiliar places anyway. After a while, even the smallest ones begin to "remember" how Daddy used to run to Grandma's cellar and hide under the stairs when they tested the fire whistle every Saturday at noon.

As we drive along, a 7-year-old will jump up and say, "See that housing development? There used to be a big hayfield there, and one summer Daddy helped load the hay wagon."

Flattered, Tom and I begin to mistake the children's willingness to "recall" events they never saw as real pride in their heritage. This illusion is quickly shattered as we are reminded of how little sense of time anyone under 10 has.

"Tell us again about the first 4th of July," says an under-10.

On the surface it's a good question and shows a proper interest in his country's birth. In a minute, however, we discover he thinks we were there. Then it is hard to explain why we are angry, and he mutters, "I thought you wanted us to care about things that happened when you were little."

It is equally difficult to explain that we expect them to have selective and discreet memories.

"My mother used to watch fireworks at the city dump when she was little," we hear one student of our history telling a neighbor. It's true. But would you expect a kid who can't remember that wonderful summer in Petoskey, to remember a thing like that?

Kids' Money
July 14, 1970

Grandma sent the boys just what they wanted for their birthdays this year--money.

The color was perfect and the size was ample, but I exchanged it anyway. I bought permanent press pajamas. The color was perfect and the size was ample, but the boys couldn't care less. They didn't say so, but you could tell they wished Grandma had sent them something sensible, like money. I didn't tell them she did.

East Lansing kids who live within walking distance of "downtown," learn the value of money early. The birthday boys I am talking about aren't allowed off their block without an older sibling or a parent, but they have friends who tell them where the real deals are.

They know, for instance, that The Scotch House has an exciting array of old-fashioned penny candy. They have sampled it often. They also know about the Sunshine Shop where beads of all shapes, sizes and color sparkle in glass jars. They have spent many blissfully quiet hours stringing chokers.

They know about sidewalk sales, too, and each year they beg to be taken to inspect all the merchandise. They aren't much interested in marked-down bikinis or summer sandals, but they find out in a minute where the cotton candy is being dispensed, and how much the popcorn is going for this year. Then they sound me out.

"Mom, did you bring any money?"

"A little," I say.

"Are you going to buy anything?" they wonder.

"Well, I thought we might find a pair of shorts to go with Mike's new shirt."

"Oh." The word drips with disappointment.

"Would you fellows like a coke and a Spudnut?" I ask, unexpectedly.

"Boy! Yeah!" they chorus.

While they enjoy their treat and I rest my feet, I sound them out.

"Did you fellows bring any money?"

"Gosh no, Mom. We don't want to spend OUR money."

I've heard about OUR money before. If you have children, you've heard about it, too. For the childless, let me explain that children's money is different from regular family money in several ways. For one thing, it is a sacred trust, to be counted, admired, added to, and guarded.

It is never, never spent for anything necessary or practical, nor for anything Mother or Dad can be talked into buying with THEIR money for you.

"Which dress do you like?" I ask a deliberating teenager.

"The red one, but it's $5 more than you said I could spend."

"How much do you like it?" I probe.

"I just love it. I like it better than anything we've seen," she answers fervently. "It's just my kind of dress. I know we'll never find another one I like as well," she sighs.

"Do you like it well enough to pay the extra $5 out of your own money?" I ask.

"MY money? NO! If we keep looking, I know we'll find something just as good," she says, tightly clutching the purse that holds HER money.

Parents occasionally find themselves in the embarrassing position of having to borrow from their children.

"Tom, do you have 75 cents for the baby sitter? All I have is a $10 bill."

"No, all I have is a fiver. Can't you pay her tomorrow?"

"I hate to ask her to wait for her money. Don't you have any change?"

"Here's 36 cents; see if you can get the rest from one of the kids."

I try.

"Mike, can I borrow 39 cents for the sitter?" I ask.

"Not MY money. I didn't even like her!"

I try a less prejudiced party of more mature years, Dale, 16.

"Can you spare 39 cents to help out your poor, old mother, Son?"

"I'd like to help you out, Mom, but I banked my whole paycheck this week. All I've got for spending money is a quarter. By the way, did you decide I could have that $15 sweater?"

HIS money goes into the bank, but I'm supposed to find $15 for a sweater when I can't even find 75 cents! As a last resort, and in spite of the threat to the national economy, I offer usurious interest rates.

"Who will lend me 75 cents? I'll pay back a dollar," I promise.

In a minute I have a taker. But there are conditions.

"Just one thing. You have to pay me back before you go shopping," demands my 10-year-old mistress of finance. "You always spend every cent you have in your purse. You really ought to learn to save like we do, Mom."

I promise to try.

Rainy Days in Camp
July 21, 1970

"Quick, what does the camping book say about children on rainy days?"

"Let's see. Rainy Day Pastimes, Page 17. Here it is. It says, 'If there are children in your camping party, be sure to pack plenty of indoor games and amusements for those inevitable rainy days. Recommended are coloring books, crayons, puzzles, cards, checkers, chess, and word games. Check your toy store for children's games in compact packages to save space.' That's all it says."

"Great. That's good advice as far as it goes, but we did all that stuff this morning, and it's still raining. What if it rains again tomorrow?"

It did. And the next day, too.

One thing about rainy days in camp, you really get to know your family. If you think "familiarity breeds contempt" is an empty saying, come around to our rain-soaked campsite sometime and I'll introduce you to a family of contemptible people.

There was a time when we camped in a tent, when we thought a trailer would solve our rainy day problems. After all, a trailer is water-tight and up off the ground, and somehow we thought that would make a world of difference.

And it does help some. There are built-ins, for instance, so you don't have to try to cook out under an umbrella, and there are fewer boxes, chests and cases to juggle around between the car, the tent, and the shady spot under the tree.

But if you've brought a passel of kids along, and a husband who thought they would all disappear into the woods and leave him to soak in nature in blissful solitude, even a trailer is too small when you hit a rainy spell.

After every kid has beat Mommy at every game twice, the thrill pales. There is a lot of unnecessary loose talk, like:

"Is it time to eat yet?"

(So far they've had breakfast, lunch and a snack, and it's only 2 o'clock.)

"You said we could swim today for sure."

(My head is swimming.)

"Has anybody seen my library book?"

(It's out in the rain, soaked like a sponge, but thank heavens, we don't know that yet.)

"How come Daddy's sitting out in the car with all the doors locked?"

(Another hour and it's my turn to go out there for parental R and R.)

"Does it always rain at Interlochen State Park?"

(Always is a long time--but 3 days with kids is longer.)

"You said we could toast marshmallows."

(Take it from me, they just don't taste the same done over a gas jet.)

Finally, unbelievably, the sun breaks through. It's "Suits, everyone!" and a joyous splash in the lake for all.

Just as we hang the last wet towel on the sagging line, the rain starts again. Things are back where they were, except that now we have 20 feet of soaking wet terrycloth to look out on.

When the rain again lets up to a drizzle, we don vinyl ponchos and take a walk to "smell the fresh rain smells" and to get away from the stale trailer smells.

One special smell intrigues us all, until we get closer and discover it's the fish cleaning house.

We come back with wet, matted leaves sticking to our feet, and add the wet ponchos to the wet towels on the line.

As we pack up to leave for home, the sun comes out and follows us all the way back to East Lansing. There we sit and swelter and wish we were up north in the woods again.

We hear the chance of rain up there is zero.

Three-Word-itis
July 28, 1970

It never fails. Right about this time every summer, separate vacations sound great to me.

"Boy, you're really liberated," gasps my neighbor, Bette. "You mean you'd actually take off without Tom? Worse yet, you'd let him go off without you?"

"Bette, who said anything about Tom? When I mentioned separate vacations, I meant separate from the kids."

That she understood.

"Boy, you and me both. You know what I said to one of my kids this morning? I said, 'Go to your room and don't come down until Labor Day.' And that was to the baby. I can't repeat what I said to the 10-year old."

At least she's still talking in full sentences. My first clue that mothering was smothering me was when I noticed that instead of speaking in usual clauses and phrases, I'm barking out short, terse commands.

No matter what the occasion, three words does it for me these days.

A typical set of commands goes like this:

"Back door please. Don't slam it. Wipe your feet. Close the refrigerator. Wash your hands. Hang your jacket. Hang it again."

Some mornings, I start out with four words. "Time to get up," but usually by the time everyone does, I'm down to "Get up NOW!"

Things are no better as the day drags on. I start with "Make your bed," dwell briefly on "Clean your room," and move on to "Time to go. Take your brother. Wear your rubbers. Button your coat. Count your change. Come right home"

Meal times are equally bright and gracious.

"Bow your heads. Thank the Lord. Pass the beans. Take some beans. Eat your beans. Beans before cake. Say excuse me. Wait up, there. Finish those beans."

Even the dog gets her share of short shrift. To her I murmur. "Stop your barking. Must you shed? Drop that meterman!"

The day I greet Tom with, "Your blue shirt? Iron it yourself," he notices something is wrong.

"What's up?" he queries cautiously.

"Not a thing," I assure him.

"Are you sure?" he presses.

"I'm absolutely sure," I affirm.

"Okay, if you say so. What are the plans for tonight?"

"Mow the lawn. Read a book. Go to bed," I suggest.

"How are the kids?" he asks, suspiciously.

"Please don't ask."

"Ha, just as I thought," he grins, "a classic case of three-word-itis. You know the cure; let's see if we can get away from the kids for a day or two."

258

"I'm already packed."

"Got a sitter?"

"You bet I have."

"See, you're better already. That was four words for sure. Anything special you want to say to the kids before we go? Use as many words as you think necessary."

"Good-bye, all."

Camping and Comfort
August 4, 1970

If camping means roughing it to you, you're one of the rare ones.

In all the long years before my introduction to camping, I was completely fooled. I watched the loaded caravans head north for the woods, and I thought, "There they go, out into the wilds to rough it."

I built up a mental image of people sleeping under the stars, eating congealed pork and beans out of a can, rationing their water, and braving the elements.

Now, as a four-year veteran of the sport, I know better. Stars? Most campers not only don't sleep under them, they seldom look up to see them. Congealed beans? Maybe once in a while, but most of the smells floating around the campsites hint at far richer fare than that.

Sure, people tell you they rough it when they go camping, but their definition of the word varies widely.

Even in our family, roughing it means different things to different people.

To the little kids, roughing it means leaving the TV set at home, having hot dogs 2 nights in a row, walking to the beach instead of riding, playing Fish with a deck that's short a jack and a 6 of diamonds, no donuts for breakfast, eating the same kind of cereal 2 days in a row, having to hang up your bathing suits instead of tossing them in the dryer, spraying on your mosquito repellent, and reading the same comic book more than once.

To the older kids, roughing it means leaving your hair dryer at home, washing your hair only twice a week, standing in line to use the mirror, getting static on your transistor, leaving the stereo at home, using a towel more than once, or having to share your toothpaste with someone younger and messier than you are.

Now, don't get me wrong. Comfort camping is my kind of thing, and frankly the thought of really roughing it was what kept me out of the woods all those years.

But Tom really would like to get closer to nature. What he does is he keeps saying, "Why don't we sell the trailer and go back to a tent?"

You can imagine the terror that thought strikes in the heart of this dyed-in-the-wood comfort camper!

To protect myself, I make an effort to at least simplify our camping. The thing about roughing it in a 22-foot trailer is that you're defeated before you start. Of course, with our brood we're be-crowded even on Noah's Ark. But with twin porcelain sinks, a gas oven, and a flush toilet, we've got more frills to begin with than thousands of people have in their year-around homes.

But my theory is that if each of us takes fewer "things" along, and we eat a lot of Spanish rice (which Tom hates), we'd all feel we were suffering just enough to fool us (and him), into thinking we were roughing it.

I ask everyone to go into the trailer and bring out things which we obviously can get along without.

Mike brings out the soap.

"Gosh, Mom, you said we should live simple, like the Indians. Who ever heard of Indians washing?"

Drew brings out a handful of toothbrushes.

"Why can't we all share one?"

Dale brings out Tom's tool box but "I left you a screwdriver, a hammer and a wrench."

"Take the tools back," orders Tom.

"But Tom, a mitre box?"

"Back."

I look over the grocery shelf and eliminate the brown sugar. ("But I wanted oatmeal," moans Beth, "and I hate it without brown sugar."); three of the four kinds of salad dressing ("That's all right for greens, but what about cabbage?" queries Ellen); a bottle of rum extract; the sweet and sour sauce; and the crystallized ginger.

(After all, the pioneers went for weeks on grits and gravy.)

To further insure my comfort, I watch Tom carefully. Whenever he starts to look at the trailer with a speculative eye, I make sure he knows how rough things really are at our campsite.

I manage to miss the newsboy when he brings the paper around, I accidentally run out of cold beer, and I hide the radio when the Tigers are playing. Then, just in case that isn't convincing enough, I make Spanish rice again.

Family Reunions
August 11, 1970

The family reunion is one of America's favorite summertime happenings. Any Sunday between the Fourth of July and Labor Day is fair game, but August is best because it's less likely to rain.

The host should always be the relative with the longest driveway, the biggest yard (a farm is great), and the best disposition. It helps if he is also generous and has a wife who makes good pie.

The first carload of guests usually arrives around 10:30, which is much too early, especially if the man is the kind who watches you try to lift a picnic table alone and says, "Say, Ed, you really ought to have help with that table. Where's your wife, anyway?"

His wife, a worried looking, tiny woman with wispy hair, is so busy keeping little Chauncey out of the beehive and little Chester from falling into the well, that she is not much help with the table setting.

Eventually, as the driveway begins to fill up, 2 or 3 efficient aunts will show up. After sending load after load of towel-wrapped goodies into the kitchen, they will take over the table setting.

After 2 or 3 moves, they will agree on the side lawn by the kitchen door as the most convenient, shadiest and most level spot for the long row of tables. And the least likely to attract the bees. (Aunt Celia isn't sure about the bees, though.)

A husband who is handy and compliant will be put to work leveling the extra tables made of planks and sawhorses so that they will not rock. Everybody remembers that Great-Uncle George got a dish of hot beans in his lap last year, and nobody wants it to happen again.

"But it was the funniest sight in the world to see him hopping around like that, and he didn't really get hurt," giggles Cousin Patsy, and the memory sends all the ladies into a round of guilty glee.

One family will be late. The men will be all for starting without them, but Aunt Genevieve will hold things off a bit longer by saying that she is sure they're on their way (it's her sister's family that is late), and besides, "the rolls aren't warmed through yet."

Finally the latecomers are spotted by little Jimmy (Minn's boy, you remember, the active one), who has climbed the big oak down by the road.

The men have to get the ladder out and young Tom Clarke, who isn't a relative but probably will marry cute, little Bev Middler, goes up to bring little Jimmy down.

Little Jimmy then objects to being seated at the children's table, but young Tom Clarke whispers something into his ear and he sits down just as quiet as you please. (Bev could do worse than young Tom Clarke, in spite of his long sideburns, and most of her aunts will tell her so before the day is over.)

Dinner will be baked ham, 2 kinds of chicken, cold tongue, baked beans (Sal makes the best ones--aim for the pot with the bacon on top), 4 kinds of potato salad, corn on the cob (2 bushels), assorted relishes, 4 kinds of cheese, 3 kinds of hot rolls, honey and butter.

Six of the kids will reject all 4 kinds of pie, the strawberry shortcake and the watermelon, and ask for ice cream bars from the freezer.

Cousin Ray, who wants to retire to a farm, will shun the iced tea, lemonade and coffee, and ask for buttermilk. After dinner the men will move their chairs under the black walnut trees and settle down to talk. The women will watch and listen as they clear the food and mind the children, each one hoping the talk won't get around to politics, religion, the war, or youth, because "it's so painful to talk about things these days" and nobody wants a family squabble today.

Katherine's family will be the first to leave (that's the blue Mercury with the out-of-state license) because they are heading back home tomorrow and they want to spend some time with Walt's dad before they go.

The Middlers would like to leave now too, but their Bev and young Tom Clarke have taken all the kids old enough to walk down to the creek to pick forget-me-nots and watch the minnows dart about. When they tramp back, Betty's little girl, Melissa, is riding on young Tom Clarke's shoulders, his handkerchief tied over the scratches on her leg. Little Chauncey was chasing Melissa and she fell into the berry bushes.

Aunt Genevieve takes the blue sweater which her sister left behind, and Ed promises to write to Katherine to ask her whether the knife with the china handle is hers.

Ed has bags of pole beans and squash for each car as it leaves, and his wife slips a jar of current jelly in each one. Grouchy old Uncle Harry, who doesn't have a wife and always brings the watermelon, gets half a black-berry pie, some cold ham and a dish of baked beans to take home. He likes Ed and his wife, but he's been grouchy so long, he just can't bring himself to say anything nice to anyone.

"Suppose you're planning another shindig like this one next year?" he grunts.

"Thought we might, the Lord willing," says Ed. "You'll come, won't you?"

262

"Suppose so," grunts grouchy old Uncle Harry, and Ed and his wife know he means he had a real good time.

Memories of Farm Visits
August 18, 1970

A farm is a nice place to visit and my children think it might even be fun to live on one.

Every child needs a farm in his memory book. There were 2 farms in my childhood. The first one was a place my family visited frequently, both summer and winter. However, I was so young at the time that my memories of it are a jumble of hand-pitched hay, lush strawberries and cream, fluffy baby chicks, fat pigs, and snow piled up to the porch roof.

Although I was an only child, and most reluctant usually to leave my mother's side, I consented to spend a week on this farm without my parents. Another little girl had been invited also, to keep me company, since the sons and daughters on the farm were in their late teens, and over.

Her name was Annie and I loved her dearly, but I felt a constant superiority since I was a godchild in the household and she was only the child of a friend. There are pictures in my mother's album of the 2 of us, up to our ankles in buttercups, with blackeyed susans in the background.

We slept on cots in a bedroom shared by 2 of the teenaged daughters. They tiptoed out in the early dawn, hoping not to wake us, but as soon as they left, Annie and I would giggle and jump up to explore their dresser.

We were fascinated by the powder and rouge, which neither of our mothers were yet "modern" enough to use. The farm daughters worked long, hard days, and only rarely found time to indulge in the makeup and scents we found. But we were too young to know.

Everyone worked on the farm, and our "jobs" were to help snip beans or shell peas for supper and to stay out of the way. We did neither very well.

But the week was a happy one. I still remember that the outhouse was a deluxe 3-holer, and that most of the time an old Sears catalog was the only "tissue" provided.

When I was slightly older, one of the married daughters of this household moved with her husband and children to a farm of their own. From then on, this newer farm was the one we meant whenever our family spoke of going to "the farm."

Of this farm, I remember more. For several summers I spent a week or 2 there. It was a "truck farm" and the season started with strawberries and peas, soon followed by beans, squash, tomatoes, corn, broccoli and cabbage.

When the big crops ripened, "day pickers" came by truck early in the morning and left before supper. A few "steady" workers stayed on the farm all summer, sleeping in a bunkhouse behind the summer kitchen, a building set off from the main farmhouse, for cooler cooking.

A couple of young girls, who slept in the farmhouse with us, cooked for the family and the steady workers, and helped to mind the small children. A bushel of corn on the cob went at a meal, and on baking days, as many as 20 loaves of hearty potato bread came from the wood-fired oven.

After supper there was always packing to do. Everyone helped with this task and it was a kind of "bee" to which we all looked forward. Often we sang or told stories as strawberry quarts went into crates, cucumbers were washed and packed, broccoli was washed and bundled, or tomatoes were carefully sorted.

For my children, a farm has been a nebulous thing, associated mainly with a one-day-a-year visit to Uncle Cal and Aunt Pauline and cousins, Deb, Nancy and Peter. This year was different. We parked our trailer in the field just down from the kitchen garden, and just upwind of the barnyard, and we stayed for a week. In that week, we learned to love the place, each in his own way.

Cal's farm is a dairy farm with no chickens or pigs, but lots of cows, a few kittens and a dog. Milk is the important thing on this farm, and every modern method of producing and marketing it is used. A huge stainless steel, refrigerated tank has replaced the old milk cans, and automatic machines do most of the milking.

But cows are still cows and keeping them clean, healthy and fed still takes most of Cal's day, in spite of help from Deb and Peter. (Nan helps Mother in the house.) Cal's herd numbers close to 50 head, including heifers, and a newborn calf, Ginger, who stole our children's hearts the first day.

Before the second day of our visit was over, our children had memorized the routine of the barn and field work, and pitched in to lend a hand. Mike and Drew helped to hitch the manure spreader to the tractor or ran for tools to help Uncle Cal. They were his constant shadows and no piece of mechanized equipment left the barnyard without one or both of them perched on top.

Beth, who is short and slight for her 10 years, pushed and shoved cows twice her size into their stanchions. The others fed the young stock or rescued the kittens from constant peril. The best part of any day was when

Uncle Cal invited all to pile into the back of the pickup truck for the ride up the bumpy, winding road to the hilltop to watch the sun set.

At night, the smaller children took turns sleeping in our small tent, pitched near the trailer, behind a spreading evergreen. On "girls' night," as many as 5 slept in the tent, but on "boys' night," Drew opted for his usual bunk in the trailer and only Mike and Peter shared the tent.

The evenings ended early in spite of the colored TV in the lovely farmhouse. Mike and Peter offered to get up at 5:30 a.m., when the cows "called" Cal, but they seldom managed to come awake before 7.

Each night the children reviewed their "wonderful!" day, and decided that this farm, set among beautiful gold and green hills, was the most glorious spot on earth, and a farmer's life, although hard, was among the best to be found.

But each of them was old enough to understand the bittersweet truth--the farm had been sold a few days before we arrived. On Friday there would be an auction to sell the cattle and machinery, and in just 3 weeks, Cal and his family would move to Virginia.

For our children, this was a first and last visit to this farm. The knowledge seemed to make each minute of each day very precious.

(Next week: The farm auction.)

Farm Auction
September 1, 1970

Our farm visit started on Saturday. On Monday, the papers carried the notice of the impending auction sale:

"Complete Dispersal," said the ad, which appeared in several dailies and weeklies in the area. It went on to state that the farm itself had already been sold, but that 50 head of Holstein cattle, large amounts of hay, complete milking equipment, and many pieces of farm machinery would be sold to the highest bidder.

On Monday and Tuesday, life was wonderful for our younger children, as they joined their three cousins, Debby, Nancy and Peter, in work and play.

At chore time, they learned to know the cows by name. In short order, they could tell you which cow was the best milker, which had a bad disposition, which had the best pedigree, which had tender teats and had to be hand-milked with a gentle touch, which was Deb's own, and which was Peter's 2-ribbon winner in the Black and White Show ("That means Holstein, Mom"), the week before.

265

They enjoyed the cows and were even helpful. But the farm machinery was something else--it was like a Christmas dream come true. There was a diesel tractor, a gas tractor, hay wagons, plows, harrows, giant combines, "haybines," grain elevators, spreaders, loaders, harvesters, and many other exciting bigger-than-life farm "toys." And if any one of them was moving, and you promised to obey all the safety rules, you could hitch a ride.

But when Wednesday morning dawned, things began to change. The milking went on as usual, because, as the children informed me soberly, "No matter what, Mom, you just gotta milk the cows." But after the milking, instead of the usual parade up the hill into the meadows, the cows stayed right in the barn.

On Thursday, men came to put up a large tent with seats for the buyers, and a runway and "stage" on which the bovine beauties would be exhibited. Meanwhile, the machinery was lined up in a green, red and yellow parade along the pasture drive. Peter, Mike and Drew helped to clean and polish the machines, climbing over the huge parts like ants at work.

Friday morning was bright and sunny. We were all up early, and before 9 the ladies from the Presbyterian Church came to set up the refreshment stand. The children found out right away that they would be selling coffee and donuts, sandwiches (the egg salad proved the best seller, with plain ham in last place), and soft drinks.

By 10:30, the highway was lined with cars and trucks. Prospective buyers who had not stopped by during the week to inspect the stock and machinery, hurried to get a look before settling down to wait for the bidding to begin,

Promptly at 11, the auctioneer started his spiel. The children, forewarned to be quiet, and not to nod their heads or wave their arms in any gesture the auctioneer might construe as bid, flitted about on the sidelines.

They dashed back and forth with the news of what price certain items had brought--and to ask if it was too soon to buy a sandwich and soda pop. They loved the crowd, and the bustle, and the importance of belonging to this gay, carnival-like adventure.

Soon, however, they began to sense the nervous anxiety among the relatives who sat watching from a circle of lawn chairs by the house. When a grandmother began to weep silently at the thought of losing part of her family to another state, the children lowered their voices, and some of the magic of the day wore off.

When it became evident that most of the machinery was sold for less than had been hoped for ("Dad, they STOLE that big Oliver!" gasped Debby), the true finality of the sale began to get to the children.

266

"Why doesn't Uncle Cal buy it himself instead of letting it go so cheap?" they asked.

"Why doesn't he just get up and stop the sale?" they begged.

"He's taken another job. He has to sell everything so he can go. You all know that. It's hard for him, too, but he made up his mind weeks ago, and now he has to go through with it. Don't make it harder for him. It'll all work out, you'll see. Today is sad, but a bright new future is just up ahead for the whole family."

We tried in words such as these to explain to the children--and to ourselves--that the day of the one-man farm is over. Cal was a success at his business, but he had gone as far as one man could go without new money or new muscle. Good help is impossible to get, and there are just so many hours of work in one man. When winter unleashed its cruel winds, the work was harder and the hours longer. If illness struck, there was still no help, and often a feverish farmer did what had to be done, and hoped he would not collapse.

But now the queen of the herd is up on the boards. The children race to report the bidding. Hooray! She's brought a good, high price. Everyone's spirits lift. Suddenly, Peter goes silent and his face turns white. His prize-winner, Ethel, is up for sale. Bidding is brisk and she too commands a fine price. Peter smiles with 10-year-old pride.

But when Deb's Countess comes up, Debby is nowhere to be seen. The children find her flushed and tearful, hidden in the heifer barn. They spill out the good news--a kind-looking Amish man in a funny hat has bought her and Deb is invited down to his farm in Pennsylvania to see her at any time.

By 3 p.m., the sale is over. Everything has been sold and already most of the stock and machinery has been hauled away.

It is a strange evening at the farm. There is no stock to care for, no field work to do. The farm children are free to play with their visiting cousins and the distraction of our presence seems to help their parents.

At bedtime, yesterday's farm family prays for a kind tomorrow.

Roamin' Law
September 8, 1970

Our gasoline bills beat us back from our vacation this year, but that's "Roamin' Law."

"Roamin' Law" (not to be confused with the ancient and much emulated Roman Law), is a capricious kind of law of the road that takes effect the moment you head out of the driveway bent on any destination further than the shopping center.

For instance, if your children talked you into one last camping trip before "our prison--er, school-term begins," and you found that half of Michigan had the same idea, that's "Roamin' Law."

If you get as far as the corner of Hagadorn and Route 78 before you discover you left one child home, that's "Roamin' Law."

If you are going to camp and you put everything into the ice chest but the ice, and you don't remember it until lunch time, that's "Roamin' Law."

More of the same:

--The second you put your head down to read your map, you pass the only road sign that matters, and miss the town you are aiming for by 15 miles.

--You look forward to driving a new stretch of freeway which eliminates 11 hairpin curves, 2 miles of dirt road, and 25 miles of bumpy concrete, but the day you are going through, a bridge is out and all traffic is rerouted over, you guessed it, the 11 hairpin curves, 2 miles of dirt road, and 25 miles of frustration.

--The festival in the picturesque little town you rush to hit on Tuesday was on Monday.

--All the gas stations you have credit cards for are on the other side of the divided (No U Turns!) highway.

--Every time you reach a stretch of 2-lane, double line highway, the driver in front of you is a little old lady who thinks 20 miles an hour is just her speed.

--Children's Day (all rides 10 cents) at the county fair where you stop to spend the day (and a fortune), was yesterday.

--The grocery store where you spend $20 is giving double stamps, of the only variety not available around East Lansing.

--No matter how you plan, connive and contrive, you hit the Big Town at 5 p.m.

--The moment you promise the children you will buy maple sugar candy at the next stand you pass, the stands all vanish from sight, and you have to drive 18 miles back to the one you rejected because "there are a million more right along this road."

--On the day you set out to make time, you are stopped in one 50-mile stretch by a 90-car freight train, 2 hay wagons going 4 miles an hour, and 40 lazy cows ambling out to pasture.

--You don't notice the out-of-order sign on the gas station rest room until your tank is full, which means you have to stop at the next one, too, and endure a stony stare as the family uses the facilities and you put a little free air into the tires.

--Steak is on sale in the town where you stop, so you splurge on 2, but by the time you find a roadside table with a grill, it is raining, and shows no sign of letting up until next year's trip.

--You carry a sweater in the car day after sweltering day, but the moment you pack it away (away under everything else in the suitcase, that is), you hit a cold snap.

--You pass up the big supermarket because it is too early to shop and end up buying your groceries at a camp store that gets its supplies by mule train and charges gold rush prices.

--After a fruitless search among the 9 people in the car, you find a quarter in the glove compartment, but you miss the toll basket, and 20 cars line up behind you as you back up to pick up the quarter which has rolled under the rear axle and wedged in a crack in the pavement.

--You use your last film just before you spot the "picture of the century."

There's only one way to repeal "Roamin' Law"--stop roaming.

When Kids Learn to Read
September 15, 1970

Most mothers agree (especially at this time of the year), that school is a wonderful thing. But there is one trouble with book-learning: it changes your whole life.

No more than 5 years ago, our family was 50 per cent illiterate. Of course, at that time, 4 of us were under 5 years of age. Nevertheless, the percentage was disturbing and embarrassing.

But each year, another child joined the ranks of those in scholarly pursuits, and all of a sudden 9 out of 9 of us can read. It makes a difference from morning 'til night.

Mother: "Eat your cereal, please."

Child: "I don't like it."

Mother: "You don't have to like it, you just have to eat it."

Child: "Why?"

Mother: "It's good for you."

Child: "It's not nearly as good as Product 22½. See, it says on the box that it has only 35 per cent of the Vitamin B that I need. Product 22½ has 100 per cent."

Mother: "We're out of Product 22½ . Eat your cereal."

Child: "What does t-e-l-e-s-c-o-p-e spell? Oh, I know, telescope! I'll eat my cereal if I can have 50 cents to send for this neat telescope."

The spell-the-important-word game doesn't work anymore, either.

Mother: "We had a note today from M-i-k-e'-s t-e-a-c-h-e-r."

Father: "Oh, oh, what now?"

Mother: "It's s-p-i-t-b-a-l-l-s."

Mike: "I didn't do it. I didn't throw any spitballs. Andy did it. Honest, I didn't do it."

There is a problem with mail, too.

Child: "I just saw Grandma's letter on the desk. Where's my dollar?"

Mother: "What dollar?"

Child: "Grandma says she sent $10 for a family gift, and I figure my share is $1.11. Can I have it in cash? The last time, you bought pillows for the couch. I'd rather have the dollar."

Mother had her heart set on a new breadbox. Next time she'll digest the news and then eat the letter.

News is something else we have problems with now that everyone can make out the headlines.

Child: "Mom, what's a pervert?"

Mother: "Go wash out your mouth!"

Child: "You said I should practice my reading."

Mother: "Go read some more cereal boxes."

In the old days, it was, "Daddy, read me the comics." Now, they can read their own comics, but they find that they prefer the movie ads. They pool their literary skills, and just from reading the ads they can tell you the plot of every X-rated film in town. I'm beginning to think it's time someone rated the ads.

In some ways it helps to have everyone in the family reading. For instance, if I expect to be late coming home in the afternoon, I can leave a note for the Bailey School crowd, our 4 youngest.

On such occasions, I write: "I will be home soon. Please change your clothes. Apples in frig. Put dog out. Stay on block."

Did you mean us?

When I come home, they are 2 blocks away, still in school clothes.

Mother: "Didn't you read my note?"

Bailey 4: "Oh, sure, but we didn't think you meant us."

Mother: "But you ate the apples."

Bailey 4: "Oh, we knew that part was for us."

Mother to Dog: "Who let you out?"

Dog: "Woff, woff" (read the note myself).

Once in a while, the tables are turned, and my young readers leave notes for me. Without exception, they are better readers and writers than spellers, and their punctuation is energetic.

"Dere Mom: I ned those new sneekers TOMORROW!!! Can you git them by noon(?) I forgot to re-mind you befour you went out. A lady named Missus Wails (Whales? Wales??? Wayles????) called."

At bedtime, Daddy is still the best reader in the house as far as the younger children are concerned. The rest of us can pronounce the words, but only Daddy can make the tigers jump out of the book.

"The noise got louder, Louder, LOUDER, and then..."

The children have heard it a hundred times. They've read it for themselves. They know exactly what comes next. But when Daddy reads it, the excitement and suspense is new each time.

Reading, now and then, brings disappointments. One of the worst kinds is when, after talking me out of the money and into the mood, they arrive at the pop machine and they can read for themselves that it is OUT OF ORDER.

Kids Evaluate Teachers
September 22, 1970

Teachers have always graded students, but more and more these troubled days, colleges and universities are offering their students an opportunity to evaluate their instructors.

Students are provided printed questionnaires and urged to express themselves on anything and everything about their classes, i.e., the clarity of texts assigned; the adequacy of ventilation in the classroom; the teacher's sincerity; or the efficiency of his deodorant.

And why not? The kids have been doing just that from K through 12, since the first school bell rang, and without benefit of printed sheets. Two days before school opened this fall, little knots of boys and girls (refreshed by 2 months of driving their parents mad), clustered in conspiratorial groups on our block.

Greasy (known as Edward to his family): "Hey, Bonehead (christened Jonathan), I hear you got ole McGrath this year. Boy, I pity you."

Bonehead: "Oh yeah, she's not half as bad as that Loud Mouth Henderson you're getting. Ole McGrath is a good teacher. My big brother had her. She lets you count on spools if you get stuck. Besides, Loud Mouth yells so loud, you'll be deaf by November. I pity you!"

It helps to know that these are second graders. By the time they reach the middle schools, their evaluations are more refined.

271

"Which team are you in? Team 99? You poor kid. There isn't an inspired teacher in the whole team. Franklin mumbles, Stone faked his way through college, and that Ellen White wears the dumpiest clothes you ever saw. Imagine, seams! She's antediluvian!"

In high school, the kids play for keeps.

"Try to get Anderson, he never takes roll."

Or,

"If you start Thomas talking about His War, you can get all your math done in history period."

Or,

"Phillips must be on drugs. He gave me a lousy D last term."

Or,

"Let's organize and get Phelps thrown out. That'll teach him to pick on me in class."

Some of the children get help from home in their evaluations.

"I stopped in to see your teacher today about your chemistry grade. You never told me 'Old Smithy' was a 22-year-old bleached blonde hussy. Does she always wear that snaky mini? No wonder you kids aren't learning anything in that class," proclaims Mother.

Dad has his opinions, too.

"If you get Bill Trumble for English, you'll really learn something this year. Honestly, that guy has the classiest drive of any golfer I know."

When all the evaluations--printed, shouted, whispered, or insinuated--are in, there is no doubt that:

--Some people are better teachers than others.

--Some people are better evaluators than others.

--Some people don't like any teachers, good or bad.

--Some teachers are people.

--One man's teacher may be another man's poison.

--Some people just never learn.

To paraphrase a cheesecake commercial, everybody doesn't like somebody, but nobody doesn't like telling about it.

Do Parents Lie?
October 6, 1970

"My father," said the solemn young man, "never lied to me."

It was a tense moment. You could tell Matt Dillon was more shaken by this youth's faith in his father's word than he was by the bullet in his own leg.

I dismissed the whole issue from my mind as soon as the show was over. After all, Dillon has been shot before, so I figured he would recover from both his injury and the tense moment, given another episode.

But that wasn't the end of it as far as Drew, Mike, Meg and Beth were concerned. The next day at lunch, the talk began in its usual happy vein.

"Do we hafta have sandwiches?"

"Would you rather have soup?"

"Naw. Can't I have chili?"

"Tomorrow, maybe. I'm out of it now. Today I'm offering ham, thuringer, salami or meat loaf. What will it be?"

"Peanut butter."

I gave him peanut butter.

"Daddy lies sometimes."

"What did you say?"

"I said, Daddy lies sometimes."

"He does not. How dare you say sucha thing, Mike?"

"Well, he lied when we crossed the Canadian border and the man asked him where he was born. He said Michigan, and he really was born in New York State, wasn't he?"

"Daddy didn't lie; he just expected the man to ask him where he was from instead of where he was born, and he answered the wrong question."

Meg rushed into the discussion.

"Daddy lied about swimming one day. He said he would take us to the Faculty Club pool, but he didn't take us."

"But, Meg, don't you remember? It rained, that's why he didn't take you."

"All I know is he promised and then he didn't do it. That's lying isn't it?"

"'No, it isn't. Lying is when you purposely set out to deceive someone. And Mother and Daddy would never do that to you."

There it was, a bald lie. I mean, there are no parents in the whole world who haven't indulged in a little deception now and then--for the children's own good, of course.

"Mama, I don't want to have a shot. It'll hurt something awful."

"No, darling, no, it'll only hurt a little bit, then it'll be all over in a second, and you can forget about it."

(Actually, the needle was 10 inches long and it hurt like fury going in and for about 4 hours afterwards. But she had to have it, she just had to.)

"Did you get the tickets? Did you? Can we go tomorrow?"

"Gosh, they were all sold out for tomorrow. I'm so sorry, but I did get tickets for next week. We'll go and have a great time, okay?'

"Okay!"

(They weren't sold out, but kids seem to understand sell-outs a lot easier than they understand special faculty conferences.)

Sometimes, it's very hard to tell the absolute truth.

"Mother, why did you lie to that man on the phone?"

"I didn't, Mike, I didn't."

"Yes you did. You told him Daddy wasn't here, and he's right out in the yard."

"Mike, I told the man Daddy wasn't in the house--and that's the truth. You understand, don't you?"

"Sure, I understand. Daddy didn't want to talk to the man, right?"

"Right."

Some parents, apparently, have managed to shade the black and whiteness of prevarication.

"Cindy's mommy lets her lie sometimes."

"I can't believe that."

"She says that if Cindy is alone and the phone rings she should say her mom is in the shower so the bad people won't come and hurt Cindy."

"Well, Beth, that isn't--I mean that's a bit different..."

"Yeah, Cindy's mom says that lying is sinful, but sometimes you have to fib a little--and fibbing is different."

Me, I'm with Cindy's mom. What's more, I think we ought to play checkers more and watch TV less.

Objectivity
October 13, 1970

Objectivity is something no household should be without.

A large supply should be laid in about the time that you are buying your first sheets and pillow cases, and a new stock should be added whenever you replace the linens.

A dictionary will tell you that to view objectively is to assess in a detached, impersonal, and unprejudiced manner. But what objectivity really is is the ability to look at your first baby while you are still full of the miracle of creation, and note that he is wrinkled, red, scaly and slightly cross-eyed.

274

A friend of mine vows that she had never tasted real objectivity until she moved last spring. The first dose came from the realtor who offered to sell her old home.

"What did you think of my ad?" asked Sir Realtor.

"We couldn't find it in the paper. We thought you didn't manage to get it in on time," said Jean.

"Here it is: 'Handy with tools and paintbrush? This little place is made for you. Owner desperate. Make an offer.' There, how does that grab you?"

"Tools? Paintbrush? This little place? Are you talking about our house? Our house has 10 rooms!"

"Well, you know, with money so tight, big barns just aren't selling these days."

Jean's new neighbors were objective too. Little Billy from next door confided, as he watched the truck being unloaded: "My mom says she's seen better furniture than yours waiting on the curb for the junk man."

Of course, all children have a kind of built-in objectivity. Turn a toddler loose at a picnic in the park, and without any prejudice at all he'll beg a cookie at one table, yank down a thermos from another, and toss sand into the casserole on another. He's impartial.

Men tend to be objective, except when it comes to themselves.

"What kind of a thing is that for a wife to say? Why would a wife want to run a man down like that? Can't understand it. A man works and slaves for his family and a wife can't even come up with a little loyalty now and then. What did you mean by that remark anyway? I mean, deep down, what were you trying to tell me?"

"All I said was that isn't the best haircut you ever got."

Women, unfortunately, are frequently the least objective of all human groups. In fact, there are some areas in which they are completely unable to be objective. For instance:

Their families: "I never said my kids were perfect, but smart--are they smart! And talented! And good-looking! And loving!"

Their homes: "I don't care what you say, I just don't like that green in Sadie's kitchen. Blue, it should have been blue. My kitchen is blue, and it's just the right color."

Their husbands: "Sarah says she'd get married in a minute if she could find a man who was good-looking, kind and successful. Say, you don't think she's got her eyes on my Tom, do you?"

Their wardrobes: "Joan's dress was too fussy for the occasion. I'm glad I wore my brown suit."

Other women: "If you ask me, nobody was ever born with hair that color!"

Writers, especially newspaper writers, are the most objective people in the world (objectively speaking, of course). To test the theory, you may ask me anything. Go ahead, ask me.

Q. How are your children, Mrs. Naybor?

A. Perfect.

Q. What kind of paper is The Towne Courier?

A. The best in town.

Q. What type of a job does your husband have?

A. Important.

Q. How does he rank in his field?

A. Tops.

Q. How would you evaluate your answers to this quiz?

A. I feel I have been completely objective.

Culture Hour
October 20, 1970

Some women are troublemakers.

Take Jean Kerr. Wouldn't you think it would be enough to raise 5 sons and a daughter, write several best-selling books, a couple of plays which ended up on Broadway and in Hollywood, win fame and fortune, and stay married to a brilliant drama critic?

Just think of the badges all that would be worth in Junior Girl Scouts!

But now I read, in her new book, "Penny Candy," about Sunday evening "Culture Hours," wherein she and husband, Walter, not only taught their children a love of poetry, but even managed to get them to commit some to memory.

How's that for a hard act to follow?

I've always felt a deep kinship with Jean Kerr, in spite of the obvious differences in our achievements.

What especially endeared her to me, in addition to her "parents-are-people-too" attitude towards bringing up children, was her comment on seeking out a size 18 maternity dress.

She said, and I had been through it, that the clerk looked at her as if no woman who already wore a size 18 had any business getting pregnant.

Another of my favorite stories about Jean Kerr is the one where, after all manner of disaster had caught up with her, and she was rushing

276

somewhere, looking like something the trashmen had overlooked, a woman came up to her and gushed, "Say, aren't you Jean Kerr?"

To which Jean answered, "Of course not. Jean Kerr would never be seen in public looking like this!"

But to get back to the culture problem, you've got to remember that to begin with, the Kerrs had to get all those kids in the same room at the same time, a feat harder than putting socks on an elephant.

There's another difficulty, too. If you tried to have a "culture hour" in your household, and it started at 7, would anybody be speaking to anybody else by 7:10? And if one of you did say something to another one, would it be poetic?

You can bet your tintinnabulation it wouldn't.

If the "culture hour" is out (take my word for it, it's OUT), what hope is there for my children? Perhaps the first step is to find out how much culture they have already absorbed (after all, they got the measles without any help from us), and plan a program from there.

"Can any of you recite a poem?"

"Sure thing, Mom, listen: 'Star light, Star Bright; Hide your face, It's a fright!"

(Score zero for poetry.)

"Let's talk about opera? Does anyone know the names of an opera?"

"How about 'As the World Turns'?"

"I don't know that one. Is it Italian, French or German?"

"Gee, Mom, I don't know about that. All I know is, Aunt Jane calls it a soap opera."

(Opera's out.)

"All right, so you don't know much about poetry and opera. I know you've all had a lot of art in school, so let's discuss art. Kate, what's your favorite medium of expression?"

"Graffiti!"

"Honestly, kids, I give up. Isn't there any form of culture you can discuss intelligently? How about drama?"

"Drama? She's fine. I just talked to Drampa on the phone, and he says Drama's just great."

(Memo to Mom and Dad: Plan to take the kids to the Lansing Civic Center between 1 and 6 p.m., on October 25 for the annual metropolitan area "Day With the Arts." It can't hurt.)

When Things Disappear
October 27, 1970

Halloween.

The coming weekend has something for everyone--All Hallows Eve, All Saints Day, All Souls Day, and even All Citizens Day, more commonly known as Election Day.

The air is filled with Halloween bats and witches, and political brickbats and witch hunts. Probably there are more prayers being said for votes than for souls.

The children will wear masks on Saturday, but next Tuesday it will be their parents who will enjoy the protective cloak of anonymity as they cast their secret ballots.

When the "all-days" are over, Halloween skeletons will go back into their closets, but a few political bones may rattle hauntingly for many months to come.

As far as I know, there are no skeletons in our closets, but we aren't All Saints either. As a matter of fact, it looks as if there may be a phantom in our "phamily."

Things disappear. Sometimes, they are never to be seen again. Other times, they reappear mysteriously and without plausible explanation.

For instance, pencils, tape, rulers, staplers, paper punches, felt markers, and even hefty scratch pads have been known to vanish from my desk right into the polluted air.

Needles, thread, thimbles, scissors and tape measures disappear regularly from my sewing basket.

Screwdrivers, hammers, bolts, clamps or awls leave my husband's tool box without human aid.

I know what you are thinking--one of the children "borrowed" the missing item and simply forgot to return it. Well, let's ask.

"Beth, have you seen my scissors?"

"You mean your favorite sharp ones that you keep in the sewing basket? I didn't take them. Have you asked Meg?"

"Meg, have you seen my scissors?"

"No, have you asked Drew?"

I ask all 7, plus my husband, plus the dog. But none of them has seen my scissors. Two days later, the scissors are back in the basket.

"Mike, did you return my scissors?"

"No, did you ask Dale?"

"Dale, did you return my scissors?"

"No, did you ask Drew?" and so on down the line to old Woof Woof.

Now, if you understand all that interplay, you know as I do that no one in the household either took the scissors or returned them.

Boiled down in a witch's cauldron, that means that a spirited Halloween ghost is making our house his permanent address--and he has creative instincts but no tools of his own.

Normally, our children are probably the world's best finders. I hide the candy and they find it--in the chafing dish, the spaghetti pot, the upper cupboard, the towel drawer, the pot holder basket, the vase Aunt Clara gave us which nobody is supposed to touch ever, the picnic basket, and even in an old varnish can.

No hiding place is safe for much more than 1½ days (the finding record is 27 seconds), and no place is good more than once.

I had real good luck once with a bag set out on the kitchen counter, and boldly marked "Trash, please take to garage." For 4 days no one saw it or went near it. But on the fifth day, a primary reader whose skills are not up to "trash" or "garage," read "Please take two," and helped himself to 2 pieces of candy and then generously passed it around.

Good as they are with candy, they seem to lose their pointing instincts when anything important is lost.

They try to be cooperative, however. The other night, after watching the news, their father growled, "Sometimes I think this country has lost its head!"

One of the children, who was just entering the room, ducked out again quickly. Soon, he had spread the word.

"Better start looking around, you guys. The 'Older Generation's' lost something again, and if I know them, the 'Youth of Today' will get the blame."

A House Is a Mirror of You
November 3, 1970

Hudson's broadcasts a musical advertisement which starts out, "Your home should be a mirror of the way that you live..."

It's a catchy tune and I found myself humming it the other day. When I remembered those beginning words, I looked around me and I thought, "My gosh, my mirror must have broken and I'm having 7 years of bad luck."

Years and years ago, when I first thought about love and marriage and family life, I had vivid dreams of the kind of haven my husband and children would call home.

I could see a living room, warm, yet serene, with lots of deep, inviting chairs, several needlepoint footstools, and colorful books on the shelves. The couch was the color of clear lemon drops.

In the dining room, my dreams alternated between Spode and Wedgwood, but always there was a sideboard of rubbed wood, and on it sat a white ironstone tureen, with matching ladle.

The beds, of course, would all be four-postered, although, in that pre-permanent press age, I did limit myself to only one canopy, in deference to the ironing involved.

Nobody expects girlish dreams to come true verbatim but mine didn't even come close.

Instead of Early American, we started out with Early Attic. We progressed from that stage, of course, and graduate school saw us neatly outfitted with Student Salvage.

As the children came (and came and came), we went through a period of wild spending. We splurged on furnishings--cribs, bunk beds, high chairs and playpens. The effect was deplorable.

From Crumby Childhood, we have stepped up our present decor, an interesting hodge-podge of things near and dear to us (let's face it--we're stuck with them), best described as Messy Miscellaneous.

In short, our interior decoration is inferior decoration.

But it's hard to know where to start to upgrade the situation. A few weeks ago, when it became apparent that our couch was in critical condition and probably wouldn't last the winter, I thought our chance had come to break through to elegance at last. But I was wrong.

You see, the couch had to harmonize with the rug (although the rug will have to be replaced next year and we'll never buy that color again!), and it had to go with the green chair (although the green chair needs covering pretty badly), and it had to go with the walls (although the walls are due to be painted soon--I hope), and it had to go with the drapes (although when we paint the walls, we'll surely have to have new drapes).

I wish I could say we bought a couch the color of clear lemon drops, but we didn't. The color is more like dusty horehound rescued from a little boy's pocket seconds before the jeans hit the wash.

It goes pretty good with the worn rug, the beat-up chair, the dirty walls and the stringy drapes. And it's a comfortable couch. If it lasts until we take care of the rug, chair, walls and drapes, the reflection in our family mirror may not be half bad.

Especially if I take the caramel apple sticks from the ashtrays, the gum wrappers from the fireplace and the gym shoe from the magazine rack.

For some mirrors, lemon drop yellow is the wrong image.

Lunch with Husband
November 10, 1970

A few weeks ago, my husband announced that he thought I should join him once a week for lunch. Not because I look as if I need lunch, you understand. (Actually, I look as if lunch once a week is all I need.) I'm not sure what brought it up.

Maybe it was women's lib. Did I tell you some of the leaders have asked me to be a test case?

If that wasn't the reason, maybe he remembered way back to when we used to be Good Friends and we looked forward to being together even if we had to eat lunch to manage it. Good Friends, by the way, was what you told "the girls" you were when they got nosey.

"Say, what's with you and Tom? It looks serious."

"Naw, we're just Good Friends."

The next day, you and your Good Friend got married, putting one over on "the girls" and, incidentally, ending a Good Friendship.

Whatever the reason, the invitation to do something together was exciting. At certain stages of wifehood and motherhood, it doesn't take much to cause excitement. A friend of mine got so excited over raking leaves with her husband that each night she'd go out to the garage, open the plastic bags and spill most of the leaves back over the lawn. He never got wise and she's looking forward to shoveling snow with him any day now.

But back to my invitation. The more I thought of it, the more excited I got. Then I started to get nervous. What would I wear? Should I have my hair done? Should I be ready on time? Should I pretend to have important things to do and leave early?

Then I thought of a problem that put all the others out of my mind. What on earth, I wondered, would we talk about?

Figure an hour for lunch. Figure about 15 minutes of that time for chewing and gulping. That leaves 45 minutes for interesting talk. How long has it been since you talked to your husband for 45 minutes straight? And interesting, yet!

Yeah, me too.

Then a thought hit me; why get so worked up? Obviously, the thing to do is to talk about things I know about.

Let's see, that includes kids, bills, broken appliances, dentist appointments, lettuce prices, stretch socks, ingrown toenails, lasagna, drain potions, stomach settlers and goodness knows what other horribly dull topics.

Of course, we could always talk about Our Family, My Day, or His Job, but come to think of it, those 3 topics are the reasons why after 20 years of marriage we need to get together once a week and go out to lunch.

In desperation I spent a whole morning "getting interesting." I watched the Today Show. I read Time. I read Holiday. I read Sports Illustrated. I even read a Mad comic I found on the floor in my teenager's room. In short, I prepared myself to be interesting on almost any topic which might come up.

At the restaurant, our appearance threw the waitress. I don't look like the kind of girl you take to lunch because it's fun to take a girl to lunch, so she concluded it was a business engagement.

"Separate checks?" she asked.

"No, just one," said my husband, and then as if to help her understand the situation, "this is my wife."

"Sure," she smiled, and you knew it wasn't the first time she'd heard that story.

Well, it was great to have shrimp salad instead of peanut butter for lunch. Tom and I both had a good time and agreed to make it a weekly date.

What did we talk about? I let Tom set the pace (maybe that was what made me endearing 20 years ago), and after we discussed the menu and the décor we got around to lots of interesting things—like Our Family, My Day, and His Job.

Victory in Fashion Wars
November 17, 1970

I don't know how it happened, but it looks as if we women have finally won one.

The battle was over hemlines--maxi, midi, mini or mama mia! There we were caught in the middle, with designers and retailers hemming us in on one side, and the girl watchers needling us on the other. The question was, to what lengths should a woman go to be fashionable?

For several months the battle raged--up and down, up and down. To everyone's surprise, women managed to come out on top with the best of all war spoils, freedom of choice.

In short, it's fashionable this season to wear what you like.

Or, if you can't afford what you like, you can even wear what you have, and still be in style. Don't tell your husband, but your closet is bulging with the latest style, even if you haven't had a new dress since V-E Day. If you can get into it, you're IN in it.

If you do have the luck to go shopping for something new, be prepared for a real thrill. No matter how long or short it is, it's just right if you like it. No alterations necessary.

You just can't go wrong. Not only can you decide on your own length, but any color is great, any neckline is acceptable, any style from A-line to feline is in. You can wear slacks when you're cold, or minis when you're bold. Everything is right for any occasion, and the only test of style is that it please the woman wearing it.

If it's your thing, you can be a leggy mod bird, a calicoed coquette, a beaded gypsy, a booted gaucho, a panted panther, a demure damsel in dimity, a svelte swinger in suede, a belle in bell-bottoms, a flapper in flounces, lethal in levis, or neat in knits.

Or you can mix and mis-match, and look collegiate.

Some say fashion reflects the time. If that is so, then there has never been a time like this in all of written history. Remember the things they said about Joan of Arc when she showed up in her tunic and tights? Today she'd go down as a nice practical girl.

And if Josephine had worn a mini now and again, would Napoleon have had so much time for war?

If Marie Antoinette had used her head and adopted the long, lean look, instead of standing there in her fat hoops offering the French cake, would they have let her keep her head and eat her cake too?

There is no doubt about it, fashion helps to shape history, as well as those who live it. If ladies had not tired of dirty petticoat ruffles we might never have graduated from dusty cowpaths to paved sidewalks.

And think of the snap Amelia's elasticized bloomers put into her followers' campaign for women's rights.

It's not hard to guess what the effect of today's freedom of fashion can mean for women. Freedom of choice is a heady tonic after the slavery of convention. Already women are deciding they ought to have it in all things. From now on it's watch out world!

Wear what you want, whenever you want! You still haven't grasped just what that means to you?

It means you can stand there in your skirt which doesn't ride up when you sit, your long jacket that hides your bulges, your sensible shoes that never get stuck in gratings, your hat that actually warms your ears, and you can look your teenage daughter right in the eye and say:

"Of course, you're right, dear. I can't go out looking like this--I almost forgot my peace medallion and I feel positively unfashionable without it!"

Fifth Year of "Family in Towne"
November 24, 1970

It seems like yesterday, if you'll pardon my grammar.

In reality, it was 5 years ago this Thanksgiving week that I introduced my Family in Towne to you.

At that time, our baby, Drew, was 2; now he is 7, and no baby. Our big girl, Ellen, was 14; now she is a young lady of 19. Between them are Dale, now 17; Kate, now 13; Beth, 10; Meg, 9; and Mike, 8. Lim Tai Hi, who lives in Seoul, South Korea, and has been a part of our family for the past 4 years through the Foster Parent Plan, Inc., is now 8.

Our dog, who 5 years ago was not even a member of the household, now rules it with a furry paw.

As for Tom and me, five years may have made us older and, hopefully, wiser, but the price has been a loss of energy and patience.

A family changes in five years. When the children were smaller, our main problems were physical--keeping them fed, clean and safe, and of course, letting them know they were loved.

Now that they are older (and larger!), our house bulges with separate lives lived under one roof. Our concerns now are with less tangible things--hoping they are challenged, understood and fulfilled, but, as before, letting them know they are loved.

It was more important in those early days to know where they were, than who they were. And if you thought it was rough keeping up with where they were, you should see us trying to keep up with who they are!

But "it seems like yesterday" is what people say when time has passed not only quickly, but pleasantly, and that's the way I feel about our five-year friendship with you.

You've been generous with calls, letters and comments, saying you've enjoyed having us in the neighborhood, and that you've been glad to provide a listening ear for our trials and our joys.

Many of you have said, "I'm not sure if all the things you write about really happened, but I can tell you that the same thing happened to us in almost the same way just the other day. When we read about it happening to you, we laughed about it all over again."

Most of the things I write about really did happen to us or our family or friends. I'm not above a bit of literary embroidery (creative snitchery, you might say), but the human race is so honestly amusing, that it is seldom necessary.

No family's existence is an unending round of gaiety, but because I knew you'd expect it of me, I leaned over backwards through the years to find a bright spot in every happening. As a family, we've had our share of worry, grief and regret, but in trying to present hopeful faces to you, we have been rewarded with hopeful hearts.

It has been fun living down the block from you and we hope to go on doing so for many years to come.

Happy Thanksgiving from our Family in Towne to yours.

Making Christmas Gifts
December 1, 1970

I hate to be the one to remind you, but it is now the first week of December.

I also hate to ask, but wasn't this the year you were going to make most of your Christmas gifts? Or maybe only one or two special things, say a crocheted vest for a teenager, or a knitted scarf for a son, or seasoned almonds for a sweet and helpful neighbor, or a furry pillow for an aunt, or a felt coat for a dog?

There is something very special about a homemade gift. Any gift is a gesture of thoughtfulness. It requires forethought, money, shopping. But a homemade gift requires an added ingredient--the time for making. In a world where the pace of everyday living is such that none of us ever has enough time, what greater gift can you give?

A homemade gift speaks up for you. It says, "I thought of something you might like; I shopped for the necessary materials; then I used some of my precious time to make it for you."

When your friend sees your gift, he knows you did all these things, and he knows you love him.

(Except in the case of that dog, who may think you hate him when you try to get him to wear that felt coat.)

But if you need a gift that will tell someone all these things, the time to start on it is now.

There are some people who start in January to make gifts for Christmas. But for me that doesn't work. I don't feel Christmasy in January, or June, or even in November.

In December--when I look at the calendar and realize there are only 20 odd days until Christmas—that's when I get the urge to make things.

Unfortunately such emotional timing rules out gifts such as jars of watermelon pickle for the neighbors, wild rose potpourri for the teachers, or gooseberry jam for Uncle George.

However, there is still plenty of time for fruited breads, a macramé belt, or a barnwood picture frame.

In fact, if you start now, there is still time to stitch, knit or crochet; to hammer, saw or chisel; to cook, bake or brew; to tole, stencil or decoupage; to paint, sketch or etch; or anything else that suits your fancy or skills.

If you have no skills, this is the perfect opportunity to learn one. No one receiving a knitted gift will say, "I can see where you dropped a stitch."

Instead, they will say, "The first thing you ever knitted? How honored I am to be the one for whom you made it."

My family will forgive all manner of defects in the gifts I hurriedly whip up in December.

Raggedy Ann's eyes cross? "I love her just the way you made her."

A piece of nut shell in the fudge? "Homemade fudge is the best there is."

The slacks are too long? "But you can fix that and they are just the color I wanted. I couldn't find ready-made slacks this color anywhere."

About the only time my family won't forgive me is when I give a "promise box" and fail to fulfill the promise.

A "Promise Box" is usually that large rectangular box on the bottom of the pile. It's always gaily wrapped. Inside is a length of fabric, thread, a zipper, and a pattern.

A note says, "I got rushed at the last minute. But I promise to make this up soon."

Last year things really got rushed. I gave out 5 "Promise Boxes," 2 for slacks, 2 for jumpers and one for a robe.

I made up the slacks during the week between Christmas and New Year's Day. The jumper fabric still sits in their boxes. I suspect the patterns are now one size too small.

The robe got cut out one zesty day last spring. Two pockets are neatly lined and finished, but somehow I haven't had many zesty days since.

Meanwhile, my husband relaxes in a tattered relic--a silent reminder of my broken promises.

If I got at it this week, do you suppose I might be able to put a robe under the tree this Christmas?

Letters to Santa
December 8, 1970

Our 9-year-old has written her letter to Santa, and from my brief look at it, I can tell you she is taking no chances.

In addition to asking for each item by its trade name, she has included the price and the catalog page number where the item can be found.

In the old days, when she was less specific but more trusting, her letters to Santa were warm and newsy. Despite many misspelled words, her affection and confidence came through loud and clear.

She used to spend considerable space and time telling Santa that she loved him, and in explaining that she had been "good, mostly." Her actual "bring list" was usually scant and sketchy. "A baby dolly" and crayons and candy might be the total of her written wants.

If she misplaced the letter before it was mailed, she would write another. This time the list, while equally short, might well be completely different, asking perhaps for "a doll bed like Cindy's," some clay and maybe ice skates, if she had happened to be reminded of them that day.

The best part of her innocence was that no matter what she asked for in her letter, and no matter how fervently she wanted it when she asked for it, she always forgave Santa instantly for the things he "forgot" to bring.

Whatever she found under the tree on Christmas morning was automatically "just exactly what I wanted most of all!"

This year her letter is more like a business order than a chat with an old friend.

After ice skates, she has written not only the size ("I think I am a 4 now"), but also specifications ("girls' white figure skates, with a soft lining, and fur tops like I had last year but don't see them in the catalog this year, but maybe you can find some to bring me").

Another toy she wants, a doll called Baby Go Bye-Bye, is in the catalog and she is precise about it being "on the lower right hand side of Page 293." However, mindful of its high price, she advises Santa that "This doll is cheaper in the discount store but just as good."

Apparently, the state of the general economy is much on her mind, because she has numbered her requests in order of preference and makes a note that "if you can't bring me all these things, please bring me the ones marked 1, 2, 3, 4, and 5, because these are the things I want most."

Not only does the catalog ease her "armchair shopping," but it helps her with her spelling. She misspells "behaveing," but every game or toy is letter perfect as copied from her official reference book.

In proper Christmas spirit, she helped her younger brother write his letter too.

"Don't lick the envelope until Mommy reads the letter," I heard her warn him.

"But I don't want her to read it. She won't let me ask for all these things," he protests, worriedly.

"Never mind that, she's got to read it," she insists.

"Why?" he asks, all the while getting his tongue dangerously close to the glue.

"She's got to fix the spelling," she tells him. "You don't want to spell any words wrong, do you? How will Santa know what you want if he can't read it?"

"Oh, yeah," he agrees, as she rescues the letter and brings it to me.

"Would you check Drew's Christmas letter for him?" she asks casually. Then she whispers hurriedly, "Boy, that dumb kid wasn't even going to show it to you before mailing it!"

I get the message, but just between you, me and Santa, I think little girls grow up too soon.

Happy Holidaze!
December 15, 1970

Christmas is full of drama, but behind the scenes in some families, a comedy of errors entitled "Santa's Helpers" is stealing the stage.

The subtitle could be "We Know That You Know, But We Won't Let on That We Know That You Know if You Don't Let on That You Know What You Know."

Scene 1. Mother and Father at home.

Father: Did you get the you-know-what for you-know-who yet?

Mother: No, I'm waiting for some store to advertise a special on it.

Father: It's $12.98 in the ad, and that's $2 off.

Mother: I know, but I think I saw it for $10.99 a couple of weeks ago and maybe we'll be able to get it for that if we wait a few days.

Father: Okay, but don't wait too long. Remember last year we waited for that one toy to come down and the last week all the stores ran out of it except one and we ended up paying $2.50 more for it than the original price, plus the gas to go 14 miles to pick it up.

Mother: Don't worry, I'm sure we can save money on it if we watch and wait.

Scene II. Mother and 4 kids in crowded parking lot.

Mother: Stay in the car, kids, while I run into the store. I'll be right out.

Kid: But, Mom, you always get angry with mothers who leave children in the car alone. Do you want us to get kidnapped or suffocate?

Mother: Suffocate. And never mind about that now, just stay in the car.

Kid: Can't we come in and look at the toys while you do your other shopping?

Mother: Sorry, they don't allow kids alone in the toy department.

Scene III. Harried Mother in store.

Harried Mother: I wonder if you could double-bag that candy so it won't break and spill in the car, and could you possibly cover both ends of that large toy box?

Saleslady: Yes, Ma'am. Oh, oh, we just ran out of large bags; I don't have anything that will cover that toy box.

H.M.: But the kids are in the car!

Saleslady: Why don't we mark it with your name and hold it for you. Can you come back for it tomorrow?

H.M.: But it's 14 miles! Wait, I have an idea. I'll bring the kids into the store and while they're looking at things I'll sneak the package out and cover it with the car blanket.

Scene IV. Harried Mother and 4 kids in store.

H.M.: Now, stay together, kids, and Mother will be back in just a minute.

Kid: I thought you said they didn't allow kids alone in the toy department.

H.M.: I made a mistake. Boy, did I make a mistake!

Scene V. Hundreds of people mill about huge store.

Loudspeaker: Would the mother who left her children unattended in the toy department please come to the service desk. We have a little lost boy who says his name is Blue. Or maybe that's Brew; he's crying a lot.

H.M.: Drew!

Scene VI. Harried Mother and 4 kids return to car (one kid clutches mother's coat for dear life).

Kid: Hey, Mom, there's something in the back of the car under the blanket.

H.M.: It's something I had to pick up for Mrs. Klein, next door.

Kid: Gee it looks just like a...

H.M.: DON'T TOUCH THAT BLANKET!!! I mean, I want it to stay clean for her, so pleeeeease don't uncover it.

Kid: Okay, but I wonder what Mrs. Klein wants with a....

H.M.: It's for her grandson---Drew, please let go of Mother so I can steer.

Scene VII. Mother and Father at home.

Father: Say, here's that toy for only $9.95, and it couldn't be more convenient--it's at that store right next to the gas station. I noticed we're out of gas again--where did you go today?

Mother: Don't ask.

Father: What's wrong?

Mother exits singing, Happy Holidaze! Happy Holidaze!

Christmas Is a Crowded Time
December 21, 1970

Christmas is a crowded time.

To make room for the tree you have to move a table. When you find a place for the table, you are stuck with an extra chair. When you bring out the crèche, you have to move a lamp. When the poinsettia arrives, your year-around plants have to fight for their place in the sunny window.

If the relatives come, you have to put up a rollaway bed in one room, make room for an extra child in another, and step gingerly over the sleeping bags on the floor. At mealtime you add another leaf to the table, get out the card table, and squeeze in as many chairs as you can manage.

In the refrigerator the eggnog displaces the milk. In the freezer coconut snowballs crowd out the orange juice. In the cupboard Santa Claus cookies and rum fruitcake push the soda crackers and cocoa into the back corner.

Pies and cakes stack up to wait their turn in the oven like planes hovering over a metropolitan airport.

In every closet large square boxes, lumpy brown bags or elegantly bowed packages crush dresses and suits into permanently pressed creases.

In the attic..."STAY OUT OF THE ATTIC, you guys, or I'll have your scalp!"

The streets and parking lots are crowded with cars, some running, some waiting, and some stuck in the snow that packs the curbs. The buses and planes are crowded with travelers, luggage and RUSH! packages.

The stores are crowded with shoppers and their counters are heaped with exciting temptations. Shopping bags bulge with gifts for him, her and home, and the colorful tissue, tags, and ties to wrap them prettily.

In the toy department an over-population of dolls try to out-smile and out-charm each other, elbow to plastic elbow. In the candy stores peppermint canes hang from the walls, ribbon candy boxes are stacked on the floor, and chocolate reindeer prance on the wrapping counter.

The children are home from school and their hours are crowded with private projects behind closed doors, unfinished puzzles on the living room floor, and miniature car speedways in the upstairs hall.

They are alternately as busy as they can be, or as bored as they can be, and always as noisy as they can be. Their hearts are bursting with the delight of anticipation and often a thunderous "I can't wait for Christmas!" crowds to the surface and spills out.

To some people, Christmas is a day, to others a season, and to some fortunate few it is a way of life.

To all who call themselves followers of the Holy Child born on Christmas, it should be a time to pause and ponder the ways of the Godman who crowded into a few short years on earth enough love to guide all mankind through eternity.

But greed has pushed that love out of our hearts and on this 1970th birthday our gifts to Him, who asked only peace on earth, are a soiled planet, pain, sorrow, poverty, injustice, hatred, brutality and war.

It isn't too late to exchange those gifts, and the process is easy--just crowd a little Christmas into every day of the year, and let peace begin in every heart.

Merry Christmas and a Peaceful New Year from your Naybors --Tom, Kaye, Ellen, Dale, Kate, Beth, Meg, Mike and Drew.

1971

"Spare Time"
January 5, 1971

"What do you do in your spare time?" asks a friend of long ago on her annual greeting.

This isn't the first time that particular question has popped up, and I have to admit that it always puzzles me. In the first place, is it really a question, or is it just another way of saying, "Seven kids! Boy, am I glad it was you and not me!"?

If it is meant in earnest and genuine interest, what makes her think I have any spare time? Of course I do, but it's better described as stolen time, rather than spare time. Spare time, if it's anything like spare ribs or spare tires, is something extra, and when it comes to time, I don't have any extra.

The kind of spare time I have is strictly a case of mind over matter--I have to convince my mind that it doesn't matter that the laundry isn't folded, the floor is dirty and I haven't started dinner yet.

Another question arises: if you do something irregular regularly (like watching a cardinal come to pick the berries off the tree next door every morning at about 9:15), is it spare time or regular time you are goofing off in?

And the things I don't do regularly, but just once in a while in my stolen moments, do I really want her to know about them? If, when she says, "What do you do in your spare time?" she is really asking, "What kind of a person have you become, and would I still like you?" then I should be careful how I answer.

For instance, yesterday in some "spare" time, I sorted out the chest that holds my tablecloths and serving things. Tell that to someone and automatically you're a "lovely, domestic worn-in, who enjoys entertaining and is a wonderful hostess."

Actually, I sorted out the chest because things were in such a jumble that a napkin was caught between 2 drawers and both of them were jammed shut and I couldn't get at the paper plates.

One day last week in my spare time, I read a 5-page article on the Johnson-Masters experiments in sexual adjustment. Does that mean I'm a middle-aged swinger? No, it simply means that the dentist's waiting room was packed, and Psychology Today was the only magazine on the stand besides Jack and Jill.

Just Tuesday morning I delivered a 10-minute impassioned speech entitled, "Man, Wake Up, You Can't Live in This Mess." So, that makes me an expert on ecology and survival? No, it makes me a mother who went to call her son and got a look at his room.

I'd like my friend to think I'm someone she would still like, an interesting person to know. So, hoping she won't read between the lines, I write that in my spare time:

I read a great deal ("These crackers are double-wrapped for extra crispness...").

I write a little ("Dear Mom, Sorry I haven't written since September but you know how

it is... ").

I seldom stay in one place for long ("And after I pick up Mike at 2:30, I'll swing around to the library and get Meg before I go for Dad...").

I've been broadened by travel (I also eat too much when I'm not traveling).

I've been giving modern art a second look of late (but I still say somebody is putting me on).

I encourage my children to be creative ("If you don't find something to do in the next 4 seconds, I'll find something for you, but you won't like it!").

I keep in touch with my old friends (By the way, what do you do in your spare time? And how come you only write once a year?).

Rules of the Games
January 12, 1971

Rules of the Games

"Would you please read me the rules again?"

"But I read them to you twice already—besides, you're old enough to read them yourself. That's why Santa left you this game this year, because you're old enough to read the rules yourself."

"Oh, all right, stop pouting, I'll read them one more time."

Santa, Smanta. Boy, he was real great with his "Ho, Ho, Ho," and his bag full of "Exciting, educational, entertaining games, guaranteed to liven up the long, winter evenings." But where is he now that the long, winter evenings are here and livened up?

He's up at the North Pole where things are peaceful and quiet, and I'm down here reading the rules "one more time."

If I had known in the middle of December what all those stimulating games would mean in the middle of January, I might have lightened Santa's load with more of those flimsy plastic toys--the kind you sweep up with the tree needles and discard.

It isn't that the games aren't exciting, educational and entertaining as advertised; it's simply that I'm not sure how much of the 3 E's I can take.

Somewhere, somehow, I got the silly idea that the greatest thing about skill games was that they kept kids busy and quiet. Through all the years of hide and seek, Cowboys and Indians, and last one down the stairs on his head is a rotten egg, I dreamed of the time when our youngest 4 would be old enough to read rules and take turns, busily and quietly.

The time has come, and even Santa wouldn't believe how un-quiet 4 game-playing kids can be, nor how busy they can keep their mother.

Did you know that chess was a noisy game? No, not the click, clack of the jumps, but the "Mom, tell him he can't do that to my knight!"

Chinese checkers is noisy too. I was an only child so I played both sides of the board. Needless to say, I played them both silently. But at our house, it's "You can't jump there, you have to follow the line. Mom! Mom! He's cheating again!"

I've read the rules to Snoopy and the Red Baron 3 times and I still can't find where it says you have to chant "Zoom, zoom, zoom," in between cries of "Curse you!" and "Good Grief."

When our 4 ante up for Michigan rummy, it sounds like an Arab-Israeli encounter. And any game that calls for spinning an arrow is automatically on my banned list. ("It is so on the line. I can see it perfectly from here, Mom! Come tell her it's on the line and I get another spin.")

Any day now I'm going to hide the Monopoly set, permanently. I've grown accustomed to the floating crap game hubbub of the roll of the dice, and I'm patient with their impatience when it comes to understanding "Go Directly to Jail."

I manage to commiserate with the wailing tycoon who has to sell his Waterworks in order to pay the inflated rent on Boardwalk with 4 houses. I even pretend not to notice when one speculator counts his money and appraises his properties with a greedy golden gleam in his calculating eye.

What bothers me is that the game never ends. It says right there on the fourth page of the directions that the last player left in the game wins, but so far we've never gotten down to a last player.

I suspect that if you left the game set up, a team of 4 could play from January to January, with time out for living, lunching and sleeping, without ever ending a game.

Mothers as Doctors
January 26, 1971

The practice of medicine was a great deal simpler in the old days. If you were slightly sick, your family treated you. If you were very sick, they called in a doctor. If you were sicker than that, they called in a specialist--the undertaker.

If the first specialist was the undertaker, then the second one was a mother. Through the years, mothers have become adept in the diagnosis and treatment of ailments to which the flesh is heir, from the cradle to the grave.

Mothers are especially good at screening these ailments and distinguishing between those which require medical care and those which don't. For instance, if an infant who has been recently fed, burped and changed continues to cry, a mother soon guesses the cause of its suffering and responds with the proper treatment, a large dose of love.

If a toddler falls and comes screaming to its mother, she can tell at one glance whether this is a case for the emergency ward, or for that cure which wards off all emergencies, a mother's kiss.

For those mothers who are new to the practice of family medicine, let me catalog some common ailments.

Little boys frequently fall victim to an ailment which paralyzes the throat and makes it impossible for them to swallow. The condition occurs most often on warm, sunny days. It usually disappears mysteriously when Mother says, "Okay, forget the rest of the sandwich. Finish your milk and you can go back out to play with the boys."

Kindergarteners sometimes experience assorted symptoms all of which can be lumped together to produce a case of the Smalls. If his head hurts too much to go to school, if his leg hurts too much to go to school, if his tummy is too upset for him to go to school, better check to see if (1) there is a large, unleashed dog on the next block; or (2) the big boys are waiting on the corner with a snowball barrage; or (3) the school door is so heavy he can't open it, so he has to wait for a big kid to go through first, and every time he does, no matter how he scurries, the door catches up with him and he gets his sleeve caught in it as it closes and he has to wait there until another big kid comes along and opens the door again.

Children of 7, 8, and 9 occasionally come down with an eye-opening illness called the Wide-awakes. This illness hits only at bedtime, and is accompanied by a bad case of the stalls, for which repeated drinks of water and trips to the bathroom are the only treatment. The illness ends the minute the young heads finally hit the pillow.

Severe headaches are found often in little girls of 8 or 9. They seldom occur during school or play time, but always strike when the child is made to wash her hair. Age plays tricks in this malady. As the young lady gets older, she is stricken with equally severe headaches when she is, for any reason, forced to skip washing her hair.

Young men of 14 are highly susceptible to a redness of the skin which begins at the neck and spreads slowly to the hairline. It is called blushing and occurs anytime anyone looks at the young man, and is especially noticeable when young ladies are present. The only cure is for the young man to turn 15.

Young ladies in their late teens at times develop despondency and depression related to an aching sensation in the hollow organ which pumps their blood. However, the heart, as that organ is commonly known, seldom truly breaks, and usually mends rapidly upon introduction to a suitable member of the opposite sex.

Boys in the 16 to 18 bracket are subject to a strange affliction which affects the lower extremities. Suddenly their legs won't work. They can't walk, run or pedal. It hit our boy the day he got his driver's license. The loan of the family car helps to curb his symptoms, but it is clear that the only permanent cure is owning a car of his own.

Many husbands suffer a disabling disease which strikes most often on Saturday and Sunday afternoons. It causes them to collapse into a soft chair from which they are unable to rise for 4 or 5 hours. The disease is called Biggameitis and the only known cure is a broken TV set. (Note: In some severe cases, it may also be necessary to break sets belonging to your in-laws, your close neighbors, and even "Ole Grouchy Blackheart" whom your husband has refused to speak to for 7 months.)

Men and women in their 60's and 70's at times are aware of a sudden tearfulness, accompanied by a lumpiness in the throat. These symptoms respond immediately to a letter, call or visit from a son, daughter or grandchild.

Any mother consulting this catalog is warned that she herself may at times fall victim to a disease called "What Am I, Everybody's Slave?" She is warned that no one else in the family has her medical perception. Therefore, if she catches this disease, she'll have to treat it herself. A good cure is to manage to spend an hour or 2 with someone else's family. Chances are that will make her family look good.

What if Mother Were a Witch?
February 9, 1971

Whenever I get to feeling sure of myself, I remember about the kid who traded his mother and a pack of gum for a Bobby Sherman record.

And his father made him give the gum back.

It isn't that my family doesn't love me; I have last year's Valentine to prove they do:

You may have faults,
You're not the best;
But as a Mom,
You pass our test.

But every once in a while, I get this uneasy feeling that if they had a choice, my children would rather have a mother with special talents--someone like Samantha Stevens, TV's mother witch.

As for my husband, I don't think he would notice I was gone if he could pour himself a spirited Jeannie, like actress Barbara Eden, from a magical bottle whenever he chose.

Even the dog gets a silly look on its face when Nanny's little bell signals another triumph over the ordinary.

Ordinary--that's me.

"Who would you rather have--Samantha or an ordinary mother?" asks my child who can't fall asleep unless I tuck in the blanket personally.

"Hey, Sam would be neat! She could zap up anything you wanted," lusts his brother who acts as if he has been betrayed if I'm out when he slams home from school.

But you can't blame the kids. Compared to the sorcery on TV these days, even the miracle of life pales. Samantha, the chief witch of "Bewitched," twitches her nose for black and white magic (no color set at our house);

298

Jeannie, the genie the world dreams of, accomplishes her magical acts with a nod of her gorgeous blonde head; and Nanny keeps her professor and his children out of harm's way simply by flashing her ravishing smile.

(It isn't enough that these gals have a special way with children, men and puppy dogs -- in addition, they're good natured, stacked, and have no cavities.)

A merely mortal woman, even a liberated and equal one, has all she can do to compete with a bedtime story nurse who "Poppins" all the toys off the nursery floor with a sweep of her hand, and a godmother who turns pumpkins into coaches.

Every child in the world, and many an adult as well, would rather sing for his supper than work for it and the possibilities of a magical mother stagger the imagination.

"Wow, you'd never have to cook again!" marvels my stomach-happy son. "You could snap your ringers and have all the French fries you could eat."

"And any time you wanted a new dress, you could zap one up," dreams a daughter who lives in constant want of a new dress.

"Or you could go to Mexico, or Portugal or anywhere in an instant," says a child with wanderlust and a good head for geography.

It never occurs to any of them that if I were a witch with all that power I wouldn't be caught dead with 7 children. I mean, why bother to have 7, even if you could zap them up, if you could have a couple with everything?

Think of the possibilities--Kate's looks, Meg's wonderful disposition, Beth's quick mind, Ellen's creativity, Dale's athletic prowess, Mike's fiery spirit, and Drew's warm heart.

But I'm stuck with their human imperfections, and they're stuck with my human limitations. But that's not all bad. Think of the things they can learn from mere mortal me.

If you had a witch for a mother how would you ever learn that:

--Pudding scorches if you stop stirring to answer the phone.

--The car battery goes dead if you leave the lights on while you shop.

--Nylon lace melts into nothing if the hot iron touches it.

--Cake tastes like sawdust if you forget to set the timer and it cooks 15 minutes too long.

--You get a tie-dyed effect if you splash liquid bleach on your son's new jeans.

--You get a weird smell from the tires if you drive 3 blocks before you remember to release the car brake.

--The dust begins to trip you if you don't get around to vacuuming more than once a month.

--Fathers don't like it if you make left-overs out of left-overs.

--House plants quietly die if you think your daughter is watering them and she thinks you are.

--You can freeze waiting on the corner of Hagadorn and Beech if your mother thinks you said the corner of Hagadorn and Burcham.

Any day now my children are going to discover the truth about me. I don't claim to be a witch or a genie or an uncanny nanny, but you don't think I manage to stay one step ahead of a crew like mine without some kind of Special Help--do you?

The Dog and Me
February 23, 1971

She still snarls ferociously at any meterman, deliveryman, or repairman who tries to enter the house. We close her up in the dining room while they are here, and after she is set free again, she sniffs suspiciously at their invisible footprints, and barks at their memory. But she is so glad to see our children come home after they have been gone, that she bowls them over in her joy.

She still finds and licks every butter wrapper I discard, no matter how deeply I bury it in the trash pail, but she has the grace to look ashamed as I pick up the spillage.

When we're alone during the day, we respect each other's habits. I let her sleep in her spot of sunlight or in front of the oven if it is on, and she keeps track of me through half-closed lids.

If I talk to myself out loud, or sputter at some annoyance, she snorts to let me know she sympathizes.

I keep her water dish full, and she lets me know that the oil truck is outside, the mail has arrived, or a stranger is coming up the walk.

The moment Tom settles into his chair, she finds her ball and nudges him until he starts to play. She never begs me to play--she knows that's not my game.

If Tom says, "Let's go out," she heads for the door. If I suggest it, she sniffs at the weather and if it's not to her liking, she hides under the table. She knows I'll say, "Okay, don't go now if you don't want to, but let me know when you're ready." And later she does.

If I get my coat out of the front closet, she knows that means she has to leave her spot on the rug, and go into the kitchen. She knows it, but she doesn't go until I insist, all the time reproaching me with her eyes. When

I return from my errand, she is still bearing her grudge, and gives me no sign of welcome.

Instead, she runs to the closed dining room door and waits for me to restore her right to roam throughout the house. Once I have opened the door, things are right with us again.

Tom and the children are her favorites, and I still think she's a big nuisance, but there is something special between us--we understand each other.

It was quite a thorough physical, and when the doctor finally looked up and said, "Everything seems to be fine," I was glad it was over.

"Overweight is the only problem I can see," said the doctor, "I suggest more exercise."

Well, I'd heard that before, only usually someone was saying it about me. I looked down at the nervous, panting dog that it had taken 2 of us to hold down on the examining table, and suddenly it occurred to me: that dog has grown on me!

Size, yes. She used to fit in one hand. Now she's got a weight problem. But more than that, she has grown on me emotionally.

I knew it the moment I started to make excuses for her.

"It's been so cold. It's hard to run her on the ice," I murmured.

For all the years that dog has lived with us, she has been a thorn in my side, and here I was making excuses for her.

Come to think of it, I was making excuses for her from the moment we entered MSU's animal clinic.

"Hold her tightly. She's nervous in this place," I said, instead of, "Get a good grip or she'll take off cross lots after a low-flying bird."

"That's good, make her sit," I said, when all she would do was sit, and right in the doorway, no matter what we commanded or how hard we tugged.

When we entered the examining room, I made excuses to the intern.

''I guess she remembers coming here before; it'll probably take 2 to hold her."

What I should have said was, "If the 2 of us don't hold her, she'll have this place in a shambles in 2 shakes of her scared tail."

Can you believe it? I who was the victim of all her puppy indiscretions; I who gave up kitchen curtains after she clawed apart 2 sets barking a the squirrels in the trees; I who trip over her 12 times a week; I who have to get down on my hands and knees to pick up the fur she sheds by the handful; I who never wanted a dog in the first place; I unbelievably have finally accepted that fool dog!

301

In truth, she's not the pesky troublemaker she used to be. Middle age has slowed her down and mellowed her.

She still rushes from window to window, barking at the neighbor's cat, leaving claw grooves behind her in the sills, but she spends a lot of her day snoozing peacefully.

Predicting the Weather
March 9, 1971

Most people blame the weather on the weatherman. Otherwise reasonable men have been heard to mutter, "If that irresponsible (polite translation) weatherman had kept his word, I'd be playing golf today instead of shoveling snow."

And many a woman is more likely to forgive infidelity in her mate than in the weatherman: "The weatherman PROMISED sunshine for Saturday, and he wouldn't DARE let it rain on Susie's garden wedding!"

To my children, the "weathermen" today are a bunch of hot heads who sit around in basements and knit bomb fuses, so they blame the weather on me.

"You said it would be warmer this afternoon and I could wear my baseball jacket to school instead of that hot old winter coat."

(That "hot old winter coat" is the same one he was wearing last week when he declared, through chattering teeth, "I froze all the way home. How come I gotta wear this flimsy rag all winter?")

My children don't know it, but I was a sort of weatherman (dealing in predictions, not bombs) once a long time ago. Everyday I prepared the abbreviated weather forecast which ran in the top left corner of the front page of the paper I worked for in New York State. The information came to us from the state capital, some 90 miles away, and my editor's charge never varied from day to day:

"Trim this to 2 lines, and for gosh sakes look out the window, will ya!"

I understand and appreciate the fact that weather prediction is an exact science, based on information gathered at substations the world around, but more often than not the "sunny skies" of the scientific bulletins I received differed widely from the heavy rains outside my editor's window. And in 2 lines you couldn't go into all that stuff about low pressure areas moving in from Canada (always Canada!), so I leaned heavily on pivotal words, such as some, possible and partly.

If there was any difference between the bulletin and the view from my window, I chose a safe middle line. I changed "sunny" to "some sunshine"; I altered "cloudy" to read "partly cloudy"; and I changed "rain," to "possible precipitation."

I'd read somewhere that similar ambiguity had assured the prophecies of the Delphi oracles, so I figured I was in good company. Whenever there was real doubt in my mind, I always chose the pessimistic view, figuring my readers would sooner forgive a sudden burst of sunshine than an unexpected thundershower. My batting average was pretty good, and once we even got a "Letter to the Editor" saying, "How come you guys always hit the weather right on the nose, and that nincompoop on the radio is always a mile off base?"

Unfortunately, we couldn't print the letter because it wasn't signed. I always figured it came from the boss of "that nincompoop," and maybe the radio station didn't have a window handy.

All ambiguities considered, it's better my children shouldn't know about this part of MY past. Of course, forecasting for children is highly specialized and calls for special knowledge such as the following:

--Boys stay hotter coming home from school than girls, because boys run, jump, hop, climb, shinny and tumble instead of walking.

--A girl who is happy about wearing her new poncho will be warm even if the temperature dips to zero.

--A boy is more comfortable in a long-sleeved shirt because it saves him the trouble of washing his elbows.

--A girl doesn't mind carrying an umbrella when it is "partly cloudy," but a boy won't wear his rubbers even if you predict a hurricane and the puddles are already up to the dog's knees.

--March may have its ups and downs, but you can tell spring is coming because the boys have their minds on baseball, and the girls have their minds on the boys.

The forecast from my window for East Lansing and surrounding towns is as follows: Some of everything; partly good, partly bad; and possibly changing.

"Everything You've Always Wanted to Know..."
March 23, 1971

The most popular items in today's newspapers seem to be the question and answer columns such as Ann Landers, the Doctor's Bag, etc. In an effort to keep up with the trend, today's column is called "Everything You

Always Wanted to Know About, But Were Afraid to Ask Because You Knew You Wouldn't Like the Answers."

Q. Is it true that love makes the world go around?

A. Yes, haven't you noticed how dizzy lovers act?

Q. What are the chances for young marriages?

A. All marriages are young in the beginning, but nothing ages faster.

Q. Do children make a marriage?

A. Usually it's the other way around.

Q. Surely a child adds to a marriage?

A. It does if 2 plus 1 still make 3.

Q. Does it really cost between $19,000 and $25,000 to raise a child to age 18?

A. Yes, and that's only the money part of it.

Q. In view of what it costs parents to raise children, don't the children owe their parents something in return?

A. There is much disagreement on this subject, mostly between children and parents, but most parents say they'd settle for a little "interest."

Q. Shouldn't parents demand a little respect from their children?

A. No. If they ask for a little, that's all they'll get. They should demand a lot.

Q. How much say should parents have in their children's lives?

A. About a third as much as they'd like to have.

Q. What is the real difference between the generations?

A. Several years.

Q. Are parents ever wrong?

A. Weren't yours?

Q. How do you judge a good teacher?

A. Discreetly, lest the teacher start to judge you as a good parent.

Q. Do you think children need as many school holidays and vacations as they are getting now?

A. No, but the teachers do.

Q. Does today's 16-year-old really need to know more than we did at that age?

A. Yes, and he'll need to know more than we do at our age, too.

Q. What period of growing up do you consider the hardest?

A. The period from hour to hour.

Q. Aren't today's kids more selfish than we were?

A. Some are more selfish; others are only more honest about being selfish.

Q. What do kids see in communes?

A. Others like themselves.

Q. What is the meaning of relevance?

A. Meaning.

Q. What makes today's kids so stubborn, arrogant and hard to live with?

A. Yesterday's kids. (Pass it on!)

Q. Will today's kids eventually turn out to be just like their parents?

A. If we're not careful.

Flying Kites
April 6, 1971

Everybody knows that what goes up must come down, but how do you get your kite to go up in the first place? Simple: You get Daddy to help you.

Simple, that is, for everyone except Daddy.

Picture the scene: It is a cool, clear Sunday afternoon in early spring, and Daddy is doing what every other child-loving father is doing on such a day. He is watching a sporting encounter on TV and ignoring the children. Occasionally, he favors them with a look of parental pride and an encouraging, "Hey, keep it down, you guys!"

The children have new kites and new string and they are busily applying the latter to the former, but this proves to be a knotty problem and before long they clamor for parental aid. By working diligently during the commercials, and missing the winning play entirely, Daddy finally gets everyone's equipment rigged for a trial run. Naturally, the kids think the time for that is right now.

Everybody knows that you can't fly a kite out in front of your house because of the danger from the power lines, so Daddy trudges up to the high school field, trailed by 4 kids, 4 kites, and 4 million yards of string.

Two hours later, the entourage returns, minus one kite, with the verdict: the equipment was worthy, the wind was great, and father should have been an octopus.

First of all, kites do not simply leap into the wind and fly. To launch a kite, one must run, hoist, aim, and let out string all at the same time. If he is properly coordinated, and does not get winded easily, a father who remembers his boyhood usually can get a kite airborne on about the fourth running, hoisting, aiming and letting-out try.

So much for one kite and one kid.

"I'm next, Daddy, but my string is all tangled up."

In a couple of wind-blown minutes, Daddy is all tangled up too. Kite becomes a 4-letter word, with strings attached. But eventually, and without too much loss of innocence, the group gets all 4 kites up.

Suddenly, one is up, up and away.

"Daddy! Daddy! It's getting awaaaaaay!"

Daddy leap-frogs over the desolate former kiter. He sprints and grasps, only to find himself with an ache in his side and a handful of air. Then, in one last desperate try, he launches his whole body skyward and just as his 6' 4" frame is settling back to earth, Mr. Wind hiccups, and the slender thread falls gently into Daddy's hand.

"He got it! He got it! Daddy got it!"

But Mr. Wind is not so easily thwarted. In a few minutes he whips playfully over the field, snaps a string, and lands a kite smack in a tree. The tree resists all manner of threat from below. It dangles the captured kite like a tantalizing morsel from a sky-scraping limit, and trembles in gustatory anticipation.

The children accept the truth--it is a kite-eating tree.

Daddy promises to buy another kite, and before the next Sunday, he does. This time he buys a box kite. He buys one and only one box kite. He has learned that he does not have arms, legs or wind enough to launch more than one kite at a time.

The box kite is a lulu. It goes higher than the kites the children had last week. When it gets going real good, Daddy has to hold tight to the little boy sailing it--so that the boy doesn't glide right up into the sky with the kite.

Helping 4 kids take turns at flying one box kite is even more exhausting than launching 4 regular kites, Daddy learns. When it suddenly crashes, he is not sorry, even though it cost 79 cents.

Before the next Sunday rolls around, Daddy gets the stilts down from the garage attic and leaves them carelessly in the garage doorway.

"Hey, Dad! Look at me, I'm tall as the sky!"

Stilts they can handle alone.

Volunteering Your Mom
April 20, 1971

One of the first things a child learns in school is to volunteer.

"Who wants to pass out the cookies?" asks the teacher on the first day of kindergarten.

She is stampeded. The second day, she posts a chart of jobs and from then on the volunteers do the honors in rotation, and hardly anybody has to go to the nurse's office as a result of being trampled.

Having learned "How to Volunteer," the children are now ready for Lesson 2, "How to Volunteer Your Mother."

For some reason, my children have shown a special aptitude for this particular subject. The first grammatically correct sentence my son with the sloppy speech habits ever put together was, "My mother will do it."

And one of my daughters has a right arm that's 3 inches longer than her left, from shooting it up in the air every time the teacher says, "Raise your hand if your mother can . . ."

The hand is up before the teacher ever gets around to mentioning the job. But no matter what the task at hand, my children are sure their mother can (and will) do it.

Don't think I'm the only mother who gets volunteered to help out. Actually there are 3 or 4 of us regulars. We smile and exchange pleasantries as we rush past each other in the school hallways.

"Driving tomorrow for the 2nd grade zoo trip?"

"No, I promised to help the 3rd graders make candy apples."

We have a lot in common, such as daughters with one arm longer than the other, and little boys with big mouths. We all have large families, too. Mothers with small families seldom get volunteered for school jobs because they usually have something better to do with their time.

"Suzie, is your mother making cookies for the class party?" I ask innocently.

"Gosh, no, Mrs. Naybor. My mother Works," pronounces Suzie, importantly.

"Ann, is your mother helping with the ear tests on Monday?"

"Mrs. Naybor, you know my mother Takes Classes," scolds Ann.

Everybody knows that if a mother Works or Takes Classes she doesn't have to volunteer. Once in a while, a Working Mother will volunteer--usually to do the telephoning to round up other volunteers. The other night, one such Working Mother called my friend, Jane, for 2 dozen cupcakes.

"Your little girl said you would make them, but if you work, say so and I'll ask someone else," said Mrs. Caller.

"Work? No, I just sit around the house all day, cooking for 10, chasing 3 kids in diapers, and presoaking the sheets from the 8 beds in this house," Jane assured her.

"Oh, good, you're the woman we want. Say, could you make that 3 dozen cupcakes instead of 2?"

One way to get your children to stop volunteering your services is to let them know that there are some things you cannot do. The smarter a parent is, the sooner she makes it clear to her children that she does not know everything, and that in some matters she is downright dumb. Right from infancy, you have to keep telling them, "I don't know." Interlace this with an occasional "I don't know why," and put special emphasis on "I don't know how," and you're in.

Then when your 4th grader comes home with the news that "They want parents to teach special skills in X-Hour," you'll be ready.

"Gosh, Mom, there are 51 skills on the list. Which one do you want to teach? There's rocketry, and macramé, and even underwater exploration!"

"Listen, all I know about underwater exploration is that if I put my hand in the washer with your clothes I'm likely to come up with anything from a petrified toad to Jacques Cousteau."

"How about teaching Indian crafts?"

"I don't . . ."

"Or sculpture?"

"I don't know . . ."

"Music composition?"

"I don't know how ... "

"Modern dance?"

"I ache all over."

"Okay. How about teaching survival in the wilderness?"

"Dear child, I'm barely surviving in civilization!"

"But Mom, don't you know anything?"

"Of course I do. I know when to say no."

"About X-Hour ...?"

"No."

Mother's Day Every Day
May 4, 1971

At 6:30 on a Monday morning
When J. P. McCarthy [a radio personality on WJR Radio, Detroit] prods me out of
The warm and dreamy half-sleep of dawn,
I have to force myself
To open my reluctant eyes
And face the start of a brand new week.

Then Tom rolls over and mumbles that
He has no meetings until 10
So he thinks he'll sleep in a while,
And one of my slippers
Is so far under the bed that I must
Get down on my stomach to reach it,

And Kate steams up the bathroom,
So that the wallpaper peels a little
Right over the mirror where I'll see it
Every morning for the next 3 years,
And Dale can find only one of
His lucky track socks for the big meet;

And we are a little short of milk
And there are only 3 eggs
And the toast burns black, automatically,
And Meg's pigtails are a snarled mess
And Beth has lost her permission slip
For the Girl Scout outing;

And Ellen calls from the dormitory
To say her tuition is due tomorrow and
Will I please remember to get
The check out today, and would it
Be possible to switch
Her dentist appointment to Tuesday;

And Mike rips the top button
Off his only clean shirt
Just as Drew barfs his whole breakfast
Right into my lap,
Then I am not sure that I am happy
Being a wife and mother.

So I think of how exhilarating
It would be to be liberated, equal,
And feminine, and wear pantsuits
To a job where others would know
That I am worth a nice big salary
And give me 2 coffee breaks a day;

And send me inter-departmental
Memos seeking my opinions
On matters of amalgamation,
Or wine and dine me up at Jake's
To try to lure me from my firm
To theirs, because they need my brain;

And in between the tasks of signing
Everything in triplicate
I'd paint or sculpt creatively,
And I'd draft a peace for now
That all nations would agree to,
And then I'd spend the evening dancing.

But it's very possible that
I would miss the nightly check I make
Of tousled, tired little heads,
And the strong and loving arms
That welcome me to bed and keep me
Safe and warm until morning comes,

So I would not, could not change.

Holiday Weekends
June 1, 1971

Some people like to whoop it up during holiday weekends; others would rather just sit back and rest.

We found out last weekend that our family splits right down the age line on the subject. All those under 21 want to keep busy every minute in a sort of marathon fun-in. Those over 21 would rather forget it.

The over 21s (way over) are Tom and I and we're outnumbered by the unders, but fortunately little things such as holding the purse strings and the keys to the car tip the balance in our favor.

If I'd had my way, the holiday part of last weekend would have been a secret. We could have had a normal Saturday, beginning with me sleeping late and the kids watching cartoons and spilling orange juice and then stepping in it.

Later we could have returned all our overdue books to the library ($2.14 in fines) and picked up my raincoat from the cleaners.

Finally, after the kids had flooded the bathroom floor and mopped it up with the guest towels, they could have gone to bed and left us to recuperate in peace.

Sunday we might have picked up some of Colonel Sander's best after church, and by the time the kids had explained the comics to each other, that day would have ended restfully too.

Monday would have been the surprise. Monday is the day none of the kids can ever seem to wake up, so this Monday I would have just let them sleep. When they finally came to, about 10:30 or 11, I would have let them get up and dress (allowing one hour for each shoe), before I broke the good news: no school today. They'd be so stunned, they'd lie around thinking about their good fortune all the rest of the day.

By the time they came to, it would have been Tuesday, and they'd have been back in school and never known they missed a chance to have a roaring three-day weekend.

But somebody goofed. Somebody told the kids a holiday weekend was coming up. (I suspect the teachers were getting even.) Naturally, the first thing they wanted to know was could they all have new catcher's mitts and/or purple peasant dresses. When we established that it definitely was not a gift-giving kind of a holiday, they wanted to know could we go swimming, camping, boating, fishing and horseback riding, with a bit of miniature golf, a baseball game and a barbeque thrown in on the side. All on the first day, of course.

Luckily the weather was uncertain. One thing you can be certain of in Michigan is that the weather will be uncertain. So we said let's play it by ear. No promises.

Children's idea of playing it by ear is listening to the neighbors' plans and filling our ears with what they hear.

"Jimmy's family is going to Mackinac. Could we go to Mackinac?"

"We'll think about it."

"Sally's mother and daddy are taking their kids on a bike hike to Ludington. Could we do that?"

"We'll think about it."

"The Quinns are going to fly to San Jewwan. Where's San Jewwan?"

"We'll think about it."

Naturally, we tend to think slowly about any kind of venture that threatens our holiday leisure and that pretty well uses up Saturday, except that we make it perfectly plain that Sunday is a day of rest and we expect them to do lots of it.

On Sunday, when they get a little bit restless, we point out that Monday after all is the real holiday and that would be the day to do something.

Of course, on Monday we've bought it. We can either plead a headache, or give in to the kids and end up with one. Either way, we're glad to see Tuesday.

By the way, how you vote is your business, but when you hear rumors about a 4-day weekend, step on them quick!

Graduation Speeches
June 15, 1971

Graduation speeches are falling on many ears this month, and each listener, even as the inhabitants of Mesopotamia, Judea, Cappadocia, Pontus, Egypt, and Cyrene, hears the miraculous flaming wind in his own tongue.

SPEAKER: ON THIS GLORIOUS DAY...

Chaplain: Lord, I hoped you'd answer when I prayed for warm weather, but is 98 degrees and sticky an answer or a judgment?

Principal: If a cloudburst would come just as we give out the first diploma, we could call the whole thing off and mail out the rest.

Grandma: If I'd known we'd have to sit in the sun on bleachers, I would have stayed at the lake and sent Junior a check,

Girl Graduate: Boy, I'm glad I listened to Susie. A bikini is the only thing to wear under these robes.

SPEAKER: WE HAIL YOUTH'S NEVER-SATED HUNGER FOR KNOWLEDGE, ENLIGHTENMENT, AND...

Mother: Ham salad, sliced turkey, cheese, relishes and jello mousse. Hmm, I wonder if I bought enough rolls--George's relatives eat like truck drivers.

SPEAKER: WHAT ABOUT TOMORROW?

Boy Graduate: I'm going to sleep until noon.

Father of Boy Graduate: If he isn't up looking for a job by 7, he'll hear a post-graduation speech from me.

SPEAKER: NEVER A GENERATION SO GIFTED...

Aunt Maude: I wonder if I should have gotten the $70 watch instead of the $55 graduate special. Harold looked so pleased..

Harold: After Aunt Maude leaves, I'll talk Mom into letting me exchange the watch. I need the bread.

SPEAKER: EYES LIFTED TO DISTANT HORIZONS...

32 Graduates: A commune in Arizona for me, man. I'm probably the only kid in this group who knows where it's at.

SPEAKER: FORMING LASTING RELATIONSHIPS...

Mother: My baby's going to be married...

Boy Graduate: What made her think I meant marriage?

Girl Graduate: Maybe he never did actually say marriage--but he will.

SPEAKER: OUT INTO THE WORLD...

Dean Of Students: Sorry about that, we really couldn't keep Clarence back another year...

Clarence: Gosh, I just learned the way to the cafeteria.

SPEAKER: FOCUSING ON NEW PROBLEMS...

Uncle Henry: If that blonde with the 2 fuzzy heads would move just a little to the right, I could get a great shot of Tommy.

Tommy: I sure hope Uncle Henry isn't stewed again. When he took pictures at my confirmation even the bishop came out tipsy.

SPEAKER: WITH GRATITUDE FOR GUIDANCE...

Principal: I wonder who we can stick as class adviser next year.

Class Adviser: Never again.

SPEAKER: INSPIRED BY LEADERSHIP...

Grandpa: And after I write 2 more letters to the editor complaining about Nixon and Agnew, I'm going to start a new series on Johnson. .

SPEAKER: BOWED BY WEIGHTY CONCERNS...

Blonde with 2 Fuzzy Heads: My girdle is killing me.

SPEAKER: JOINT EFFORTS AND SHARED JOYS...

Athlete: Sure, I set up all the plays and old Tanglefoot got the award.

Coach: Next year we'll rebuild the team. And next year, and the next...

SPEAKER: THIS TIME OF DECISION...

Graduate: Like I got principles. But for $8,500 a year I might even consider getting a crew cut.

Vice president of the bank: Hair or no hair, his father's the president, so he gets the job.

SPEAKER: ZELDINA ZABLEWSKY, CONGRATULATIONS AND GOOD LUCK!

Audience: Wake up, Grandpa, it's time to go.

Summers Can Be Too Long
June 29, 1971

To the poet, summer is a fleeting moment. Even to ordinary mortal Michiganders, it sometimes seems that June and September are back to back.

But that is an illusion; summer progresses one day at a time, just like any other season. In fact, there are even some occasions when summer looms too long, too hot and tedious, too.

For instance:

--When the "creative" child from down the street, who knows more ways to be noisy than a firecracker, tells you his family isn't going away this summer, and he'll be around every day.

--When there is drought all around, but the day you plan a garden party, it rains.

--When your children, whom you've promised to take swimming at 3, start asking at 10 if it's almost time to go.

--When 3 different sets of relatives promise to spend the night with you on their way west--the same night.

--When your daughters sort their closets of everything that doesn't fit, leaving them each with 2 semi-decent outfits, and a tremendous need to shop.

--When the students in the house down the block mount a stereo speaker in their window--facing out.

--When a squirrel develops a fascination for your dog and sits out front wagging its tail while the dog goes loudly mad, running from one window to the other.

--When the mint you wanted just a patch of goes wild and takes over the flower bed.

--When you could strangle the parents of the kids bellowing outside your window at 7 a.m., and they turn out to be your kids.

--When your weekly hairdo, which normally keeps you respectable for 4 or 5 days, wilts after 2.

--When, just as your cousin's 5 kids arrive, the club pool needs draining, and is closed for the week.

--When a window which usually won't stay open, jams and won't close during a 10-minute monsoon.

--When the huge supply of cold drinks you buy for the month disappears after 4 thirsty days.

--When the trash men miss one can (the one you filled with watermelon rinds, potato peels and chicken innards the day the disposal broke down), leaving you with foul odors, flies and maggots.

--When the kids gather in a circle around you, shutting out the feeble breeze, and moan listlessly, "What can we do now?"

--When construction starts up the way, and 30 dump trucks take turns rumbling by from dawn 'til dusk, blowing liberal samples of 15 kinds of Michigan dirt through your windows.

--When you take a cottage 400 miles away to get away from it all, and you discover you brought it all with you.

The Appraisers Are Coming!
July 13, 1971

There is something about having appraisers in town that makes every homeowner feel as if he ought to hide something--if only dust.

Ever since the city council announced that they hired 4 men to go door to door evaluating property, homeowners have jumped at the doorbell.

Take Carolynn Curtiss. Carolynn is your average East Lansing good citizen, most days. One morning Carolynn stopped to talk across the fence with Bernice.

"I suppose they'll be over on your block next," said Bernice.

"Who?" asked Carolynn.

"The appraisers," said Bernice. "One was here yesterday. Went all through the house and...Carolynn, where are you going in such a hurry?"

Carolynn never answered. She dashed home, slammed the door, locked it, pulled down the shades and called Bert at the office.

"Bert, come home!" she wailed.

"Carolynn, what's wrong? For Pete's sake, Carolynn, stop saying 'Come home!' and tell me what's wrong."

"Oh, Bert, they're coming. They were at Bernice's and they'll be here anytime now. Oh, Bert, what are we going to do?"

At this point, Bert gave up trying to figure out what the crises was and ran the 6 blocks home. He pounded on the door, wondering if he should have alerted the police or called an ambulance.

"Carolynn, let me in! Carolynn, can you hear me?"

Carolynn opened the door slowly and looked up and down the street.

"Do you see them? Hide the car and come in, quick," whispered Carolynn. "They mustn't see we're home. We can't let them in."

Bert, bursting with fear and worry, exploded, "Who? Carolynn, who are you talking about?"

"The appraisers, Bert, the appraisers are on our street and I refuse to let them in until you paint that downstairs bathroom. I've been after you for 3 years and now I've had it. No appraiser is going to see our house with a cracked ceiling in the downstairs bathroom."

"But, Carolynn," said Bert, when his rage subsided and he could talk again, "a cracked ceiling is the best thing in the world for an appraiser to see. You know how high our taxes are now!"

Carolynn looked confused.

"But Bert, what will he tell his wife?"

In another part of town, the Jaggers took the news with outward calmness.

"Appraisers in the neighborhood," said Nick to Sally.

"I know, Dear. Jane and I have it all worked out. All 12 kids will mill around in her house when they come to her door, and then the mob will come over here and follow the appraiser from room to room. With all those kids around, things are bound to look shabby."

"Suppose they catch on that they are the same kids?"

"Come on, Nick, sometimes even you can't tell which are Jane's and which are ours."

"I guess you're right. Anyway, be sure you leave the beds unmade and don't clear the table, and scatter toys around on the stairs. Maybe it'll take their mind off the new aluminum siding."

Mabel Schale looked forward to the appraiser's visit.

"Come in, Dearie. Are you Bill, Bob, Russ or Roy? I can't help feeling I've met you boys before. Something about those names. How about some tea? Tell me, Roy, oh sorry, Russ, what did you think of the Rogers' property? Ever see a mess like that before? Imagine asking $39,500 for that shack!

"Now the Jones place is older, but they've added on; cost them a pretty penny, too. What would you say that's worth, give or take a few thousand. I know you're not supposed to say, but I'm so interested."

"Shame about the Wilsons. They didn't tell you? Well, just one thing after another went wrong, and they've had to put in a new furnace, 2 new bathrooms, a new kitchen and they put down new floors in 2 other rooms. But at least they'll have something worth selling if they go ahead with the divorce. Noticed a little coolness, I suppose, when you spoke to them?"

"My, you are a close-mouthed one. Well, let me know if you can't get in some of the houses down below. I can tell you all you need to know."

"And more," muttered Roy--or Russ--as he scrambled out the door.

At the Davis house, little Marvin answered the door.

"Is your mother at home, little boy?"

"Naw, Who are you?"

"I'm the appraiser. Is your father in?"

"Yeah, in the shower. Whatta ya want?"

"I want to look at your house to see how much it's worth. But I can come back in a little while."

"Oh I can tell you that. We paid $42,500, but Grandma says Daddy got rooked on it like he does on everything he buys. Grandma says Daddy never... Hey, Mister, don't cha want to hear about the house?"

At our house my husband commented on the fact that I took the appraisal right in stride. What he said was, "Hey, how come all that dust is gone from under our bed?"

Mother Gets a College Education
July 28, 1971

A mother learns a lot when her daughter goes to college.

In my own case, my daughter hadn't been at MSU a week before I took a new interest in books. The first book I found myself studying was my checkbook.

I brushed up on my math, but I need not have bothered. I know now, as she finishes her second college year, that checkbook math, on the college level, is very simple: first you pay for tuition, board and room, and books, and then the family scrapes along on what's left.

One book leads to another, I always say, and my empty checkbook led me automatically to volumes such as "Cooking for Less Than Nothing," "Last Year's Midi is This Year's Mini," "How to Make Hot Pants Out of Torn Pants," and "Walking is Good for Your Health" (especially when it's a choice between gas and food).

After rediscovering math and reading, I turned to vocabulary and spelling.

"What's the word from our college girl?" asks Grandma in all her letters. "What do you hear from her?"

I get out the dictionary and write back:

"The word from our coed is good, but multi-syllabic. What I hear is a syncretistic cacophony about interpersonal relationships, national conscience, structural fluidity, moral commitment, cross-cultural communication, immediate withdrawal, projected psychological manifestations, corporate connivance, morphology, sociology, anthropology and cafeteria goulash, interspersed by an occasional "wow!" and a frequent "I've got to run now, I'll call you back."

The most startling word I heard from my daughter all term was mononucleosis. Mono, as most people refer to it after looking it up twice (once to find out what it is, and once to find out how to spell it in that letter to Grandma), isn't exactly required in college. But hardly anyone manages to graduate without it.

Our coed was fortunate. She got mono during Spring Break.

"What a lucky break," we kept saying.

"What a lousy break," she kept mumbling.

But it was a light case and soon she was back in the dorm.

Speaking of dormitories, and who isn't these days, I used to have trouble remembering which wing was for boys and which was for girls. But I have that solved now.

If you walk along a hall and see someone with lovely long blond hair, who is dressed in a ruffled shirt, bell-bottomed jeans and sandals, that is a boy and this is the girl's wing.

If you are walking along and you see what looks like the same person, only instead of a pretty ruffled shirt it is wearing what looks like a dye-stained copy of Wallace Beery's undershirt, that is a girl. Naturally she and you are in the men's wing.

Another thing I learned since my daughter went to college is not to jump to conclusions. Once I called her dorm room at 6:30 in the morning.

"Lo," said a sleepy bass voice.

"Wrong number, I hope," I gulped, and hung up immediately.

I spent the rest of the morning trying to decide whether to try dialing again, or whether to call cither a policeman, a priest, or Grandma.

Later in the day my daughter called me.

"Hi," she yawned into the phone.

"Humph," I humphed.

"I didn't get much sleep last night," she said.

Where did I go wrong, I asked myself and Saints Veronica, Cecielia, Anastasia and Lucia.

"Cindy's kid brother was here so he took my bed and I went up to sleep on the floor in Carol's room," she went on. "But poor kid, he didn't get much sleep either. Some weirdo woman got him out of bed at 6:30 to answer a wrong number. Gosh, some people!"

My daughter has 2 more years of college to go. By then my education should be complete.

Summer Cottages
August 3, 1971

"Thank God, that's over! I've never been so glad to see the end of anything in all my life!"

If you overhear a woman making the above statement, is she glad because:

A. She has just been granted a divorce, or

B. Her son and daughter-in-law and their 6 children have just left after a 3-week visit, or

C. She and her husband have just sold their summer cottage.

Answer A is right if when she spoke she had a slight twinge of uncertainty in her voice.

Answer B is right if she had a minute touch of guilt about her.

But if her voice was bright and clear, her tone was firm and positive, and her resolve was unmistakable, then the answer is C.

The summer cottage is a strange phenomenon. Frequently, after a family has acquired a 2nd child, a 2nd pet and a 2nd car, they begin to feel the need for a 2nd mortgage.

Some couples start to prepare for this acquisition early in their married life. When they buy their 2nd set of everyday dishes, they carefully pack away the first set "for when we buy a cottage." When their first refrigerator breaks down, they have it repaired and keep it in the basement, for the cottage. Eventually, the house becomes so crowded that a 2nd one is no longer a luxury, but a necessity.

A cottage can be anything from a lean-to with a one-holer, to a house 2 feet smaller than the White House. Whatever its size, there is one thing it must have: water. Not running water, necessarily, but water for swimming, boating, fishing, or at least watching.

In Michigan, it is possible to own a fancier summer house than a year-around house. In the northern areas, there are hundreds of lovely mansions built by the very wealthy as "cottages." Some have as many as 10 to 20 rooms, and servants' quarters. Many of these have been abandoned by the rich for more fashionable shores, and while their ownership is now less prestigious, their facades are not.

Having acquired a summer place, the next move of the owners is to let everyone know about it. The announcement goes something like this:

"We're going to be away all summer. We've bought a new place up north. It's beautiful--we can't wait to start fixing it up a little. You MUST come to see us. We insist! We'll be so lonely up there. There's plenty of room; bring the whole family. We've got a boat too."

Now if you can find all the errors in that paragraph, you're smarter to begin with than most cottage owners.

Mistake 1: "All summer..." Some summers you'll hardly get to the cottage at all, but you'll pay the taxes on schedule anyway.

Mistake 2: "A new place..." When you start to fix up the place, you'll realize how very old it actually is and how expensive it is to repair even fine-quality old things.

Mistake 3: All the words from "You must come," to "whole family." If you insist on making such invitations, you will never have time to be lonely. You'll be too busy commuting to work to make enough money to feed everyone who comes. Also, if there's "plenty of room," how come you're sleeping out on the screened porch?

Mistake 4: "We've got a boat . . ." That may have looked like a boat the day you signed on the dotted line, but when your visitors line up for the maiden voyage, you'll discover it's really a precious old antique and should never be moved, for fear of instant disintegration.

Children's reactions to cottages are mixed. Before you buy one they think they are deprived and announce that an early death would be preferable to another summer without one. After you buy, they spend the next few winters thinking up excuses for not going to it every summer.

"We went there last year."

"There's nobody groovy up there."

"I think we ought to travel and broaden our horizons."

"My girl is down here."

Or even, in desperation, "I'm thinking of getting a job."

After they marry and become parents, their attitude changes.

"You're not thinking of selling it? All my childhood memories are up there. I want my sons to enjoy it as I did. How can you look at that view and think of giving it up?"

Most of these remarks condense to "Where else can I take my family so cheaply?"

Which brings me to my final observation on cottages: They're a nice place to visit, and you're lucky if you have a relative who owns one.

Travel Advice
August 10, 1971

Everyone who takes a trip comes home a travel expert. With thousands of feet of film, hundreds of slides, or even his collection of restaurant placemats, he is ready to tell you where to go, until you want to tell him where to go

Wherever you are thinking of going, he has been there, or he had a friend who went there once, and honestly, you wouldn't like it.

"I could write a book about my travel experiences," he gushes, after his weekend in Kalamazoo.

So why should I be any different?

Experienced writers tell me that the title of a book is frequently the last order of business. But since it's the first thing a person reads, I firmly insist it's the first thing one ought to write. So I wrote a title.

To give the reader an idea of the kind of travel experiences I've had, I'm going to call the book "Home Sweet Home."

The Table of Contents alone should be required reading for anyone planning to travel even across town Read on:

Chapter I: Hints on Packing. Sect. A: If you take all that along, you might as well rent the house unfurnished. Sect. B: Don't worry about forgetting a necessity, because you will anyway.

Chapter II: Planning Your Route. Sect. A: Doesn't anyone in this family know how to read a map? Sect. B: A detour seldom if ever is a short cut. Sect. C: One thing about railroads, they never went to Cuba.

Chapter III: Understanding Signs. Sect. A: Wherein we learn about understatement (Hairpin curve, No guard rails, Use lower gear), and that strange feeling in the pit of your stomach is fear.

Chapter IV: Foreign Countries. Sect. A: Drink the water, eat the food, and talk to strangers. Sect. B: Nobody said you had to live forever.

Chapter V: Traveling with Children. Sect. A: Laundromats I have known. Sect. B: How to ask for Pampers in French. Sect. C: How to get the smell of vomited milk out of the car upholstery.

Chapter VI: Come Fly with Me. Sect. A: Spandex is not a girdle, it is a Spanish airline (but when you see how tight the seats are packed in, you may wish it was a 2-way stretch. Sect B: But, Darling, she is speaking in English. Sect. C: No, you can't get there from here; yes, you can get there from there, but you can't get there from here. Sect D: Madame, this IS first class.

Chapter VII: Finding a Restroom. Sect A: Would you believe under the front stairs at the Lincoln Memorial? Sect. B: Save those big British pennies for Victoria Station. Sect C: When in Rome don't be surprised if His and Hers turn out to be Everybody's.

Chapter VIII: Food on the Go. Sect. A: If Colonel Sanders hasn't come to town, why did we? Sect B: The supermarket is open 24 hours a day in El Toro, California. Why did we come to Florida? Sect. C: Anguila means eel. Pay the man anyway.

Chapter IX: Wild Woods Beckon the Nature Lover. Sect. A: Back-packing is pretty rough on the little woman, but don't worry, one more day and she'll be too tired to complain. Sect. B: Worm recipes for unlucky fishermen. Sect. C: Mosquitoes, gnats, black flies, spiders, and other friends of the forest. Sect. D: Matches versus Boy Scouts.

Wilderness Survival
September 7, 1971

Every time I pick up a paper, I read about an experiment in survival. For me, just getting from one day to the next is an experiment in survival. But these people are doing it the hard way--no combs, razors, tooth paste, sleeping bags, food, TV--not even foot powder!

At MSU several students went off into the wilds to live off the land. Elsewhere, young couples went native to measure their marriages. (Marriage--that's the real test of survival.) In another part of the forest, several families are trying their hand at roughing it as a community.

I find it all very interesting, but it makes me uneasy. What, I wonder, do they know that I don't know? And, if they do know something, do I really want to know about it?

I'm just not the survival type. Even with 3 meals a day, a foam rubber mattress, arch-support shoes, and a lifetime supply of penicillin, I don't expect to survive to sign up for Social Security.

And if I were stranded on a desert island with enough water and bananas for 20 years, I'd probably become allergic to bananas the first day and die within a week. I suffered just reading Robinson Crusoe.

The specifications for the MSU group were too stiff for me to begin with. The prerequisites were "Stability and maturity," and "the ability to live off insect larvae, snakes, frogs, snails, snowshoe rabbits or grouse."

"My problem is that I am too stable and too mature to start living off creepy crawlers and squiggly things. I'm pretty good at pretending I don't see the fly in my dinner but if the fly IS the dinner--well, there'd be no sense in my getting it down. It wouldn't stay down long enough to turn into protein anyway.

There is a lot to be said for a vegetarian diet, especially if you've ever had to kill a chicken or smelled the hot blood and guts of a freshly killed hare. Years ago I remember eating woodchuck stew. The meat was tough, stringy and gamey, but it had been camouflaged by a hot, spicy tomato sauce, onions, carrots, potatoes, peas, mushrooms, a liberal sprinkling of parmesan cheese and a smart dollop of white wine.

I remember telling my mother that it would have been just great if she had left out the woodchuck. I suspect she agreed, but the hunter had come home with his kill, and like many good wives before her, she had made the best of it, woodchuck cacciatore.

Of course vegetables can be tricky. Somehow the pictures of the poisonous mushrooms look just like the pictures of the coveted morel to me. My education in the toxicity of flora and fauna is sorely lacking. I never knew, until I read it in an Agatha Christie thriller, that yew berries can kill. (I'm almost sure I ate a few of those when I was younger.)

The MSU group were allowed to carry a 6 by 8 by 3 inch pack, including a poncho and matches and a knife. I'd be tempted to fill my pack with good Scotch, about 125 proof, strong enough to unpollute any water I might find, or to pollute me enough so I couldn't care less.

If I had my choice of any small, compact item I could be marooned with, I'd pass up the poncho, the matches and the knife, and pack up an 8-year-old boy to take along. Small boys have just enough guile to track a frog, just enough agility to trap one, just enough curiosity to kill one, and just enough hunger to eat one.

But if he could manage the rest, I might be able to manage the hunger.

What I Did Last Summer
September 21, 1971

There was a time when every school year started with the same assignment: Write a composition on "What I Did This Summer."

The kids hated it. Some even managed a slight temperature the first week to get out of doing it. But it gave the class something to do while the teacher learned all the first names and checked in the new supplies, and otherwise got things organized for the real work.

Reading the reports was usually kind of fun for the teacher, and informative in more ways than one.

Billy Brown wrote:

"I dint do nuttin this summer cause my mom had a new baby and I had to be gud cause she crys a lot."

From this the teacher learned that she has a pupil with a spelling problem; that the Browns had a new addition; and that Billy could use a little extra tenderness for a few weeks until he gets used to having a new sister.

But compositions about summer fun are out of fashion now. The people who know about such things say that it stunts a child's creativity to be given such a limited topic. I suppose they are right, but I hate to see the custom

323

go. You know, for me there were times when that "limited" topic actually stirred my creativity.

In the neighborhood where I grew up, the only "vacation" most fathers got was in "slack" times, and time off meant layoffs and weeks of worry rather than summer fun. My father was one of the lucky ones; he worked all summer, and summer was little different from winter for me, except that sometimes I was lonesome for my school friends.

Mostly, we celebrated summer on Sundays. Every Sunday when the weather was good, we piled food and drink into the car and went on a picnic. Probably my teachers would have been pleased to hear about the places we picnicked, or the smell of my mother's homemade sausage roasting on a spit over a charcoal fire in the woods, but I never wrote about those outings.

I read a lot in those days, and down deep in my heart I knew that a real summer vacation was going to the shore, or the mountains, or The Lake. (In the books I read people were always going to The Lake. They never said which lake it was, but all the other people in the book always seemed to know even if I didn't.)

Things being what they were, and beyond my power to change, I summoned all my creativity and lied a lot. There was almost always a river or creek where we picnicked, so I always wrote that we went to The Lake, and if I was questioned about its name, I conveniently couldn't remember.

When I got older I discovered that it was fashionable to visit farms in the summer, and since we always did that (for strawberries, corn or canning tomatoes), I adopted The Farm as my favorite theme. I hardly had to lie at all and I almost always got an A for "What I Did This Summer."

Ask my children what they did this summer and they'll probably find it hard to remember. They went to the shore, the mountains, and The Lake (its name is Michigan), but they do most of that every summer, and as far as they are concerned, it's not worth writing about.

This year we sandwiched visits to relatives in between our regular travels, and when and if the kids talk about their trip, it's those visits which they tell about. Often their reports are almost as creative as mine were.

"We met this little kid, I guess she's my mother's second cousin from New York, and gosh, did she talk funny!" (Soytanly, she was from the Bronx.)

"My aunt has a new house in Virginia and boy, you should see the bugs in the bedroom." (The boys left the window open, the light on, and the screens aren't up yet.)

"We went to see my dad's old, old friend from way back in the olden days when he was in graduate school." (Ten years ago is the olden days?)

"I liked my grandma's house, but when the company came and they all started kissing, I ran and hid in the bathroom." (He came out for the cake and ice cream fast enough.)

"My sisters had to take turns sitting in the back of the station wagon, but I got to sit in the front all the time." (The troublemaker sits where I can reach him.)

"Us kids were having a great time at Grandma's, and we wanted to stay longer, but Momma said Grandma would remember us better if we stayed shorter." (What I said was, "Grandma is always glad to see us come and glad to see us go.)

"I went to Williamsburg with my cousin. The houses? Yeah, they were okay, but the best part was I found a dime in the pay phone." (Kids should be seen but not toured.)

"We had gelati, spumani and "lemonade" like my mother used to have when she was little, but I really wanted a popsicle. (Tell me, have you ever wanted to twist a kid's neck?)

Seeing "National Velvet"
October 5, 1871

There are lots of things you can do on a dark and rainy Sunday afternoon. You can read, or work on your hobby, or listen to a concerto, or sit and dream. Or, if you have children, you can sit around and watch your blood pressure rise as you alternately break up fights and bribe kids with treats from the freezer.

It was a fight-and-bribe kind of day at our house when someone read on the movie page that "National Velvet" was playing at the Campus Theater. In some households where there are children the movie page is ripped out when the paper arrives and filed under "P" for Probably Pornographic. To see it you either have to show a note from a teacher that it's part of your homework, or you have to prove by at least 3 forms of identification that you are over 21.

At our house we take our chances and leave it right in the paper, alongside the news from Vietnam and Washington. Sure, it's an ugly world, but it's got to be better to find out about it at home.

To get back to "National Velvet," the ad was marked Children's Matinee, which are the first 2 words children learn to read these days, apparently because even the slow reader got the point on the first sounding out.

I vaguely remembered that it was a pretty good movie when I saw it way back in the days before Elizabeth Taylor was afraid of Virginia Woolf. To show you how vaguely I remembered it, however, I thought Velvet was the horse.

"Can we go?" begged my Formidable Four, who are the Younger segment of our Sonorous Seven.

"Well, I don't know," I stalled.

"You said the next time a children's movie came we'd get to go," remembered Beth, whose turn it is to be 11 and in love with horses.

It's true, I did say that. But frankly, I thought I was safe. You can go 2 years in this town without running into a children's movie. As a matter of fact you can go almost 2 years without seeing the marquee change.

"Okay, I'll see if Kate will take you," I relented, noting the "All Seats 75 Cents" notice.

"Why would I want to go see a horse and Elizabeth Taylor with braces on?" asked Kate. (Kate is too old for children's movies and too young for adult movies, but she's seen "Gone With the Wind" twice and she's happy.)

Later, when I was standing in a line that went clear around to Ann St., I got around to wondering why I was going to see a horse and Elizabeth Taylor with braces on. It didn't help that I could feel my hairdo go flat in the drizzle, and a kid in front of me kept standing on my toe and yelling, "When I stand like this I can almost see the ticket seller."

Somehow they managed to squeeze every kid in town into the theater. Maybe it wasn't EVERY kid in town. All I know is that on Monday in the 3rd, 4th and 5th grades at Bailey School Show and Tell was a replay of "National Velvet."

On the way home, the kids all agreed that it was a great movie. At first Mike and Drew couldn't quite understand how the doctor knew Elizabeth Taylor was a girl just by unbuttoning her blouse, but we cleared that up in a hurry.

Meanwhile, Meg and Beth were aghast that Velvet was disqualified as the winner of the race just because she was a girl. Shades of fem lib!

All 4 were overjoyed that there wasn't any "mushy stuff" to spoil the action, and they all agreed that the part they liked best, next to the candy bars and peanuts I passed around, was the exciting race scene. It was exhilarating, especially since every kid in the place was cheering Velvet on with every last breath in his body. In fact, it was a most responsive audience and hardly anyone noticed that I went through 3 tissues and sniffed and blew my nose a lot.

"National Velvet" was made before the day of ratings, and if you rated it now you'd probably have to give it a "C" for Corny. But at that it was better than staying home and watching a husband watching football on TV. And you know what really choked me up? When the movie ended, every kid in the place clapped. How long has it been since you saw a movie worth clapping for?

Bowling
November 3, 1971

"To everything there is a season, and a time to every purpose" goes the phrase from Ecclesiastes. And it is true. Some things, for instance are better begun in youth.

I like to think that the human being is flexible and adaptable, but the older I get the more I begin to suspect that youth and old age are the times to experiment. Before 25 you can do anything you can try, and after 65 you can try anything you can do.

The time in between had best be dedicated to meditation, spiritual enrichment, and developing the hobbies you started in younger days, such as chess or child-rearing.

Take sky-diving. The best of all times for that is after 65. What can you lose? But if you're interested in driving, say, or maybe sex, it's best to start young and hope for improvement through time and Experience. All of which is why I think I've come too late to bowling.

The bowling alley in my hometown was not so much a place to bowl with a bar attached as vice-versa. I was in it 2 times--once when I was too young to drink beer and once when I wasn't. Both times it was hard to see the pin boy through the smoke, and I didn't learn much about bowling except that it took stamina. Even breathing was hard in a place like that.

Bowling alleys have come a long way in the years between those experiences and my new determination to take up the sport. The pin boy has been replaced by a machine that is quicker and more dependable, and everything else is cleaner, prettier and bigger than I remember. The emporium in my memory had 10 alleys; the one I went to the other day had about 50. And when I let go of that first ball, I could swear that the alleys are half a mile longer these days.

Letting go of the ball, apparently, is the most important part of the whole game.

How you do it and where you do it make the difference. On my first attempt, beginner's luck was with me all the way, and I rolled a perfect gutter ball. Don't laugh. I wasn't sure I was even going to be able to let go of that thing when I walked up for my turn. As a matter of fact, after a couple of turns, I really got nervous and my thumb froze in the ball.

A couple of throws later, I relaxed so completely that the ball rolled away on my backswing, luckily missing my teammates and a sleeping baby.

I noticed that some people start with their left foot and others their right, so I decided to experiment on my next turn. It was a mistake. The moment I remembered I had feet I was in trouble. Suddenly both of them were too big and in the wrong place. To add to my problems, my arm resented losing my attention and sent the ball bouncing down the lane, thumpity, thumpity, thumpppp!

People were kind; they turned away and pretended not to notice.

About midway through the game, I accidentally struck 3 pins. I was so embarrassed at my triumph I didn't know how to act. Two frames later I got a strike. Horns tooted, lights flashed, bands played and confetti flew--all inside my head, of course.

From then on, it was all downhill. I scored 44 in my first game, and the less said about the second the better (it was in 2 figures, but just barely).

So now I'm sitting here nursing my sore arm and stiff wrist and wondering when the swelling in my thumb will go down. My son, concealing his horror at my scores, says I'll do better next time, especially if I take the time to find a ball that fits me. My daughter says it would be pretty hard to do worse.

I'd like to believe it's never too late to learn (or at least that it's better late than never), but my muscles are saying "You can't teach an old dog new tricks."

Bow-wow.

Winter Leaves Me Cold
November 16, 1971

I am not ready for winter. My condition is chronic. It flares up yearly around the first of November and lasts well into April.

Strangely, Big Business, which knows all about my iron-poor blood, has a remedy for my sour stomach, a cleaner for my dingy floor tile, and protein for my undernourished hair, feels no urge to prepare me for winter.

"Get your car ready for winter!" urges one ad. "Is your house protected against winter's blast?" inquires another. Nobody advertises, "Winterize your mother in 3 easy steps!" Nobody offers to change my oil, clean my plugs, insulate my walls, regulate my humidity, or even zip in a new personality to fortify me for the months ahead.

And to show you how unprepared I am for winter, there are 2 pairs of shorts and a sleeveless shirt in the "Urgent" section of my ironing basket. My neighbor says I should try to meet winter half way, but deep down in my heart I'd rather by-pass it altogether. Anyway, her system of crossing out mosquito repellant, barbeque sauce and briquettes on the shopping list and writing in rock salt, new shovel and medicinal brandy doesn't seem to do it for me.

Every time I think "White," I also think "Cold," and "Long," and I am chilled by the certainty that the game plan for winter includes:

--The day the dog romps joyously in snow up to her neck and then shakes it all off in the living room.

--The cry, "I need dry mittens." Dry mittens are something you find in the drawer in July. From November to April, all mittens are wet.

--The battle on the morning the thermometer drops to 15 degrees and the kids say, "Aw, why do I need a hat? There's no snow on the ground even."

--The disappointment that day in December when the trash man leaves half the garbage frozen in the bottom of the can.

--The smell that day in January when the warm spell thaws out December's garbage.

--The expense when one shoe disappears completely until after you buy your poor boy another pair. Then it turns up in the galosh he lost at school, and has since been replaced with another pair.

--Darkness any day at 5 p.m.

--Bumps and ruts in the street (any street, but especially yours), and corners slicker than a greased griddle.

--The coat that feels paper thin when you wait on the street corner, but weighs a hot ton in the store.

--The solid mass of ice right in the middle of your windshield, which you can't reach no matter how you stretch up over the hood.

--A frozen nose and numbed toes.

--The search for the shovel which was out all night and which is right about here or maybe there, but under 4 feet of snow.

--The thrill of being passed at 60 miles an hour by a blind fool who can't possibly see out of any of the car windows he didn't bother to clear off.

.

--A collection of skis, boots, and poles, dripping wet and tripping people in the front hall.

--Chills, aches and a fever in any one of the kids on the day of the Big Luncheon.

--No school because of ice and snow the day of the Big Luncheon.

--No luncheon, the day of the Big Luncheon.

--The furnace splitting its fan belt during the night, the same night the thermometer hits zero.

--The nice big fat heating and repair bill that arrives the same day as the Christmas bills and the orthodontist's estimate.

--The kids demanding to go out in sub-zero weather.

--The kids demanding to stay in, in the sub zero weather.

--The kids going in and out in sub-zero weather.

Some people like winter. It leaves me cold.

What Was the First Thanksgiving Like?
November 30, 1971

Santa is back in town. Talk about eat-and-run! Can you imagine the nerve of that guy taking off like that after his Thanksgiving dinner and leaving Mrs. Claus with all that leftover turkey, dressing and cranberry sauce. Well, one good thing, she has a big enough freezer--the whole North Pole.

I've often wondered whether the Pilgrim Fathers, or rather mothers, had a problem with leftovers after the original Thanksgiving feast back in 1621. Cooking being the chore it must have been back then, they probably spent more time worrying that there wouldn't be enough than that there would be any left. Especially since the feast lasted 3 days. Can't you just hear the admonitions:

"When you carve the venison, make it thin. It's got to last until Sunday. And pass the cornbread only once, or you'll have to chop down another tree for firewood."

That celebration must have been quite a party when you think back on it. I can just imagine the talk the morning after.

"Wow! Three days of feasting, prayer and singing! Have you ever seen such a great party?"

By the way, whose bright idea was it to put Chief Showemhow next to old Grandma Sharptongue? He's so proud of his 10 words of English, but poor Grandma's so deaf she kept saying, "Eh? Speak up, boy. Sounds like you're saying Digum hole, plantum seed, makeum raindance, pickum corn, and eatum over and over again."

"That wasn't so bad. I'm still trying to explain to Purity Wiggles that Graywolf was really paying her a compliment when he slapped her on the bottom and laughed and laughed."

"I know. And did you see what happened when I passed the wild pheasant to that squaw? She smiled, put the whole thing on her plate and ate it."

"Our people weren't any better. Did you see Sarah Righteous put away that whole jug of wild grape wine?" "Jus a lil'digessive tonic," she kept saying.

"The kids were good, though."

"All except Jonathan. He behaved like a little Indian--oops, I mean troublemaker."

Our family visited in Plymouth last summer, and went aboard the replica of the Mayflower which lies at anchor there. That experience filled me with new wonder at that first small band of pioneer settlers. How 102 people ever fit on that tiny ship to begin with, much less ate, slept and worked on it for 65 days, is beyond my comprehension. At least 90 of them must have had the patience of angels, and the other 12 must have been out and out saints.

There isn't anyone in our family of 9 who would have qualified to make the trip. Tom would be out automatically. At 6 feet 4 inches, he couldn't stand up straight anywhere but on deck. Ellen would never have survived. She uses more water for each shampoo than that ship could carry altogether. Dale would have had claustrophobia--the Civic Center makes him feel penned in.

Beth, who managed to trip over her own feet in the school gym last week, would probably have snagged her foot in a coil of line and plunged headlong overboard. Meg gets seasick in the plush new motionless elevator at Jacobson's--enough said.

Mike would probably have been thrown overboard by the crew after about 5 minutes worth of his How? and Why? and When? Drew, who was on thirds of turkey and mashed potatoes last Thursday when the rest of us were deciding on pumpkin, mince or pecan, would have starved to death without question.

As for me, with my husband left back on shore, my children dying off all around me, what would I have had to be thankful for?

(Kaye's note: Descendants of that first ethnic gathering are asked not to see red, or go white, as no malice is intended, and are asked not to picket our doorstep.)

Letter to Santa Is a Stretch
December 14, 1971

Our 8-year-old thinks it would be terrible to live in Holland where children are reported to put their wooden shoes out for the Dutch version of Santa Claus to fill on Christmas Eve.

"What's so bad about wooden shoes?" asks an older sister.

"They don't stretch at all," protests our opportunist.

Santa is the fella who knows all about stretching, especially when it comes to the truth. His mailbag tells it all.

Dear Santa,

I have been good this year. (Compared to last year! And besides, what Santa doesn't know won't hurt him.)

Lots of times I helped my mother with the housework. (Once he took out the garbage--under protest.)

One day I washed the floor. (He spilled the baby's bath water.)

I took care of my kid brother last Thursday. (The doctor took 4 stitches in the brother and prescribed lots of aspirin--for the mother.)

I learned a lot in school this year. (He can get to the principal's office with his eyes closed.)

I didn't start any fights with my friends. (Who fights with friends? You should see his enemies.)

I heard that you think sharing is important, so I did a lot of sharing in my family. (He shared his sister's candy, his father's tools, and the sofa with his brother when his mother made him.)

I was polite to older people like my mother wants me to be. (After he ran into old Mr. Sharp with his bicycle, he circled back and helped him get up.)

I didn't steal anything from anybody. (He learned a new word--borrowing.)

I didn't tell any lies, purposely. (He's accident-prone, verbally.)

I kept my bedroom neat. (Compared to a bear's den, that is.)

I hung my clothes most of the time. (From the chandelier, the bed post, the curtain rod--you name it.)

I made my bed almost everyday. (Some days he made it into a raft, other days it was a trampoline. Last Friday it was a bomb shelter--after the bombing.)

I will try to be even better next year. (There's no way to go but up.)

I want a few things for Christmas. (A few games; a few toy cars; a few toy trains; a few balls, bats, helmets, and gloves; a few skates, skis and sleds; a few clothes--very few; a few candy bars and other treats; and a few crisp green dollar bills.)

Say "hello" to Mrs. Claus. (It never hurts to appeal to a higher authority.)

Love,

Everyboy

P.S. Jimmy says there ain't no Santa Claus, but what does he know? (Hope springs eternal.)

Gifts That Last
December 28, 1971

"Package for Naybors," says the parcel post man at the door, and immediately a crowd collects.

"Is it for me?" is the question on each face as everyone strains for a look, and chills run up and down several small spines.

It turns out to be Daddy's underwear from the tall man's shop in Boston, but the magic lingers on.

"Gee, it's fun to get a package in the mail," says one child. The mob disperses, still smiling.

For many years a special package came during every Christmas season--a huge carton, wrapped in brown paper, tied across, and then across again, and then the other way, and then again, with the sturdiest of twine and the strongest of knots, and plastered with dozens of stamps, and always carefully addressed in precise Palmer Method script.

Grampy did the wrapping and tying and mailing, but Mimi did the shopping and packing. Along with hand-knit mittens for everybody, there would be pajamas, or sweaters, or blouses or nighties, and always a game for the whole family, something sweet-smelling for a teenaged girl, and a can of special toffee or buttermints for everyone to share.

Mimi's special gift was a cake mix for the children to bake for "Jesus' birthday," and Grampy's was a tightly-sealed canister of butternuts for our Christmas fudge, each kernel plucked patiently from its tough shell by hand, after a smashing blow from Grampy's special butternut-cracking hammer.

But for the past few years, a check has come instead of a package. Mimi usually jots down some ideas, and I do the shopping and the wrapping. The sizes are better than when she shopped ("Is he that big already? He seemed so much smaller when you were here in August."), and more things are "just what I wanted!" but the special excitement of receiving and unpacking that big, clumsy package is lost.

This year, Mimi has been ill and the letter that came with the check held a special note of poignancy. "We'd like the children to have something lasting from us this year. Can you think of anything they might like?" she wrote.

We've sent her some ideas--birthstones, charm bracelets, cuff links, books, etc., but the question of what is "lasting" haunts our hearts.

Gifts that last come in many shapes and sizes, but few of the most lasting gifts that loving grandparents give their grandchildren over the years can be bought in a store or mailed in a bulky brown package.

They don't ever come at special times of the year. Most often they are presented without fanfare, and the children are not even aware of them at the time.

There is no gift card when Grampy says, "Let him go; he'll be all right," as a grandson climbs the gnarled old apple tree in the backyard and spends most of the afternoon up there dreaming lofty dreams.

"When Daddy was a little boy," says Mimi, beginning a tale that intrigues her audience and is indeed a present, although there are no fancy wrappings.

Once in a while a child will come home, sniff a bit, and say, "Um, smells like Grandma's house in here," and go off, gifted again in smiles.

A lasting gift? Maybe it's a hammock in the backyard. Or a rhubarb pie lovingly baked and frozen in summer and saved for an out-of-season visit. Or a box of Daddy's old trains in the attic. Or Grampy's tools, each respectfully cleaned off and hung in the proper place. Or Mimi's warm welcome: "I was hoping you'd get here early!" Or Grampy's robust "Who's for picking blackberries on the hill?" Or a half-whispered, "I prayed for you."

Our children have had a lifetime of lasting gifts. We wish the same for yours.

334

1972

Two Kids Become Adults
January 18, 1972

We have 2 new adults in our household. To the rest of us they don't look like new adults; they look like the same old kids we had a few weeks ago.

But the law says they are adults now, and who can argue with the law?

Right from the start I was all for adulthood for 18, 19 and 20-year-olds. In a way, I may be partially responsible for the new law. Way back when I was part of the New Generation (now called the Old Generation), I stood up in formal debate and argued successfully the resolution "That 18-Year-Olds Should Have the Vote."

World War II was the current unpleasantness in those days, and the clinching argument was, "If they're old enough to fight, they're old enough to vote," a refrain that re-echoed through the gunfire of Korea, Viet Nam and Cambodia.

As I remember it, I also declared that an 18-year-old is mature and reasonable and deserves to share the rights and responsibilities of adulthood.

Of course, the 18-year-old I had in mind at the time was me!

Little did I dream that by the time the nation acted on "my" suggestion, I'd be an old adult with 2 newly certified young adults of my own, and 5 more in training. Now I kind of wish I'd kept my mouth shut.

Everyone from the President on down has carefully spelled out what it means to be a new adult. But as the parent of new adults, I want to know, what about the parent of new adults?

For example, now that my son can legally "make binding contracts for goods and services," can I refuse to wash his socks unless he turns them right side out before putting them in the laundry?

And when he calls in the middle of the night to say his heap won't creep, do I still have to leap into ours and mush to his rescue?

And when he says "Keep the dinner hot," but doesn't show up for 3 hours, can I sue him for breach of casserole?

And now that he can "write wills leaving property to whom he wishes," can I safely tell him to clean the mess in his closet OR ELSE!?

My new adults have taken it upon themselves to help me understand how this new juggling of rights and responsibility works. The way they tell it, I'm home free!

Now they can eat, drink and be married, and I don't have to worry.

Now they can sign on the dotted line for anything from a car to a house, and I don't have to worry.

Now they can admit themselves to a mental hospital, and I don't have to worry.

Now they can serve on a jury, and I don't have to worry.

Now they can be employed as security guards, and I don't have to worry.

Now they can sell goods to a secondhand dealer without my consent, and I don't have to worry.

Now they can represent themselves in proceedings, and I don't have to worry.

In addition, they can go without their galoshes, skip breakfast, lunch and dinner, be late for classes, freeze their thumbs, jay-walk, and vote as they please--and the best part is that I don't have to worry.

You know what? I don't have to worry, but I do.

A Visit to the White House
February 1, 1972

Somebody has been going all around town telling people that I dropped my spoon at the White House. What a nasty thing to say!

Well, yes, my spoon did drop at the White House. But what a nasty thing to say!

Besides, it wasn't my fault. I was standing in the Blue Room holding my empty teacup and reflecting that among the many things my mother never told me was what to do with an empty teacup in the Blue Room of the White House.

I had about decided to hide it behind a flower bowl when a butler held his silver tray towards me. I placed the cup, saucer, spoon and napkin deftly on the tray and was just about to congratulate myself on my party manners when the butler shifted the tray and dropped the spoon.

I wanted to yell out, "The butler did it!"

I settled for turning red, looking guilty, and explaining to everyone for the rest of the day that "ordinarily I don't take a spoon with my tea--just a little lemon."

In spite of that trauma, I had a great time. I had never been to the White House before. Usually we go to Washington in summer, and there is always an uninvitingly long line for the 10 to 12 a.m. tour. Also, I'd heard that the tour isn't much, a quick sprint through roped-off corridors with a brief view of rolled-up carpets.

I had decided to wait until I could go in style. (I have 3 sons and 4 liberated daughters, and who knows when political destiny may swing towards Michigan.) However, when the invitation came to attend a reception given by Mrs. Nixon at the White House, I decided not to wait for fate. I accepted--along with about 299 other women.

From the moment we stepped off our chartered bus, it was apparent that we were guests, not tourists. Attractive young men (White House police with "degrees" in etiquette) extended us a welcome with white-gloved hands. Liveried attendants took our wraps. A string ensemble composed of 6 Marines in flashy red coats played show tunes in the entrance hall. Old-fashioned Williamsburg-type bouquets of fresh flowers brightened tables in every room.

The red carpet was out--literally. We sat on the chairs, examined the fireside F.D.R. made famous, admired the portraits, and gazed out the windows at the sweeping lawns and fountains. A few bold ones even tipped their cigarettes in the ash trays.

On the bus ride over, we had joked about our chances of actually seeing Mrs. Nixon. The reception was 2 days after her return from Africa, and we were convinced that our reception committee would be "an aide to an aide to an aide."

We were wrong. Mrs. Nixon stood by herself in the center of the state dining room, wearing a long-sleeved red dress and black pumps, and shook the hand of each guest and exchanged a few words with her. An attendant told us that one afternoon she had shaken hands with each one of a group of 2,000, between 1 and 5 o'clock.

But, honestly, I've got to talk to my mother. Another thing she never told me was what to say to the First Lady of the land as she shakes your hand and smiles at you.

Just before my turn came, I tested a few comments inwardly:

"I just love your house."

"I didn't vote for your husband, but may I shake your hand anyway?"

"They really kept the place up while you were gone. I noticed how the windows sparkle."

"Could I have the recipe for these yummy nut bars?"

"What do you hear from Julie and Tricia?"

At the crucial moment I came up with "We enjoyed watching your African visit on TV. Especially the part where they dressed you up in the native skirt and hat. I'm sure children all over the country loved that scene."

Mrs. Nixon was gracious in the face of such inadequacy. She said, "It was fun."

When my turn had passed I looked on as she greeted some of the others. She was on her 200th hand by then, but she still looked fresh. Her hair is redder than I had expected, a sort of strawberry blonde. She is extremely thin. She looks much younger than her 58 years, except for her neck and hands where her thinness betrays her. She smiles a public smile, but she keeps what writer Jessamyn West (a shirt-tail relative of the President) has called "a private face."

On the bus back, the ladies buzzed their verdict. Mrs. Nixon, most felt, is not a warm person, but she is attractive, polite and correct, and greeting us was above and beyond the call of duty--even in an election year.

As to the White House, the general feeling was, it's a nice place to visit, but...

Rising Meat Prices
February 15, 1972

A housewife in Walnut Hills is still ecstatic over her Valentine's Day gift from her husband. Usually he sends her a dozen long-stemmed red roses. This year he sent her an 8-pound rib roast of beef and this note:

"My love is like a red, red rose-t."

She was so happy she cried in the gravy.

Another couple I know came close to separation last week. The only thing that kept them together was 250 pounds of beef in the freezer. The marriage counselor said the only sensible thing to do is eat together for a few more months and then see how prices are.

At our house, one of the little kids cried for 2 hours before we found out what was wrong.

"Mommy doesn't love me anymore," he sobbed.

"Of course I do, whatever gave you that idea?"

"You never yell at me to eat all my meat anymore!"

Strange behavior indeed, but the steady rise in the cost of groceries, especially beef and other meats, has everyone in town acting peculiarly.

One man from Okemos couldn't find his wife for 2 days. Finally, the police spotted her on campus trying to lure a duck out of the Red Cedar.

One mother was arrested after she abandoned her 8-year-old son at the back door of the meat market with a note pinned to his jacket saying, "Forgive me, I can't keep him. He asks for seconds on chops."

Sales went up on electric knives (the thinner to slice with), catsup (the thicker to cover with), and candles (the darker to eat by).

The drug store ran out of its supply of Quiet World, and the MSU Extension Service reprinted 20,000 more copies of its booklet, "How to Be a Vegetarian, and Like It."

A snowmobiler who scared a farmer's bull so that it ran around in circles was fined for the loss of 10 pounds at $5 a pound.

Young newlywed students sublet their new apartment and moved back to live in their dorms and eat in the cafeteria.

A professor in poultry sciences decided it was time to test his theories and went into chicken- raising.

The ladies at one church in town sponsored a spaghetti and meatball supper and lost $150 on the meatballs.

Two middle school girls ran away from home after their mother put a little chopped pickle and mayonnaise in the canned dog food and made sandwich spread out of it.

A large family went to the store en masse so that everyone could vote on how to spend the week's meat money.

A woman was treated for shock when shoppers found her standing by the meat counter shaking her head and muttering "75 cents for hamburger ... 75 cents for hamburger ... 75 cents for hamburger ..."

I could go on and on, but I've got to run now. I just heard about a secret address that's being passed around from hostess to hostess. They say all you have to do is knock twice and say, "Jo sent me..."

Explaining Leap Year
February 29, 1972

It's that day again, February 29, and I have the awful feeling I'm going to blow it again. It's slipping away minute by minute, and here I am cooking, washing dishes, and making beds, as usual.

I spent most of breakfast time trying to explain Leap Year to a kid who hasn't figured out New Year's Eve yet. In less time I could have discussed human sexuality, euthanasia, and President Nixon's response to the ballet he saw in Peking.

"Why do they call it Leap Year?"

(It's a good year for frogs?)

"Why does it come in February?"

(Boy, that's what I want to know. February would be long enough if we skipped it entirely. How about an extra day of June or July instead?)

"Why does Beth giggle and spell it out when she's talking on the phone?"

(Ask your father.)

An extra day in the year ought to be something special. To begin with, you shouldn't call it Tuesday, or Wednesday, or whatever day it happens to fall on. It ought to have its own special name, something that makes it stand apart from all the ordinary Tuesdays and Wednesdays of the year.

Maybe Catch-Up Day would be appropriate. After all, the only reason for the day occurring each 4th year (except in century years not divisible by 400, such as 1500), is to get the calendar squared away with the solar system. (I know that because I looked it up at breakfast time.)

I'm never quite sure which is ahead, but the day is necessary for one or the other to catch up. And if Catch-Up Day is so important to the calendar and the solar system, just think what a Catch-Up Day could do for the average human being, who normally runs just about 4 years behind in everything (especially ironing, entertaining or having that little talk with your son).

It would be "found" time, and goodness knows that if there's anything humanity needs, it's to find time.

The day could be everybody's some day, you know, "SOME DAY I'm going to write a book; give that kid what's coming to him; soak in the tub for 2 hours; head west and just keep going; make hash browns for breakfast; balance the checkbook; make a baked Alaska; give them a piece of my mind; order a whole lunch of pastry at the Olde World Restaurant;

buy a new bathroom scale; go on a diet; sail off into the blue; or maybe just collect my thoughts.

The more I think about a Catch-Up Day, the better I like the idea. With a little bit of effort I'll bet we could get Congress to go for it. I'll spearhead the drive--as soon as I find a little time SOME DAY.

Leaving the Kids
March 15, 1972

As a parent of 7, I've had my share of sad farewells, but now that our "babies" range in age from 8 to 20, there are seldom any pangs on either side when there is an occasion to part.

"I'm leaving," they yell as they head for school, work or play.

"Thank goodness," I mutter.

When I leave I say, "Please be good until I get back."

"Then can we be naughty?" one is sure to ask.

It wasn't always that easy. Our first child we left only with her grandparents, and we made them sign an oath of loyalty, wash in Phisohex, and pass an eye and ear test before we gave them custody of her.

When our second child came along, we had our first real sitters--bonded registered nurses, of course, with on-the-side training in fire control, civil emergencies and behavioral sciences. We left highly detailed instructions (10 pages in triplicate).

But of late, leaving home for a few days has become a fairly simple operation. All I have to do is bring in $60 worth of groceries, cook up 2 or 3 batches of reheatables, leave the recipe for a few others, make a timetable of everyone's whereabouts, alert several neighbors and a doctor, do 8 loads of laundry, re-weave a new chain for the dog, and have my hair done, and I can go.

If I have a few qualms about how they will make out, I am instantly reassured by the young adults in the household.

"Everything will be fine. Go and have a good time. What can happen? Besides, we know the way to Sparrow Emergency as well as you do."

I know lots of things that can go wrong, but for my own sanity I don't think about them. I mean if you've already spent next Sunday's pot roast money for theater tickets in Chicago, you might as well go and enjoy the show, and then come home and worry about stretching the chipped beef.

The first night away from home you play the old game: shall you call tonight or shall you wait until tomorrow night? On the pro side is finding out how things are, and getting a good night's sleep. On the con side is finding out how things are, and worrying all night. Usually, you opt for not calling. What this does is reaffirm your trust in your children, and gives you about half a night of good sleep and half a night of worrying.

The next day, of course, you wait until after 6 to call. This is because phone rates are lower after 6, and also because it gives you a chance to do a little sightseeing before you find out the worst. Finally, you call, collect. As the operator does her bit you hear a familiar voice bellow:

"Somebody on the phone wants to talk to collect--shall I say wrong number?"

"Operator, tell him it's his mother calling," you insert, hurriedly.

The phone dangles on its cord and after about 3 minutes another child picks it up and hangs up. The operator tries again, and this time you get through.

"Hi, this is Mother. How's it going?"

"Hi, Mom. Gosh, everything's fine, considering. Hey, did you find a red jumper to buy me? Have you seen the show yet? What does it mean when the meat thermometer explodes a little? Guess what the dog did. Did you say not to open the French vanilla? Want to talk to the older kids?"

You panic.

"What do you mean 'considering'?" Explode? Did you say explode? Let me talk to anybody. And hurry!"

Anybody turns out to be the next youngest, who says, wistfully, "When are you coming home? Nobody tucks my sheet in right. Is it all right if I wear one brown sock and one blue? I can't comb my hair because all the tooths fell out of my comb. Isn't somebody supposed to God Bless me at night?"

The vision of this untucked, unmatched, uncombed and unblessed orphan is almost enough to send you hurtling out to charter a private plane for instant flight. But by this time, an older child has gotten the word that you're on the line and a cool, calm voice says, "Hi, how's it going?"

It turns out there was one crisis. They had to use diced tomatoes instead of tomato sauce in the Spanish rice and one child objected to the bumps and ate a peanut butter sandwich instead.

So you stop worrying about the kids and worry about the cost of the phone bill instead.

Spring Shopping with Daughter
March 29, 1972

If a woman with tightly drawn lips, a glazed look in her eye, and an aura of panic in her movements bumps into you in the store this week, please forgive her. She's probably only a mother out shopping with her teenage daughter for a new outfit for spring.

Normally, this same woman is a kind, warm, gentle person who takes shopping in stride and spreads sunshine as she meanders in the malls. But shopping with today's Junior Miss has a strange effect on mothers--it shakes them out of their tree. I know. I have 4 tree-shakers of my own and I land on my well-upholstered convictions regularly.

Part of the problem, at least in our family, rests with the mother. And her mother, and her mother's mother, and Eve, who didn't know how to say no to a fig leaf. I mean if you were brought up believing that spring meant black patent leather Mary Jane's, a flouncy dress, a pastel coat and a straw hat with flowers, ribbons and veiling on it, it's pretty hard to get with a fringed poncho over red and blue hot pants with white stars on the "pot holder."

My spirits lift a bit when a daughter stops by a window on E. Grand River to look at a gingham and lace confection reminiscent of great-grandma's Gibson Girl days.

"Wow!" she whispers with what I hope is longing.

"It's yours," I shout, propelling her into the store.

"Gosh, Mom, it's expensive. You said I shouldn't even look at anything over..."

"Never mind what I said. Try it on and I'll have them wrap it up."

"I guess not."

"NOT?"

"It's just too pretty. I don't have anyplace to wear it."

As if styles weren't bad enough, daughters also have trouble with sizes. The man who sets measurements for readymade garments--and I know it's a man, one without daughters, at that--is high on my list of trouble-makers. How can there be peace in the world if a 14-year-old girl can't find a pair of slacks that fit around the waist and don't end at the middle of her calf? Of if the top of a size 9 dress bags and droops, and the hip seams threaten to split?

Shoe salesmen hurry into the back room when they see me coming with one of my daughters in tow.

"My, my. Long and narrow. Well, well, well," they mutter, when the manager lures them out.

"You do have something?" I ask, hopefully.

"No problem, no problem. Great selection."

The persimmon pump and brown suede brogue he brings out leave mother and daughter close to tears.

Luckily for mothers, today's Easter bunnies do not wear hats. Even the vocabulary of hats is fast fading from the language. Breton, toque, sailer, turban, skimmer, cloche, pill box, Milan, raffia, horsehair--"What does that mean, Mother?"

Girls today do wear headgear, but the words that describe it are wooly, floppy, felt, leather and plastic.

I'm truly sorry about the milliners' slump, surely the lowest in the history of heads. The hat industry was always good to me. Even when I was 9 months and 2 weeks pregnant no hat saleslady ever said, "I'm afraid we don't have your size. Why don't you come back after the eleph--er, baby--is born."

They always pulled out 2 chairs, motioned me down and said, "I have just the thing for you."

Mothers, by the way, do recover from their shopping traumas. But if you hear one intone an extra Halleluiah on Easter morning, you can figure she's asking for the extra grace she knows she's going to need to face the next family crisis--bathing suit season.

Income Tax Time
April 12, 1972

When the kids procrastinate, it's stalling. When mother does it, it's biding her time. When the head of the house does it, it's income tax.

Why not put off until tomorrow what you can do today, especially if it makes it easier to get through today?

The trouble with working out your income tax is that if you're in a good mood you sure don't want to spoil it doing that pesky job, and if you're in a bad mood already, you'd be surprised how much worse things can get.

In some households, when the tax forms come in, that's the signal for the children to go out. Out of hearing range at least.

"Where do you wannus to go?"

"Try Grandma's."

"But she lives 500 miles away."

"Walk, don't run. I'll call you when the worst is over."

At other houses, it's different.

"Call the children, I'm doing the tax tonight."

"What do you want me to call them?"

"Call them immediately, the little darlings."

"Even the 'worthless' one you banished yesterday?"

"Yesterday he was worthless; today he's a $675 deduction. Call him."

Twice the children are counted.

"Wasn't there another one? Let me see, 1951, Joe; 1953, Harry; 1957, George --what happened to '55? I remember bailing you out of the hospital in '55, where's the kid?"

"Sorry, I guess they don't give you one when you have your gall bladder out."

"But we had twins once didn't we?"

"No. It just seems that way."

The matter of the brother-in-law comes up, but after a while everyone concedes that inviting a relative to dinner once a week doesn't make him a qualified dependent.

Taxwise, there is no reward in being healthy it seems.

"Where are the rest of the doctor bills?"

"All we've got are in that envelope marked 'Ouch!' "

"Is that all? Didn't anybody break a leg last year? Honestly, you gotta speak to those kids. Do they think deductions grow on trees?"

"Spencer had 4 wisdom teeth removed…"

"That's more like it! Did you hear about the Coopers' tragedy--their daughter got married. In January! She couldn't wait until October or November like a good dependent should."

"The ungrateful wretch."

"But the Smiths really have it made this year. Imagine, triplets in December!"

"Some people have all the luck."

"Yeah. Say, what would you think about having…"

"Pay the tax, Charlie. It's worth it, believe me."

Going to the Dentist
May 3, 1972

If you get the feeling you've bitten off more than you can chew, it's wise to let the dentist pull his hand back out of your mouth.

That thought for the day comes to you courtesy of my recent oral spring cleaning. One thing about going to the dentist, it gives you plenty of time for thought.

I thought in the waiting room. (Why do they say 10 when they mean 10:37½ ?)

I thought in the chair. (Chair? Can you call it a chair if your feet are higher than your head when you "sit" in it?)

I thought most when he said, "Open wider." (I thought I'd die!)

A current advertisement asks a resurrected R. E. Olds, "How did you happen to invent the Oldsmobile?" A squeaky voice answers, "I didn't want to be a dentist."

My kids don't want to be dentists either.

"Catch me putting my hand in anybody's old mouth!"

"Yeah. And sometimes you have to get down real close. S'posing it's a girl!"

Some people were born to be dentists, but don't find out until it's too late. We had a man in my hometown named Dr. Mollar. He was a gynecologist.

My neighbor's kid was considering dentistry, but he didn't qualify. He couldn't break par. Golfers and dentists actually have a lot in common--they both get excited when they spot a hole in one.

Choosing a family dentist is a very serious matter. Never do it blindly. Go to the man's office and check first hand on all the important things. For instance:

1. Can you get in his parking lot during rush hours?

2. Can you get out of his parking lot during rush hours?

3. Are the chairs in the waiting room comfy enough to let you forget you've waited 45 minutes?

4. Does he subscribe to anything besides Dental Health? (Special features: "Tooth is Stranger than Fiction," "The Tooth, The Whole Tooth, Nothing but the Tooth," "A Tooth, A Tooth, My Kingdom for A Tooth!" And for a centerfold, "The Naked Tooth.")

5. Does he give out rings? (One of our former dentists gave out rings. The kids liked the rings. They didn't like the dentist, mostly because he sang while he worked. "Boy, I never heard of any of those songs he sings. What's an Amapola, anyway?")

6. Does he use a vacuum hose to suck away the moisture in your mouth? ("Gosh, Mom, why can't we just spit? That vacuum cleaner feels like it's gonna suck out my tongue and my tonsils!")

7. Is he married? (If he's young, good looking, well-dressed and unattached, your husband may resent him--especially when the bills come.

Probably the most important thing to investigate is whether his receptionist comes from a large family. She's got to understand that only 2 members of the family can have appointments in one month.

If more go, it won't matter how bad our teeth get. We won't be able to afford to eat anyway, by gum.

Anti-War Demonstrations
May 17, 1972

Last Wednesday morning the world outside our window was blue and sunny, and as we awoke, we heard birds gossiping in the trees.

After breakfast our doorbell rang, and we heard our 9-year-old greet his friend. As they headed off to school, our boy said excitedly, "Hey, guess what. I went to the riot last night. I saw the police come in a big bus. There was about a thousand of 'em. You shoulda seen 'em!"

Mentally I corrected "riot" to "demonstration," and listened for the drone of the police helicopter which had hummed an uneasy lullaby through most of the night. I reflected unbelievingly that 2 blocks from the school playground where our children would play today, clouds of tear gas filled the air the night before.

If you are truly a family in town, and live within hailing distance of downtown, as we do, one of the great things is that your children can go on their own to most of the places where children need to go: school, the barber shop, the library, the drug store, the post office, the book store. Or even, if no one is looking, to an anti-war protest rally.

The house rules are simple--tell somebody where you are going. So when Kate, our 14-year-old who knows more about the American Revolution than 9 out of 10 adults, decided to get a first hand look at democracy in action, she told the person least likely to object (our 8-year-old) and left with 9-year-old Mike, a revolutionary in his own right, in tow.

Before the word got to us that they had gone, Kate had returned without Mike.

For 1½ hours, Tom and I walked around downtown, searching fearfully among the groups of student demonstrators for a small boy on a bike.

"I'm sure he's perfectly all right," we told concerned friends. "He knows his way around town, and he's got on a white jacket so we should be able to spot him easily."

But as our eyes began to water from tear gas, our hearts chilled with unspoken fear. In spite of the apparent peacefulness of the protesters and the restraint of the police, we wished fervently that our child were home in bed.

We searched down by the drug store, a friendly, familiar spot suddenly made sinister and frightening by a row of uniformed police, wearing gas masks and holding clubs. The store lights were on and the proprietor was inside, but the doors were locked.

We walked to *The Towne Courier* office and used their phone to call home on the chance that Mike may have come back. About half an hour later, the welcome news came: Mike was home and safe.

The next day, strangely, life went on as usual. Late in the afternoon, as some of the main streets were blocked off, strange traffic wove past our house. Several neighbors who watched from the corner took note of the speed of the increased traffic and decided that protesting the proposed peripheral route had been the right thing to do.

Protest--it is hard to explain to children the need or the method. But when you live only 5 blocks from the action, you can't pretend it isn't happening.

"Why are the policemen here?" asks one child.

"They have to protect property," you answer.

"Are we for the police or for the students?" asks another, in confusion.

"This isn't good guys against bad guys," you explain, badly. "It's simply students trying to be heard, and police trying to do their job."

"Are students the only ones who want to be heard?"

"No, but grown-ups have gotten used to not being heard, and most of us have stopped trying," you admit.

"Does somebody hear the students?"

"Probably not," you answer, unhappily.

"Tomorrow will it be safe to go to the book store again?"

"We'll have to wait and see."

"They said at school not to go downtown. I think it's scary when you can't go downtown, don't you?"

"Yes, I think that is scary," you answer.

Protest is hard to explain to anyone. But when children ask, you feel you have to try. So you say that protesting national violence with mob violence is scary, and protesting mob violence with police violence is scary, but that not protesting violence at all is the scariest thing of all.

When Summer Vacation Begins
June 14, 1972

For every school teacher who will wake up on Monday morning and chirp, "There's no school!" there will be 25 mothers who will pull the covers over their heads and groan, "There's no school?"

Psychologically, no mother is ever ready for the end of school. A few try to deal realistically with the impending disaster, but success is rare. For most mothers, the school year is just about 3 months shorter than they had hoped it would be, and the end always comes as a traumatic surprise.

Normally women have a great sense of timing. They can smell a marriage proposal 6 months off and arrange to have it come off on schedule--theirs. On the job, they can cram 15 errands into one lunch hour and get back 10 seconds before the boss. As teachers, secretaries, and wives they keep the world running with precision, give or take a minute or 2, allowing for traffic jams on E. Grand River.

Motherhood, however, distorts a woman's chronological perspective. First there are those 9 months of waiting. No woman has ever been able to get through those in less than a year.

Then come the feedings. In the book it takes about 15 minutes every 3 or 4 hours. In real life, each feeding takes 3 or 4 hours, and leaves her arms numb for 15 minutes.

Just as she's about to recover her time values, along comes the year of the Terrible Twos. It lasts at least 27 months.

About this time, friends start to offer succor.

"When your children are in school, you'll have all day to catch up on your housework/mending/reading/volunteer work/beauty treatments/ Yoga/loafing/ etc.," her friends assure her.

"All day" turns out to be time for a swift turn with the dust mop in the morning, and a dash to the grocery store after lunch, if she doesn't dawdle over the asparagus.

At school conferences the children's teachers talk reassuringly about "the rest of the year."

"Sally's only in Chapter 8 of her math book, but I don't think you need to worry. After all, she has the REST OF THE YEAR to complete the next 4 chapters," says one, in May yet!

If a mother were really on her toes, that phrase about the rest of the year would sound a warning bell and she would know it's later than she thinks.

Remember? It's the same wording the shoe salesman used when he talked her into buying the higher priced sneakers for Freddie the Footdragger.

"The best part about these sneakers is that they will last the rest of the year," he said.

In 7 weeks, tops, Freddie has reduced each shoe to a flapping bit of rubber, 3 eyelets, and a set of laces made out of his sister's slip straps.

Of course, he meant the fiscal year. Whatever that is.

The experts (my mother-in-law and her neighbor, the one who squints) say the only thing a mother can do is take this period of trial and tribulation (otherwise known as summer vacation) a day at a time.

After all, each day has only 26 hours in it--or is it 28?

Weddings Aren't What They Used to Be
June 28, 1972

One of our friends is due to become the mother of a bride this month, and at this point we're all a little worried that she won't make it.

When her *Towne Courier* arrives in the mail on Thursday morning, she turns to the family page, reads each wedding, word for word, and weeps.

"Everything's so different these days," she moans, meaning she wonders what her friends will think when they get the invitations. The young couple printed them themselves with a linoleum block, in white on rose-colored paper.

"Share Our Joy," they urged, instead of the usual "So and So Requests the Honor of Your Presence."

"Well, it's their wedding," says the mother, nervously, meaning she can't understand how any daughter of hers could have picked a sheer embroidered caftan over a satin body suit for her wedding gown. She also plans to wear a halo of fresh daisies and ivy instead of her mother's veil and Chantilly lace. And what will Grandma think?

"I just know it will rain," worries Mama, out loud, meaning "That beautiful new church, all air-conditioned and carpeted--but no, they had to pick a 'Cathedral in the Trees'! I know the mosquitoes will find it, but will the guests?"

"Well, at least the refreshments will be good," she concedes, meaning she is secretly proud and pleased that the young couple hunted up the recipes for the same wine punch and golden fruit cake which were served at her own wedding.

"The strange thing is that they are both having so much fun planning it all," she ponders, remembering that she was so tired and tense at her own wedding that she almost cried out, "I can't, I won't, I don't!"

She got married in a time when premarital always went with whirl. Now it goes with s-e-x. (And I don't know why I think I have to spell it; even the dog's too bored to look up if you yell it.)

All in all, it sounds to us as if it will be a lovely wedding. A bit unusual, but not strange, as today's ceremonies go. One invitation we heard of said, cryptically, "Shoes may be worn." Inquiries revealed it was being held at a nudist retreat.

An invitation we received recently cost 24 cents to mail. Besides an outer envelope and an inner envelope, there was a formal invitation to the church, a bid to the reception, a card to r.s.v.p. on a stamped envelope to r.s.v.p. in, and another card bearing a scale map of the Borough of Queens, highlighting the location of the reception hall.

It was overwhelming. I'm still wondering if the pewter salad servers we sent were up to the invitation.

I couldn't bring myself to mark an X before Cannot Attend, so I wrote a friendly little note about the piano recital, the dentist appointment, Tom's work, and the distance to Queens, and a few other reasons why we couldn't be there. Then I soaked the stamp off the r.s.v.p. envelope and put it on my note and mailed it.

I bundled up the rest of the invitation and sent it off to be recycled.

All I can say is everyone has his own ideas of what's right, I guess, including the couple we heard about who invited their friends to their "non-wedding," where they didn't get married, followed by a reception celebrating the fact that they didn't.

But that's going a little too far. After all, there's a lot to be said for marriage--and some of it's even good.

House Swapping
July 12, 1972

I'm intrigued by the advertisement of a company which specializes in arranging international house swapping on a temporary basis.

"List your requirements," says the ad.

Simple. A cottage in Cork, a house near Hampstead Heath, a villa in Vichy, a bungalow in Barcelona, or even a garret in Greece. I'm not fussy when it comes to getting away.

But there's a catch.

"List the features of your house and area which make it attractive to foreigners," urges the ad.

I can't even think of any features that make it attractive to me. Sure, home is home, but even employing the power of positive thinking, all it boils down to is "a comfortable two-story colonial in a small town in central southern Michigan."

Of course, if someone actually got interested in coming here (instead of New York which has theater, or Washington which has monuments, or San Francisco which has charm--or even Traverse City which has that great view of the bay), I'd be willing to be more specific. A helpful (and truthful) letter might read:

Dear Swapees:

First of all, be sure you don't buy at that 24-hour store down the block. Convenient, yes, but they'll charge you 33 cents for a 21 cent can of corn.

The light at the bottom of the cellar stairs works, although it almost never goes on when you push the switch. Give it a tap on the glass and say, firmly, "Let there be light." My husband says you don't need to say that, but I find it helps.

The sheets are color-coded according to bedrooms. Check the chart on the linen closet door. (Oops, I almost forgot--we switched the blues from the yellow room to the green room, and the pinks go in the blue now. Or, gosh, use your own judgment--but one yellow pillowcase is gone. My son used it for a duffel bag.)

The double bed in the master bedroom (that small, dark room on the second floor) has a board under the mattress. Feel free to remove it, if you please. Frankly, it doesn't do much for my husband's back ache, but it makes the bedspread hang better.

My advice in regard to the worn spots on the living room rug is to entertain at night by candlelight, and make the first round double strength.

The man from Bill and Ernie's came about the disposer. I told him it sticks and I have to jiggle it with that funny little tool to get it started. He fussed with it for half an hour and then he said, "It sticks. Try jiggling it with that funny little tool when you start it." Then I wrote him a check for $11. (The trash man comes on Tuesdays.)

The small TV in the kitchen is not hooked up to that expensive aerial on the roof. To get Channel 12 in the kitchen (Password is our favorite—11 a.m—don't miss it!), you have to rest the nub of the telescoping aerial on the top right curlicue of the trivet which hangs on the wall just above it. It won't work on any other curlicue.

352

One of the greatest things about our house is the neighbors. There are good neighbors to the right of us and to the left of us. (Yes, politically as well as geographically, but don't antagonize either, please, because they're so good to the kids.)

You'll be happy to know that it isn't necessary to keep up with the neighbors in any way on our account. We settled that business when we had our 7th child. Nobody wanted to top that.

If you're wondering about the town, it comes with an attached university, although there are those who would put that vice-versa. The university gives the town a place to go for education, art, music and sports. The town gives the university a place to go for life's basics, such as food, clothing, traffic jams, parking tickets and riots.

Most of the time, it's a nice place to live. I'm only eager to leave because a little change now and then is good for everyone.

P.S. I won't go into particulars about the frig or the lawn mower or the garage door, because it would all be wasted if we don't swap after all. But if we do, I'll leave notes on everything. Except the dryer--all you have to do is kick that.

Grandmother Dies
July 22, 1972

One of the special joys of our children's lives has come to an end. The loss is permanent. Their father's mother, the grandmother they called Mimi, is dead.

Mimi had suffered from a heart ailment for the past 2 years, and she and we knew that her years were numbered. Some of her days were good, others were very bad, but each new morning was a kind of triumph.

I wish I could say that death came quietly while she slept. It didn't. She died of violent injuries suffered in a head-on automobile collision, an accident which happened because the young driver of the other car was, in his words, "momentarily distracted." His car swerved directly into the path of Grampy's car, and the impact brought death hours later to our Mimi.

The other driver and his passenger were hurt and hospitalized. They are young and their scars will heal.

"Cookie," a sweet, gentle, little old lady who had been Mimi's best friend all of their lives, was on the critical list for 4 days. Glass still sparkles from between her thinning hair, and her forehead is dotted with angry sores where she was peppered with glass splinters.

"How is Margaret?" she asked, when she woke to find herself in a hospital with broken legs and other painful injuries too many to mention.

"Mimi is in good hands," we assured her, and only 5 days later did the doctor allow us to add, "the hands of our Lord."

Grampy suffered a broken hip, broken ribs, numerous deep cuts on his face, arms and legs, painful bruises on his chest, and a great void in his life.

In 1970, he and Mimi celebrated their 50th wedding anniversary. Their marriage was little different from that of any other couple who came together in 1920. They raised 3 sons, bought a little home, planted large gardens, never had quite enough money to do very many special things, but they worked together and stayed happy.

She was deeply religious and while he respected her beliefs, it was only in the last few years that he was able to equal her faith and rejoice with her in God's word.

Now he is able to say of the other driver, "May the Lord have mercy on him."

Our oldest child will always remember that Mimi's idea of a pretty school dress was red plaid. She sent her three different red plaid dresses in as many years. It was our private family joke. Our second oldest will remember her magic touch with pastry. Her rhubarb pie was second to none.

Our third child took it upon herself to write to Mimi every week and tell her the crazy escapades of our active family. Mimi's last letter in return arrived after she had been buried.

Our 4 younger children remember her visits, new mittens every winter, exciting birthday packages or checks, picnics in her backyard, her cookie jar and her candy treats.

My husband and I will always remember her last gift to those who loved her. Before her death she wrote carefully her wishes in regard to her funeral and burial. For us this was a true gift of love. By this thoughtful act she simplified our hard task, and granted us the peace that comes with knowing you have done what a loved one desired.

Many people, old and young, find it hard to regard death as part of life. They cannot think about it or talk about it. This is a selfish indulgence which burdens survivors with unnecessary agony at the time of death.

Remember that someone you love will have to do difficult things for you when you die. Accept that fact and make their job easier when the time comes. Don't tell them your wishes, write them down, and distribute copies so there is no danger that they will not be found.

Mimi's wishes were simplicity itself. We were honored to carry them out with dignity. Her thoughtfulness was her final gift to us.

Swim Suits
August 2, 1972

People watching is fun. And in the summer, at the shore, lake or pool, it can be a revelation.

There is this about a modern bathing suit. It offers visible proof that all men and/or women are not created equal.

The human body, say some, is a beautiful thing. But others ask, compared to what? Both groups get to say "I told you so" at water's edge.

In all, men suffer most when the camouflage of daily clothing falls away. A well-cut suit can make princes out of physical paupers. Shoulder pads add width, long lapels add height, and a loose jacket hides everything from pot bellies to xylophone rib cages.

Women's street clothing, on the other hand, keeps few secrets. A bulge is a bulge is a bulge, in a sheath as well as a bikini. And Flat Flossie is a big nothing either way.

The truth is that the girl you thought would look great in a bathing suit, does. And the rest of us just have to grin and bare it.

You can almost always spot a first-bikini wearer. The man bursts dripping up out of the water. His hands reach down to his waist to re-adjust his trunks. There's nothing there! Swoosh! Splash! Then up to the surface again.

He's remembered, just in time, that (a) he can't swim, and (b) bikinis ride real low on the hip.

Adolescent girls solve their first-bikini insecurities the simple way. They walk around with their towels draped over their arms, neatly covering the view from waist to toe, while their firm, young backsides delight the rear guards.

Towels are a bit like nautical signal flags. If you pay attention, you'll get the message. For instance:

Towel spread over legs while sunning: Varicose veins.

Towel wrapped around middle: Ruptured navel.

Towel draped casually over shoulders: Wing-shaped shoulder blades.

Towel wrapped around hips: Oh, where is my 18-hour girdle now?

Towel rolled up and tucked under flowing locks of long, wavy red hair: I'm beautiful and I don't care who knows it.

Towel applied briskly to arms, legs and torso: So I'm fat, 40 and frumpy--well, so what? I like to swim!

Camping with Kids
August 16, 1972

One thing about family camping, you can count on the kids.

Yes sir, you can count on the kids to find the only patch of poison ivy within 5 miles, and fall into it.

You can count on the kids to tell you the nearby water faucet doesn't work, after you get the camp all set up.

You can count on them to be dying of hunger, and then disappear just as the meat is done.

You can count on them to blow up an air mattress--but not 2, or 3, or 4.

You can count on them to tell you that something sure smells good, something the people next door are cooking.

You can count on them to hang up their swimming towels, in full sight of that fussy camper next door after they drag them through the swamp on the way home from the lake.

You can count on them to show you the easy short cut to the beach, after you take the long way that winds over the mountain.

You can count on them to be bored to tears all week, and suddenly find they love the place the day you're due to pull out.

You can count on them to wear out every battery you brought along playing Spotlight Tag, a nighttime version of Hide and Seek.

You can count on them to become "very best friends" with a kid whose last name they won't remember by September 1.

You can count on them, also, to get you and your spouse into a good old-fashioned fight, usually over the ax.

Now, no family can go camping without an ax, and no child figures he's been to camp unless he got to wield it.

Because of the nature of their sex, there are certain things fathers feel they have to say in regard to children and axes. And because of the nature of the difference of their sex, there are certain things mothers just have to say on the same subject.

Father: "I used one when I was a kid, and I never got hurt."

Mother: "But he's only 9!"

Father: "Every boy needs to learn to use the tools of survival."

Mother: "The hospital is 57 miles away!"

Father: "Let me see the edge on that ax."

Mother: "At last you're coming to your senses. I hope it's good and dull."

Father: "You don't understand, the sharper it is, the better."

Mother: "Oh, I understand, all right. You wish you were still a carefree bachelor with a fur-lined pad."

But even when the fur is flying, you can count on the kids to solve the problem.

Child: "I don't wanna chop any more wood. I'm going to go out in the motor boat all by myself."

Father and Mother, together: "Oh no you don't."

Visiting Museums
August 23, 1972

It came as a surprise to me to learn that most museums are open all year around.

"What are you doing this winter?" I asked my friend who makes dioramas.

"The Boston Tea Party needs redoing," she said, and I figured she was knee-deep in some of this student activism.

We got it all straightened out, eventually, but I've got to admit I've never been in a museum when it wasn't 132 degrees Fahrenheit in the Egyptian tomb room. I always figured the mummies got that way by baking, like ceramics in a kiln. No ancient secrets about it. By the third tomb room, I can feel myself crusting on the outside like French bread.

We average about 5 museums each summer, give or take a village restoration or 2, and depending how often it rains while we are camping. By the 3rd one, the bloom wears off for the kids, and they march through like Sherman through Georgia.

"Hey, come back here and see this old English armor," I suggest, sweetly but firmly, grabbing a determined campaigner just north of Atlanta.

"Aw, we saw old English armor last week. Let's go buy some Coke."

"You just had lemonade."

"I know, but I like Coke better."

"Look, we came to this museum so you could absorb some culture, and all you're soaking up is soft drinks."

"Kin I help it if it's hot in here?"

Restored forts are the boys' favorite type of museum.

"Wow! Lookit that squashed up bullet. It's still got blood on it! Sure, it's blood. See how it's all splashy and gooey looking."

All of a sudden I can really feel the heat--right in the pit of my stomach. "See that arrow? How'd ya like to get that in your ole chest? Ugh! Oh, I'm hit. Hey, Mike, watch me die. Ohhhhhhhh... hey, Mike, see if I watch you when you get a razor sharp arrow right over your heart and your blood and guts come gushing ...Oh, Mom, whadda want to leave now for?"

The girls prefer restored mansion houses with canopied beds, hand-painted chamber pots, candle stands and other vestiges of genteel living. It's great while it lasts, but for a week afterwards they roam around the house in resigned dissatisfaction, and you get the distinct feeling that something smells bad.

For my money, the best museums of all are the wax museums. I hate the exhibits, but at least the buildings are air conditioned.

First Lessons at School
September 12, 1972

School has been in session for only a week, and already everybody has learned a lot.

One kindergartner isn't happy about what he learned the first day. Answering alternately to Sonny or Stinky at home, he found out in school that his real name is Archibald. Knowledge like that could make a guy drop out at a very young age.

Names have always been a problem at the start of the school year. If a kid isn't spelling out Presticiacomo 13 times an hour, he's explaining patiently that he's really Ralph George, not George Ralph.

The middle school syndrome is name-changing. All of a sudden Reynaldo becomes Ray, Peter becomes Pete, and Philomena becomes Mia.

High school girls give the computer indigestion by varying their name from card to card. Kristin comes out Crystyn, Laurie becomes Lorry, and Rosalind becomes Rozlynnde. Burp!!

Lyle Thomas, however, stuck it out, and managed to get transferred to girl's gym, in spite of the computer's insistence that she is a boy.

Another problem beset young Kenny Walters, who hasn't conquered his lisp yet. He solved it by calling Mrs. Wisniewskivitch "Teacher."

And in the fourth grade, a youngster who shall be nameless, solved a different kind of problem by calling Miss Sherman, "Ole Sourpuss." Under his breath, of course.

Teachers get smart early in the term, too. One of the first things they learn to spot is the troublemakers. Their early strategy of counter-attack is known as the Seating Chart.

"Bud and Mick and I all had to sit right up front. What a bore! I told Ole Lady Clark I needed to sit in the back by the door for air, but she said we had to follow the Seating Chart. Gross!"

Another bit of information which teachers pick up at the start of the term is what is referred to in the faculty lounge as "the family situation."

Translation: The inside story on the latest separations, divorces and settlements.

"My mother gave my dad all the books. She said he was really married to them anyway, and if he didn't find a job pretty soon he could always burn them for fuel. But she kept the dog. She said IT loved, honored and obeyed, and it didn't leave wet towels on the bed. I like the dog, but I miss Daddy."

Educators have always maintained that a lot of learning takes place outside the classroom, and who can disagree? One youngster on our block learned several lessons without setting foot in the school building.

On the playground he gained a bit of insight into social studies, physics, biology and psychology.

In short, he laughed at a big guy who was getting the worst of a scuffle, suddenly found himself the object of the loser's wrath, lost a bluff, got socked in the nose, bled mightily, and attracted the succor of several pretty girls.

At home, his big brother added to his knowledge with a bit of arithmetic:

"Next time, bring your fist up like this and give him the old 1-2."

Losing Wisdom Teeth
September 27, 1972

Mike lost a tooth last week. As he put it under his pillow, he wondered loudly if the Tooth Fairy would come. In the morning he found a dime where the tooth had been.

Ten-year-olds have it made. I lost 2 teeth last week, and all I got for my trouble was a sore mouth, a large bill, and a hole in my jaw big enough to cradle a pregnant elephant.

They call the molars I lost wisdom teeth. You can call them wisdom teeth if you want to. I call them a pain in the neck--and jaw--and head. They hurt coming in and they hurt coming out, and if man were really wise, he'd figure out a way to stop growing them.

"Mama had a lost weekend," one of the kids told a friend.

Weekend? I lost a whole week. Plus my sense of humor, all hopes of being able to afford that slenderizing suit I had my eye on at Jake's, and the ability to chew soup.

Besides all that, I felt I had been betrayed. If my teeth can give me that kind of grief, what can I expect from my heart and my head? Most people expect a little trouble from their teeth. I don't. I was 28 and the mother of 3 before I had a cavity. I have an overbite, my teeth are not quite white, not quite straight, but they are solid.

Dentists swoon when they look into my mouth, and not just because I like garlic salt in my salad dressing.

"My, what a beautiful mouth," they murmur, breathing just a little bit faster.

Even the oral surgeon allowed himself to rhapsodize briefly before he got down to business. First he inserted something uncomfortable between my teeth. He said it would taste awful. It did. Then he hit me with an arsenal of needles. He said they would sting. They did. Then he slit the gum and extracted the teeth. He said I'd feel it when they came out. I did.

Frankly, I hated the whole bit!

The surgeon was gentle, efficient and expertly effective. He kept telling me what a good patient I was, which really worried me because if he had any sense at all he'd know I was nervous, tense and scared to death.

He seemed to know what he was doing in spite of his poor assessment of my cowardly character, but I had the distinct feeling that he was catching my tongue in the stitches. I couldn't figure out why the nurse didn't speak up.

When the surgeon and his nurse took their hands and feet and equipment out of my mouth, I breathed a sigh of relief. After I tested my tongue and found it free, I congratulated the surgeon on his skill--and myself on the fact that it was all over.

As I left, the receptionist gave me a sheet of instructions, touching on hygiene, diet, hemorrhaging, swelling, nausea, pain, drowsiness, bone fragments and immediate dentures, hinting that it wasn't quite all over. I followed instructions and hit the jackpot; I had trouble with all of them except the last two. (Next time, for sure.)

A week later I went back to have the stitches removed.

"How have you been?" asked the surgeon.

"Wretched," I felt free to admit. "I didn't expect to have so much pain so long. I thought it would be all over in a day or two."

"It would have," he said, "if you were 18."

Well sure, and if I were 10, the Tooth Fairy would have left me 2 dimes.

Grocery Shopping
October 25, 1972

I dashed into a grocery store on the other side of town the other day for bread.

I bought a loaf of white sliced, a loaf of Pepperidge oatmeal, one thin-sliced New York rye, 2 packs of hot dog rolls and some bran muffins.

Then I decided that maybe I ought to think ahead a day or 2, so while I was at it I doubled up on everything, substituting some hamburger buns for the extra hot dog rolls.

At the meat counter, I picked up 3 packages of cold cuts, 2 pounds of hot dogs, 2 English roasts, 6 pounds of hamburger and some bacon.

Then I saw a special on Cold Power so I bought 2 big ones. And 4 rolls of toilet tissue, and 5 kinds of soup, 3 cans of each. I remembered eggs, and bought 4 dozen, plus a gallon of oil, the large size Bisquick, 3 pounds of whipped margarine, and a piece each of cheddar, Swiss and brick.

I was standing there wondering whether we needed another bushel of apples when I suddenly realized the check-out girl and the bag boy were giggling at me.

"Say, Lady, are you the one?" asked the bagger.

"What one?" I asked, wondering if I'd gone around the last aisle too fast again and broken a quart of mayonnaise.

"You know, the one in the paper who shops once a year."

"Once a year? Not me. I just came in for bread," I said, pushing the 2 carts with my 9 bags out to my car.

I read the story. Some woman who has better things to do than shop for groceries (and anything is better, believe me), makes a once-a-year trip and picks up some $600's worth at a crack.

"What a great idea!" I thought when I read it.

Of course $600 wouldn't feed our family for much more than a month, but imagine shopping only once a year instead of once a day. As a matter of fact, I can't imagine it.

Years and years ago, when I was an Army bride, I shopped once a month. I made friends with the commissary butcher one month, only to find he'd been decorated with gold lamb chops and honorably discharged by the next month.

As my tribe, and their appetites, increased, I found it necessary to shop more often. First it was once a week, then twice a week, and then even more often. Last month I hit my peak--once a day with emergency runs in between.

I'm a little self-conscious about it. At first I went to the same store all the time, but that got to be embarrassing. What do you say to a clerk when she says, "Your sister was in this morning. How does it feel to be a twin?"

Also I kept meeting my friends.

"I see you shop every Tuesday just like I do," said one. ("And Mondays and Wednesdays and every other day," I mumbled.)

Now I make the rounds. If I'm in the A & P in the morning, I drop in at Eberhards in the afternoon. Saturdays I visit Meijers, Thursdays it's Kroger's, and in between I spread my favors among Wrigley's, Shop-Rite, and the Seven-Eleven.

I have to be careful about stocking up. We use 4 cans of niblet corn at one meal. Sometimes when there is room on my shelf, I buy ahead. One day I put 12 cans of corn into my basket. When I went to check out, I heard a man asking, "'Where's the sale corn. I see you stocking up, but I can't find where they've got the special."

Another time, anticipating a spree of baking, I bought several bags of sugar. A woman watched me load up, grabbed an extra bag, and whispered, "Have you heard about a shortage coming? Oh, those Republicans!"

No doubt about it, yearly shopping is out of the question for large families. The clerk would strangle in the cash register tape, and the national economy could never absorb the shock.

But computerized shopping is coming, I hear. I figure they might as well plug me in right at the bank. My husband never sees any of his money anyway.

School Pictures
November 8, 1972

"Hey, Mom. You were right!"

The yell is followed by a slamming door, so I can recognize the yeller as a 10-year-old male with muddy feet before I see him. What I can't guess is what I've done right.

After all, in the past 2 weeks, I have been wrong about:

--The elections ("My vote can make the difference," I said.)

--The number of trick-or-treaters on our block ("Gee, Lady, is Saltines all you got left?")

--Our Spartans ("You can do it, boys!")

--The weather ("It can't rain again, today.")

--My waistline ("One little teeny spoonful of hot fudge can't hurt.")

--My gas tank ("Sure I know E means empty. I just didn't realize how empty.")

--The roast beef ("There'll be plenty left over for sandwiches.")

--The time ("Relax, we're early--oops, my watch stopped.")

Being right is harder for mothers than it is for other members of the human race, so I mop up the mud without scolding and ask, "What was I right about?"

"My pictures. We got our school pictures today and you were right. I came out swell!"

I've got to tell you how it is with school pictures. Purchased regularly, they grow into a visual record of your children's coming-of-age.

In this one you've caught the Jack-O-Lantern smile of the first grader losing his baby teeth. In another, the tightly clenched lips of the hesitant brace-wearer. Then there's the year your daughter cut her hair, and your son didn't. Pimples! And where did the baby fat go?

You don't have to buy them, but you always do. They're cheaper and less bother than studio portraits. And on those 2 counts alone a parent who remembers sittings highlighted by mild hysterics, curdled vomit and bitten photographers, figures it's worth it.

All you have to do the morning of school picture day is find a shirt without ring- around-the-collar, and send your child off to school with the admonition to "Smile pretty." If the cameraman gets close enough to get his finger bitten, that's the school's worry.

In spite of the informality of the occasion, or, perhaps because of it, school pictures usually come out great. Or so you and the grandparents agree.

With the children, acceptance diminishes with age.

The kindergartner says, "That's me, Momma, do you like me?" Momma's delight is good enough for him.

The third grader is more critical.

"I think I closed my eyes just a little bit. Nancy says I look squinty."

The fifth grader (he of the muddy shoes) worries in advance.

"I'll bet mine comes out awful. Do they make you buy them if they're rotten?"

The middle schooler gets a bit emotional.

"Please don't buy them, Mother. They're terrible. Okay, buy them, but promise me you'll burn them. Oh, if they use that in the yearbook, I'll positively die. Can't we move away?"

The high schooler takes things into her own hands.

"Pictures? Yes, we took some. No, I didn't bring them home. I didn't like them so I didn't buy them. What are you so upset about? You've got plenty of pictures of me. Remember that cute one of me in my sandbox?"

I have to agree with the fifth grader, his picture came out swell. Right from his unmanageable hair, to his impish grin and pinpoint freckles, the camera has caught our unpredictable, mischievous, lovable little boy.

"Hey, look at that!" he exclaims after a closer look. "You can see where my neck is dirty. See that green spot right there? That's my dirty neck. Gee, I didn't know dirty necks photographed green, did you?" he asks, in wonder.

You know, you get a mother in just the right mood and a green spot on a boy's neck can really choke her up.

Being Thankful
November 22, 1972

10ᵗʰ Anniversary Issue of *The Towne Courier*

"A Mother's Thanks."

See the busy Pilgrim housewife kneading dough for bread.

See her puréeing a home-grown pumpkin for pie for the great Thanksgiving Day feast.

See her plucking tail feathers from a scrawny wild turkey.

See her carrying wood. See her carrying water.

See, you've got more to be thankful for than you realized.

If nothing else, you can be thankful that the Pilgrims ate as well as they did. How would you like to celebrate with a traditional woodchuck?

Like the Pilgrims, we've been through hard times lately, but there's always something to be thankful for. The problem is that we tend to reserve our thanks for big things, such as peace, prosperity, medical miracles, or at least a lottery windfall.

Kids are smarter. They live one minute at a time, and they're willing to be thankful for one little thing at a time.

True, kids are seldom thankful without prompting, but they catch on quickly.

"What do you say?" asks Mother, her hand still on the cookie.

"Pa," gurgles baby, capturing the treat.

One Thanksgiving Day, we skipped our usual grace and invited each member of the family to tell what he was thankful for. With the smell of turkey and dressing under their noses, and the memory of assorted pies glimpsed in the kitchen, the children made quick work of their thankfulness.

"I'm thankful for turkey," said one.

" I'm thankful for cranberries and mince meat," said another.

"Isn't anyone thankful for good health, a good home and a happy family?" I sputtered.

"Oh, yeah, good health," said one child. "Sure I'm happy my teeth finally grew back in so I can eat nuts."

Like the kids, I'm thankful for little things such as:

---Days when the streets are clear and I don't skid at the corners.

--Stainless steel flatware that doesn't need polishing.

--My disposal, in spite of its tendency to gag on my cooking.

--Cake mixes that taste good even when I add the wrong amount of milk.

--Self-service stores where I can poke, pinch and handle, to my heart's content.

--Neighbors who don't ask what my kids are doing outside in their pajamas when the temperature is 25 degrees.

--An occasional movie that's witty and full of fun, such as "1776."

--Slips that don't cling.

--Youngsters who present me with a soft cheek for a good-night kiss.

--Teenagers who give me the benefit of the doubt, not because I'm right (sometimes), but because I'm their mother.

--My husband, who understands that once in a while I just have to nag.

--God, who understands when I forget to be thankful enough.

Christmas Shopping Madness
December 6, 1972

There ought to be a warning posted at the entrance to all department stores, malls, and super-duper discount emporiums saying, "Warning! Christmas shopping may be injurious to your health."

The known hazards are many, including:

Shopper's Elbow--the best bargains are always just a prod and a push beyond another shopper.

General De-feet-ism--Corns, bunions, falling arches and moaning, which, roughly translated, comes out, "I knew I shoulda worn my sneakers."

Price-eye-tis--"My eyes can't believe these prices!"

Loss of Appetite--"All right, we'll get the Norwegian sweater for your brother. But I hope you realize that means canned hash for Sunday dinner this week."

Dizziness and Disorientation--"I'm sorry, Madam, but that's a Sears charge card you're giving me. This is Knapp's."

Congestion--Boy, I'll say!

On second thought, that warning probably ought to read, "Injurious to your physical and mental health."

If you don't think Christmas shopping is a mental strain, listen to the way we talk about it:

"I'm going out of my mind trying to find something for Aunt Seraphina!"

Just an expression, you say?

"I paid $29.75 for this, and I don't even know what it is--I must be crazy!"

How about that?

"What do you mean, you think I've flipped? I think a set of purple shorts and T-shirts for Grandpa shows a lot of imagination."

Convinced?

In addition to physical and mental agony, Christmas shopping can also gum up family relations. Only the strongest units can survive the strain.

Stand under the clock in a large department store any day in December and you'll get an idea of the jeopardy.

Husband, rage rampant on his usually peaceful mien: "Well, it's about time. I thought you said we'd meet here by the clock at 2. Do you realize it's 3:15 and I've had to go out twice to feed the meter?"

Wife, tears streaming down her cheeks: "I've been here twice and when I couldn't find you, I thought you meant the other clock and I walked all the way over to the west end of the store carrying this set of encyclopedias and my arms are breaking and I got a run in my stocking when I went past the hockey sticks and if you say one more word, I'll scream!"

Husband's still annoyed, but willing to forget: "Hey, look, I'm sorry. It was just a misunderstanding, I guess. Here, give me the books, and let's go home."

Wife: "We can't. Don't you remember, we've got to wait for Sally and Jack. Have you seen either of them?"

Husband: "No, but Sally said she'd be in Cosmetics, and I think Jack headed for Sporting Goods. You stay here and I'll see if I can round them up."

Wife, slightly revived: "I'll just browse around the stationery while you're hunting."

Husband: "You leave this spot and you'll celebrate Christmas alone!"

Two hours and one parking ticket later, the family is reunited. The daughter is not talking to the brother. The brother is not talking to the mother. The mother is not talking to the father. The father is not talking, period. And the worst of it is they still haven't found a present for Aunt Seraphina.

The Meanings of Peace
December 18, 1972

Peace is the wrong shape to fit into a Christmas stocking.

It's hard to make, harder to grasp and even harder to hold.

Sometimes it's the shape of a smile. At other times, it resembles a handshake, or an arm reaching out to help. It can be the size of a sacrifice, or the depth of forgiveness.

It can be any color in the rainbow and brighter than the most spectacular bird.

It's made up of love and faith; of reverence for the old and delight in the new; of the victory of faith over doubt; of the joy of sharing.

Peace is the complete absence of fear.

Peace is elusive. History records almost no periods of world peace, and even personal peace comes and goes.

When you are one year old, peace is a warm place in Daddy's lap, a smile from Mommy and a friendly teddy bear to hug.

When you are 5, peace is a kindergarten teacher with a warm and ready smile and a coat hook you can reach without standing on tiptoe.

When you are 10, peace is knowing all the words on the spelling test and making the late bus home after tribal sports.

When you are 15, peace is an invitation to the big dance and no pimples that week.

When you are 20, peace is a full gas tank and a high draft number.

When you are 25, peace is the new baby finally sleeping through the night.

When you are 30, peace is discovering it's someone else's week to drive in the nursery school car pool.

When you are 35, peace is making it to pay day with $2.34 to spare, and the knowledge that your snow tires will fit on your new car after all.

When you are 40, peace is the last car driving in, the last light going out, the last child home safely one more time.

When you are 45, peace is losing those 10 extra pounds, and no worries about your blood pressure.

When you are 50, peace is a paid-up mortgage and the arrival of your first grandchild.

When you are 55, peace is ushering your last daughter down the aisle and turning over to another man her hand and her bills.

When you are 60, peace is a cleaning lady once a week and a gynecologist with a large parking lot.

When you are 65, peace is Florida in the winter and a pension check every month.

When you are 70, peace is a small apartment with no attic, no basement, and no guest room.

When you are 75, peace is a friend, a nap, a cup of hot soup, and a sweater with a pocket for your hanky.

When you are 80, peace is respect.

At any age, peace is the fulfillment of the promise Christmas offers.

Merry Christmas--and peace--to all, from your Naybors, Tom, Kaye, Ellen, Dale, Kate, Beth, Meg, Mike and Drew.

1973

What Time Is It?
January 3, 1973

The new year arrived at our house a little late.

There was good old 1972 all packed up and ready to go and none of us could tell him the right time. No 2 clocks or watches at our house ever agree, and boy, can that be confusing.

"Happy New Year!" enthused one member of the family.

"Hey, it's still only 7 minutes to 12," objected another.

"That's not right," said another, "the kitchen clock says 10 after."

"Gosh, I've got 11:45 on the nose," chimed in another.

Finally, just as we were about to settle for an average, someone switched on the TV set, and we got in on the celebrating. For us, 1973 began at about a quarter after midnight.

Probably no family in town is so well equipped to have the right time, and less likely to.

True, the sundial is under the lilac bush and never sees the sun, but over the years we've acquired quite a few clocks and watches.

At last count there was a kitchen wall clock, a stove clock, great-grandfather's mantle clock, 3 bedroom clock radios, 2 cheap alarms, one rhinestone studded alarm, 3 travel alarms, one Swiss cuckoo, one Black Forest cuckoo, one digital clock.

In addition, the 9 of us own 22 wrist watches, in various stages of repair, including 2 that Santa just dropped off last week. Also, 4 turnip-style pocket watches.

You've got to admit that ought to get us to the church/ school /or office on time.

Hah! Time is a perpetual problem.

"Mother, will you speak to Kate? She sets her alarm for 5:30 and wakes us all up.

"Why do you need to get up at 5:30, Kate?"

"I don't. I have to get up at 6:30, but I like to have my alarm ring early so I can roll over and sleep another hour."

The kitchen clock causes its share of confusion.

"Hey, Mom, I left when the kitchen clock said 12:10, but when I got there it was only 11:50 and I had to wait out in the cold for 20 minutes."

By dialing 487-1212 we are able to synchronize the kitchen clock.

The next day another son protests.

"Do you know I was late for my exam? Who's been fooling with the kitchen clock?" At this point we call a family conference.

The consensus of opinion is that life can't go on unless the kitchen clock is 10 minutes fast at all times.

"Can't you simply start out earlier?" I plead.

"No!!"

No sooner does everyone get used to the situation when a well-placed (and highly illegal) softball collides with the clock and the hour hand snaps off.

For about a week we try to make do. "It's 10 after something, Mom. Is it time to go yet?"

Then the man of the house tries to glue the hand back on. Unfortunately, he glues it to the other hand. Neither works.

Well, no matter, there's always the stove clock.

"Mom, my watch says 2:35 and Beth's says 2:20 and we don't know what time it is."

"Check the stove clock."

"The stove clock? Where's that? Oh, I see it. It says 350 degrees Fahrenheit."

We buy a new kitchen wall clock, but even that doesn't solve all the problems. At least one member of the family still needs help.

"I want you ready to go in exactly 5 minutes," I tell Drew.

"Sure, Mom, but by whose watch?"

"Drew, it doesn't matter whose watch. Five minutes is 5 minutes on any watch."

"Are you sure?" demands Drew.

How can I be sure? My watch may be right on the dot, but it's also upstairs on the bathroom shelf where I forget it every morning when I shower.

TV at Dinner Time
January 17, 1973

The CBS News is as much a part of our family supper as bread and butter and spilled milk.

Our Prayer of Grace varies from day to day, but it usually ends with "…through thy great love, Amen. Turn up the volume and adjust the horizontal hold a bit."

If God is the unseen guest at our table, Walter Cronkite is very much in sight.

At first I fought against this uncivilized intrusion into what I had always envisioned as an hour of family communion, enlivened by the interchange of stimulating ideas and happy banter. But supper with 7 children being what it is, I've almost come to look forward to having the news as background music.

If nothing else, it makes the normal mealtime calamities seem trivial.

"Mom, Drew spilled his milk all over my meatloaf!" moans Beth.

"I know, dear," I soothe, "but you can soak it up with your bread. Just think of those poor people caught in that awful flood."

"Yeah, you sure can't soak up a whole flood with a slice of bread," agrees Drew, an expert on spilling and flooding.

On those occasions when I scorch the main course, I draw on the news to bail me out.

"Overdone? You should complain. Did you hear that Cleveland has been without electricity for 2 days? Overdone has got to be better than raw."

There have been some embarrassing moments. The other night at a dinner party I pulled the hostess back to the table and cautioned her, "Wait for Harry to finish his story, Honey. You can go to the kitchen for the salt during the commercial."

Naturally, the news makes a deep impression on the children.

"Gosh," moans one, "some days life is just one disaster after another. Mom, is it all right if the dog eats up the spaghetti I spilled?"

And whatever it is Daddy does for a living, Charles Kuralt has him beat all hollow.

"Hey, kids, he's in Wyoming tonight. Whadaya bet he's at a rodeo again, the luck! "

"Yeah, he has it made. I liked it last time when he visited that lumbering camp and everybody chopped down trees and ate steak and hash browns for breakfast."

"Boy, imagine getting paid for touring around in a motorhome and having fun!"

But for Mike, who wanted to be the weatherman until he discovered he couldn't stand the squeak of chalk, the TV news has opened up a completely new horizon in the field of careers.

For weeks now he has been studying Henry Kissinger's technique and he thinks he has peace-making down pat.

"Hey, watch me operate," he urges. "Here comes Fuzzy Miller up the walk. I'll leave the door open just a crack and then I'll disappear into the other room. Now, whatever you do, don't yell 'Come in'! "

Fuzzy stands on the doorstep uncertainly for a moment, then seeing the open door, he pushes it and walks in.

"Hey, Mike, are ya still mad at me for the iceball I gotcha with?"

"Naw," says Mike, at his diplomatic best, sticking out his leg and tripping Fuzzy.

The boys leave the house together, but they don't smile, frown or touch. Peace? Not a chance. Leaving together may be protocol, but according to Mike and the Kissinger manual, "that don't mean nuttin."

When it comes to veiled secrecy, Mike is almost as much of a pro as Henry.

"What happened in English today?" I ask.

"I had it 4th period," says the budding diplomat.

"I know that," I fume, "but was your report a hit?"

"I have English again tomorrow," says Mr. Close Mouth.

"Great, at least that means you didn't get thrown out. But how about a hint--are you going to pass English or not?"

"I understand the great responsibility thrust upon my shoulders..." begins Mike, with just a hint of a German accent. But this time I refuse to take No Comment for an answer.

"Cut it! Cut it!" I interrupt. "Now hear this--pack up your attaché case and report to your commander-in-chief immediately--in the kitchen!"

It's possible I am spoiling a good thing. After all, there's one thing you can say about peace-making--there's always a need.

Flu Epidemic
January 30, 1973

"What's an epidemic?" asks Drew. I don't even have to look it up. An epidemic is what's coming when there are 9 people in your family and one comes down with the flu.

At our house it comes under Naybor's Theory of Relativity: Anything you can get, I can get sooner, harder and longer. Maybe this time, maybe just this once, I thought, we might miss it. Which shows you there're still dreamers in this world. But at least the suspense is over. The waiting and wondering can be almost unbearable. But now that one of us has it, the other 8 can just relax, take our books back to the library, and otherwise set our affairs in order.

The only question now is who will be next?

The first victim is Kate. With some people it is hard to tell they are sick. But with Kate it was simple.

"Kate, Stina's here. Time for school!" I yell up the stairs.

"Unrahab," answers our 15-year-old.

"Unrahab?" I puzzle, grabbing my fever thermometer and dashing up the stairs.

Kate joined the debate team at the high school last fall, and is now known affectionately among members of her long-suffering family as Lily the Lip. Affirmatively or negatively, the Kate we have come to know and tolerate talks resolutely, positively and constantly.

She speaks with conviction and clarity all the time. She does not say "rahab."

By the time the 9th one of us gets the flu, I probably will be an expert on the care and cure of this particular virus. At present I know only that the doctor and penicillin have no clout against it, and it's every mother for herself.

At the Kroger supermarket I notice a display marked, "Cough, Cold and Flu Center." Thoughtfully, it is right by the door where the afflicted can stumble in and out quickly. In the hope that they know something I don't, I study the display.

Featured are Vicks cough syrup, Nyquil, aspirin and tissue. Obviously we've been trained by the same authoritative TV commercial.

The display has one hopeful aspect--there isn't an ounce of Kaopectate in sight.

My neighbor recommends bed rest, paper cups and isolation for Kate, to which I answer, "She is, we are and no way."

Isolation has lots going for it, but until they bottle it, this family is out of luck.

"Can't you keep Meg and Beth out of here?" moans Kate, and that's when she isn't even sick.

But sick or not, her room is their room and the best I can offer is, "Turn over, everybody, and try to breathe in different directions."

Meg and Beth do not scare easily, especially since at the middle school where they go it's in to be out.

"Karen's mom had to come get her this morning. Boy, was she sick in English!" relates Meg, wistfully.

For once I feel I can offer hope.

"Your turn will come," I start to promise just as Beth comes down with a message from Kate.

"She says she feels better now and maybe it wasn't the flu after all."

I don't know whether to laugh or cry.

Names
February 14, 1973

All things considered, our kids think you'd have to be a saint to put up with a name like Valentine.

It does no good to point out that the word has its base in the Latin word Valere which means to be strong, healthy and masculine. Or that 3 Roman emperors bore a version of the name, as well as one 3rd Century Christian martyr, to whom, incidentally, they owe thanks for the heart-shaped candy they've been enjoying all week.

With kids there are 2 kinds of names, names they like and names that are "rotten." In the first category fall their own names (usually), their father's name (always), and their mother's name (unless they have just been scolded, in which case their mother's name is mud, and "rotten").

Valentine, needless to say, smells of pinks and reds, and hearts and flowers, and satin and lace, and is rotten.

Kids have an answer for everything, and their answer to rotten names is simply to change them. A man I know was named Rudolf Valentino by his impressionable mother, who then proceeded to call him Val. The kids on his block changed it to Teeny, and that's the name that stuck, even when he grew to be 6 feet tall, and weighed 211 pounds.

The problem of names is hardly trivial. So serious is it, in fact, that literally hundreds of books have been written on the meanings of names, the selection of names, and as night follows day, the changing of names.

The most thumbed literature in an obstetrician's waiting room is one called "What Shall We Name the Baby?" For the better part of 9 months, couples worry and argue over their selection, and some are still worrying and arguing after the baby comes.

One mother I know admits her son's name was her 12th choice. It was her husband's 15th choice, but it was the first name that showed up on both lists, so they pounced on it.

The boy is 11 now, and his mother still wishes she could have named him Peter. Actually, it doesn't matter. I hear the boys at school call him Frog.

Nicknames are a natural evolution of rotten names. Some are descriptive, such as Squinty, Shorty, Red or Fats. Others are friendly, like Sonny, Buddy, Honey, Muffin or Sis. A few are downright unfriendly, such as Killer, Hulk or Bear.

It's possible that behind every Killer, Hulk or Bear, there is a personality problem. But more likely, the problem is a set of parents who got carried away and wrote Theobald, Rutherford or Claude on a birth certificate.

Fortunately, most people outgrow their nicknames and make a separate peace with their given names. A few even develop a feeling of pride in their names, especially if they see it on checks often enough.

As for Valentine, you can be sure another February 14 baby got it this year. But as the kids pointed out, it could be worse. Suppose the poor child had been born on April Fool's Day, Ground Hog Day, Bastille Day, or Halloween?

Dialects
March 14, 1973

Our children don't remember dialect jokes. They've grown up in a time when the only ethnic group you can laugh at is the cave man--and him only because hardly anyone wants to admit be was a relative.

But every family has its own collection of "in" jokes, and one of our favorites has to do with Great-grandfather's unsuccessful battle with the English language. Born in Italy, he spoke what he called "broken," and often the fracture was delightful.

He was the shopper for his household, and his specialty was fruit. He bought the largest peaches, the mellowest melons and the juiciest oranges. When it came to apples, he thought nothing surpassed what he called the "merican Dutch."

Once when he was housebound with a cold, Great-Aunt Grace decided to surprise him with some of his favorites.

"I'll take 3 pounds of American Dutch apples," she told the grocer.

"Gosh, that's a new one on me," said the man.

"But my father has always bought them here," protested Grace.

"No, we don't have anything like that. I know your father all right--he's the guy who told me my lemons were 'alla skin, no juice.' But he never bought any American Dutch apples here. I never heard of them."

"What kind do you sell him?" asked Grace.

"Well, sometimes he buys Golden Delicious, but his favorite seems to be the MacIntosh."

Great-aunt Grace was half-way home before it hit her that in great-grandfather's "broken," MacIntosh was 'merican Dutch.

Great-grandfather never tired of telling the joke, nor of laughing at it.

A friend who comes of Pennsylvania Dutch stock assures me that her people, too, are actually proud of the humor their Germanic, or "Dutch" dialect produces, and enjoy being quoted. Here are a few of her favorite sentences:

"The butter won't reach and the jelly is all."

"Eat your mouth empty before you say."

"The pie is all, but the cake is yet."

"Fritz, come in to eat; Ma and Pa are on the table and Johnny has et himself already."

"Is it raining out? It listens like it."

"It's hands-in-the-pocket weather."

"His off is all." (His vacation is over.)

"There's 2 roads to town. They are both the same as far, but one is more the hill up."

"Go the bridge over and the street a little up."

"Don't horn the machine so. You'll blow the baby awake."

"Aunt Emmy's wonderful sick."

"You don't look so good in the face."

"Go out and tie the dog loose."

"Throw Papa down from the hay-mow, his hat."

"Go look the window out and see who comes the yard in."

"Lena's wearing new shoes on the baby."

"I'd like to get went with, but the boys ain't so for me."

"In town today I bought myself poor."

'Buying new shoes reaches me so in the pocketbook."

Many Pennsylvania Dutch proverbs have found their way into kitchens across the country, brightly painted on colorful trivets or breadboards. A few which may be destined to catch the eye and wrath of women's libbers have to do with women.

"Better it is to single live than to the wife the britches give."

"A woman can throw out with a spoon more than a man can bring in with a shovel."

"A plump wife and a big barn, never did any man harm."

"Kissin' wears out--cookin' don't."

"Nothin's more beautiful than a woman working."

"No woman can be happy with less than 7 to cook for."

I've saved 2 of my own favorites for the end. One is a warning. "We git too soon oldt und too late schmart."

The other is a blessing: "May your friends be many, your troubles few, and all your sausages long."

Weddings Today
March 3, 1973

[Editor's note: This was a feature story for a special issue of The Towne Courier on weddings.]

Among the many good news/bad news jokes which are making the rounds is one in which a daughter tells her father some good news and some bad news.

The good news: "Tom and I have decided to get married."

The bad news: "Tom and I have decided to get married."

Many fathers agree that marriage is good news morally, but find out in a hurry that financially, it's strictly bad news. In 1971, the American wedding industry was a $7 billion-a-year business, and it shows no signs of falling off this year.

All weddings, according to local consultants, will cost more this year than last year or the year before as a result of rising costs in clothing manufacture, food and services. There is still a choice between high, medium and low cost weddings, but even at the bottom of the scale, where the bridegroom wears jeans, the bride carries one field daisy and the guests drink May wine, the price has gone up. Have you priced jeans lately?

Traditionally, Father has always paid the wedding bills, and few brides are interested in denying him that privilege. However, Mother's role as planner and manager of the affair, has gradually given way to her modern daughter's desire to have a ceremony which reflects her own personality rather than Emily Post's.

"It's up to her, it's her wedding," is the word from most mothers, according to area wedding consultants Ernestine Sorber of Jacobson's, Natalie Schubel of Bride's Showcase and Mrs. Howard Bennett of The Wedding Secretary.

Most girls still confer with their mothers, say the consultants, but practicality and good taste are their rule of thumb rather than yesteryear's code of etiquette.

One area girl whose 2 sisters had large, gala weddings chose, instead, to elope because, "I felt Bob needed a new winter coat more than I needed a long white dress I'd never wear again." But it wasn't really a run-away wedding; the couple invited both sets of parents to go down to the county seat in Mason with them for the wedding.

If mother still has a role, it's as chief worrier. Brought up in a period when there was a right way and a wrong way, *she* worries most about *her* daughter's inclination to have it "my way."

But if she is afraid that "my way" means a barefoot wedding on the Capitol lawn followed by wading in the Red Cedar, she can put her heart at rest. Weddings may be way-out in some parts of the country, but so far area brides have shown restraint and decorum.

Out-of-door weddings have been popular in the warm months, with home gardens, the horticulture gardens at Michigan State University and Francis Park's rose garden in Lansing as the favorite sites. But inside or out, most of the brides have shunned garish garb for traditional apparel.

Recently an area go-go dancer was married in red, according to Mrs. Bennett, but all consultants we spoke to agreed that candlelight, ivory and white are still the top choices. Occasionally a touch of pink, blue, yellow or lilac shows up in ribbons or other trim.

Susan Imshaug, a designer and dressmaker at a shop in Free Spirit in Lansing, reports she is working on medieval-styled dresses in royal purple jersey for one bride and her attendants, but she admits this is the first such order she has had.

The West Coast may see its share of Palazzo pants parading down the center aisle, but locally the look is pure Victorian. Long sleeves have it 10 to 1 over short or sleeveless styles, and high necks have scoop necks beat by a mile. Lace is in this year, including a new cotton variety called Cluny, which looks a lot like great grandmother's Sunday best tablecloth.

Banlon, which is washable, is popular in bridesmaid's dresses, and "a dress I can wear again" is usually what the girls are looking for. Pastels are still popular for attendants, but bolder navies and reds and small prints are selling too. Surprisingly, brown is now a good color, and one bride had a black and white wedding recently, according to Mrs. Schubel.

A new trend is the substitution of hats for veils as the bride's headgear. Mrs. Sorber reports the sale of many picture hats, and Mrs. Schubel says her shop makes many 'Bobby" hats, styled after the hats of London policemen, with matching parasols.

Some local florists report that the "nature girl"—one-rose style of wedding favored in some circles—is costing them a large loss of business. But others say the wedding flowers business has never been better. To cut costs, brides are urged to order seasonal flowers rather than exotic blooms which must be imported.

One bride ordered paper flower bouquets from Bride's Showcase recently, and the owner of Fran's Floral Craft, which makes flowers out of wood fiber cut from the stalk of a plant imported from Formosa, reports she sometimes serves as many as 6 weddings in one week.

The fiber comes in 3-inch squares, and can be dyed all colors and is treated with glycerin for permanency. The shop reports the cost of the custom-made flowers is about half the price of fresh flowers. Also, they are non-allergenic.

At one wedding held recently, the bride's sister caught the bride's bouquet.

"Ah!" sighed her mother.

"Oh no!" groaned her father envisioning another financial setback.

Spring Cleaning
April 4, 1973

From October on, all my letters, Christmas cards, notes to my children's teachers, and memos to the milkman end with the same phrase: I wish you love and peace and an early spring.

I'm sincere about the love and peace, of course, but as a Michigander, the early spring part is where my heart is.

When I say early, I mean the day we finally get around to taking down the Christmas tree--or January 31--whichever comes first.

And when I say spring, I mean flowers, sunshine, gentle showers, and fresh green sprouting underfoot and budding overhead.

I don't mean mud, potholes, thundershowers or spring cleaning. But because the first 3 are acts of God, I tolerate them. Spring cleaning is something else. If God had meant for us to do spring cleaning, he'd have given us mop heads, pail faces, and sudsy spit.

On that theory, I usually feel free to put off my spring cleaning as long as possible--say until fall. Then, what with school starting, the holidays coming, and the days so dark and short, I usually manage to put off my fall cleaning until spring.

Scratch a little deeper and you'll find that my true feeling on the subject of spring or fall cleanings is that if the house needs it that badly, it may be time to move out. Which brings me to today's problem. I'm 3 falls and 4 springs behind in my cleaning and we aren't going to move out.

The answer, my man of decision assures me, is to throw out. When it comes to what to throw out, he's all out of decisions.

"How about all those books on needlework?" he suggests.

"How about some of your notes on Thoreau?" I counter.

We compromise, which means we decide to keep all the old coffee cans (for his painting), and all the old corn cans (for my drippings), and tell the kids they've got to throw out everything that's on the floor of their rooms.

This works because they really aren't attached to what they find on the floor. For one thing, they haven't seen it in 6 months and they've forgotten they own it.

While they are throwing out, I rescue 3 socks, (none matching), the bottoms of Mike's spare PJ's, which we thought were lost in the Adirondacks, 43 cents in pennies, nickels, dimes and Japanese yen, an invitation to a birthday party which Drew forgot to go to, and a note from a teacher marked, "Please let me know today," and dated last November 23.

Everything goes smoothly until I try to throw out 387 baseball cards, all last year's, which belong to Mike.

"Can't you tell the good stuff?" he asks. "And how come you don't make Ellen throw out some of her stuff."

Ellen--read that pack rat. A dedicated arts and crafts nut, Ellen can find a use for any kind of discard you can think of. As a result we save grocery bags, plastic bags and onion bags. And the rolls from toilet tissue, wax paper, and gift wrap. And the round boxes from oatmeal, salt, and cheese crock refills.

And the colored boxes from facial tissue, eggs, and imported chocolates. And scraps of fabric, foil and fancy paper. And odd buttons, yards of yarn, and colored wire. Also lace, rick-rack and ribbon. And beads, sequins and sparklers.

We save bottles of all shapes and color, including those that break into interesting pieces. Also caps from milk bottles, pickle jars and tartar sauce. And milk cartons. And old candles. Pieces of crayons. Dried weeds, pods and cones. Curtain rings, old umbrella handles and wine-stained corks. And cardboard--thin, fat, or corrugated.

Last week she asked me to blow my eggs from now on so she can color the shells for Easter projects. And she told the kids she has to have the sticks from their popsicles and candied apples. She even saves the seeds from watermelons, grapefruit and cantaloupe.

Whenever I see a sign by the roadside that says "Jesus Saves," I think, well, Ellen's in good company.

But last week she went too far.

I walked out into the kitchen after supper and found her whirling something in the blender.

"What are you making?" I asked, eyeing the murky brown liquid in the blender.

"Fertilizer," she said. "And by the way, would you mind saving your garbage from now on? I thought I'd liquefy it and save it in a bottle and feed it to my plants."

I saved my answer for the privacy of my room.

Taking Kids to Church
April 18, 1973

It is Holy Week, and if that is a time for taking stock, all I can say is, "Lord, we are trying."

They say that the family that prays together stays together, but for a long time I have had my doubts.

Take Sunday mornings--and how often I've wished someone would!

When I was little I had a church calendar which showed a picture of Christ surrounded by children. The caption was, "Suffer the little ones to come unto me."

I was enchanted by the picture, but the words puzzled me. Not until I started "unto-ing" with little ones of my own did I understand about the suffering. At our house, it begins on Saturday night.

"Bath time," I say.

"Aw, can't I skip it? I'm too tired."

"Then you'll be too dirty to go to church tomorrow," I reason.

"OK," he says cheerfully.

After a few minutes the cheerfulness sinks in and 1 ask, "What do you mean, "OK?"

"OK, I won't take my bath and I won't go to church."

By morning, I have regained my composure and my good intentions.

"Dear Lord," I promise in my silent prayer, "today will be different. No scoldings, no arguments, and I will keep my temper. I will bring them unto you smiling and happy, just like those beautiful little charmers on my old calendar."

An hour later we march, tight-lipped and sullen, into church. In the interim I have twice dissuaded Cain and Abel from mortal combat. I have ordered their sister to wipe up the orange juice from the fertile soil of my kitchen floor before it takes root and flourishes.

I have assured a 15-year-old lily of the field that her raiment is neither too long, too short, nor too old.

I have also reaffirmed my belief that the Devil gets paid double time under his wages-of-sin contract for Sunday work.

Enroute to church only one muddy foot lands on a best Sunday coat, and there are only 2 arguments over the merits of air conditioning versus open windows.

Once in church, it takes a computer to seat us so that the boy who sniffles is well away from his sister who glares at him when he does, and the girl who wears perfume is downwind of the girl who is allergic to it.

I seek refuge in the comforting rhythm of the Mass, confident that mine is a forgiving God.

"Lord, have mercy," I plead, my eyes closed tightly, my mind pondering the mystery of God's greatness, and my heart bursting with the wonder of His everlasting love.

Suddenly a kneeler drops with a thud.

"Lord, have mercy," I plead again, this time adding, "Stop that!" in what I hope is a subtle whisper.

All the way down the pew my children blink, straighten up in their seats and give the priest their undivided attention---for a minute.

The one sitting closest to me leans over and asks, "Wha'd I do?"

"Pray!" I command, ignoring his question because by this time I have come back to earth and I know the thud came from 2 rows behind us and, along with the wiggling, coughing and fighting back there, it's another mother's problem.

By the time the priest urges us to clasp hands and exchange peaceful greetings, I am serene and full of love. My children aren't so bad, I convince myself. Look how quietly they sit, and how reverently they pray. I turn lovingly to those on either side of me and say, "Peace be with you."

As I withdraw my hands from their loving caress, I find a wiggly black plastic spider in one, and enough freshly chewed gum to stick 2 of my fingers together, probably permanently, in the other.

Like I said, Lord, we are trying. The trouble is that children are easier to pray for than with.

Feasting in the Merry Month of May
May 16, 1973

Every culture has a food-sharing ceremony. Whether it's a ritualistic breaking of bread, or simply the splitting of a prune Danish over coffee, it's usually more symbolic of trust and friendship than of real want or hunger.

From childhood on, man's instinct is to get a group of people together over food and drink. It starts with a lispy, "Leth have a tea party. I'll make mud pieth," and ends with, "The funeral's at 1. I'll bake a ham."

Whether engaged in celebration, consolation, or even devastation, refreshments and fellowship go together.

"We won! Let's go find a pizza with pepperoni!"

"You lost--how about some beer and pretzels?"

"Aye Lads, lower yon battering ram anon, whilst we tackle a meaty joint and quaff our fill of this fine brown ale!"

In modern America, the custom peaks in May. There are more reasons to eat, drink and be merry in May than there are days in the month. In May nobody eats alone, hardly anyone eats at home, and almost everyone eats too much.

On Sundays and holidays families get together, first here and then there.

"We went to Aunt Lotte's for Mother's Day, so that means we'll go to Cousin Harriet's for Memorial Day. Unless Don and Marian get the plumbing fixed at the cabin, in which case we'll go to Harriet's on Saturday, Jake's on Sunday and the cabin on Monday."

Those who get the formula mixed up and forget where to go, simply have a picnic of their own in Uncle Dan's yard.

During the week, the family splits up.

There's a band banquet for big sis to attend, a Scout cookout that little sis wants to go to. The boys are at a sports banquet (Monday, hockey; Tuesday, track; Wednesday, basketball, etc.). Dad's at a bowling bash, and mother's at a bridal shower.

And that's just your average stay-at-home type family. On a good day a truly sociable type could join others for breakfast at 8, coffee at 9, brunch at 10, lunch at 12, dessert at 2, tea at 4, cocktails at 6, dinner at 8, a reception at 11, and a midnight snack at 12--if his digestion is good.

The baby, who usually doesn't get asked to the retiree's banquet, the farewell pot luck, the wedding wingding, church salad luncheon, school outing, Friday fish fry, membership tea, club coffee, or luncheon with the girls, already has the instinct and finds a friend of her own to eat with.

The puppy shares his dog biscuit with her in exchange for 2 gulps of her zwieback.

This horrifies her parents, who immediately call a neighboring couple to come over and tell them what to do over over coffee and cake, of course.

Everyone looks forward to June, which could be one long burp.

Watergate Talk
May 30, 1973

In addition to all the other trouble the Watergate affair has caused, it is making gamblers out of some of my best friends.

As I arrived at a gathering the other evening, I heard 2 very proper matrons making bets on how long it would take the party talk to turn to Watergate.

"Two minutes," said one, "no more than 2 minutes. Just as soon as the clam dip starts around, you'll hear someone talking about immorality in government. I'll give you odds."

"I don't know," hedged the other. "At one party it never even came up--but, come to think of it, most of the guests were Republicans."

Intrigued, I looked at my watch. Three and a half minutes later, just as the dip (avocado this time), started around, it happened. But morality wasn't really the issue.

"Boy, aren't those Watergate hearings something?" asked one lady between chips.

"Terrible!" agreed another. "Terrible, just terrible!"

"Honestly, I couldn't wait for the recess," said the first woman. "Do you know Harry's mother called me every afternoon the hearings were on TV and bent my ear for 2 hours about how she didn't think it was right?"

"Oh, I know. The older generation's really shocked by corruption in high office," said her friend.

"Well, it wasn't the scandal that had her all upset. After all, she's probably old enough to remember Harding. No, she was just mad about missing her favorite serials every day."

In another corner, where there really was some clam dip, 2 men who had lived and worked in the capital clucked sadly over the matter.

"You ever been in that Watergate monstrosity?' asked one.

"A few times. It's a mess considering the rent they charge. You know I tripped over a place where the hall floor is buckled and almost broke my neck," said the other.

"I believe it," answered the first.

"You know, termites I would have expected, but bugs!"

One hostess, who usually prepares elaborate entertainment for her gatherings, says she's given up all that. Now she passes through her guests whispering key words and phrases such as "secret funds," "CIA," "Cuban cause," "immunity," and "for the good of what country?" and then lets them take it from there.

It works great, she says, except when she gets a group of state employees together. All they want to talk about is something called the "Rule of 3," she says.

In talking to our children, I've discovered that most teachers have avoided the topic as much as possible. Can you blame them? Most of them haven't recovered from such key words as "Vietnam," "bombings," and "amnesty" yet.

"There's no use talking about it in our class," says Meg. "Those who like Nixon are against the hearings, and those who don't are happy about them. It all kind of depends on things like measles and mumps. Whichever group has the best attendance wins the argument," she says, explaining the process of democratic discussion in the 6th grade.

The topic was a flop in Beth's class, too.

"We almost had a skit about it, but no one wanted to be the Republicans," she reports.

Our high school history buff has already put the affair into perspective.

"Ten years from now they'll reduce the whole mess down to 2 sentences in the history books. By the time they cross-index it under Watergate, Nixon, Republicans, Bugging (electronic), and Naughty-Naughty, there'll be more in the index than in the book!"

Mike, our 10-year-old, who has trouble understanding the difference between a trial and a hearing, and probably the whole judicial system as well, had a question no one wanted to try to answer.

"Did they find anyone innocent yet?" he asked.

Chickadees in the Fencepost
June 13, 1973

You've heard of the empty nest syndrome? We're suffering from a classic case.

No, not our children, although two have left us for the summer and Tom keeps looking around the dinner table at the five who are left and saying, "Where is everybody?"

Our problem is that our birds have flown away. Literally. One day there was happy chirping and noisy squabbling and the next day there was only silence and emptiness.

The children, as usual, were the first to spot the new family on our block.

"There's a bird's nest in our fence," said Drew.

"In the tree by the fence?" I asked.

"No, in the fence. Right in the hole where the rail fits into the post," said Drew.

"You're kidding," I said. "That hole can't be more than 1½ inches high. No birds could fit in there."

I was wrong. Not only had 2 tiny chickadees picked our fencepost to call home, but they had built a nest in the cavity behind the rail.

We were landlords! And honored ones at that. According to a natural resources bulletin published by Michigan State University's Extension Service, the presence of chickadees in a neighborhood indicates excellent natural environmental quality.

According to the bulletin anyone can attract sparrows and starlings, but chickadees frequent only elite areas which abound in "clean air, greenery, and have few people and little noise."

Obviously the chickadees never read the bulletin.

Little noise? There must be 30 children on our block and every one of them has the lungs of a Welsh tenor. Two or 3 times a day each one came by to check on the birds and the 7 jelly bean-like eggs which appeared one day.

From morning until dark lusty town crier voices rang out.

"Hey, Mike, Come see the birds. The mother's sitting on the eggs, all right!" Amazingly, she continued to sit.

By this time I was beginning to feel a burden of responsibility for our tenants.

"Those eggs will never hatch," I worried. "If the kids don't scare the mother bird off, they'll break the eggs," I prophesied gloomily.

Tom shared my dim view of their prospects, but refused to feel any responsibility.

"Dumb," he muttered. "It's a dumb place to build a nest, right in the middle of town and only 3 feet off the ground. Talk about dumb birds!"

One morning, soon after this pronouncement, he sprang from his bed and ran to the window. He pulled on his pants and shoes and dashed outside. Within a few minutes he had encircled the fence post with wire fencing.

"There," he said, "That ought to take care of that cat."

I could see responsibility was beginning to set in.

To our great surprise the eggs hatched eventually and squeaky chirps came out of the hole. It was difficult to count noses, but the children were certain there were at least 5 babies and maybe more.

Whatever the actual number, there were enough open beaks so that the mother and father birds spent every waking hour flying in food for the family. Nothing stopped the airlift. Dogs barked, children yelled, mothers called, lawn mowers coughed, cars braked, but still the birds swooped down and vanished into the hole.

The sounds from the nest were louder every day, signaling, presumably, the advent of adolescence.

To me it sounded like home:

"Why can't I have a room of my own?"

"Hash again?"

"What do you mean am I eating again? That was Mike you gave the cookies to a little while ago. I haven't had anything to eat in hours."

"How can it be my turn to carry the laundry again? I just did it yesterday."

"It's not my fault you had to go and have such a big family. I wish I were an only child."

One morning when I walked to the corner to check on the tenants, an ominous silence greeted me. The birds were gone.

For one awful moment my heart sank.

The cat! Did the cat come back again after all this time and eat the whole family for breakfast? I searched for "crumbs," hoping not to find any.

There was no trace of a struggle or hasty meal and we decided that the birds had merely flown their coop. If we had hoped for a farewell or a forwarding address, we were out of luck.

Whenever I pass the fence post, I peek in at the empty nest. How clever of birds to know that nests are for babies, while the sky's the limit for young birds testing their sturdy wings.

Clear skies and happy landings, Mr. and Mrs. Chickadee, to your young adventurers--and ours.

Plans for a Restful Summer
June 27, 1973

There are always some scoffers.

Say "energy crisis" and half the people in the room will laugh it off. Not me. It doesn't take 3 closed gas stations in one block for me to know about being out of gas. I live with the situation every summer.

Just let the thermometer rise above 75, the humidity register about the same, and the kids fight over whose turn it is to clear the table, and all my energy deserts me. From mid-June to early September it's strictly "all systems slow" with me.

But I figure why fight it? If you don't count all the things I didn't get done last fall and winter, you've got to admit I've earned the right to a nice quiet restful summer, and that's what I decided this one should be.

I was hard at work convincing the children that if they could possibly be nice and quiet I could be restful, when Mike broke the spell.

"Whadda we gonna do about my birthday?" he asked, as a subtle reminder that the anniversary of the day we all awaited so eagerly 11 years ago is upon us again.

(Looking back on it, I have to admit that I was the one who waited eagerly, especially the last couple of weeks when I was overweight and overwrought and he was overdue. As far as the rest of the family was concerned, they agreed he was cute--for a 6th child--and went on about their business.)

Mike repeated the question and I was tempted to say, "Well, we could make a novena in atonement."

But the last thing an 11-year-old boy needs is a wise-guy mother, so I mustered enough adrenalin to say all the right things, like how about hamburgers and swimming, or maybe a "G" movie, if they've made one lately.

"Sounds okay to me," said Mike racing his motor.

I made a mental note that there are 3 more family birthdays during the summer and was just slipping slowly back into sloth when I heard that an 86-year-old woman from Saginaw attended last week's College Week for Women at Michigan State University.

Birthdays my brain handled while it idled, but for this news I shifted into low gear. My brain ground slowly. My first thought was amazement that she could make it. My second was confusion over why she wanted to.

I looked again at the seminar offerings. Certainly the many titles were intriguing. The accent was on insight and a woman with questions about the law, taxes, food, children, design, sexuality, marriage, or even that fascinating topic, Woman, could find answers.

But what, I wondered, is there that an 86-year-old woman doesn't know? Me, I've got 7 children who already know all the answers, and only 2 of them are even old enough to vote.

And, supposing there is something she's missed, where does she get the energy to care?

I was really curious as to how she stood the pace of all that stimulating interchange, and I was going to go over to ask her. But it got to be 2 o'clock and I was afraid that if I missed my nap I'd never make it through supper. So I wished her well and resigned myself to the fact that some people just seem to hold together better than others.

Some doctors say that heredity has a lot to do with it. My children's great-grandmother died when she was 92. She and her housekeeper, a younger woman (of 84), lived alone and did for themselves with the help of a youth of 76 from down the block who went to the store for them and kept their walks shoveled.

Unfortunately for me, this heritage is on my husband's side of the family. But from the racket that's coming from the yard I can tell that every one of our kids got some of those genes.

I wonder how many kids it would take to keep an air conditioner running.

City Water
July 10, 1973

When you first move into a town, all its shortcomings hit you in the face.

You were hoping for a town square with little white churches and pretty picket fences? How does a 6-lane state highway, divided by a median landscaped with jaywalking students hit you?

You get high on a view of the mountains? There's always the Lansing Ski Club hill.

You're longing for a whiff of sea air again? Have you been out to Lake Lansing yet?

389

But you can get used to anything. After a few weeks, your emotional scars heal, and you notice that the houses are pretty, the neighborhoods are friendly and the shopping centers are convenient.

After 15 years in town, I've forgiven East Lansing for most of its Haves, a lot of its Have-Nots, and even some Might-Have-Beens. What I couldn't forgive was the water.

"How long did the realtor say this house had been empty?" asked Tom, as we settled into a rented house.

"A few months, I guess. Why?"

"It must have been longer than that. The water tastes stagnant."

I took a sip.

"Urgg. Well, let it run for a while. It's got to get better."

It didn't.

We mentioned the water in a letter home. A few months later my dad came to visit. He brought my mother, a couple of suitcases, some home-made chili sauce, and 5 gallons of well water.

"What's with the water?" asked Tom.

"You said your water tasted funny," said Dad. "You never said that about the water where you used to live, and it was awful. I figured if you had noticed it, it must really be bad."

"Oh, it's not all that bad," said Tom, mustering a bit of new-hometown loyalty. "Here, have a taste."

Dad took one whiff and decanted the well water.

A short time later, Tom's folks came out to visit. His mother was more tolerant.

"I'm sure it won't hurt to cook in it," she said cautiously, "but maybe you should give the baby an oil bath."

We talked to other residents. Those who had lived here for a long time said, well, yes, the water was a bit hard, but we'd get used to it.

We got used to it, but our plumbing never did. Two years ago we bought a new faucet guaranteed not to drip for 10 years. We replaced it last month. No, it didn't drip, but it didn't pour either. Our water had eaten the insides out of it. The sight of the corroded remains brought suspicious pains in my own pipes.

When we lived in that first rented house, we decided the real problem was that it was a new development. Then we moved into an old development. There we decided the trouble was probably old pipes. Then we moved into this house, and after 8 years, we've gradually eliminated all the old excuses.

Now we know what the real problem is--lousy water.

In the beginning I did a lot of scrubbing. I hit the tiles and tubs and toilets a couple of times a week, but I had a strange feeling that the creeping crud was gaining on me.

When we came back from our vacation last year, I knew I'd been beaten. Even the shower curtain--abetted by the neglect of an 18-year-old boy--had turned yellow. And from blue that ain't easy.

At last relief is in sight. The city's new water treatment plant is ready to give us clean, clear, soft water (after a suitable period of transitional sludge, of course).

Clean, clear, soft water. Well, as I said, you can get used to anything.

Air Conditioning
August 1, 1973

"It was too hot to sleep. Blaine tossed restlessly on the bare cot, his mind troubled by the events of the day. Finally, he gave up. He had to think. He needed air to clear his head. He dressed and tiptoed quietly down the stairs and let himself out the backdoor. Suddenly, 2 shots rang out..."

You can scratch that plot. Today's hero, troubled and mystified, takes 2 aspirins, turns up the air conditioner and conks out the second he hits the polyester-packed pillow.

Writers have it hard these days. "Central air" may be the biggest thing on the real estate market, and "factory air" may make the day for a used-car dealer, but the take-over of air conditioning has ruined more good plots and outdated more dependable phrases than there are degrees on a thermometer.

"The screen door has been slit. There must be an intruder in the house!"

Forget it, nobody bothers with a screen door anymore.

"I heard voices through my bedroom window," she said.

Not with the windows closed tighter than a drum, she didn't.

"Elementary, my dear Blatson," said the master sleuth. "It was 93 in the shade, but every window in the apartment was tightly shut. Clark couldn't have been there as he said, so he's our killer."

So much for that keen observation.

Gone is the stray breeze fluttering the curtains and stirring the ringlets on our heroine's head.

Gone are the moist curls at the back of Celia's neck, which drove young Peter wild with desire.

Gone is the shy promise in Melissa's eyes as she peers boldly over her fan, its pale violet lace reflecting the soft velvet of her eyes.

Gone is the tête-à-tête in the shade of the old apple tree, the tryst on the cool veranda, the kiss on the porch swing, and the iced lemonade in the stuffy front parlor.

Instead we have Joe and Jane Cool (in hot pants, of all things), untouched by the heat of the day or night, and still cool and dry after a bout with the afore-mentioned wild desire.

The writer has to stay on his toes to be believable. There are no more salad days when it's too hot to eat or too hot to cook. No flies buzz, no mosquitoes zero in, no moths flutter about the lamp.

Ladies no longer faint from the heat, or take comfort from cool cloths on the brow or the tingle of cologne on the wrists.

Both sexes resort to the layered look with long sleeved shirts, knitted vests and cardigans to add or subtract, according to the degree of frigidity at Consolidated Drudgery Inc. All winter long the steno pool resounds to the click of knitting needles as secretaries produce shawls and ponchos for the cold air-conditioned days of summer.

Writers who used to prod a muscular he-man into stripping to the waist in moments of tense drama, now have to remember to provide cabana tops to go with his swimming trunks.

Except for that scene in the boiler room, no exposed flesh can be warm, smooth and shiny. Even topless dancers are dotted with goose bumps, and "getting into something comfortable," now means the girl is putting something on, rather than taking it off.

It used to be that the poor sweated in hot factories and the rich perspired on the tennis court or golf links, but now neither does either. The factory and the clubhouse are air-conditioned, and everybody stays dry except the man who makes dress shields. He's soaked with tears shed over his lost business.

Of course there is a slender silver lining. While some plots are doomed, new ones are possible.

With air conditioning you can suffocate a whole building full of people by pulling the plug, make a surprise entry or hasty retreat *through* the ducts, or even control a whole city during a brown-out.

"It was midnight in the metropolis. Stealthily a shadowy figure made its way towards the massive cables. The moonlight flashed on an object in the intruder's hand. Pliers!"

Somehow it doesn't quite come up to that cat on a hot tin roof in the heat of the night having a hot time in the old town tonight.

What's Heaven?
August 15, 1973

It's one of those days you yearned for all winter. You're lying on the beach enjoying the sun, the sand and the lap of the water nearby.

Lazily you turn over and look at the small boy digging in the sand by your elbow. His hole is almost 2 feet straight down. You giggle and ask, "Reached China yet?"

Anybody can make a mistake, especially a mother. He doesn't know what you're talking about so of course you've got to tell him. Before you are through you've rummaged through the lunch bag for a spotted peach on which you point out the North Pole, Michigan, China and other points of interest.

You think he's got it when he asks, "How can I dig down through the pit in the middle?" and you have to start all over again.

Finally, to change the subject, you point out a fleecy cloud and say "What does that cloud look like to you?"

"Rain?" he asks worriedly.

"No," you say with annoyance, "I mean what does its shape look like to you?"

"Oh," he says, looking again. "A baseball glove," he says, with certainty this time.

"Bosh," you splutter. "How can you look up at that heavenly blue sky and that enchanting cloud and see a baseball glove?"

With that you turn back over away from his ditch and try to tune back in to the gentle waves.

No soap. Now that he's been to China and back, he's interested in more far-out places.

"Is Heaven really up there?" he asks.

You answer without thinking, a mistake common to mothers.

"Well, it always was when I was a little girl, but I'm not so sure now."

"If it isn't up there, where is it?" he wants to know.

You give up on the waves and turn over towards him again.

"I'm not sure where it is," you say. "It's easier to say what it is."

"What is it then?" he persists.

"A clean soap dish," you answer rashly.

"Aw, you're kidding me."

"No, I'm not. You don't think soap dishes turn grungy in Heaven the way they do in our house, do you?"

He concedes your point and says, "What else?"

"Little things—like no jelly on the woodwork. And no bicycle grease on my best guest towels. And pairs of socks that come out even in the wash. And marinated asparagus for supper, often."

"Gosh, your Heaven sounds like there aren't any kids in it," he accuses.

You start to speak and then backup and start again.

"No, it wouldn't be Heaven without kids. It's just that in Heaven things are easier for kids and mothers. Take milk. In Heaven when milk spills it congeals instantly into a sheet of foil-like substance. You just roll it up and toss it out. Of course there are kids in Heaven, but it's a little like strawberry cream pie--in Heaven it has no calories. Understand?"

"Yeah. How about a popsicle?"

"Sure," you say excitedly, "if that's what turns you on. Now that you are getting the swing of it, you got any more ideas?"

"I meant how about buying me a popsicle?" he says.

"I thought you were interested in Heaven," you protest.

"Sure, but I'm more interested in a popsicle right now."

You give him the dime.

Back from Vacation, Back to School
August 29, 1973

Each year I think we'll be sensible and get back from our summer trip in time to unpack, do the laundry, shop and relax a bit before school starts. Each year I am wrong.

The kids could care less. The best part of the whole vacation for them is that last week or two when they spot school buses plying the roads in neighboring states where school starts earlier. They watch in quiet fascination as the buses stop to take on groups of clean-looking kids, loaded down with books, lunch boxes and assorted band instruments.

"You mean school has started here already," one asks in disbelief. "Boy, I'm glad we live in good ole Michigan!"

Despite good intentions, we put off the return to reality until the very last minute and we haul into town about 10:30 the night before school starts.

The first morning is unbelievable. No one has slept well. After a few weeks in a trailer, it is hard to adjust to beds with sheets, rooms with doors, and floors which are not coated with gritty sand, swamp grass or mud.

You intercept the first child who comes down on the way to the breakfast table. "Change!" you order, holding your nose and shoving him back up the stairs. "But yesterday you said this outfit was good for two or three days yet," he protests.

You shove harder.

"That's what you did tell him yesterday. I heard you," says a sympathetic sibling.

"Yesterday," you say in carefully measured pre-breakfast tones, "we were deep in the mountains, miles from anything human--and more important--miles from a launderette. Eat your noodles."

"Noodles? For breakfast?"

"Would you rather have rice? I thought noodles would be better with the gravy."

"Noodles? Rice? Gravy? What happened to bacon? Eggs? Cornflakes?"

"We're fresh out," you mutter.

"Toast? English muffins?" he tries, hopefully.

"Noodles," you repeat.

"Coffee?" asks Dad, fresh on the scene in his last clean undershirt, the one with the wild blueberry stain from Maine on it.

"'Tea--iced?" you propose.

Three of the children go to the middle school this year and two of them think they need a lunch. A search of the trailer produces three end pieces of bread, two black bananas, four ears of cold corn on the cob, and almost all of "that stinky cheese we went five miles out of our way to buy in New Hampshire."

"Ask Dad for money," you suggest.

"Will they take a traveler's check?" asks Dad. "All I had left after we paid that last bridge toll were two Canadian pennies and a token from that trolley museum in Connecticut."

Finally, you smooth down a cowlick, check again for matching socks, and watch the last child limp out the door.

"Come back here a minute. What's with the limp?"

"I dunno. Something's wrong with these new sneakers we bought on sale," he says,

"Wrong? What can be wrong? I know you didn't like the color but they were a great buy at that end-of-the summer sale we stumbled on. And if you remember, you got your other ones all soggy and the smell of fish didn't come out even when we bleached them."

"I know, I know, but something's wrong with them," he persists.

It turns out he has two left sneakers.

"Wear the smelly ones and sit by the window," you advise. "I'll take these back."

"Back?" asks your husband.

And you remember in horror that "back" is a store whose name you never knew in a town you can't remember in Massachusetts--or was it Pennsylvania?

Homework on Vacation?
September 12, 1973

Understanding is a big thing in education these days. Not only is it important for the child to understand his teacher and the teacher to understand the child, but it helps if the teacher understands herself, etc., etc., etc.

When school ended last spring we congratulated ourselves on the fact that one of our children had had a teacher who rated A-Plus in Understanding.

This teacher is great. She looks at kids and she really sees them. And because she understands them, she gets through to them and all sorts of marvelous things happen in their heads. Well, judge for yourself--Mike finally learned his times tables!

And she cared. We got enough Glad Notes about his success with the sixes and sevens to paper the den.

I mean she really cared. She cared so much that she gave him two math books to take home to work on over the summer so that he wouldn't lose his hard-earned skills.

Which brings us to the etceteras--or the chapter entitled, "Gosh, Teacher, Did you Flunk the Test on Understanding Parents?"

Did it ever occur to her that if Mike had the kind of parents who were organized enough in the summer to get him to take a peek at his math book once or twice, he would have learned his tables long before he got to her?

We thought the math books were a great idea, too, and we explained to Mike that it was a special privilege to be trusted with them. He understood and was proud.

The important thing, we all realized, was to set aside a period each day for the work. As it turned out, that was what we did--each day we set it aside and managed to do *something else* instead.

The days went by so fast. First there was that dirty room to take care of, and then there was baseball, and then there was swimming, and then there was our trip, and then there was that dirty room again.

And would you believe it, that math was on our minds every minute? I was trying to figure out how to get him on it, and he was trying to figure out how to get out of it. He simply out-figured me.

Last week we returned the books via Mike's younger brother. I started to write a note, but I couldn't get past the first sentence, "Thank you so much for letting Mike have these books."

After that it was nothing but false starts.

"He got a lot out of them," seemed such an outright lie, mostly because it was.

"He used them several times," gave way to "He took them out several times," and finally to "We dusted them often."

I thought of telling her that we took them on our summer trip, which was true enough. We carted them some 3,000 miles and they kept falling out of the trailer book rack which was designed for paperbacks, not textbooks. Every time we wanted something, those darn math books were on top of whatever it was we wanted. We wore them out, moving them.

In one way Mike did get a lot of benefit from having them along. They were just the right height to prop the fan so it cooled his upper bunk.

Things To Be Thankful For
November 19, 1973

Our teacher asked us what we have to be thankful for, says Drew, between bites of an after-school apple.

"Oh? Anyone have any good ideas?"

"Yeah, I guess so."

"What are you thankful for?

"I'm thankful she didn't call on me," he says.

I suspect Thanksgiving Day is kind of lost on children. They're great on turkey and dressing, and pie and nuts, but too short on memory to do much with the spirit of the day.

Grandmothers are a different story. Thanksgiving Day was made for them. Grandmothers have longer memories than anybody (except possibly grandfathers, and they can find something to be thankful for even in the bad ones.)

"Last year at this time, Jake was in the hospital and I was sick with worry," Grandma says dismally. "They brought his tray with turkey and all the trimmings and he couldn't eat a thing. But you know, I tasted his corn scallop and it had the best taste. I figured out later they put a touch of nutmeg in it and I sent the recipe to a magazine and got $50 for it."

If their family comes for the holiday, grandmothers cook a huge turkey and get out all the best china, which has to be washed before and after dinner, and they're thankful. If the family doesn't come, they're just as thankful because it means they can go to their favorite restaurant for lamb chops, which they like better anyway.

A grandmother has lots of little things to be thankful for too---little girls and little boys, and little pink pills to take after the little girls and little boys have spent the afternoon at her house.

One grandmother I know says she is thankful for stretch stockings.

"I'm an inch and a half taller now that my girdle and my nylons don't pull in opposite directions," she says.

Another, whose memory goes back to a farm childhood replete with wood-burning stoves, outhouses, chickens to pluck, pigs to butcher and miles to walk to anywhere, says she is thankful for what she calls "women's liberators."

"You mean NOW and Betty Friedan and Germaine Greer?" I asked.

"Them too," she says, confiding that she tells her grandchildren all about Adam and Eve, and hopes that soon things will be so equal that all anyone will have to worry about is human lib.

"But what I'm really thankful for are flush toilets, electric stoves, disposable diapers, dishwashers, frozen foods, washers and dryers, and second cars--you know, the real liberators!"

For those who are not old enough to understand what she means, here's a hint from the Visitors Center in Smoky Mountain National Park. It's a copy of a pioneer mother's letter to her daughter telling her how to wash clothes, back in the "good old days."

"Build a fire in the backyard to heat a kettle of rain water. Set tubs so smoke won't blow in your eyes if wind is present. Shave whole cake of lye soap in boiling water. Spread tea towels on grass. Hang old rags on fence. Pour rinse water in flower bed. Scrub porch with soapy water. Scrub privy seat and floor with soapy water caught from porch floor scrub. Turn tubs upside down. Go put on a clean dress. Smooth hair with side combs. Brew up tea, set and rest a spell and count your blessings.

Made in the USA
Middletown, DE
21 December 2014